The Closet and the Cul-de-Sac

POLITICS AND CULTURE IN MODERN AMERICA

Series Editors
Margot Canaday, Glenda Gilmore, Matthew Lassiter,
Stephen Pitti, Thomas J. Sugrue

Volumes in the series narrate and analyze political and social change in the broadest dimensions from 1865 to the present, including ideas about the ways people have sought and wielded power in the public sphere and the language and institutions of politics at all levels—local, national, and transnational. The series is motivated by a desire to reverse the fragmentation of modern U.S. history and to encourage synthetic perspectives on social movements and the state, on gender, race, and labor, and on intellectual history and popular culture.

The Closet and the Cul-de-Sac

The Politics of Sexual Privacy in Northern California

Clayton Howard

PENN

UNIVERSITY OF PENNSYLVANIA PRESS

PHILADELPHIA

Published by
University of Pennsylvania Press
Philadelphia, Pennsylvania 19104-4112
www.upenn.edu/pennpress

Printed in the United States of America
on acid-free paper

10 9 8 7 6 5 4 3 2 1

Library of Congress Cataloging-in-Publication Data

Names: Howard, Clayton, author.
Title: The closet and the cul-de-sac : the politics of sexual privacy in Northern California / Clayton Howard.
Other titles: Politics and culture in modern America.
Description: 1st edition. | Philadelphia : University of Pennsylvania Press, [2019] | Series: Politics and culture in modern America | Includes bibliographical references and index.
Identifiers: LCCN 2018044568| ISBN 9780812251241 (hardcover : alk. paper) | ISBN 0812251245 (hardcover : alk. paper)
Subjects: LCSH: Privacy, Right of—California—History—20th century. | Sexual rights—California—History—20th century. | Gay rights—California—History—20th century. | Suburbanites—California—Social conditions—History—20th century.
Classification: LCC JC596.2.U5 H69 2019 | DDC 323.44/8097940904—dc23
LC record available at https://lccn.loc.gov/2018044568

To Catherine

Contents

Introduction

From the Straight State to the Culture Wars

In October and November 1978, an unlikely duo went on tour in California together. That year, openly gay San Francisco Supervisor Harvey Milk met State Senator John Briggs, a conservative from suburban Orange County, to debate a ballot initiative that aimed to ban openly gay teachers in California's public schools. The measure, alternately known as Proposition 6 or the Briggs Initiative, was the first statewide referendum on gay rights in U.S. history, and the two politicians fought over the issue in community centers, television studios, and school gyms across the state. Briggs predicted the ban would spark a conservative revival that would draw a "moral line" against homosexuality, while Milk later declared, "Gay people can never go back into their closets."[1] Together, the pair seemed like divergent responses to the sexual revolution of the 1960s and 1970s and embodied two of the most important social movements of the late twentieth century: Gay Liberation and the Religious Right. Progressive versus conservative, urban versus suburban, and gay versus straight, the debates over Proposition 6 could easily be seen as some of the opening shots of the coming culture wars over homosexuality.

Yet the conflicts over gay rights were never just a struggle between two sides of the political spectrum. Instead, the culture wars included a wide range of people beyond the two social movements. They included activists and policymakers, to be sure, but also married men and women who supported gay rights because they desired privacy in their own bedrooms and straight-identified Americans who never joined the Religious Right but who disliked homosexuality. In 1978, approximately 60 percent of Californians lived in suburbs, and while Briggs found enthusiastic support in some of the conservative "megachurches" along the state's highways, not all suburbanites agreed with him.

Many Californians expressed ambivalence—rather than hostility—toward openly gay people like Milk. In the lead-up to Proposition 6, pollster Mervin Field asserted that "the broad middle group, 50 to 60 percent, is in conflict. It's the kind of issue where there is some instinctive feeling, but the feeling is that it's highly discriminatory and not the way to do it."[2] Just a year earlier, a national poll indicated that while most Americans believed that employers should not discriminate against gay men and lesbians, they nevertheless overwhelmingly opposed hiring them as schoolteachers or members of the clergy.[3]

The history of the culture wars is best comprehended, then, not as a two-sided fight over the legacy of the sexual revolution but as a multisided debate over the boundaries of the closet. Most Americans have primarily understood the culture wars as a dispute about the definition of "privacy." In the late twentieth and early twenty-first centuries, people across the political spectrum saw sexual privacy as a fundamental right, yet majorities also believed heterosexual marriage was superior to other kinds of relationships. Confronted with the gay rights movement of the late twentieth century, many straight-identified people struggled to define the right to privacy and the extent to which society should accept homosexuality. They argued about where and when openly gay, lesbian, or bisexual people should express their sexuality and how much public officials should tolerate same-sex relationships. In these debates, straight-identified Americans sometimes argued that the government should respect the private lives of all of its citizens and in other cases that gay relationships violated their own right not to know what others allegedly did in their bedrooms. The specific language of privacy appealed to so many, in part, because it seemed like common sense, and partisans used the same language to support numerous positions. Invocations of the term could justify eliminating discrimination against gay men and lesbians, compelling them to conceal their identities, or both.

The contours of how this discourse worked can be seen in the debate over the Briggs Initiative. The Bay Area Committee Against the Briggs Initiative warned in 1978 that Proposition 6 "would authorize the government to regulate the private lives . . . of teachers outside the school."[4] John Briggs, meanwhile, told a cheering crowd, "What teachers do in private is their own business. But what they do in California's classrooms is our business."[5] Privacy was neither progressive nor conservative, and many straight-identified moderates used the discourse to express their ambivalence. During the Briggs debates, J. E. S. Tyson in the San Francisco Bay Area suburb of Los Gatos told the *San Jose Mercury*, "As a heterosexual person, I view this measure as an invasion of privacy . . . [but] I am certainly not condoning the public flaunting of one's sexuality, homo- or hetero-."[6]

The outbreak of the culture wars in the 1970s thus signaled neither the arrival of total equality for gay men and lesbians nor the opening of a uniquely conservative period in American politics. The question of homosexuality surfaced again and again in the late twentieth and early twenty-first centuries. Proposition 6 ultimately failed at the polls, but its sponsor made at least one accurate prediction: "Homosexuality," Briggs declared, "is the hottest social issue since Reconstruction." In subsequent decades, gay rights activists and religious conservatives became seemingly permanent and linked fixtures in national politics, clashing over topics such as the AIDS crisis, gays in the military, and same-sex marriage. Their prominent place in the culture wars, in fact, even prompted a pair of journalists to dub the social movements "Perfect Enemies" in 1996.[7]

Yet, like the Briggs Initiative, almost all of these battles hinged on the question of privacy, and the moderate consensus developing around the idea of privacy influenced their outcomes to a significant extent. Though employed to dramatically different ends, the discourse united people across the culture wars, and Americans used it to justify pushing gay men and lesbian back into the closet as often as they used it to combat prejudice. At the height of the clashes over same-sex marriage in the early 2000s, for example, the San Francisco–based National Center for Lesbian Rights alleged that gay marriage bans violated same-sex couples' "right to privacy."[8] President George W. Bush, meanwhile, declared, "What they do in the privacy of their house, consenting adults should be able to do. This is America. It's a free society. But it doesn't mean we have to redefine traditional marriage."[9] In 2013 and 2014, polls found that 30 to 45 percent of Americans viewed homosexuality as a "sin," yet a stunning 80 percent or more of them believed people had a "right to privacy" in their bedrooms. When gay rights advocates and conservatives clashed over same-sex marriage in the 2010s, they alternately framed the issue as either one where the government denied couples their right to express their private love or one where the state denied people the right to express their private religion.[10] And in its landmark 2015 case legalizing same-sex marriage, the U.S. Supreme Court invoked the discourse in its majority opinion, extending the rights found in the Fourteenth Amendment's due process clause "to certain personal choices central to individual dignity and autonomy, including intimate choices that define personal identity and beliefs."[11]

Privacy and the Legacy of the Straight State

The durability of the conflicts over gay rights and the particular interest in privacy are the contested legacies of the state's support for heterosexuality and marriage in postwar America. In the two decades after World War II, adults publicly involved in normative "straight" relationships, particularly heterosexual marriage, enjoyed the fullest benefits of American citizenship, while those who engaged in sex with others of the same sex risked social isolation, economic deprivation, and legal prosecution. Government authorities had regulated Americans' sex lives before the 1940s, but the war spurred the creation of a new legal regime that tightened earlier policing strategies, specifically targeted homosexuality, and promoted heterosexuality as a form of mental health.[12] As numerous scholars have shown, World War II caused the mass migration of people to urban centers; disrupted numerous racial, gender, and sexual norms; and created what one historian described as "something of a national coming out experience" for millions of gay men and lesbians.[13] The conflict, however, also served as an important watershed for Americans with normative sexual identities. Politicized by what they saw as the chaos of the war years, many Americans in urban centers petitioned public officials to protect what they saw as normal family life, and authorities responded by rewarding people for marrying and by penalizing those who broke sexual norms.

This combination of policy penalties and benefits—or what historian Margot Canaday calls the "Straight State"—cast a long shadow across the postwar period. It tolerated same-sex relationships in private but incentivized people experiencing same-sex desires to mask their feelings in public.[14] It reinforced personal prejudice, encouraging Americans to see heterosexual marriage as the only relationship worthy of collective celebration, and pushed citizens to see homosexuality as a problem in need of a remedy. It expanded and fortified racial and gender inequality by rewarding white men for marrying while denying benefits to most women and people of color, regardless of their marital status. And for almost two decades, officials at all levels of governance helped make everyone's private life a public concern, subjecting even straight-identified people to scrutiny over the possibility of being queer.[15]

Powerful forces undermined this regime almost as soon as it came into being, in part because of contradictions in the system itself. The local, state, and federal policies that made up the Straight State contained two goals that sometimes reinforced one another and sometimes came into conflict. On one hand, public officials rewarded Americans for marrying and punished them for deviating from marital heterosexuality. Police arrested people for wearing gender-nonconforming clothing and harassed or closed gay bars. State-sponsored sex education campaigns encouraged Americans to think of marriage as a sign of good mental health and to worry about dangers posed by homosexuals. And the postwar housing policies that fueled suburban growth pushed banks to give mortgages to white married men while forbidding them to lend to people they suspected of homosexuality. Yet, on the other hand, authorities encouraged Americans to have sex in private. Policing never completely eradicated same-sex relationships; it merely drove illicit sex behind closed doors. Sex education not only celebrated marriage; it also encouraged young people to respect their parents' sexual privacy. Government support for the suburbs required developers to build private master bedrooms and offered homeowners one of the only acceptable places to have sex in postwar America. These housing policies, designed to help married couples have private sex, also allowed for other illicit relationships, including homosexual ones.

Authorities designed these policies with heterosexual married couples in mind, believing that sexual privacy helped build healthy families, but they simultaneously undermined the Straight State. Civil libertarians critiqued the most punitive elements of the postwar heteronormative legal regime and argued that laws forbidding consensual sex between adults threatened the private sex lives of married couples. The police, they contended, could never truly know what happened behind closed doors without an elaborate surveillance system. Sex educators, too, adopted similar ideas and reasoned that while heterosexual marriage remained the healthiest kind of relationship, other private consensual sex acts between adults did not necessarily warrant punishment. Beginning in the mid-1960s, state and federal courts gradually accepted these arguments and issued a series of rulings that guaranteed Americans a right to privacy when it came to contraceptives, pornography, and, in some cases, homosexuality. For numerous gay men and lesbians, many of whom were barred from the suburbs and lived in older cities, this liberalization of the Straight State offered an important opportunity. Much of the early gay rights movement borrowed the discourse and emphasized the importance of sexual privacy.

As the postwar Straight State eroded, however, Americans across the political spectrum breathed new life into it, hoping to prevent the complete collapse of the state's support for heterosexuality. In the late twentieth century, straight-identified liberals, conservatives, and moderates spoke about "privacy" to police the boundaries of sexual respectability, and their use of the term concealed the government's ongoing role in shaping Americans' sex lives. Conservatives such as Briggs stoked opposition to gay rights in "family-friendly" churches in the suburbs and argued that openly gay teachers violated their own "right" not to be confronted with homosexuality in public. Meanwhile, many self-identified moderates criticized what they saw as discrimination and violations of privacy, even as they distanced themselves from what they saw as the excesses of pride parades or gay-friendly sex education. Even some white middle-class gay men and lesbians spoke of privacy to distinguish themselves from others they deemed less respectable than themselves. Privacy allowed gay activists to challenge elements of the Straight State, but it also encouraged them to avoid associations with Americans who seemed less able to assimilate to mainstream ideas about acceptable sexuality, including transgender people, radicals who advocated for revolution, or the queer poor who lacked bedrooms altogether. Neither inherently conservative nor progressive, discourses about privacy in the late twentieth and early twenty-first centuries defied easy categorization and transcended the clear left-right binary of the culture wars.

The Straight State, the Culture Wars, and the San Francisco Bay Area

The Closet and the Cul-de-Sac chronicles this history by focusing on the cities and suburbs of the San Francisco Bay Area. Between World War II and Proposition 6, the postwar Straight State, mass suburbanization, and a sexual politics centered on the right to privacy transformed San Francisco and nearby San Mateo and Santa Clara counties. Traveling to work in defense industries or to fight in the Pacific theater, migrants flooded San Francisco in the 1940s and caused older residents to demand that public officials preserve social order. During the 1950s and 1960s, San Mateo and Santa Clara counties underwent economic and population booms while the city lost residents and revenue to the suburbs. In this period, San Francisco witnessed an influx of tens of thousands of poorer residents, people of color, and unmarried people, including many gay, lesbian, and transgender migrants, while millions of white, married middle-class couples moved to the suburbs to have children. This sifting process not only produced new evangelical churches and gay communities; it also led to growth in mainline Protestant congregations, Catholic parishes, homeowners' groups, and parent-teacher associations. Over time, these communities produced multiple politics related to sexuality, religion, and the state. By 1978, the Bay Area included one of the most well-known middle-class gay neighborhoods in the country that elected Harvey Milk to office in San Francisco, a dozen evangelical megachurches that enthusiastically backed John Briggs in Santa Clara County, and numerous other communities that sat between them politically, ideologically, and even geographically.

Many writers have dismissed or celebrated the Bay Area as an exceptionally liberal place, and in many ways, San Francisco deserves its progressive reputation as a "Left Coast City."[16] San Francisco has a long tradition of radical and liberal politics, and since the 1960s, it has boasted one of the largest lesbian, gay, bisexual, and transgender (LGBT) populations in the country.[17] Yet the city also developed in ways remarkably similar to other parts of the United States. By the 1970s, suburbanization had transformed urban centers nationwide, San Francisco included. Cities as diverse as Jackson, Mississippi; Chicago, Illinois; Flint, Michigan; and Miami, Florida, all encompassed a mixture of gay neighborhoods, red-light districts, queer bars, and politically active LGBT voters.[18] These spaces and communities varied from place to place, but they all underwent spatial and demographic shifts in alignment with those taking place in San Francisco in the same period. "San Francisco is exceptional," editorialized the *New Republic* in 1979. "It is exceptional, however, in the sense of being in the vanguard, not of being a mere fluke. . . . What happens to the gay population of San Francisco . . . is a portent of what awaits the nation as a whole."[19]

At the same time, the evolution of the Bay Area suburbs, particularly those in San Mateo and Santa Clara counties, paralleled trends visible in other places. The second largest metropolis in the nation's most populous state, the Bay Area's history includes more than just its central city. Originally conceived as "bedroom communities," the suburbs of the San Francisco Peninsula and South Bay experienced enormous postwar growth. Similar to "crabgrass frontiers" across the country, these areas witnessed an influx of new homeowners in the postwar period, almost all of whom were white, middle class, and married.[20] Cold War defense spending helped fuel population booms across the American South and West, including the Bay Area, and Santa Clara County received the most military-related funds in

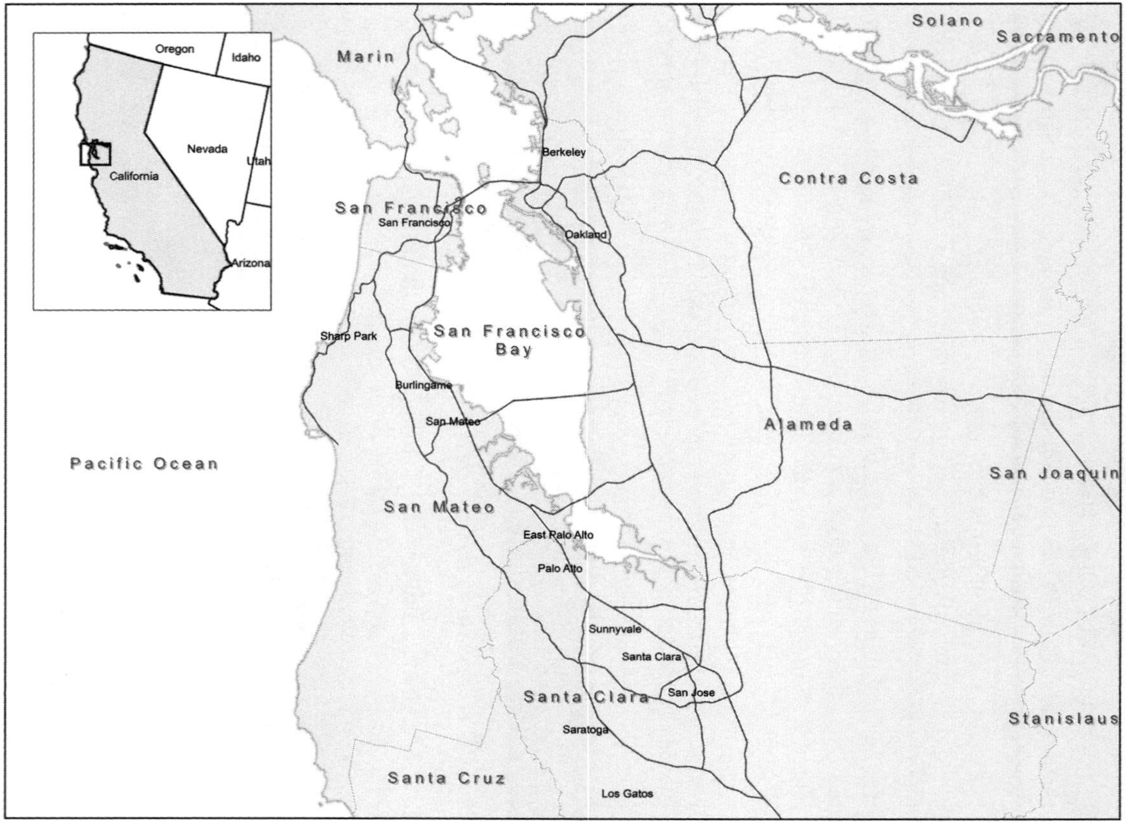

Map 1. San Francisco Bay Area. Center for Urban and Regional Analysis, Ohio State University.

California after Los Angeles and San Diego.[21] Thirty years of growth eventually turned the relatively homogeneous bedroom communities of the Peninsula and South Bay into a polynucleated, "postsuburban" landscape in the 1970s comparable to places such as Orange County, California, or the "Research Triangle" near Raleigh, North Carolina.[22]

But it was, perhaps, early participants in the culture wars themselves who articulated the most important reason to study the Golden State and the Bay Area in particular. Harvey Milk understood that his visibility as an openly gay official extended far beyond San Francisco, and he promised to bring hope to "young gay people" in places like "Altoona, Pennsylvania," and "Richmond, Minnesota." John Briggs, meanwhile, campaigned in California's suburbs, including the Bay Area towns of Santa Clara and Mountain View, promising to "Save America." And onlookers from *Newsweek* to the *Wall Street Journal* watched Proposition 6 with interest because they believed what happened in California could transform the nation.[23] The story of the Bay Area, therefore, is also very much postwar America's story: a history of cities and suburbs, cul-de-sacs and red-light districts, gay professionals and conservative evangelicals, sexual nonconformists and sexual traditionalists, and voters spread across the political left, right, and center. While no example can truly stand in for every place, San Francisco and its suburbs offer both a unique and representative vantage point from which to observe the origins of the nation's culture wars.

Sexuality, the State, and the Postwar Metropolis

The story of the Milk-Briggs debates, in many ways, epitomizes the ways that most scholars have conceptualized political conflicts over homosexuality in late twentieth-century and early twenty-first-century America. Too often, historians have defined the struggle over gay rights narrowly as a clash between traditionalists and radicals over the meaning of the sexual revolution. Political histories that mention sexuality primarily underscore the importance of the Religious Right and Gay Liberation, beginning their narratives just before the rise of the two social movements in the 1960s and 1970s. Recent work on conservatism, in particular, has often framed the issue in binary terms, ceaselessly replaying the duels between figures such as Briggs and Milk. In some cases, scholars have argued that a backlash against feminism, gay rights, and the "hippie counterculture" fueled the New Right and allowed conservatives to seize power.[24]

The Religious Right and Gay Liberation, undoubtedly, represent two of the most important social movements of the late twentieth and early twenty-first centuries. Yet stories about the culture wars that begin in the 1960s and rely on a clear left-right binary obscure as much as they reveal. Most notably, they often mystify the postwar liberal state's role in stigmatizing deviant sexuality and obscure the privileges enjoyed by the vast majority of self-identified heterosexuals who never joined the Religious Right. Decades before the culture wars made national headlines, local, state, and federal officials rewarded Americans for marrying and punished people who had gay sex. That regime affected nearly everyone, not just the opposing sides of the culture wars. Many Americans in the late twentieth and early twenty-first centuries felt strongly that heterosexuality represented the only healthy, natural kind of relationship. A broad range of Americans supported political, social, and economic rewards for heterosexual married couples. Framing the issue of gay rights as a two-sided culture war conceals this broad consensus, focusing scholarly attention solely on the most vocal participants.

Blending some of the key insights of metropolitan history and LGBT history offers a more compelling framework in understanding these conflicts. Historians have frequently relied on national frameworks for explaining American politics, and scholarship has often isolated the Religious Right and Gay Liberation from larger trends in postwar history. Bird's-eye views on the culture wars tend to reify divisions between liberal coasts and the "Bible Belt," blue states and red states, erotic cities and vanilla suburbs. Yet historians can best see the complex interplay of sexuality, race, gender, class, and politics at the metropolitan level.[25] The field of postwar metropolitan history, however, has only begun to include an analysis of sexuality.[26] Histories of lesbian, gay, bisexual, and transgender life have long focused on cities as places in which people experiencing queer desires or who have deviated from middle-class social norms have found one another.[27] More recently, historians have begun "queering the state," demonstrating the ways in which public policies have promoted heterosexuality and policed homosexuality, yet this scholarship has primarily focused on national policies.[28]

Together, these literatures enable a more nuanced understanding of the origins of the culture wars. Beginning this history in the 1940s and setting it in a metropolitan context reveals a number of diverse sexual communities and the important role the state played in promoting marital heterosexuality. After the New Deal, federal policies shaped two of the most important internal migrations in U.S. history—the outward movement of married white couples to the suburbs and the influx of a racially diverse cohort of unmarried people, including many gay men, lesbians, bisexuals, and transgender people, to older cities. The government's intervention in the postwar housing market was a crucial pillar of the postwar Straight State, and the sorting of people by the Federal Housing Administration and Veterans Administration based on their perceived sexuality paralleled and reinforced their racially exclusionary practices. This process never operated with the rigidity of racial segregation; self-identified and closeted gay men and lesbians have always lived in the suburbs, and private bedrooms allowed numerous seemingly "straight" suburbanites to engage in queer sex.[29] But the penalties embedded in the postwar housing market placed significant barriers to openly gay people wishing to buy a new home and, therefore, created a divided landscape in which some places allowed for the freer public expression of same-sex desires than others. Restrictions based on marital status and sexuality, furthermore, reinforced racial segregation since California banned interracial marriages until 1948 and many other states banned them until 1967, and public officials frequently stressed the ways in which racially homogeneous neighborhoods nurtured strong families.

These federal policies set the stage for a number of local actions. As urban areas took on a greater share of their regions' residents of color, poorer people, and unmarried residents, including many gay men and lesbians, worried mayors in cities such as San Francisco cracked down on "vice."[30] Bar raids and police sweeps of parks grew out of a larger fear that "sleaze" hurt downtown investment and encouraged businesses and white middle-class families to relocate to the suburbs. Federal policies that divided the Bay Area and other regions along sexual lines, therefore, intensified competition at the metropolitan level.

At the same time, school and health officials tried to promote marriage through education campaigns about sex and parenting.[31] Suburban school districts, often filled with thousands of new mothers and fathers, offered adult courses on childrearing that included teaching children about sex and marriage. These classes not only served as important avenues for disseminating scientific knowledge about sexuality to a wider public but also nurtured new communities of middle-class parents. Eager to use expert advice to raise "better" families, many new suburbanites in places such as Santa Clara County came together in book clubs, parent-teacher associations (PTAs), and church groups to discuss the works of writers like Dr. Benjamin Spock and to meet others like themselves.

From the mid-1940s through the 1960s, these policies garnered enormous public support, enabled the creation of new social communities built around sexual norms, and mobilized voters in defense of those norms. During the war, middle-class, primarily white parents in California and elsewhere forged a new relationship with the state, demanding that authorities repress the increasingly visible queer people in major cities and promote heterosexual marriage in public schools. Over the course of the 1950s and 1960s, suburban homes, schools, and churches represented key counterparts to urban gay bars and bookstores, bringing communities of like-minded individuals together. In the long postwar period, many of these groups served as the most ardent supporters of classroom-based sex education. Although almost all suburban residents agreed that heterosexual marriage represented the only socially acceptable place for sex, they disagreed over whether schools or churches could best supplement lessons taught in the home. In the twenty years before the battles over classroom-based sex education in California attracted national attention in the late 1960s, suburban parents debated the issue in their PTAs, congregations, and neighborhoods.[32]

Examining controversies over homosexuality and sex education in the homes, schools, churches, and neighborhoods of postwar America, therefore, reveals longstanding concerns about the importance of heterosexuality and marriage and hostility to same-sex relationships. It embeds the Religious Right within the state's larger, longer support for heterosexual marriage and helps explain how the postwar period can be remembered both as one of the most "liberal" periods in American history regarding the expansion of the welfare state and as one of the most "conservative" eras in terms of its gender and sexual politics. One of the principal consequences of the postwar expansion of the state was the dramatic mobilization of parents across the political spectrum in defense of marriage, childrearing, and heteronormative sex. Telling the history of those movements not only helps explain the rise of the Religious Right in the 1970s, it also reveals the consensus in American politics about the importance of preserving heterosexuality and marriage. As bedroom seclusion became a popular expectation of many postwar homeowners and renters, large numbers of self-identified "straight" voters distanced themselves from what they saw as the "excesses" of both the sexual left and right by emphasizing the importance of "privacy."

Contested Consensuses and the Normative Center

By delving into the social, cultural, and political fabric of a metropolitan area and broadening the history of the culture wars beyond Gay Liberation and the Religious Right, *The Closet and the Cul-de-Sac* challenges historians to look beyond the left-right binary of American elections and to see moderation as an ideology with its own politics and history. Some of the best studies of the suburbs have underscored the ways in which many middle-class white Americans have more frequently identified themselves in nonpartisan terms such as homeowners, taxpayers, and school parents than as ideologically coherent liberals or conservatives.[33] Identifying labels such as "heterosexual," "husband," and "wife" worked precisely in this manner after World War II, and similar to other seemingly neutral suburban identities, these terms have masked varying degrees of racial, gender, sexual, and class privilege. Numerous historians have demonstrated that the homosexual-heterosexual binary that dominates the present-day "common sense" about sexuality only came into existence in the late nineteenth century.[34] As late as World War II, relationships between two men or two women did not invariably provoke hostility from the wider society or even define someone as "homosexual."[35] The growth of the postwar Straight State, however, consolidated heterosexuality and American identity and reinforced the notion that same-sex desires represented a problem in need of a collective solution. This regulatory system defined heterosexuality and homosexuality in exclusionary and hierarchical terms, giving many Americans a "possessive investment in straightness" that transcended the left-right axis of electoral politics.[36] No study of liberalism or conservatism alone could fully encapsulate the widespread faith in heterosexual marriage that has animated multiple sides of the culture wars.

Understanding the consensus around straightness requires recognizing a moderate rhetorical tradition in U.S. politics. Since the 1940s, white, middle-class suburbanites, in particular, have frequently embraced a centrist rhetorical style that valorizes the middle and has rejected "extreme" points of view. The merits of any given issue have varied, but activists' and policymakers' ability to persuade others has often rested on their ability to convince the wider public that their proposal was "in the middle" and "balanced." Self-identified moderates have not necessarily sat idle, waiting for direction from others. They have, instead, actively crafted their own centrist politics with its own ideology, contradictions, and self-interest.[37]

Moderation as a rhetorical frame has defined the culture wars as often as polarization and understanding the tensions within centrist discourses necessitates investigating what historian Wendy Wall calls the "politics of consensus." Even when Americans have expressed seeming agreement over words like "freedom" or "the American Way," they have often clashed over definitions. Opponents have frequently used similar language to reach different goals.[38] Moderate politics since World War II have functioned precisely in this manner with Americans sharing common words, even as they have disagreed about their meaning. Deciphering the language that they have used matters greatly because "balanced," "middle," and "extreme" represent relative expressions that have changed over time. Moderates have refashioned the boundaries of centrist discourses in response to pressure from social movements as well as a means of preserving their own self-interest. These middle-class voters have also sometimes revised their points of view out of genuine sympathy for a given cause. On other occasions—or even on the same occasions—they have changed their rhetoric as a means for preserving their own interests. When, for example, historian Matthew Lassiter studied school integration in the Sunbelt South in the 1960s and 1970s, he found numerous suburban whites who expressed sympathy for the goals of the civil rights movement but who also opposed "extreme" measures like busing students across neighborhood lines. Whites' rhetorical support for "colorblindness" often simultaneously reflected a genuine antipathy to Jim Crow and a convenient rhetorical tool for preserving segregated schools.[39] A close analysis of the discourse of moderation, therefore, not only helps historians see Americans' attitudes change over time but also unmasks varying degrees of privilege and ideology masquerading as common sense.

Sexual Moderation and the Postwar Public

This book follows two of the most important moderate discourses that middle-class Bay Area residents and policymakers used to define their relationship to sexuality, the city, and the state. In the years immediately after World War II, San Franciscans or suburbanites rarely mentioned a right to sexual privacy. Instead, people across the ideological spectrum spoke about marriage and childrearing as collective projects and described "homes, schools, and churches" as the building blocks of a moral order that protected so-called normal families. Many white middle-class Bay Area residents called this trinity of institutions "preventative agencies," which helped discipline people. When the home, school, and church failed, voters and public officials looked to the police or other law enforcement to punish sexual misconduct of any kind. Ideally, the three institutions taught similar, reinforcing messages, and postwar moderates frequently spoke of homes, schools, and churches as a unified front against sexual delinquency and disorder.

The migration of people to cities during and after World War II seemed to test the strength of the Bay Area's homes, schools, and churches and triggered a new round of reforms reminiscent of the antivice campaigns of the early twentieth century.[40] Population growth in ports such as San Francisco, in particular, expanded older LGBT communities and communities of color, alarmed many middle-class residents, and prompted a crackdown on prostitution and gay bars. Unlike earlier campaigns, however, the antivice efforts of the 1940s unfolded amid the expansion of the New Deal state, and residents worried about homosexuality and sexual promiscuity found a sympathetic audience among public officials. Authorities after World War II called for unity between the home, school, and church, offering voters a mixture of classroom-based sex education, information about human sexuality for parents, and school prayer. The state's support for character-building programs effectively democratized elite ideas about sexuality, broadening the number of people who saw heterosexuality as a form of psychological maturity.

By contrast, moderate discourses about sexual privacy were newer developments that first appeared after World War II and grew in popularity after several decisions by the Warren Court in the 1960s. A small number of liberal lawyers and researchers such as Alfred Kinsey spoke of the "right to privacy" after the war to push back against laws restricting multiple kinds of nonmarital sex, including homosexuality. Most often, these liberals spoke about dangers to civil liberties and the practical difficulties police faced in trying to monitor behaviors that took place behind closed doors. Some gay rights groups in this early period spoke about privacy to try to limit harassment from law enforcement.

But a larger set of middle-class gay activists used the discourse to win limited freedoms after Supreme Court decisions in the 1960s such as *Griswold v. Connecticut* and *Stanley v. Georgia* made "privacy" a basic legal right for Americans using birth control or viewing pornography. Beginning in

1965, federal courts gradually extended the Fourth Amendment's guarantee of protections against "unreasonable search and seizure" and the Fourteenth Amendment's "due process" clause to offer Americans limited sexual freedoms. These decisions primarily restricted the state's ability to police its citizens, rather than establishing an unfettered right to sexual freedom. Nevertheless, after these rulings, many gay men and lesbians argued that their disproportionate arrest, loss of employment, and discrimination in housing represented a violation of their "privacy." Groups such as the American Civil Liberties Union subsequently used the discourse to justify nondiscrimination ordinances in employment and a halt to the arrest of Americans for "victimless crimes."[41]

Equally important to the rise of the privacy discourse were a series of Supreme Court rulings in the early 1960s that made it difficult for parents to treat the school and church as interchangeable pieces of a moral order. In *Engel v. Vitale* and *Abington v. Schempp*, the U.S. Supreme Court curtailed teacher-led prayer and Bible readings in public schools. These decisions did not mean that religion disappeared from public education altogether, but they triggered local debates about whether open expressions of religion violated the privacy of nonbelieving students. Numerous conservatives argued that the church and school needed to reinforce lessons given in the home and that prayer bans endangered young people's morality. Many moderates and liberals, by contrast, contended that schools should teach "facts" about sex and that young people could learn their own private morality in the church and home.

A few years later, these arguments overwhelmed conservatives at the dawn of the sexual revolution. Worried about premarital sex, homosexuality, and drug use, middle-class Bay Area parents across the ideological spectrum asked the public schools to contain what they saw as immorality and convinced the California legislature to require family life education for all high school students. For liberals and moderates, education about "facts" violated no one's privacy, even if teachers told students that homosexuality was a mental disorder. Conservatives, now on the defensive, argued that mandatory teachings about sex violated their right to privacy. Convinced that the secular school system corrupted students, many conservative parents opted to teach their children at home or in private religious academies.

By the late 1960s, however, gay activists increasingly split over privacy's value as a rhetorical tool. Many gay men and lesbians worried that emphasizing privacy allowed officials and employers to require them to conceal their relationships in order to gain the benefits of a nondiscrimination policy. Instead, they emphasized the public dimensions of sexuality, calling for people experiencing same-sex attractions to "come out of the closet." Their fears were well founded because many straight-identified Americans increasingly spoke about privacy to justify their own ideological positions. Some moderates, for example, affirmed that they opposed discrimination against gay men and lesbians because they believed in "privacy," but they opposed "public" displays of homosexual affection in parades or on the street. Others claimed that nondiscrimination ordinances themselves violated the public's right not to have openly gay teachers in the classroom. Many middle-class gay activists continued to emphasize privacy's liberal elements, therefore, and argued that gay men and lesbians barely differed from straight people except for what they did in the bedroom. This claim gave many gay people a measure of acceptance, but it also sharpened the line between those most able to conform to middle-class gender and sexual norms and those who could not. Most transgender people, sex radicals, and the queer poor who sold sex for a living or lived on the street still faced accusations that they violated others' privacy.[42]

Focusing on these two moderate discourses reinforces and disrupts the longstanding view that the 1960s represented a crucial turning point in the development of the culture wars. Both before and after the 1960s, Bay Area residents clashed over the meaning of a united "home, school, and church" and the "right to privacy" even as they used the phrases again and again. Moderates, for example, alternately spoke of "privacy" to support gay equality, condemn homosexuality, or justify a middle ground on the issue. Proponents of unity between the "home, school, and church" shared a belief that parents, teachers, and clergy should work together. Yet they also differed on how to mediate the needs of those groups. Some voters argued that unity between "home, school, and church" required greater sex education in children's classrooms, while others used it to justify more religious instruction. Local clashes over classroom prayer and sex education played out against the backdrop of a seeming national consensus about the importance of normative marriage and the value of religion in public life.

A history of these two discourses furthermore reveals ongoing and continuous support for marriage and heterosexuality before and after the 1960s. All sexual relationships have public dimensions, and many straight-identified people have used "privacy" in a way that has obscured the state's ongoing support for heterosexual relationships, particularly marriage.[43]

Scholars have traditionally thought of legal arguments about "privacy" as a kind of "negative liberty"—or a claim about the "right to be left alone" from government interference. This understanding of the term has often accompanied a broader explanation of the freedoms that came with the sexual revolution. Court rulings, such as *Griswold*, that affirmed the right to privacy opened the door for legalized contraception and the repeal of laws against gay sex.[44]

Yet Americans at the grassroots level in the late twentieth century primarily used privacy to demarcate the boundaries of sexual respectability and to reinforce straight privilege. In this context, same-sex couples have repeatedly faced accusations that open expressions of their relationships violate others' privacy. The central questions surrounding gay rights in this era have usually been the following: who has the right to openly express their sexuality, and which relationships deserve public acknowledgment? While marriage ceremonies or heterosexual dates have rarely generated controversy, for example, same-sex couples have often faced extra scrutiny for public displays of affection. In its most liberal form, the right to privacy has carved out important legal protections for LGBT people. But it has also left other kinds of consensual adult relationships, such as polyamory or people who engage in casual sex, outside those protections and beyond the bounds of respectability. Even with antidiscrimination laws, many LGBT people have felt pressure to conceal their relationships in their neighborhoods, workplaces, or schools.[45]

More importantly, the frequent invocation of privacy has concealed numerous "positive rights" offered to heterosexual married couples. Although the Straight State decisively weakened after the 1960s, it cast a long shadow across the twentieth century, and public officials passed new laws that promoted heterosexuality and reinforced marriage often in the name of privacy. Between 1993 and 2011, the military's "don't ask, don't tell" policy required people engaged in same-sex relationships to conceal them from their commanding officers or risk discharge and a loss of benefits. Even as states such as California banned same-sex marriage, bipartisan coalitions in Congress and state legislatures launched marriage promotion initiatives for heterosexual couples in the nation's schools and churches. Married couples in the early twenty-first century benefited from numerous advantages in housing, insurance, and tax policies.[46] Throughout these debates, few people acknowledged that the government has long offered married couples benefits that it has denied to the unmarried or that LGBT activists were responding to a long history of "special rights" conferred on people who conformed to heterosexual norms.

To be sure, many straight-identified Americans expressed sympathy for gay rights in the late twentieth and early twenty-first centuries. However, they often qualified that support either by also emphasizing the importance of marriage between a man and a woman or by offering their support to gay couples who most looked like them and shared their attitudes about sexual respectability. White, middle-class, monogamous gay couples were best positioned to claim the sympathy of straight-identified Americans who shared their larger adherence to other gender and sexual norms. Yet even they faced discrimination. In the twenty-first century, proponents of same-sex marriage not only needed to redefine marriage as a private relationship devoid of any support from the government but also needed to convince the wider electorate that "marriage equality" would violate no one's privacy. The postwar Straight State no longer universally discriminated against all people in same-sex relationships in the early 2000s, but it nevertheless continued to shape many Americans' expectations about who deserved public support and who did not.

The history of the origins of the culture wars thus reveals the importance of moderate voters who disavowed discrimination, even as they embraced a fundamentally discriminatory worldview. Tracing the evolution of public policies, the changing language of the political center, and the transformation of metropolitan space helps make this worldview visible. By the time Californians debated Proposition 6 in 1978, a majority of Americans had benefited from the economic redistribution of goods through processes such as homeownership, had supported heteronormative sex education, and had joined new communities defined by common social characteristics like marriage. The creation and subsequent liberalization of the postwar closet transformed more than just the conservatives who would later make up the Religious Right. It also gave millions of middle-class, self-identified straight voters a shared hierarchical vision that enabled the dismantling of the most repressive elements of the postwar closet and the reinscription of a tiered division between heterosexual and homosexual relationships. Even as gay activists clashed with religious conservatives, the "right to privacy" emerged as a bipartisan discourse designed to limit both the egalitarian agenda of gay liberation and the rightist vision of figures like John Briggs.

PART I

The Family and the State

Chapter 1

Sex and the Crowded City

Many San Franciscans and millions of other Americans believed they were witnessing a sexual crisis in the nation's cities in the 1940s. *Newsweek* editor Harold Isaacs surveyed urban America in 1947 and condemned what he saw as the "widespread neuroticism, juvenile delinquency, sex crimes, venereal disease, wholesale promiscuity and the rising divorce rate" unleashed by World War II. Cities like San Francisco seemed sexually chaotic—even dangerous—to many Americans. Journalist Howard Whitman warned *Collier's* readers that "sex variants" and molesters threatened to abuse children in "alleys or rooming houses." The perceived crisis generated such concern that conflicts erupted over how to address it. Urban residents across the country demanded more from the police. Some called for a religious revival. Others hoped modern psychology might build stronger families. Magazines claimed that "never before has a more favorable opinion existed" for sex education in public schools. Yet the sex education provoked "bitter community arguments" in places like San Francisco over whether it would encourage "self-restraint" or "morbid curiosity and experimentation." When a writer for *Better Homes and Gardens* looked across the country, he allegedly saw numerous communities "scream alarm" at the many "wayward girls, young sex offenders [and] unmarried mothers" in their midst.[1]

World War II triggered much of this anxiety, and San Franciscans felt the war's effects more than most other Americans. The conflict magnified social trends apparent in cities since the nineteenth century, and as a major port and production center, the Bay Area witnessed particularly large changes. The war intensified a sexualized youth culture, brought millions of middle-class women into the paid labor force, and expanded gay life. Seemingly, everywhere San Franciscans looked in the 1940s, the war had shifted the city's sexual norms. Teenagers necked in movie theaters. Married women danced and drank in bars. Prostitutes solicited customers on the street. And gay sailors flirted with men downtown. The war had dramatically shifted the city's demographics, bringing a large influx of African Americans and unmarried people of all races to the West Coast. These newcomers strained San Francisco's tight housing market and sparked shortages that lasted well past V-J Day. Sexuality became more public in these circumstances, as crowded conditions encouraged people to pursue courtships out of the home and exposed residents to the sex lives of their neighbors, roommates, and families. Although urbanites had experienced similar phenomena in other eras, the sheer scope of the war mobilization exposed an even greater number of Americans to the erotic pleasures and perils of modern city living.[2]

Many San Franciscans relished these newfound freedoms, but the war also motivated people to contain what they saw as the excess of the war years and to demand that authorities mitigate the crisis. Living amid a "sexual revolution" in the 1940s, many city residents organized a counterrevolution designed to limit the sexual autonomy of their fellow citizens, and understanding their work first requires understanding San Francisco's sexual geography. Since the nineteenth century, downtowns exhibited the most diverse array of people, households, and dwellings in American urban centers. Residential hotels, apartments, and tenements attracted transient workers, and numerous businesses, including bars, catered to nearby residents and commuters who traveled in and out of downtown.[3] In San Francisco, the wartime sexual revolution largely took place in these spaces, as hundreds of thousands of people flooded the central business district and adjacent neighborhoods. The counterrevolution, by contrast, largely unfolded in "respectable" neighborhoods in the western half of the city. In the late nineteenth and early twentieth centuries, white, middle-class married couples across the country migrated to suburban districts away from downtown. Residents in these areas frequently enjoyed more living space, and the privacy and order of their sexual lives helped them distinguish themselves from what they saw as the sexual "clutter" of poorer districts.[4] While residents near San Francisco's downtown loosened some of the rules around sex, groups in these western "family-friendly" neighborhoods such as the Sunset District worked to stop them.[5]

Supporters of this counterrevolution did not speak with one voice, however. During the 1940s, a wide consensus on the meaning of "family" united

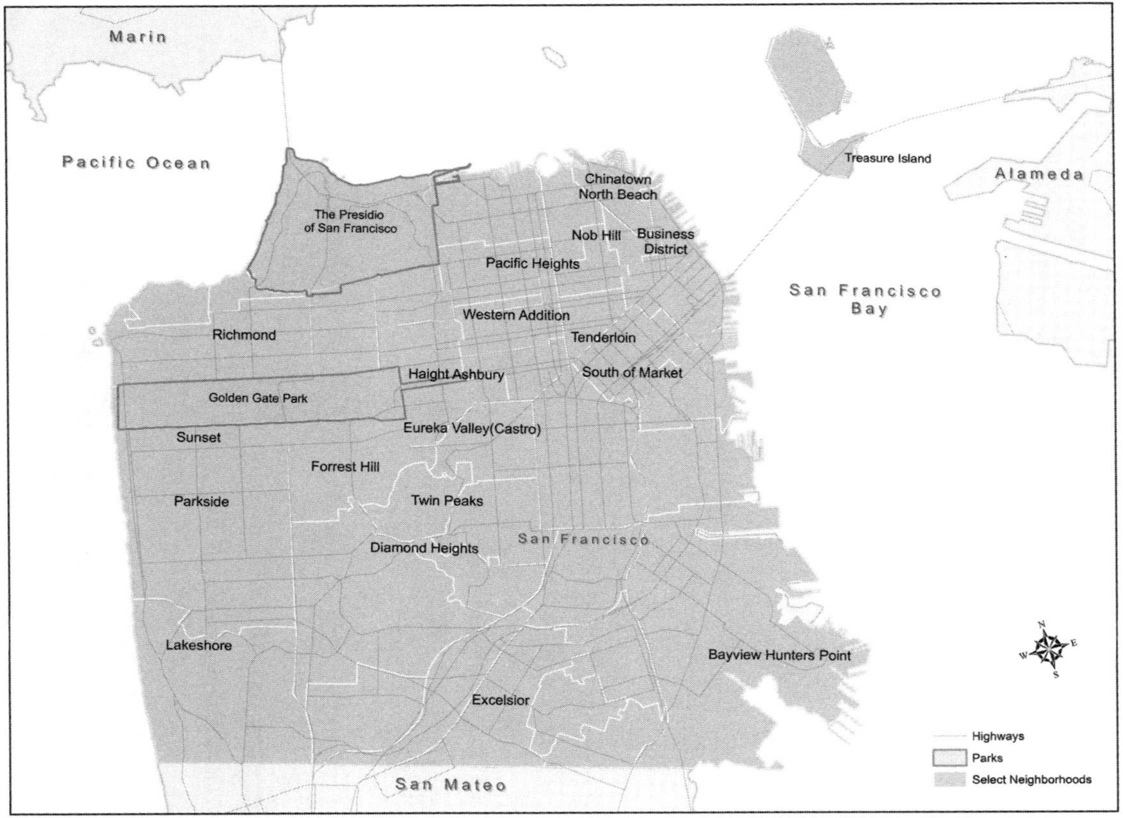

Map 2. Select San Francisco neighborhoods. Center for Urban and Regional Analysis, Ohio State University.

middle-class San Franciscans. Few challenged the assumption that men and women played separate roles in society, that sex should occur within marriage and in the home, or that homosexuality was a dangerous vice. Yet many people who shared this normative vision of family life also disagreed about how to create it, and no issue revealed those fissures more than sex education. During the 1940s, a coalition of psychologists, middle-class women's clubs, and liberal churches pushed for the dissemination of scientific information about sex, marriage, and childrearing. They hoped that greater education for both adults and high school students would build stronger marriages and "clean up" the city. They encountered stiff resistance from conservative clergy and parents who believed sex education in the public schools would encourage young people to experiment with sex and to ignore the teachings of their church. Even as many San Franciscans, therefore, worked to stop the sexual revolution unfolding near downtown, they also clashed about how to halt it.

In short, World War II and the housing crisis opened a window of greater sexual freedom in cities like San Francisco, but they also provoked a movement intent upon closing that window. That counterrevolution was not monolithic. It included significant debates about which institutions could best educate the public about sex. Yet these disputes only underscored the popular consensus in support of normative family life and highlighted the fact that rules governing sexual behavior stem, in part, from the exercise of political power. All of the sides in the debates over sex education, for example, fundamentally agreed on the importance of marriage and the dangers of other kinds of sexuality, including those involving consenting adults. The arguments both for and against the issue contributed to the larger grassroots mobilization of middle-class San Franciscans in favor of limiting others' sexual autonomy. In the wake of these protests, public officials at the local, state, and federal levels would respond with a series of important laws designed to reinforce sexual norms.

The Privacy of Crowds

World War II helped blur the boundary between public and private sexuality for most San Franciscans. Millions of soldiers and war workers moved through the city and crammed into aging housing near its downtown. These crowded living conditions breathed new life into San Francisco's commercial spaces and public places. Eager to escape roommates or families, residents socialized in the city's many bars, cafeterias, streets, and parks. Numerous gay men and lesbians, in particular, took advantage of the semi-anonymity of these crowded spaces. The war brought many people who were attracted to others of the same sex to the city, and they found one another in some of the packed bars and streets. Queer communities largely blended in with the wider populace, and in some cases, the sheer volume of people sometimes freed them to have sex in semi-secluded places without garnering unwanted attention. Crowded housing, furthermore, forced many San Franciscans to adjust their expectations of their roommates and neighbors at home. While judgmental families and neighbors compelled some to have sex in public, others benefited from the ways that crowded apartments forced residents to adjust their expectations of sexual privacy. Cramped apartment dwellers often kept a respectful distance from their roommates and neighbors' relationships. Even as public spaces allowed some people to escape into urban anonymity, packed living conditions also forced many residents to expect to be exposed to a certain amount of other people's sex lives at home.

San Francisco had enjoyed a reputation as a "Wide Open Town" since the nineteenth-century Gold Rush, but World War II fundamentally transformed the city.[6] As an embarkation point for the war in the Pacific, San Francisco experienced an enormous population boom.[7] Between 1940 and 1943, close to 314,000 people migrated to the Bay Area, and in 1945, San Francisco's population soared to an all-time high of 825,000 people.[8] Many of these newcomers were young and unmarried. One survey found that almost 40 percent of new residents were between twenty and thirty-four years old, and 18 percent of them were under the age of fifteen. State officials declared that the war had "flooded" California with young transients and concluded that many of them had migrated due to unhappy or "broken" homes.[9] Furthermore, the boom in industrial employment dramatically shifted San Francisco's racial makeup. The number of African Americans in the city grew tremendously during the conflict. Whereas approximately 4,800 black inhabitants lived in San Francisco in 1940, almost 25,000 resided there in 1945.[10]

This influx of war workers and military personnel provoked a dramatic shift in sexual and gender norms. Across the country, the mass migration of people from small towns to major cities pushed members of the armed services and wartime industrial workers into sex-segregated environments far from home. City bars served as key gathering point for increasingly self-aware queer communities in San Francisco.[11] At the same time, large numbers of women entered the paid labor force. Although many women worked for pay before the 1940s, the shortage of men during the war pushed an unprecedented number of female laborers into traditionally male industries. According to one estimate, women made up between 36 and 41 percent of all government workers in California during the war and 40 percent of the personnel on some of the military bases in the Bay Area.[12] This surge in employment gave San Francisco female workers an unprecedented amount of social autonomy. Contemporaries frequently commented on the large numbers of women living on their own in downtown rooming houses, out at bars, or walking the streets. Lesbians in particular benefited from the ways that paid labor allowed them to live independent from hostile families, and the wartime boom helped create an environment where some women felt freer to love other women.[13]

Although the war affected all of San Francisco, it transformed older neighborhoods near downtown more than other districts. Like other major cities, the areas around the central core provided most of San Francisco's rental housing and nightlife, and they exhibited the starkest racial and class divides in the metropolis. Three of the most affluent predominantly white neighborhoods—Nob Hill, Russian Hill, and Pacific Heights—dotted inclines north of downtown. In general, residents in these districts enjoyed a fair amount of personal privacy thanks to the sheer size of their homes. Gilded Age millionaires like Leland Stanford erected enormous houses in Nob Hill, inspiring Robert Louis Stevenson to dub the area the "Hill of Palaces." Developers built only slightly more modest luxury apartment buildings in Russian Hill and Pacific Heights in the 1920s, offering residents doormen and units that sometimes encompassed an entire floor of the building.[14]

San Francisco's poorest areas, by contrast, were scattered around the business district's other edges. The South of Market and Tenderloin districts housed much of the industrial workforce that labored along the waterfront and factories south of downtown. Like other cities, race defined San Francisco's housing markets. Real estate discrimination and restrictive covenants ensured that almost every single person of Chinese descent in the city in 1940 inhabited just two crowded census tracts on downtown's northeastern side. The relatively small prewar African American community in San Francisco lived relatively interspersed throughout the city, but some whites dubbed the small cluster of black-owned businesses northwest of downtown in the multiracial Western Addition "Little Harlem." In all of these neighborhoods, personal privacy often seemed like a luxury. Residents frequently lived with people outside of their immediate families and carried out their social lives in public spaces. High unemployment, public drinking, and the frequent congregation of men on street corners in one strip of the South of Market, for example, prompted wealthier residents to label the area a "Skid Row."[15]

San Francisco's prewar sexual economy roughly mapped onto these class and racial divisions. Downtown theaters, bars, and restaurants offered some of the primary sites for middle-class, heterosexual dating in the city. Middle-class couples went to movies at cinemas like the Paramount on Market Street, dined at white cloth restaurants in downtown neighborhoods like North Beach, and drank cocktails in hotel bars in Nob Hill. Like many cities, San Francisco police tolerated prostitution, gambling, and unlicensed alcohol sales in predominantly black and Asian American neighborhoods. Therefore, many white San Franciscans looking for exotic, racialized thrills away from respectable entertainment went to speakeasies in the Western Addition and cabarets in Chinatown.[16] Similarly, gay bars flourished after the end of Prohibition, bringing queer men and women to neighborhoods like North Beach and the Tenderloin. Mona's, near Chinatown, was one of the West Coast's best-known lesbian bars. Although the city's respectable classes disdained these queer businesses, many patrons nevertheless sought them out. Drag shows at bars like North Beach's Finnoccio's garnered large numbers of "slummers" interested in gawking at the performers. Police occasionally raided these establishments for violating codes against female impersonation or "lewd" behavior, but a desire to protect San Francisco tourism and rampant graft minimized trouble from authorities.[17]

These downtown neighborhoods strained to accommodate the wave of new residents in the 1940s. With war-related industries siphoning off labor and raw materials, home construction stalled across the country at the exact moment that people flooded cities such as San Francisco. Public Health Director J. C. Geiger told federal investigators that the population boom had pushed San Francisco's residential hotels to the limit, with many of the lodging houses "occupied almost entirely by shipyard workers who have come here from other parts of the country."[18] City and federal officials struggled to house newcomers in the city, and the shortage lasted well past V-J Day. In 1945, Northern California's biggest builder announced that waiting lists for new homes ran ten to twelve people deep, and San Franciscans complained about high rents, picky landlords, and cramped living conditions as late as 1949.[19]

The shortage particularly hurt poor San Franciscans, including most people of color. Economic circumstances had long forced the poor to live with other people, and the wartime boom only magnified this problem. In one particularly egregious instance, city health inspectors found a Western Addition basement divided into seven apartments by old wood and cardboard and inhabited by thirty-four people.[20] A study of Chinatown in 1947 found that dwellings in the neighborhood averaged one toilet for every twenty-eight people.[21] Housing discrimination denied most people of color the option to live in most neighborhoods, and segregation ensured that many African Americans, Asian Americans, and Latinos struggled to find places to live well after the crisis abated for most native-born whites.[22]

This housing crunch, however, marked an exceptional period in San Francisco and the nation's history. Poor residents suffered the worst hardships, but the severity of the crisis affected an unprecedented number of people living near downtown. Only the truly wealthy escaped the crisis altogether. Magazines described upscale San Francisco hotel lobbies "packed with dejected people" and relayed horror stories about hardworking families living in converted mortuaries.[23] Profiteers divided up Nob Hill mansions and turned them into apartment houses.[24] In fact, for many journalists, the difficulties of relatively well-off people were precisely what made the "shortage" a "crisis." "But now it isn't only the one third ill-housed who must make do with cast-off, filtered down housing," complained two writers in *Collier's* magazine in 1947. "Now the great American middle-class . . . must get their houses secondhand."[25]

Many working-class people had long conducted part or all of their courtships in public, but the housing crisis in the 1940s meant that even many well-to-do San Franciscans thought about privacy in ways comparable to the poor. Sometimes couples wanted to keep their relationships secret from their parents or neighbors. Sometimes they shared homes with so many people that a crowded street, bar, park, or movie theater offered them more privacy. Sometimes the briefest meeting on a busy corner appeared to offer the possibility of romance and adventure. Moviegoers complained about "young men and their girls making love" in theaters, and academic experts claimed that small apartments offered "no privacy," compelling couples to "conduct their courtships on the streets" and other public

Figure 1. Servicemen sleeping in hotel lobby, 1943. Fang family *San Francisco Examiner* photograph archive negative files, BANC PIC 2006.029:105872.06.5—NEG, box 832. © Regents of the University of California, Bancroft Library, University of California, Berkeley.

spaces.[26] Health authorities in San Francisco noted an upsurge in young men and women meeting in commercial spaces like bars. These experts worried that young women, in particular, moved in with girlfriends in hotels after a "chance meeting on a streetcar or in a dance hall" and that "such living arrangements were conducive to unstable, promiscuous behavior."[27] San Francisco's district attorney reported that "transient" young people were living in "flop houses" and going home with "friendly truck drivers or other chance pick-up acquaintances."[28]

The housing crisis and the larger revolution in public sexuality framed the specific expansion of gay life in the city. In the early twentieth century, busy parks, street corners, and cafeterias had masked a semi-visible subculture, and gay men had found one another in the semi-anonymous spaces of the modern city.[29] Similarly, lesbians and gay men who came out during the war frequently recalled the crowded living conditions of the 1940s, and many of them rejoiced at the semi-anonymity offered by San Francisco's crowded streets, bars, and theaters. Pat Bond remembered living with "ten dykes" in an "old beat-up house" in San Francisco when she got out of the Navy after the war. They threw wild parties, caroused on Grant Street, and went to bars in North Beach.[30] Jim Kepner hid his sexuality from his father and sister when he lived with them in a one-bedroom apartment near downtown in the 1940s. His first sexual experience came after a sailor picked him up near the financial district. The two men saw one another regularly and slept together in the sailor's converted "utility room" in a rooming house downtown.[31]

Living with parents or roommates pushed many San Franciscans' courtship into public spaces, but crowding also facilitated other kinds of sexual encounters. In some cases, the crunch facilitated new relationships merely by bringing many people under the same roof. While soldiers slept with others of the same sex in cramped barracks and train cars, residents in crowded tenements and rooming houses adjusted their expectations of sexual privacy.[32] Living in rooms with thin walls or with many roommates meant fewer San Franciscans could expect to escape others' sex lives, and many of them learned to keep a tolerant distance. Roland Bianchi, for example, worked for a North Beach grocer in the 1940s, and he wrote in his memoir about a time when he discovered a young woman from the neighborhood having sex with a man in his store's basement. "What audacity," he recalled thinking, "But then the romantic in me thought Nina took her boyfriend here because she has no privacy at home." Bianchi felt voyeuristic curiosity and revulsion upon finding the lovers in the basement, but he ultimately pretended not to have seen them.[33]

No example illustrates the ways cramped housing shifted many San Franciscans' expectations of sexual privacy better than the experiences of William Gaddis. A white gay man, Gaddis served in the Navy officer corps, avidly took part in Oakland and San Francisco's booming nightlife, and wrote letters detailing his sexual exploits to friends in the early 1940s. He and his large social circle benefited from the semi-open sexual culture of the war years, and their racial and class backgrounds allowed them to travel across the metropolis. They attended drag shows at cabarets like Finnochio's, patronized gay bars in North Beach and the Tenderloin, and crossed the color line on slumming excursions to "Negro spots" in neighborhoods like West Oakland. Gaddis and his comrades picked up sailors on busy streets, and their flirting often took place in full view of other people. On one occasion, he and two companions "put on a good show" as they ate at a Tenderloin diner, and Gaddis noted that other patrons were "really getting us," including a "Queen and soldier who were standing outside watching."[34]

Gaddis lived outside San Francisco, but he frequently stayed in cheap hotels or at friends' apartments after long nights of drinking in the city. Unable to drive home, he and some of the men he knew often shared rooms and slept together. In some cases, crowded conditions forced them to navigate the awkwardness of trying to have sex when they did not necessarily know everyone in the shared space, and his letters reveal some of the ways that San Franciscans allowed for sex, even gay sex, amid the housing shortage. After one night of drinking, for example, Gaddis and a group of sailors moved their party from a bar to a friend's apartment. When they arrived, they found the friend's sister, her boyfriend, and a group of companions having a celebration of their own. The sister, according to Gaddis, was "hep to the situation," but her boyfriend took "too astute an interest" in the gay sailors who were drunk, "carryin' on," and "dancing together." In order to distract her boyfriend, the sister convinced her group to leave the apartment and freed the sailors to drink in peace. Later, Gaddis retired to a bedroom with a man he had met earlier in the evening. They tried to have sex, but his friends kept drunkenly bursting into the room and interrupting them. Finally, Gaddis persuaded them to leave him alone with the man, "which enabled us to finish our party in privacy."[35]

All of these letters underscore sexuality's social dimension. Busy streets, crowded diners, packed bars, and full movie theaters granted San Franciscans a certain degree of anonymity, and even though Gaddis flirted with other men in full view of others, they tolerated his behavior as a part of downtown's larger nightlife—at least among whites. Observers may have found his "show" in the diner amusing, confusing, or repulsive, but they nevertheless left him alone. Similarly, many friends, family members, neighbors, and roommates looked the other way when they confronted sex in crowded housing. Gaddis's story about the late-night party has two examples of this kind of tolerance. First, the sister steered her boyfriend and companions out of the apartment when the gay sailors showed up. It is not clear if her brother's friends embarrassed her or if she wanted to help them. But she did not care enough about their behavior to scold them or call the police. Second, Gaddis saw the "privacy" he enjoyed with his date as the result of others' decision to leave them alone. Rather than the product of a locked door or other obstruction, he gained a long-awaited moment of intimacy after his friends finally agreed to stop bothering him. In all of these cases, other people were at least partial witnesses to others' sex lives. The privacy that people like Gaddis enjoyed came thanks to a mutual agreement that they continue undisturbed. Far from secret, sex in these stories happened thanks to the willingness of others to look the other way.

During the 1940s, therefore, the in-migration of new people and crowded housing reshaped the ways in which many San Franciscans understood sex and personal space. Residents frequently noted the ways that the lines between public and private sexuality appeared to blur during the war years. For many San Franciscans, these circumstances represented a kind of liberation. Although taboos against homosexuality or extramarital relations did not fall away entirely, the 1940s were a brief period when some city dwellers learned to tolerate behaviors they might have otherwise condemned. Rather than a clouded secret, many San Franciscans occasionally encountered others' sex lives on the streets, in bars, and even in their own homes during the war and its aftermath.

The Dangers of the Street

While many lesbians and gay men experienced the war and the housing shortage as a moment of increased freedom, most residents in the city's middle-class districts saw the era differently. Many of them interpreted the public displays of a new dating culture, unsupervised teenagers, and queer sexuality as signs of moral decay. For decades, white middle-class families had drawn a sharp line between the feminine, private world of the home and the masculine, public realm of the street. This ideology justified the movement of relatively affluent parents with children away from downtowns, and it sustained a number of social movements dedicated to upholding the importance of marriage and sexual respectability. During the war, white middle-class San Franciscans in the outer districts mobilized to counter what they saw as the disorderly world of the street, calling upon civic authorities to crack down on the sexual revolution near downtown.

The origins of this countermovement lay in the bifurcated sexual ideology through which many middle-class San Franciscans understood the city. From the early to the mid-twentieth century, increasing numbers of middle-class Americans subscribed to what historians have called "sexual liberalism." Fewer people saw sex primarily as a procreative function, and more and more of them viewed it as a pleasurable act that built stronger relationships and led to greater personal satisfaction. However, this "liberalization" applied only to married couples. Even as they broadened the definition of acceptable sex, many middle-class Americans grew more critical of extramarital relations, "redrawing the boundaries" between "moral" and "immoral" sex. More married couples used birth control and thought of intercourse as an act of pleasure than ever before, but growing numbers of people also condemned pornography, teen sexuality, homosexuality, and prostitution.[36]

Many San Franciscans mapped these distinctions onto the urban landscape. For many, "homes" signified the ostensibly sacred world of marriage, family, and children. Mothers, in this ideology, did not work for pay, and their nurturing domestic labor allegedly differed sharply from the commercial, masculine world of downtown.[37] When it came to sex, the "home" had two important functions. First, it represented the only place where socially acceptable sex took place. Sexual liberalism's promise of pleasure within marriage rested on a distancing of the marital relationship from other kinds of relationships. Discourses about the home expressed this separation, celebrating marital sex as an exceptional form of intimacy best expressed in private. *Let's Tell the Truth About Sex*, a popular 1948 sex education manual for parents, made this view explicit and described sex as "something which is very private and very sacred. It is the mother's and father's special expression of their love and it has meaning only for them. It would not even occur if anyone else were present."[38] This was an ideal and not necessarily a reflection of the lived experience of actual couples. Yet it reveals the popular belief that marital sex was "special" and needed to be expressed apart from the wider world.

Second, the "home" was the place in which parents, particularly mothers, taught children about marriage and respectability. Young people allegedly learned how to establish their own households and how to avoid temptations by witnessing their parents' marriages and by formal instruction from their mothers. Many white middle-class Americans believed in the importance of "character," which children allegedly learned unconsciously by observing their families and thanks to explicit teachings given by their parents. The "home," therefore, not only signified the private world of the family but also symbolized a kind of sexual respectability passed on from generation to generation. According to one of California's leading advocates for sex education, "A child's basic character is established in the home, and if it is not established on a sound emotional basis, it leads to habits and attitudes in later life injurious to the individual and community."[39]

This private, nurturing world of the home stood opposed to what many middle-class San Franciscans saw as the dangers of the "street," "alley," or "gutter," and they used these terms interchangeably to describe different perceived threats to the family. Sometimes these places signified urban vice. Working-class bars, brothels, dance halls, erotic bookstores, and gambling houses, in particular, attracted well-to-do residents' contempt because of the supposed dangers they posed to young people. During the war, unsupervised kids in San Francisco prompted an expert on juvenile delinquency to complain about children "roaming the streets" and "low places" in search of "adventure, excitement . . . gambling, and sex."[40] At other times, the terms referred to youthful peer pressure and unsupervised children. "The boy with an inadequate home life goes out in the street [and] joins a gang," complained one juvenile expert.[41] And in yet still other cases, middle-class residents used the terms to explain the physical dangers posed by violent adults. Cities by their very nature allegedly gave people anonymity, they argued, and some people took advantage of that freedom to break rules. Popular author and San Francisco psychiatrist Joseph Catton warned readers in 1940 of a broken court system that pushed killers "out onto the street over and over again."[42]

People who used these terms often spoke of them figuratively, imposing a moral order onto the chaotic landscape of the modern city. They represented an ideal, which did not necessarily reflect the actual experiences of real-life people. But this ideology nevertheless had real-world effects in cities like San Francisco. In the two decades before World War II, for example, the nascent field of urban planning translated this ideal about "homes" and "streets" into theories about the built environment. Clarence Perry was one of the most celebrated planners of the United States in the late 1920s and 1930s, and he worried that the shape of contemporary cities, particularly downtowns, hurt marriages and childrearing. Haphazard planning, he contended, forced parents to rush to distant schools and stores. Married couples with children lived in large apartment complexes where they never knew their neighbors and raised families in relative isolation. Distant parks meant that children sometimes wandered far from home to play while the shortage of yards in urban areas forced them to go into dangerous areas. When "children are forced to obtain their play opportunities and character development from the street," Perry claimed, "then his conduct is not unlike that of the cuckoo which lays eggs in other birds' nests, for strangers to hatch." Adrift in a sea of strangers, children encountered all manner of role models and dangers in cities.[43]

Perry claimed that better neighborhood design could solve these problems, and notions about literal and figurative streets guided much of his thinking. City builders, he argued, should pool amenities that married couples with children needed, such as schools, churches, and playgrounds, in residential areas, and they should exclude most commerce. Busy roads should surround the neighborhood like large moats, while winding lanes and cul-de-sacs connected individual houses to the rest of the city. This traffic system not only kept speeding cars away from areas with children but also gave neighborhoods clearly demarcated boundaries. Perry believed that the combination of institutions like schools and churches with the child-friendly street system would foster strong communities of married couples with children, resisting the dangers of the modern city. He, therefore, forbade developers from building structures that might draw "large crowds of strangers," and he contrasted his idealized "family-friendly" neighborhoods with the allegedly alienated "bachelor men and women" in downtown rooming houses.[44]

Perry's ideas about what he called the "neighborhood unit" were only starting to gain a wider audience when builders began to develop San Francisco's western residential districts, but his theories clearly influenced some of their shape and composition. Three steep inclines—the Twin Peaks and Mount Davison—contained most housing construction close to downtown for most of San Francisco's history, but the opening of streetcar tunnels in 1918 and 1922 spurred a building boom on the city's west side below Golden Gate Park. Here during the 1920s and 1930s, ambitious developers built rows of white houses and neighborhoods with bucolic names like the Sunset, Parkside, and Forest Hill, hoping to attract middle-class parents with children. By the time San Francisco implemented its first citywide plan in the early 1940s, planners tried their best to incorporate Perry's ideals. They pushed traffic in the Sunset to major roads, for example, and they limited commercial development in the neighborhoods. Even amid the worst housing shortage of the twentieth century, San Francisco officials allotted ample space west of the Twin Peaks for single-family detached homes with yards and made it harder to build apartments in the area.[45]

The construction of these neighborhoods west of downtown prompted an influx of white, middle-class couples with children, and the area gradually gained a reputation as a "good place" for family living and social conformity. Racial covenants and unwritten segregationist agreements covered most of the neighborhoods, limiting occupancy to members of the "Caucasian race," and residents were often married and relatively prosperous. Even as crowded conditions near downtown enabled a sexual revolution, census tracts west of the Twin Peaks boasted some of the highest percentages of married couples with their own households in the city. Many of the newer, mass-produced homes offered families modest amounts of personal privacy, boasting at least two bedrooms, a living room, and backyard. Neighborhoods often included small commercial strips with stores and movie theaters, but much of the area's social life revolved around education and religion. The local Council of Churches called the West Side "San Francisco at Its Best," thanks to its high attendance at Sunday services. In order to accommodate the area's many children after the war, the Board of Education built four new elementary schools in the Sunset District alone. By the late 1940s, the area west of the Twin Peaks had earned such a reputation for social and physical homogeneity that Herb Caen, the *Chronicle*'s snarky columnist, dismissed it as a bunch of "little white new houses" parading like "stucco lemmings" into the sea.[46]

San Francisco did not look exactly like the drawings in Perry's books, but his ideas about neighborhood cohesiveness nevertheless circulated among the city's realtors, builders, and homeowners. Residents in places like the Sunset or Parkside believed that neighborhoods should foster environments good for marriage and children while screening out undesirable strangers. The West of Twin Peaks Central Council united several area homeowners groups in the early 1940s and opposed most commercial development, vowing "to keep the section residential."[47] Concerns about property values frequently overlapped with childrearing concerns, and parent groups worked with homeowners associations to fight unwanted development. West Side parents, for example, attempted to limit bars near their homes because they might "attract undesirables." One resident opposed a tavern since "people move to our area to live and raise children—not to drink."[48]

Homeowners associations have long drawn historians' attention for the role they played in perpetuating segregation. San Francisco "improvement clubs," like their counterparts elsewhere, closed most housing markets to

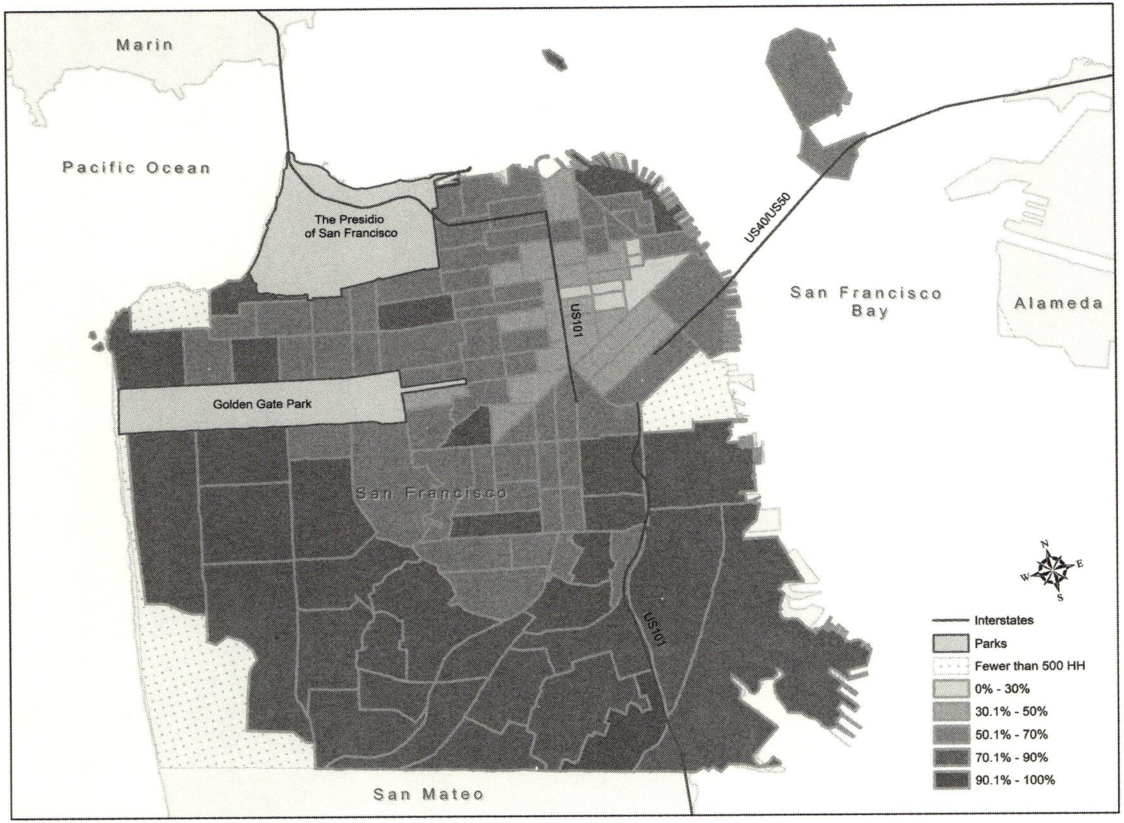

Map 3. Percentage of married couples with their own household in San Francisco by census tract, 1950. This map does not include information for tracts with fewer than 500 households. Center for Urban and Regional Analysis, Ohio State University.

nonwhite residents. During the war, homeowners associations west of the Twin Peaks fielded rumors that African American and Filipino renters sought to move to the area, and their commitment to close their district to nonwhites sprang from concerns about the dangers of the "street."[49] Many whites naturalized the vice trade in places like the Western Addition and assumed that black residents threatened to spread illicit sex and crime to other neighborhoods. One civil rights investigation in San Francisco found that homeowners associations resisted integration, in part, because they believed black men "linger on sidewalks and street corners" and wanted to be "around white girls."[50] When whites organized in a southwest district to bar African Americans from the neighborhood, they alleged that black people brought "crime, delinquency, and unsanitary conditions" with them. "The future of our community, our property, and our children is at stake," they declared.[51] When the U.S. Supreme Court invalidated racial covenants in 1948, therefore, white homeowners in places like the neighborhoods west of the Twin Peaks continued to discriminate against most people of color.[52]

During the 1940s, anxieties about changes in the city prompted many of these residents to organize against what they saw as the sexuality of "the streets," and their connections to City Hall helped them immensely. Many of the officials in charge of policing sex, in fact, themselves lived west of the Twin Peaks. When these authorities heard complaints about sex and the city, they often heard them from their families, friends, and neighbors. Public Health Director J. C. Geiger and District Attorney Edmund Brown, for example, lived near each other in Forest Hill. Geiger worried about the morals of "streetwalkers" and "young patriotic girls," while Brown called the "growing number of homosexuals" in San Francisco during the war one of the most "alarming problems" he faced. George Reilly, the head of the city's liquor licensing agency, lived in the Sunset District and closed several bars during the war for allegedly catering to gay men and prostitutes.[53] In 1942, Geiger and Deputy Police Chief Michael Riordan—both residents of the West Side—proposed an ordinance to the city Board of Supervisors that would have made it a misdemeanor for someone to have intercourse "with a female not the wife of the male or . . . with a male not the husband of the female."[54]

The history of Geiger and Riordan's bill, in particular, reveals the ways that some residents west of the Twin Peaks saw even consensual sex between adults as a matter of public concern and that those concerns were focused specifically on San Francisco's downtown. Initially, their proposal would have criminalized all sex between unmarried people. It included punishments for those who "transported" or "received" people who had that kind of sex, and it applied to all acts committed "near any thoroughfare or in any public or private place."[55] Some of the supervisors, however, objected to what they saw as the vagueness of the bill, and they revised it to make it more specific. The new version continued to punish sex outside of marriage, but their changes underscore their particular concerns about downtown. The board removed the word "private" but kept language from the previous bill that punished anyone who "knowingly receives, offers, or agrees to receive any person into any place or building for the purpose of assignation . . . or knowingly permits any person to remain there for any such purposes." Whereas the stricken word "private" might have applied to all indoor extramarital sex in the city, the latter language primarily applied to hotel managers and landlords who allowed residents to sleep together on their property. Therefore, if unmarried San Franciscans had sex in homes that they owned, then the law did not apply to them. But if they rented a room or apartment and their landlord or hotel manager knew they were having sex outside of marriage, then the latter had a responsibility to turn them in to the police. With the matter clarified, the board unanimously passed the bill into law in November 1942.[56]

A second example of middle-class residents' concerns about the wartime sexual revolution emerged in a plan to combat juvenile delinquency submitted by Supervisor Chester MacPhee a year later. All members of the board campaigned for office citywide, and no supervisor represented an individual district. Yet MacPhee had strong ties to the area west of the Twin Peaks that helped him stay in office from 1941 to 1953. A realtor and insurance agent, he profited heavily from the construction boom on the West Side and bought a home for his family in the St. Francis Wood neighborhood. In 1943, he worked with dozens of community groups to develop what he called a "Master Plan for Youth." In a report submitted to the Board of Supervisors, MacPhee blamed the housing crisis, wartime migration, and working mothers for the destruction of "well regulated homes" and the abandonment of youth to "outside places" where "temptations abound."[57] He called for money for playgrounds, recreation facilities—including a half-million-dollar Sunset District community center—and "more emphasis on moral and spiritual values" in public schools. This project would not only guide young people toward healthy role models but also displace some of the "persons of immoral character" who were frequenting some of the city's parks.[58]

Support for this proposal came overwhelmingly from the middle-class and affluent parts of San Francisco. MacPhee thanked eighty-nine concerned citizens for their contributions to the plan in his report to the board. Fourteen of those citizens either did not live in San Francisco or were not listed in the city directory. Thirty-four of the remainder resided west of the Twin Peaks, twenty of them came from the wealthy neighborhoods north of downtown like Pacific Heights, and seven lived in the Richmond, an older streetcar district north of Golden Gate Park. Only thirteen of the remaining citizens named in the report came from other parts of the city, and just two of them came from an area adjacent to downtown, like the Western Addition. In other words, just under half of the people with known addresses in the city thanked by MacPhee lived west of the Twin Peaks, and 80 percent of them came from the city's wealthy and middle-class districts. And while many of the citizens named in the report had economic interests downtown, almost none of them lived there.[59]

The most dramatic example of the mobilization of San Francisco's middle-class "family" districts, however, took place amid a wave of anxiety about child molesters that erupted across the country in 1949. Ever since the start of the war, the influx of newcomers and seemingly fluid sexual morals of the city had set many of San Francisco's white middle-class parents on edge. In 1947, San Francisco's Second District Parent-Teacher Association (PTA) worried about gay cruising and possible molesters in neighborhood parks and asked city officials "to curb the sex perverts" and for more supervision at playgrounds.[60] Their anxiety seemed justified when several brutal crimes, including the rape and murder of a six-year-old in Los Angeles, grabbed national headlines two years later. Although officials across the country noticed no statistical uptick in crimes against children, magazines and newspapers painted American cities as dangerous places overrun by "psychopaths." *Collier's* magazine alleged that in city after city, children "were becoming hunted game, stalked by the molester." Narratives like this one highlighted the dangers of dark alleys and deserted streets and encouraged parents to bring their families inside after dark.[61]

Historians have aptly attributed the heightened anxiety about molesters to the chaos created by the war. The in-migration of workers, the racial turnover in many neighborhoods, the flood of women into the paid labor force, the sexual revolution, and the housing shortage of the 1940s prompted fears that streets full of strangers endangered children. Yet the most forceful example of the panic in San Francisco came in the most homogeneous and least congested part of the city. Residents west of the Twin Peaks had long worried about the threats posed by outsiders. Not long after the national press began its exposés of sex crimes, San Francisco newspapers reported that a man had tried to abduct a kindergartner near her Sunset District elementary school. The Second District PTA responded by holding meetings across San Francisco and organized a committee of West Side residents to force officials to pay more attention to the dangers of molesters. Parents pressed city officials for greater surveillance of playgrounds and parks, and they asked Governor Earl Warren and San Francisco Police Chief Michael Mitchell to do background checks on all adults working with young people, including teachers. Mitchell responded to the outcry over the attempted kidnapping by ordering officers to watch for suspects "loitering in the vicinity of schools."[62]

The immediate issue that prompted these meetings was the fear of child molestation and violence. But the anxiety about molesters sprang from larger concerns about sex in the city. The scare at the Sunset District elementary school seemed to confirm many residents' beliefs that the war had somehow unleashed dangerous sexual forces in San Francisco, and they did not limit their complaints to the specific issue of pedophilia. Instead, they waged a broader campaign to tighten the social rules governing sex in the city. Just one month after the scare at the Sunset District elementary school, for example, San Francisco grand jurors demanded more police to crack down on night clubs, homosexuals, and prostitutes.[63] Four months later, Supervisor Chester MacPhee tried to pass a bill that would have required the parents of "delinquents" to appear in court to explain the misbehavior of their children.[64]

The molester scare in 1949, therefore, represented an extreme example of neighborhood activism designed to protect children, marriage, and the family. Figures like MacPhee exemplified a "family-centered" movement from residents in western districts who worried about what they saw as the loosening of morality near downtown. The panic about child molesters represented the most dramatic example of this social activism, but middle-class voters west of the Twin Peaks pursued multiple strategies to limit the dangers of the "street." These included greater policing, new parks, and penalties for the parents of delinquent children. These campaigns overlapped because voters did not necessarily differentiate between child molestation and premarital sex, prostitution, or homosexuality. These issues all appeared on a continuum of loosened morals and threats to normative family life.

Sex Education in the Home, School, and Church

Discussions about the dangers of the "street" revealed a consensus among many white middle-class San Franciscans that the turmoil of the war years had upset the moral order of the city and that the government needed to crack down on sexual expression outside of marriage. However, many residents disagreed on how to best protect children and marriage, and no issue better exemplified those disagreements than the fights over sex education. Proponents of the issue argued that public education represented the only way to bypass "problem parents" and reach all of the families in the city. Their opponents saw the issue as an attempt to usurp the authority of religious institutions, like the Catholic Church, and as a slippery slope toward pornography. Teaching young people about sex, they argued, would only encourage them to experiment and to sample the vices of the "street." However, both sides of the debate agreed that more needed to be done for marriage and the protection of children.

Although many later associated "sex education" primarily with instruction in public schools, its supporters originally defined the term more broadly. Campaigns for sex education began in the early twentieth century amid widespread anxiety that urbanization had eroded the family and ushered in a more sexually permissive society. Many medical professionals and middle-class city dwellers, including in San Francisco, worried about the dangers of the "street," such as prostitution, premarital sex, pornography, interracial sex, and venereal disease. These reformers believed that the three key "preventative agencies," the home, school, and church, could roll back these dangers and encourage marriage. "Sex education" in this context meant teaching youth to resist the temptations of urban vice and pushing parents to teach their children responsibility. Proponents of the issue in San Francisco in 1915, for example, declared their intention to speak to many different people, including "young manhood and womanhood," "those who were taking on the cares and responsibilities of matrimony," and those "assuming the burden of parenthood." Reaching these audiences meant that the "school and home" would need to cooperate with "religious, social, and industrial agencies."[65]

World War II reinvigorated many Americans' support for this broader, disciplinary vision of sex education and underscored the issue's history primarily as a question of public morality. Lester Kirkendall, one of the nation's foremost authorities on sex education, complained in 1944 that "war experiences have swept away restraints . . . and have led to promiscuity and sexual freedom." Young people, he alleged, who had "comprehensive home, school, and church training" were less likely to engage in premarital sex.[66] Unlike Americans in later decades who would invoke an individual "right to privacy," sex education's supporters in the 1940s fervently believed that the dangers of sex required collective solutions. Even ideal parents needed help from the state, in the form of the public education system, and organized religion. Schools reached almost all children, and they promised to create future generations of good citizens. Churches provided sacred wisdom that helped people discern right from wrong. Together, they allegedly offered compatible and reinforcing messages for city residents. Kirkendall claimed that homes, schools, and churches all served different needs and all had "certain contributions to make."[67] The danger of weak parents, however, made cooperation between the three agencies more crucial. If Americans left sex education solely to parents, they risked young people learning about sex from the "street." According to Kirkendall, "All parents are concerned when certain parents fail in their responsibility," and therefore "each of the institutions—church, school, and home—should encourage the effective participation of the others."[68]

The drive for sex education in San Francisco in the 1940s brought together a coalition of three different groups of activists built around this imagined trinity of institutions. The first group included large numbers of psychologists and experts in related fields like education and social work. The Mental Hygiene Society of Northern California (MHSNC) was San Francisco's largest collection of mental health professionals, and it included several experts who saw sex education as a public health necessity. Like the burgeoning field of psychology across the country, these professionals believed that mental health could be examined, recorded, and, subsequently, replicated. The Society's mission lay in not only studying the origins of what they called "normal mental and emotional development" but also disseminating knowledge about its causes in order to build a better society. MHSNC's members, therefore, came together as leaders in a public health campaign to promote "normal" human behavior.[69]

Sex education lay near the center of this desire to encourage healthy norms, and the Mental Hygiene Society updated the disciplinary tendencies long associated with the issue with the latest psychological theories. Most psychologists in the 1940s, including leaders in the MHSNC, argued that human sexuality moved through stages, evolving as a person aged. According to the reigning orthodoxy in the field, infants and children often experimented with autoerotic pleasure. Adolescents, meanwhile, often felt strong homosexual attachments to others of the same sex. Those feelings allegedly usually fell away by the time a youth entered high school, and experts claimed that older teens replaced the homoerotic longings of adolescence with more mature feelings for the opposite sex. Those emotions allegedly ultimately culminated in marriage and the launching of a new cycle when a couple had children of their own.[70]

People frequently moved through these steps with little or no problem, but sexual traumas or negative role models could stall them. Psychologists in the 1940s often equated children with sponges, unconsciously absorbing attitudes and ideas about sex. Poor role models, like bickering parents or obsessive teachers, could derail the healthy march toward marriage without even knowing it. Experts, therefore, called adult relationships other than marital heterosexuality "deviations" or "variants" because they represented forms of "arrested development," a kind of straying away from the normal evolution toward marriage. For most doctors, "sex education" meant teaching these theories to parents and other adults who worked with children in order to avoid this problem. Hale Shirley, a leading member of the Mental Hygiene Society, claimed that doctors could treat "sexual problems" emanating in childhood by using education to correct the "disturbing environmental conditions" that created them.[71]

Most of the MSHNC's directors and officers lived in exclusive neighborhoods near San Francisco's largest hospitals like Pacific Heights, but they found allies among the many PTAs west of the Twin Peaks.[72] World War II represented a watershed moment in which increasing numbers of Americans looked to psychology to solve everyday problems, and the largely middle-class women who volunteered for the PTAs had long engaged in "scientific motherhood," the attempt to perfect childrearing with assistance from medical and scientific elites.[73] Moreover, as early as the 1920s, the city's Second District PTA had championed "parent education" as a means for helping mothers speak to their children about sex, and during the 1930s, the organization brought in speakers from groups like the MSHNC.[74] During the war, Society members like Hale Shirley published brief articles on sex education in the state PTA's magazine, the *California Parent-Teacher*, and units west of the Twin Peaks brought in experts to lecture on the subject.[75] In 1948, the Mental Hygiene Society and the Second District PTA sponsored an evening film called *Human Growth* for parents in the western

Figure 2. Members of the Mental Hygiene Society of Northern California speaking to San Francisco parents about sex education, 1948. Fang family *San Francisco Examiner* photograph archive negative files, BANC PIC 2006.029:038187.02.01—NEG, box 2701, sleeve 038187_02. © Regents of the University of California, Bancroft Library, University of California, Berkeley.

Richmond District.[76] One expert who frequently spoke about sex education with PTAs in the 1940s called her students "first and foremost . . . parents who are interested in becoming better parents."[77]

If many Second District members valued knowledge about sex education for its practical value, they also saw it as a public health issue that particularly concerned middle-class mothers. A Depression-era survey conducted by the California PTA found that 93 percent of its members listed "homemaking" as their sole occupation. Although San Francisco's Second District had a "father's council" and approximately thirteen thousand members in 1947, not a single man held a governing position in the organization in the 1930s or 1940s.[78] Since the late nineteenth century, maternalist groups like the PTA had played an influential role in politics by arguing that cities needed "municipal housekeeping." Playing on the idea that the sexes occupied "separate spheres," many middle-class white women argued that their unique roles as wives and mothers compelled them to reform urban institutions like hospitals or schools. Sex education fell well within this tradition, and many PTA members believed that they needed to spread the latest psychological ideas on the subject to the entire city.[79]

Middle-class women's groups provided the bulk of grassroots support for sex education, but they found sympathetic ears in a third piece of the coalition: some of San Francisco's churches. Sex education polarized religious groups in the war decade, but a significant number of liberal Protestants took an interest in the issue. Beginning in the 1940s, growing numbers of ministers used psychology to bolster their traditional mission to strengthen marriage, avert divorce, and prohibit premarital sex. Psychologically informed sex education meant longer, happier marriages and a new way to teach young people about marriage's significance. As these ministers perused the latest medical expertise on this topic, they increasingly came to see homosexuality as a problem that needed both religious and scientific remedies. If premarital relations or sex with others of the same sex went against God's commandments, then what better way to combat these sins than to adopt the latest ideas in mental health? In the late 1940s, pastors like Methodist minister Lawrence Whitfield from the nearby town of Millbrae forcefully advocated for greater psychologically informed sex education in San Francisco.[80]

Like the "scientific mothers" in the PTA, the church leaders interested in the issue saw it through the lens of their own needs. Theories about mental health and family life overlapped with many ministers' concerns about church growth. Clergy like Whitfield understood that psychology's ideas about sex and family offered a popular tool for building congregations. A planning study commissioned by the San Francisco Council of Churches in 1947 concluded that Protestants faced an unprecedented opportunity to evangelize to the tens of thousands of newcomers to the city. Yet doing so required correcting lopsided congregational membership. The study noted that several churches in the central business district, like the Tenderloin's Glide Methodist Church, had over 1,700 members. Meanwhile, some neighborhood congregations struggled to fill the pews because nearby would-be worshippers often traveled downtown to attend Sunday services. The solution, according to the study's authors, lay in tailoring programs that served "the needs of particular neighborhoods," and the study's authors saw family-related programming as a good tool to build churches west of the Twin Peaks. By the end of the 1940s, many Protestants in the Bay Area hoped to specifically attract young parents with children by promising them sex education based on traditional religion and modern psychology.[81]

The MHSNC, middle-class women's groups, and liberal ministers, therefore, came at the issue from different vantage points, but they all found common cause in their dedication to building stronger marriages and families. In the five years after World War II, this coalition drew growing numbers of adherents in San Francisco. The Mental Hygiene Society convinced the city schools to offer courses for parents, and classes such as "Sex Interests in Childhood" and "Teaching Adolescents About Reproduction and Sexual Behavior" drew approximately five hundred adult students every week. The city's PTA cosponsored a lecture series on "The Adolescent—His Needs," and almost two thousand people attended them.[82] In the late 1940s, the San Francisco Council of Churches cosponsored a ten-part series on sex and marriage given by lecturers from the University of California, and in 1948, the group joined the PTA and other organizations to offer a similar series on "Youth and Marriage" that drew almost a thousand people.[83]

Most of sex education's supporters were adult volunteers, and their outreach to parents generated little controversy. Yet many of them followed their arguments to their logical conclusion: if strong families averted delinquency and "deviations" like homosexuality, then all young people, not just adult volunteers, needed to learn about sex before they married. Sex education's supporters ascribed the rise in extramarital sex, divorce, and homosexuality to other parents' failure to equip their children with proper knowledge about the importance of marriage. These were the families that sex education allegedly needed to reach. Schools were one of the few institutions with a nearly universal reach, and proponents of the issue hoped that mandatory instruction on family life, including sex, could bypass what they saw as other adults' reticence to talk about sex with their children.

In this regard, the pro–sex education coalition met stiff resistance, particularly from the Catholic Church. Although not all foes of sex education in schools were Catholics and not all Catholics objected to the practice, the San Francisco Archdiocese represented the largest institution opposed to it. Since the 1930s, Archbishop John Mitty had led a drive to combat what he saw as the secularization of the city's workplaces, politics, schools, and other public places. Mitty and his allies argued that true believers needed to bring their faith into the public realm, and their "Catholic Action" campaign included protests against doctors who prescribed birth control and businesses that sold "indecent" entertainment.[84]

The Catholic Church drew adherents from across San Francisco, but many of its most outspoken leaders on marriage, sex, and church law lived and served parishes in the streetcar suburbs west of the Twin Peaks. San Francisco's parochial school head James O'Dowd organized Christian youth programs on marriage, loudly opposed sex education in public schools, and lived in the Richmond District.[85] Thomas Bowe, a member of the Archdiocese's marriage court, similarly spoke out against the issue and resided deep in the Sunset.[86]

The Church's concern about secularization undergirded much of its opposition to sex education in schools. Leading Catholic thinkers in this period saw the teaching of sex as yet another way for secularists to push religion out of public life. "A great segment of modern educators regards sex as merely a biological function, having no moral aspect whatsoever," complained one writer in a Catholic periodical in 1944. "But for us sex is not purely material and sensory. It is something sacred—and dangerous."[87] Many Catholics, furthermore, worried that sex education in the public schools would undermine parents' authority. "Christian sobriety . . . must be taught and practiced primarily in the home," declared the nation's largest group of Catholic women in San Francisco in 1949. "Sex education should come only from the mother and has no place in the public schools."[88]

This concern overlapped with a second argument against the issue: society already allegedly overemphasized sex, and instruction on the subject in classrooms would blur the line between the school and the street. Opponents of classroom-based sex education shared the anxiety about the apparent immorality of the war years, and like their adversaries, they complained about "back-alley discussions" and "instruction in sex from 'gutter sources.'"[89] Yet they saw mandatory sex education in the public schools as an extension of the "gutter," not a defense against it. One San Francisco mother opposed any plan to offer courses on the subject in schools because "adolescents are adventurous, reckless, quick to experiment with danger. Is it hard to believe that advanced sex knowledge, now emphasized all out of proportion to its importance, will be put to a test at once?"[90] Rather than mitigating corrupting influences on the young, San Franciscans like this mother worried that mandatory sex education merely collapsed the lines between "school" and "street."

Opponents of classroom-based sex education, therefore, often supported an alternative plan that empowered religious authorities. The Archdiocese joined the city's Protestant Council of Churches in the 1940s to propose that students leave their classrooms once a week for an hour of religious instruction in their family's faith. Churches around the country favored this "released-time" plan because they believed it circumvented constitutional prohibitions against teaching religion in the public schools and because it would teach young people sexual morality. During the war, Reverend John Leffler, San Francisco's chief supporter of released time, argued, "Our kind of society depends for its success upon the kind of moral integrity contained in the Ten Commandments, and upon those attitudes of justice, tolerance, and good-will which religion requires of its sincere followers."[91]

Even as the Archdiocese and its allies fought back proposals to require sex education in public schools, a nationwide survey in 1943 found approximately 68 percent of Americans favored sex education in high schools, and urban residents favored the issue in even greater numbers.[92] These reports emboldened supporters of the issue across the country, and in San Francisco, parents from west of the Twin Peaks lobbied Supervisor Chester MacPhee to investigate the possibility of offering sex education in the city's schools. Lawrence Arnstein from the MHSNC pleaded to the Board of Supervisors for basic instruction on "venereal disease" in 1944 and complained that "if you're looking for sex education in the San Francisco schools, there is none." Father James O'Dowd testified against the plan, however, calling it the "parents' responsibility" and stating flatly that "it opens up points in regard to morality and brings the religious aspect into the public school."[93]

The Board of Supervisors ultimately declined to endorse the proposal, but sex education returned to the city again in 1949. That year, San Francisco's PTAs joined others from across California to lobby for mandatory sex education in all of the state's public schools. San Francisco's School Board formally opposed the 1949 state bill, with Catholic board member Joseph Alioto declaring that "sex education belongs in the family not in the schools."[94] In the very same meeting, however, the board also opposed a state law requiring five minutes of Bible study in California's public schools. Karl Schaupp, one of the supervisors who opposed both sex education and the Bible reading law, used similar language to oppose both and claimed that the second bill "tries to relieve parents of what should be done in the home and in the church."[95] Both bills were defeated at the state level.

Debates like this erupted across the country in the 1940s, and both sides launched bitter volleys at their adversaries. The vitriol in these disputes, however, risks obscuring some of the commonalities that supporters of sex education in schools shared with their opponents. Most notably, all participants in the debate saw themselves as guardians of middle-class sexual norms. Proponents of sex education in the public schools supported the issue because they wanted marriage strengthened, not because they opposed it. Their adversaries worried that secular classes would tip the scales toward immoral behavior. When it came to the issue of religion, the lines grew even blurrier. Supporters of sex education in the public schools sometimes also supported classroom prayer and released time. After all, a disciplinary impulse to limit promiscuity and promote marriage lay near the heart of all of these proposals.

The venom in the debates also threatens to conceal the widespread support for sex education in other contexts. Middle-class Catholics, like many other San Franciscans, spoke about the importance of the "preventative agencies" in promoting youthful morality. The "Catholic Action" campaign, for example, was, among other things, a cooperative attempt to teach children proper behavior through the teachings of the Church.[96] They spoke of a specific church with a capital "C," but they too believed parents needed help from educators and clergy to teach young people about sex. "Sex education?" asked one Catholic editorialist in 1949. "Yes, by all means! The Church (is this news to you?) has never opposed it—it has opposed types of it. The best type . . . is through parents who . . . ought to be helped to do the job calmly, efficiently, and lovingly."[97] Although proponents of sex education in schools dismissed such statements as wishful thinking, many Catholics were arguing for discussions about sex within the home even as they opposed it in the schools.

* * *

Taken together, the campaigns for and against sex education, the calls for a religious revival, and the demands for more policing of the "street" comprised a larger social movement to roll back the sexual freedoms of people living in and near downtown. They not only underscored the broad consensus in favor of marital sexuality but also revealed the essential fact that politics played a crucial role in producing sexual norms. The rules governing sex did not erupt solely out of a momentary "panic." Instead, organized constituencies debated them and waged campaigns to turn them into law. Sometimes these constituencies were elites like the doctors in the MHSNC or the Archbishop. Sometimes they were grassroots organizations, such as the PTA, homeowners groups, or churches. But the social rules defining what constituted socially acceptable sexual behavior ultimately required some measure of popular support to exist, and such support came out of long, sustained campaigns.

The political dimensions of these struggles became even more visible at the state level in the 1940s. At the end of the decade, California put together numerous conferences to plan the state's postwar future, and many of them touched on issues related to the government's connection to sex and the family. In 1949 alone, the State Assembly held conferences on sex crimes, juvenile justice, and mental hygiene. Legislators solicited testimony from expert witnesses and the wider public, and their hearings revealed the widespread anxiety. Parent groups like the PTA, psychological associations like the MHSNC, and churches from across California told legislators and the governor's office that they worried about premarital sex, homosexuality, prostitution, and "obscene" literature. Some of these concerns erupted in the state's investigation into child molesters in 1949, but they also appeared in conferences on mental hygiene, delinquency, and family life. Ultimately, the groups that organized around these concerns and the legislators who responded to these groups produced a legal order uniting sex and the state. In the late 1940s and early 1950s, cities like San Francisco, states like California, and the U.S. government worked to create incentives for people to adhere to sexual norms, including marriage, and to establish penalties for those who deviated from those standards.

Chapter 2

Public Policy and the Right to Privacy

The protests around sex education in places like San Francisco sparked a vigorous debate about how the government could best promote marriage and eliminate so-called sex deviance. In the decade after World War II, officials in California and across the country launched investigations that raised questions about the role of the state in the sex lives of its citizens. The California Subcommittee on Sex Crimes' 1950 report, for example, concluded that "sex deviance" rarely occurred in "happy, well-adjusted persons who were reared in happy, well-adjusted families." The state, therefore, had an interest in creating "normal" marriages that would create future "normal" citizens. Yet some of the nation's leading researchers on sex and the law challenged that conclusion. Most notably, Alfred Kinsey told California's Subcommittee on Sex Crimes, "Ninety-five percent of the males of any population could be committed to state penal institutions if their behavior were known and they were apprehended."[1] Although homosexual acts or premarital sex violated California law, most men who engaged in them did so out of public view and never faced arrest. Passing new laws against consensual extramarital sex acts like homosexuality, Kinsey cautioned, would not change this reality.

This exchange offers a window into two important shifts in postwar American sexual politics. First, the Subcommittee on Sex Crimes exemplified California's version of what historian Margot Canaday has termed the "Straight State." In the two decades after World War II, public officials at all levels of governance created new ways to reward Americans for marrying and new tools to punish them for engaging in sexuality outside of marriage.[2] These reforms built off policies from earlier eras, but the outrage of citizens like those in San Francisco's middle-class districts in the 1940s fueled a police state that dwarfed earlier regimes. Furthermore, the Cold War prompted officials to enlist the help of psychologists for help engineering "normal" families that would produce future generations of healthy citizens. Unlike previous eras, however, this postwar regime singled out homosexuality as a set of behaviors in need of regulation. Community groups and local officials in places like San Francisco had sometimes treated same-sex desire as a vice problem akin to prostitution, but as officials integrated psychology into public policy, they further stigmatized and penalized people they suspected of homosexuality. In some cases, the Straight State's policies were punitive in nature. City police raided gay bars, state investigators revoked the licenses of teachers they suspected of immoral behavior, and federal officials barred unmarried tenants from new public housing projects. In other instances, government officials employed "softer" methods such as offering material incentives for marriage or education campaigns that equated heterosexuality with mental health.[3]

Second, a small number of critics like Kinsey helped popularize the notion that Americans had a sexual "right to privacy" and criticized the Straight State for what they perceived as its excesses. Kinsey alone treated nonmarital sexuality with respect and condemned the hypocrisy of a government that punished consensual behaviors discretely practiced by millions of citizens.[4] But many of his contemporaries, including several liberal lawyers in the 1940s and 1950s, spoke of the privacy in more limited ways. The state, they argued, could never stamp out any behavior that took place in secret, and therefore, policing Americans' sex lives misused resources. Unlike Kinsey, they avoided suggesting that all kinds of consensual sex were equal. Instead, they argued that laws penalizing homosexuality wasted taxpayers' money while subjecting "normal" people to unnecessary surveillance. Almost two decades before the U.S. Supreme Court spoke of a right to privacy, a few liberal lawyers argued that while not all forms of sex were equal, the government had no business policing the sex lives of its citizens. These advocates honed a limited critique of public power that would gain adherents in later years.

The Straight State and the "right to privacy," therefore, emerged in tandem in the postwar era, and it was no coincidence that critics like Kinsey spoke about privacy in particular. The state itself, in numerous ways, encouraged Americans to think of sexual privacy as an important value and a defense against its policing powers. The penalties policymakers levied against lesbians and gay men, obviously, never eradicated homosexuality.

They merely pushed individuals to conceal their relationships. The Straight State's power lay in its ability not only to punish people who engaged in same-sex relations but also to encourage a far broader group of citizens to hide their desires. Under this regime, the day-to-day reality of what future generations would call "being in the closet" was itself one of the state's primary goals.[5] Privacy afforded people experiencing same-sex desires a measure of security against imprisonment or loss of employment, but it also ensured that the government and the wider public would not have to recognize their relationships or even their very existence.

At the same time, the Straight State itself promised sexual privacy to its citizens. Eager to produce "happy, well-adjusted persons," government officials tried to guarantee married couples the ability to sleep together away from the prying eyes of children or neighbors. Authorities believed that wartime crowding had exposed urban residents to the sex lives of others, and they required public housing agencies and private developers to seclude bedrooms from the outside world. Government-led sex education campaigns, furthermore, promoted the idea that healthy, marital sexuality took place in private. Thus, when Kinsey and other liberals spoke about privacy, they did more than merely point out the impracticalities of policing sex that happened behind closed doors. They challenged the state using language employed by the state itself. These early critics of policing only sometimes referenced sex education and never mentioned housing policies. But they honed their critique at a time when growing numbers of middle-class Americans came to expect sexual privacy. Postwar sexual liberals, therefore, not only shared the Straight State's assumption that marital heterosexuality represented a social good in need of public support but also borrowed some of its language to critique it.

Policing and the Disciplinary Powers of the State

Although authorities had punished same-sex sexuality in earlier decades, the postwar era witnessed an unprecedented degree of penalties for it. These punishments included arrest, imprisonment, confinement in a mental hospital, loss of employment, and public humiliation. These actions devastated the lives of people directly affected by them, but they also served as a warning to others. The mere threat of termination or arrest encouraged people to at least pretend to conform to the sexual norms of postwar America and to try to keep their relationships private. Negative consequences alone might have pushed people to hide in "the closet," but the policing regime itself encouraged Americans to think about privacy as a means of self-preservation in other ways. Officials saw arrests, detentions, and hospitalizations as prohibitively expensive. As long as people adhered to sexual norms in public, authorities often hesitated to pursue their targets. This combination of harsh punishment and leniency was particularly visible in California's schools. After World War II, state officials launched a campaign to root out so-called sex deviates in the public education system. Their work cost hundreds of people their jobs and subjected thousands more to surveillance. Yet authorities also hated publicizing their work, fearing criticism that they had allowed homosexuals in classrooms in the first place. Consequently, California officials often offered to protect suspected gay teachers' privacy in order to save themselves from censure.

These complicated dynamics emerged out of earlier forms of policing by the state in the sex lives of Americans. In the late 1930s, states like California passed so-called sexual psychopath laws, which allowed for the indeterminate hospitalization of people convicted of any crime and whom officials believed were likely to commit a new one. Legislators passed these laws to control pedophiles who hurt children, but authorities often made no distinction between violent and nonviolent offenses involving adults, and they often specifically targeted gay men.[6] World War II was a watershed, however, in the state's treatment of sexuality. For the first time, psychologists worked with military officials to monitor soldiers and sailors for homosexuality. They screened conscripts and discharged personnel who they suspected of having sex with others of the same sex. These policies resulted in roughly four to five thousand rejected inductees and over nine thousand discharges for men and women in the armed forces.[7]

In the years after the war, the state's interest in policing homosexuality expanded to an even greater degree. During the Cold War, many Americans believed that gay or extramarital sex made public officials vulnerable to blackmail from Soviet agents, and authorities barred anyone suspected of homosexuality from federal employment.[8] The government tightened the military's prohibitions against gay personnel and extended it to postwar welfare policy, forbidding anyone discharged from the armed forces for homosexual conduct from acquiring benefits through the G.I. Bill. Immigration officials, meanwhile, began to deport people for same-sex relationships and denied suspected homosexuals from entering the country.[9] California, like many states, increased the penalties for sodomy convictions to twenty-five years to life in prison, while local authorities across the state responded to public outrage about the sexual revolution of the war years. A study conducted in 1952 noted that San Francisco police arrested over twelve thousand people between 1945 and 1950 for sex crimes alone, averaging five to six arrests per day. Only 15 percent of men in the sample faced charges of a coercive nature like rape or sex crimes against children.[10]

Police and other officials often charged gay men and lesbians with status crimes like "lewd vagrancy," which applied to people whom authorities deemed "out of place." Law enforcement authorities saw homosexuality and gender variance like crossdressing as offenses against public decency, and they did not make exceptions for the spaces in which they occurred. Vagrants, by definition, were always "out of place." Although the police might need a warrant to enter someone's house, one could face a vagrancy or similar charge in one's bedroom as well as on the street or in a bar. Yet authorities could not arrest someone for a crime that they did know was happening, and not surprisingly, people who broke the law in their own homes faced considerably less scrutiny than those who did so in more public places. Although government officials did not yet recognize a right to privacy, discretion and staying out of the sight of police made it more likely for lesbians and gay men to evade sanction.[11]

Authorities may have seen the sex lives of citizens as public matters, but they nevertheless believed their own work warranted privacy. Government officials faced enormous pressure to purge gay men and lesbians from sensitive positions of employment, but publicity around their firing sometimes stirred up controversy. News about the termination of gay workers might also suggest that an employer had failed to recognize the employees' homosexuality sooner. Consequently, authorities sometimes worked quietly, revealing the firing of lesbians or gay men on their own terms. State Department officials, for example, often investigated alleged homosexuals discretely and encouraged suspects to resign without a public trial or hearing. This strategy eased the government's burden, allowing it to conserve resources, but it also meant holding back private details that could potentially embarrass the state.[12]

Damage inflicted by these policies went far beyond the people arrested or fired from their jobs. Anxiety about homosexuality crisscrossed multiple realms of life, stigmatizing same-sex relationships in many social interactions and reinforcing private discrimination.[13] Even more important, people did not need to sleep with someone of the same sex in order to face scrutiny. Numerous Americans faced queer-baiting to varying degrees, and therefore the combination of policy and social stigma incentivized most people to disavow any relationship that might seem "abnormal." This meant that even gay men and lesbians who escaped notice paid a penalty. Access to employment, public benefits, friendship, and even in some cases the ability to move freely in the city often meant camouflaging potentially damaging affiliations. This does not mean that everyone who felt attracted to others of the same sex constantly hid in the closet. To be sure, many lesbians and gay men lived relatively open lives in the postwar era. It does mean, however, that most lesbians and gay men understood that they faced penalties or lost opportunities if the wrong people knew the details of those lives. One of the most damaging legacies of this era, therefore, lay in the energy and sacrifice it took to hide.[14]

The history of suspected gay teachers in California illustrates many of these dynamics. Although superintendents technically had the power to terminate teachers, California's licensing system served as the state's principal tool for barring employees who deviated from sexual norms. The Department of Education required all teachers to obtain a credential, and it used the licensing process to police teachers' sexuality. The legislature did not specifically forbid the employment of gay teachers until 1952, but the Department of Education first directed local administrators to report employees it suspected of homosexuality as early as 1948.[15]

This directive set in motion a wave of firings and helped establish a system that remained in place until the late 1960s. During this time, top school officials revoked the licenses of anyone arrested for or suspected—but not necessarily convicted—of violating the state's laws against sex between adults of the same sex, and they clandestinely investigated teachers who their colleagues or superiors believed to be gay.[16] In a 1960 review of the Department of Education's credentialing policy, administrative advisors working for the state noted that concerns about teachers fell into three categories: "professional training," "health," and "character." The last category was by far the largest, and their conception of character problems included professional misconduct, affiliation with the Communist Party, criminal violations, and an elastic conception of mental health that allowed state authorities to revoke credentials if they suspected that an employee's behavior would adversely affect the psychological development of children.[17]

Policing teachers thus required a dramatic expansion of the state's bureaucracy. A review conducted by the Department of Education in 1960 noted that since the legislature approved the fingerprinting of school employees, the agency had processed 70,000 applications and produced 4,000 arrest records for a number of different infractions.[18] These cases included rape, child molestation, and numerous other violent acts, but the overwhelming number of them pertained to teachers engaged in consensual homosexual acts with other adults caught up in dragnets set by local police. In 1952, the Department of Education created its own staff of internal investigators to look into allegations of misconduct brought by school employees or parents. Although it is impossible to determine exactly how many teachers lost their credentials for gay-related sex crimes, an internal investigation undertaken by the department in mid-1963 revealed that in the previous three and half years, the state's Commission of Credentials had revoked the licenses of 109 teachers for sex crime convictions alone. Although administrators revoked credentials for other offenses, sex-related incidents made up 71 percent of the total.[19]

Most sex crimes investigated by the commission involved homosexuality, and they particularly focused on men. Their overwhelming interest in male teachers no doubt reflected the prevailing belief that men had innate, aggressive sexual impulses and, therefore, possessed a greater danger to students. Furthermore, most teachers in California were women, and men may have attracted more scrutiny by working in a predominantly female profession. In the files currently retained by the California State Archives, only three cases focused on possible lesbian relationships. In one case from 1954, the superintendent of an elementary school district in Merced County reported that two female teachers working for her had engaged in activities "alleged to be of a homosexual nature." The evidence amassed by the administrator included the fact that the two women lived together, had joint bank accounts, had purchased real estate together, and mysteriously alleged that "during a television show in discussing their mode of living, they stated that they wore each others [*sic*] underwear."[20]

The Department of Education also subjected heterosexual women, particularly single ones, to increased scrutiny. During the postwar era, California and many local jurisdictions prosecuted women for sex outside of marriage, and these arrests frequently came to the attention of the Department of Education. Female promiscuity, like male homosexuality, potentially justified the denial or revocation of a teacher's credential, and the state looked into several cases involving women arrested for heterosexual sex outside of marriage. In a 1959 case from San Francisco, it responded to a note written by a teacher's husband, who alleged that his wife had moved in with another man and who thought that "a person who does this is unfit to supervise children and adults especially in the school system."[21]

Women undoubtedly faced a double standard when it came to extramarital sex; few men were scrutinized for heterosexual affairs. However, state officials viewed such indiscretions merely as unacceptable extensions of an otherwise "normal" heterosexual impulse. Even in some cases involving female homosexuality, they presumed that women's less aggressive sex drives kept them from hurting children. In its probe of the two female teachers who lived together in Merced County, for example, the state concluded that "further investigation has failed to reflect sufficient evidence to substantiate the allegations contained in the report that the Subject[s] [were] immoral person[s]."[22]

Although these investigations cost numerous teachers their jobs and likely deterred many people from pursuing careers in education, some teachers contested their expulsion. Their efforts reveal the ways that the state wanted, above all, teachers to at least outwardly appear heterosexual. In 1958, after lengthy deliberations, the California Board of Education voted to restore the credential of a Bay Area teacher whom the police had previously arrested for a homosexual solicitation. State officials made their decision based on the fact that the incriminating incident had taken place in 1952 and that the teacher had not committed any "deviant" acts since then. In order to prove his rehabilitation, the instructor reported that he was married, had two sons, and regularly attended church, and he provided numerous letters of support from psychiatrists, his spouse, employer, and two ministers, including the Episcopal Bishop of California. Despite these documents, commission officials still denied his request for a license to work as a speech pathologist. Only in 1958, after an extensive debate within the Department of Education, a hearing officer counseled the board to reinstate his credential based on a psychiatrist's recommendation and the alleged fact that his homosexual encounter "was an outgrowth of marital difficulties" and that, since then, he had "led a normal happy married life."[23]

The specifics of whether or not teachers retained or lost their credentials can conceal the larger consequences of these investigations. By making an instructor's sexual conduct a prerequisite for employment and by exposing some teachers to public shame, the Department of Education compelled all employees and their families to hide behaviors that might expose them to legal action. In order to uncover potential misconduct, state investigators examined every relationship in a teacher's nonprofessional life. When a state agent looked into allegations that a male vice-principal in the Los Angeles area had molested high school boys, he reported numerous examples of what he saw as suspicious activity. The vice-principal was married, but the investigator noted that his "reputation in that area is that he is a homosexual." He also reported that the police had once arrested the vice-principal's wife for "lodging at a hotel with a sailor" and that another teacher "under suspicion as a lesbian" currently rented one of his former apartments. Together, these seemingly unrelated rumors helped the state build its case.[24]

Even as investigators documented the personal details of the lives of people like this vice-principal, they strove to keep their work quiet. Local and state officials worried about the embarrassment of a sex scandal in California's schools, and consequently, officials frequently pushed employees to "voluntarily" terminate their credentials. In a 1948 letter, an administrative advisor at the State Department of Education advised an instructor who had been arrested in Oakland and San Francisco for "moral delinquency" before World War II that "under the circumstances it is best that you immediately request the State Board of Education to revoke all credentials issued by the Board and held by you."[25] In exchange for their compliance, the state offered teachers suspected of sexual misconduct a pledge to protect their privacy. These "voluntary" revocations made up an even larger share of the credential terminations than so-called compulsory ones. In its own internal inquiry, the Department of Education concluded that 158 of the 199 "voluntary" revocations it oversaw between 1960 and 1963 "involved sex misconduct."[26] The commission also retained correspondence with local superintendents who carried out their own investigations. These included a superintendent in the Bay Area city of Richmond who found no "concrete" evidence that one of his teachers had had a homosexual affair with another teacher, but he nevertheless obtained the employee's resignation after confronting him with rumors about it.[27]

These so-called voluntary revocations not only reveal that officials used multiple methods to police the behavior of its employees but also demonstrate that the state itself sought to conceal its actions. Forcing teachers to opt to terminate their own licenses preserved the illusion of fairness and kept the government's work out of the public eye. Files compiled by investigators included numerous press clippings related to sexual misconduct by teachers, and local and state officials tried to avoid accusations that they had allowed homosexuals to work in schools. In a 1955 letter to a Southern California man, for example, a special agent for the Department of Education revealed that voluntary revocations protected the interests of both the teacher and the state: "This procedure . . . voids the necessity of appearing before a State Hearing Officer . . . as well as preventing adverse publicity to all concerned."[28] The investigators succeeded in avoiding "publicity" so well, in fact, that they had difficulty defending themselves against accusations that they were not performing their duties well enough. When conservative politician Max Rafferty took over as California superintendent in 1963, he criticized what he saw as the liberal leanings of the Board of Education by claiming that it had failed to completely eradicate "sex deviates" from the state's schools.[29]

These secretive policies subjected even senior administrators to state surveillance. In the most dramatic case of the purge, California investigators quietly engineered the resignation of a high-ranking education official in San Francisco in 1955. The high-ranking administrator first came to their attention in 1950 after an informant relayed rumors to them that the male official had allegedly carried on an affair with a man from an educational film company.[30] After conducting their own inquiry, state investigators passed along their findings to the San Francisco Board of Education in the hopes that they would terminate the administrator.[31] When, for unknown reasons, the board failed to act, the state officials orchestrated a defamation campaign to pressure board members. First, they leaked a compromising letter about the allegedly gay school administrator to a prominent minister in the city. The clergyman, in turn, passed the investigators' note over to San Francisco District Attorney Thomas Lynch and to parent groups. In 1954, the city launched a grand jury investigation of the school administrator, and in 1955, newspaper columnist Herb Caen reported, "Scurrilous anonymous letters about a top S.F. official are being circulated among 22,000 members of the local [PTA]."[32] Just a year later, the administrator resigned.[33]

These investigations led to thousands of ruined reputations and lost careers, but the state's interest in secrecy sometimes allowed teachers accused of more serious crimes to escape prosecution. In 1952, police reported to the commission that they had arrested two male teachers living together in Palo Alto for having sex with "juveniles." The men first came to their attention when some of the "youths" confessed to having attended "sex parties" at their home, and as a result of these admissions, the police secretly installed microphones in the teachers' residence. They allegedly recorded the suspects discussing having sex with minors, and authorities arrested them in March 1952. The county prosecutor reported feeling confident about his ability to convict the teachers of sodomy and sex with a minor, but they refrained from going forward at the behest of the teachers' superintendent, who worried that the case would anger parents. According to an investigator on the case, the superintendent asked the police to "settle the affair with as little publicity as possible and thereby save the school department and all the persons connected with it the embarrassment and publicity of a public trial." In April, the two men resigned their positions but escaped prosecution.[34]

Although teachers sometimes contested their termination, evasion was frequently a more successful tactic. The Department of Education notably found enforcing its policies difficult. In 1963, Assistant Superintendent Everett Calvert complained that the 1952 law requiring all teachers to submit fingerprints to law enforcement officials had "created a 'monster' within the Department of Education" and that the "workload is insurmountable."[35] In 1957, for example, the *San Francisco Examiner* reported that two local teachers had worked in the city school system undetected until recently, despite previous arrests for soliciting sex from other men. In one case, the police failed to report the teacher to state authorities because he "mentioned nothing about being a schoolteacher," and the Department of Education only found out about the arrest after the *Examiner* published its story on the scandal.[36]

The fact that some employees evaded state surveillance, however, did not mean that the system had little effect. The postwar Straight State not only scrutinized teachers' sexuality but also offered an important inducement for people to at least appear to conform to sexual norms. In this case, the example of the teacher who waged a multiyear campaign to keep his credentials is the most revealing. It is impossible to know how he felt about his wife and marriage or whether or not his homosexual encounter merely resulted from a bout of depression. It is clear, however, that the state required evidence of a happy marriage and a disavowal of his gay past as evidence of his rehabilitation. Regardless of his particular circumstances, his arguments before the credentialing committee showed that working as a teacher in California necessitated at least the appearance of normative heterosexuality and a monogamous marriage. Part of the damage inflicted by this system, therefore, lay in its ability to convince people that some kinds of sex required concealment and that no one really suffered for having hidden it. By inadvertently allowing some gay teachers to pass undetected, public officials preserved a larger social and legal order that sanctioned some relationships between consenting adults but not others.[37]

Promoting Healthy Citizens

Governments do not merely repress sex they do not like. They also promote norms that they deem beneficial to society. In the two decades after World War II, the federal and California state governments tried to promote heterosexuality and marriage through instructional campaigns modeled after public health initiatives. Sex education, alternately framed as "parent" or "family life" education, acted as one important avenue through which authorities promoted what they viewed as sexual norms. They helped popularize expert ideas about human sexual development, broadened public awareness of the dangers allegedly posed by homosexuality, and encouraged citizens to speak about marriage and other desirable norms in their communities.

The state's educational campaigns also encouraged Americans to think about the importance of sexual privacy. Officials argued that married couples should expect to have sex in private and teach their children about the importance of respecting others' privacy. Indeed, even though many Americans in the late twentieth century, therefore, would come to see the "right to privacy" as an absence of government involvement in their private lives, one of the institutions that helped popularize that notion before the 1960s was the state itself. Psychologists and sex educators valued privacy as a sign of respectability and health, and the state's dissemination of their work helped popularize these ideas among the parents of the Baby Boom.

Government support for teaching citizens about sex emerged at the same time that cities such as San Francisco erupted over the question of whether or not the subject should be taught in the schools. After World War II, professional groups of psychologists across the country, including the Mental Hygiene Society of Northern California, lobbied state and federal administrators to dedicate more funding to mental health, which included normative ideas about sex.[38] Some of the nation's leading child developmental experts, including psychologists who testified to the Mid-Century White Conference on the Child in Washington, D.C., called sex education "essential to the personal integration of the child." Yet many Americans, including the leadership of the San Francisco Archdiocese, opposed teaching it in public schools. Their discomfort stemmed not only from their belief that information would cause young people to experiment out of wedlock but also because the issue seemed to symbolize a government takeover of a "private" matter. California State Senator Jack Tenney, for example, called sex education in schools a "communist-inspired" conspiracy in 1947.[39]

Government officials who saw the issue as a necessary public health matter searched for other ways to promote sex education without appearing to expand the government, and they consequently worked through intermediaries.[40] Congress passed the National Mental Health Act in 1946, for example, which funded new community clinics, trained new psychologists, and educated the wider public about psychology. The law created the National Institute for Mental Health, but it also gave grants to state governments, universities, and professional groups. Relative to the wider federal budget, the act was small. But the law required states to create or expand their own mental health agencies and to raise their own funds to match those from the federal government. Whereas only twenty-four states had mental health programs in 1945, all of them had them by 1951. In 1948, California won approximately $140,000 for training, new clinics, and outreach.[41]

Because psychologists saw homosexuality as a "deviation," expanding mental health funding also meant expanding concerns about homosexuality. San Francisco's Langley-Porter Psychiatric Clinic added new training programs thanks to the National Mental Health Act, and when the California legislature awarded the clinic $100,000 to research "sexual deviation" in 1950, it became one of the nation's leading places to study homosexuality.[42] This government money helped make psychology respectable to the wider public, and as health professionals integrated insights from the field into their work, homosexuality joined a growing list of disorders that allegedly needed treatment and prevention.[43] Since many psychologists rooted "abnormal sexuality" in early childhood experiences, they believed parental education offered one of the best ways to prevent conditions like homosexuality. Researchers at the Langley-Porter Clinic argued that law enforcement alone could not solve the problem. Instead, the state needed to address it through an aggressive public health campaign. California, they contended, needed "programs of adult education in mental hygiene principles," which included "effective sex education and effective preparation of youths for marriage."[44]

Figure 3. Dr. Karl Bowman and Dr. Langley Porter meet with California Director of Mental Hygiene Dora Shaw Heffner at the opening of a new psychiatric clinic, 1943. Fang family *San Francisco Examiner* photograph archive negative files, BANC PIC 2006.029:124510_01.3—NEG, box 895.

Federal and state officials, conscious of the ways that teaching sex in schools in places like San Francisco generated controversy, launched a campaign specifically aimed at parents, teachers, medical professionals, clergy, and other authorities responsible for children. Their pamphlets, books, radio broadcasts, lectures, and other materials covered a wide variety of topics, such as when to tell young people about sex or whether parents' nudity harmed children. But they almost always included either warnings about homosexuality or information that reinforced the idea that heterosexuality was a desirable yet learned behavior. The U.S. Children's Bureau's booklet *The Adolescent in Your Family*, for example, warned readers about the dangers of girls who refused to give up crushes on their female peers, boys or girls who veered too far from gender-appropriate styles or fashions, and teenagers who overzealously pursued sex. Parents could head off these problems by telling teenagers about their expectations for them and letting their own relationships act as models for their children. Federal officials warned that too many boys and girls had to "depend on poor or false" sources on information about sex. Parents could help their families by giving "their sons and daughters . . . full and accurate knowledge, and the example of a healthy outlook."[45]

These materials also communicated contemporary ideas about race. Most books, films, and pamphlets written by postwar psychologists, including those published by government agencies, spoke to a white audience and celebrated middle-class norms such as breadwinning fathers, homemaking mothers, and monogamous marriage. They largely avoided the racist rhetoric of the early twentieth-century eugenics movement, yet they regularly contrasted white, middle-class norms of "American civilization" with the "primitive" beliefs of societies in other parts of the world. Postwar psychologists and their audiences frequently understood normative sexuality through the lens of race, describing monogamous, heterosexual marriage with separate gender roles as important markers of European-style scientific progress and human evolution. The film *Human Growth*, for example, dramatized a middle-class, white family's first conversation about sex education and used racial difference as a way to introduce the topic. The movie opens with a boy reading a textbook about American Indians, and his curiosity about their nudity allows his parents to tell him about the physical changes he will experience in adolescence.[46]

These texts also notably emphasized privacy. Postwar psychologists and their government sponsors advised parents on when they should start covering up in front of their children, the importance of separate bedrooms for boys and girls, and the need for adolescents to have a space of their own, free of their parents. Writers with the U.S. Children's Bureau suggested that Americans will know when their children have a "new awareness of sex" when they have a sense of "modesty" and no longer want to share the bathroom with their parents.[47] The most important advice on this topic given by psychologists and their government sponsors, however, involved the sex lives of parents themselves. Experts repeatedly told mothers and fathers to be honest when their children asked them about sex, but they also warned that too much exposure to adult sexuality could interfere with their children's healthy development. One California educator, for example, told parents to tell their children, "It is common courtesy that if a bathroom or bedroom door is closed, anyone desiring to enter knocks and awaits permission. . . . The desire for privacy varies with individuals and with age. [But] It should be respected."[48]

The State of California launched its own sex education campaign for adults, and it primarily worked through intermediaries. At the bequest of the state's PTAs, officials in Sacramento created a "Bureau of Parent Education" in 1926 with funds from the Rockefeller Foundation. In its early years, the bureau offered material for mothers on a variety of subjects related to homemaking, such as sewing and budgeting. This agency had long included sex education as an important topic for parents, but the issue grew in importance when the state appointed Ralph Eckert to run it in 1946.[49] Eckert, a former family counselor and junior college dean, ardently believed that psychological ideas about sex could help parents raise healthier children and build stronger marriages. "The problems are too complex for parents alone," he declared. "We must move as rapidly as possible to supplement the home's influence."[50]

His bureau's significance lay not in its tiny size—Eckert was its only full-time employee—but in the way in which it mobilized parents at the grassroots level. In the five years after Eckert took over the bureau, the agency sponsored annual summer workshops on sex and family life for volunteers interested in leading discussions back in their communities.[51] Eckert and his allies hoped these volunteers would serve as "lay leaders," setting up discussion groups, distributing literature on sex and family life to their neighbors, and serving as instructors in local classes on the subject.[52] The state government subsidized many of those classes, allowing the city of San Francisco, for example, to offer free parenting classes for most of the late 1940s and 1950s.[53] Thanks to state support, the city's Division of Adult Education subsidized a conference for San Francisco groups interested in learning about sex and family life in 1951, including the PTA, Episcopal Church, and Mental Hygiene Society of Northern California.[54] Eckert forged a particularly close relationship with the California Congress of Parents and Teachers (CCPT), speaking at the group's meetings and crediting it with leading the "way in broadening the concept of sex education to its present scope."[55] Most important, the CCPT's magazine, the *California Parent-Teacher*, carried numerous articles written by state experts.[56]

In later years, many Americans would see sex education as the product of groups like the PTA and professional experts. Few would see it as the result of state action, and in fact, many of them would argue that education offered a better way to address sexual "deviance" and "promiscuity" than policing. In fact, education and policing expanded together after the war as two strategies that policymakers used to promote what they saw as healthy sexuality. Federal and state officials sponsored much of the research that sex educators relied on in their work and published texts for the wider public. Since the question of whether or not to teach the issue in schools sparked controversy, authorities often worked through intermediaries like the Langley-Porter Clinic or the PTA. Privacy was a key piece of these campaigns. Authorities directed parents to discourage their children from bothering them when they were having sex and to knock before entering their bedrooms. Shielding young people from adult sex allegedly would help create healthy families, and married couples should expect to have sexual pleasure free of intrusions from children or nosy neighbors. Even as government authorities helped raise awareness about heterosexuality and so-called sexual deviance, they also promoted the idea that parents deserved sexual privacy.

Housing Healthy Families

Policing and education represented two crucial elements of the Straight State, but housing played perhaps the greatest role in popularizing the importance of sexual privacy. During the New Deal, the federal government launched multiple housing initiatives to try to overcome the Depression. After the war, Congress expanded these projects in an effort to relieve the shortage in places like San Francisco, and all of them encouraged the construction of private bedrooms. Housing theorists and architects read many of the same psychology texts as contemporary sex educators, and they believed that secluded bedrooms built stronger marriages, reformed the sex lives of the poor, and created healthy children. In the case of the federal officials' subsidies for postwar for-profit housing, these factors helped the government support the construction of homes that they deemed worthy of mortgage insurance. Even as the Straight State expanded its policing of Americans' sexuality, it also encouraged the construction of private bedrooms that would make it harder for authorities to know if Americans broke sexual norms.

Beginning with the New Deal, the federal government subsidized two kinds of residences in the United States. First, so-called public housing served the poor as a part of the social safety net. Cities opted to create their own housing authorities and used federal money to build low-rent developments. At the same time, the Federal Housing Administration (FHA) and, later, the Veterans Administration (VA) underwrote home loans and created a new mortgage market that made it easier for private developers to build homes. Policymakers designed this second set of policies to encourage homeownership and to subsidize new residences for the nation's white middle class. Both tiers began in the Depression, but they expanded considerably in the 1940s and 1950s. Cities like San Francisco, worried about the housing shortage, used federal money to build low-income projects. Private developers, meanwhile, primarily used subsidized FHA and VA loans to build new houses outside the city limits. While both "public housing" and federal involvement in the mortgage market involved government subsidies, the latter involved a much larger share federal spending and affected a greater number of Americans.[57]

These two tracks would have dramatically different histories in postwar America, but they shared several important characteristics. First, they expanded the Straight State's policing system. Federal housing officials rewarded people for marrying and punished them for deviating from sexual norms. In 1954, the Home and Housing Finance Agency (HHFA), which oversaw both public housing authorities and the FHA, fired sixteen employees for suspected "perversion," including six women whom internal investigators had accused of engaging in "abnormal sex practices."[58] This policing applied to Americans who sought benefits through the government as well. HHFA officials limited tenancy in federally subsidized, low-income apartments to "at least 2 or more related persons" and defined "family" as people related to one another by "blood, marriage, or adoption."[59] The San Francisco Housing Authority (SFHA) limited tenancy to "stable" families in its early years, which meant two parents and their children.[60] The FHA's mortgage policies offered even more explicit instruction. Hoping to insure loans that they believed borrowers would pay back, government officials required banks to give preferential treatment to married men.[61]

This preference for married men reinforced explicit discrimination against single people, gay men, and lesbians. The 1944 Servicemen's Readjustment Act, which gave low-interest home loans to veterans, specifically barred anyone discharged for homosexual conduct during the war from receiving housing or educational benefits under its provisions. By some estimates, the VA ultimately denied approximately 9,000 servicemen remuneration under the act for homosexual acts.[62] Eager to safeguard their investment in the housing market, FHA officials similarly warned lenders to investigate the "character" of applicants and to give borrowers unrelated to each other by blood or marriage a "low rating." No marital or blood ties meant potential "disagreements," which might jeopardize the investment in the home and cause foreclosure.[63]

This screening process did not necessarily eliminate everyone who had ever deviated from sexual norms, obviously. It did, however, mean that applicants for both public housing and federally insured mortgages needed to at least appear to conform to postwar sexual norms. Public housing authorities sometimes made this an explicit goal. During the 1950s, officials across the country debated how to handle so-called problem families, which included unmarried mothers, cohabitators, and prostitutes. Although most officials opposed admitting "problem families," some of them also saw housing as an opportunity to change the sex lives of the poor. According to one official, this system gave applicants an opportunity to reform themselves and that "these families [now] recognize that they must meet some goals of acceptable behavior if they are accepted."[64] Few records from the SFHA survived flooding at the local branch of the national archives, and it is unclear if the agency pursued a similar strategy. But it did see reforming tenants' families as one of its goals. Similar to the California Parent Education Bureau, the SFHA hired a "consultant" to give low-income San Franciscans advice on how to raise their families.[65]

The preference for married applicants and discrimination against unmarried ones further reinforced gender and racial inequalities in postwar housing policies. The FHA told male borrowers that the government did not recognize their wives' wages as "real income" because they assumed they would leave the paid labor force to raise children.[66] At the same time, postwar housing policies promoted segregation and reinforced white privilege. The SFHA maintained a "separate but equal" policy, admitting nonwhites into just two of its eleven projects until 1954.[67] The VA and FHA, meanwhile, required developers to use racially restrictive covenants until the U.S. Supreme Court banned them in 1948 and mandated a whites-only policy for their mortgage programs well into the 1960s.[68]

The sexual, gendered, and racial limits federal officials imposed on tenants and borrowers did not merely unfold at the same time. Rather, they reinforced one another. By limiting loans to married men, mortgage programs encouraged women to marry in order to access beneficial housing programs. The U.S. Housing Authority (USHA), FHA, and VA's use of marriage as a marker of financial reliability constituted a form of racial as well gender and sexual discrimination. A whites-only policy penalized intermarriages even after states like California legalized them. Similarly, federal officials subscribed to a theory of property that prized harmony within neighborhoods. Their efforts to exclude people of color from the postwar housing market reflected their belief that integrated areas created social strife that threatened the well-being of married white couples and their children.[69] By making "congenial" families the target of their intervention in the postwar real estate market, they not only discriminated against people outside of normative relationships but also cast racial or socioeconomic integration as a threat to white middle-class couples with children.

Officials in both housing tracks, therefore, expanded the policing capabilities of the Straight State, but they also shared a common desire to expand Americans' sexual privacy. Slum reformers in the early twentieth century ascribed what they saw as antisocial behavior to poor environmental conditions such as overcrowding, and they frequently asserted that better housing could forestall divorce, prostitution, and juvenile delinquency.[70] During the Depression, parenting and family life experts amplified these concerns by arguing that overcrowding gave children unhealthy attitudes about sex. J. S. Plant, for example, argued that a lack of sexual privacy not only created "mental strain" among adults but also destroyed children's "illusions about sex" and caused them to overvalue the "physical" aspects of relationships.[71]

Over the next decade, the concerns of people like Plant moved to the center of national discussions about housing and mental health. Organizations like the American Public Health Association (APHA) told homebuilders and government officials that new dwellings needed to offer residents adequate privacy in order to ensure that children did not witness adults having sex. In 1939, the APHA's Committee on the Hygiene of Housing argued that "a room should only be occupied only by persons of the same sex except for married couples and young children." Meanwhile, "toilets, bathrooms, and bedrooms should be accessible from halls of living rooms without passing through other bedrooms or bathrooms." Housing activist Edith Elmer Wood built off the APHA's claims by proclaiming, "Immorality is closely connected with overcrowding, lack of privacy, and use of common toilets by a number of families. . . . Sexual matters are thrust on the attention of children at an abnormally early age by the impossibility of privacy within a 1- or 2- or even 3-bedroom dwelling."[72]

Federal authorities incorporated these concerns into all of their plans for home construction. Public housing officials particularly hoped that sexual privacy could change the behavior of the poor. The USHA, which oversaw federal support for low-income housing, cited the APHA's claim that "lack of privacy . . . is certainly undesirable for the best mental, moral, and spiritual development" and required local authorities to make sure that residents could access bedrooms "without passage through another room."[73] The SFHA recruited tenants by telling them, among other things, that they "Need Better Housing" if their current homes were "crowded, without privacy, or had an average of more than two persons per bedroom."[74] The agency tried to design units that protected the sex lives of tenants from both their children and neighbors. A survey conducted by the SFHA in 1946 concluded that most residents valued concrete walls in their buildings for their "soundproofing qualities."[75]

FHA and VA officials similarly set rules for banks and homebuilders that required new houses to have bedroom privacy. These agencies primarily worked with middle- to upper-class homeowners, and therefore they worried less about reforming the behavior of the poor than about insuring homes that would have high resale values. At the same time that slum reformers called for better low-income housing, architects hoped to build spaces to improve the erotic possibilities of marriage. Architectural critic Lewis Mumford argued that designers needed to take into account the ways that many Americans saw sexual satisfaction as a sign of marital success: "Every part of the dwelling must be arranged equally with an eye to sexual privacy and untrammeled courtship," he declared. "Sexual intercourse must not be forever doomed, except for the luxuriously rich, to take place only, like burglary, under cover of darkness."[76] Government officials helped democratize Mumford's ideas after the war. FHA guidelines from the period, consequently, told mortgage assessors that "a high degree of privacy . . . enhances livability and continuing appeal."[77] The FHA underscored the need to avoid "exposing the bedroom to bathroom passage or the bathroom to view from the living portion of the dwelling" in new homes and counseled builders to arrange "windows or exterior planting to prevent the intrusion upon the privacy of one family unit from the windows of another."[78]

A concern for sexual privacy, the policing of the sex lives of Americans, and racial and gender discrimination thus united the two tiers of U.S. housing policies. But the tiers also differed in crucial ways. Most important, they enjoyed significantly different funding realities and reputations in postwar

America. Federal officials gave low-income housing significantly less money than the subsidies they gave to builders and banks through the VA and FHA. According to one estimate, the federal government spent approximately $4.2 billion to encourage suburban home construction between 1948 and 1954 alone.[79] Yet most Americans, particularly white, middle-class Americans, identified public housing as a "government handout." Critics even described public housing as a form of government overreach and "communism," not unlike the denunciations lobbed at sex education in schools. Although much larger, the VA and FHA mortgage programs faced no such accusations. Numerous Americans, particularly homeowners, saw suburban housing purely as the product of their proprietors' work, free of government support.

This discrepancy emerged for multiple reasons. Americans explicitly called low-income housing "public," and federal and local officials promoted these programs as a way that government could solve social problems. Public mortgage subsidies worked through intermediaries, such as banks and developers, just as sex education programs worked through universities and parent groups. Homeowners did not meet with public officials directly. Instead, FHA and VA officials preferred to work at one step removed from their programs' beneficiaries. The FHA, in particular, actively downplayed its large contribution to the postwar housing market. Worried that congressional conservatives would label it a "communistic" program, the administration launched a marketing campaign that described itself merely as an "assistant" to the free market, rather than a government agency that had defined and created that market.[80] Just as significantly, so-called public housing faced greater stigma because it served poor people. Mortgage subsidies primarily helped the middle class and pushed wealth upward. Similar to California's parent education program, which also targeted middle-class families, the much larger FHA and VA programs benefited a more powerful demographic, less inclined to see their benefits as the result of public policies. Over time, suburban homeowners would increasingly define themselves as hardworking contributors to society and public housing tenants as people who unfairly benefited from government assistance.

The Right to Sexual Privacy

In many ways, the private bedrooms called for by housing advocates in the 1930s, 1940s, and 1950s represented a potent metaphor for the "closet" in postwar public policies. Reformers who pushed for homes that shielded children from the dangers of the street and the sex lives of their parents reinforced normative trends in postwar public policy, intending to help young people develop "healthier" attitudes about sex. Yet by promoting bedroom privacy, they revealed a double standard at the heart of the Straight State: how could government officials police behaviors that took place behind closed doors? Beginning in the early 1950s, several academics and lawyers argued that states like California should decriminalize all sex acts that took place between consenting adults in private. With the notable exception of Alfred Kinsey, these critics accepted the notion that marital heterosexuality represented a healthier and more "normal" relationship. Legal experts like Morris Plowscowe and the American Law Institute (ALI) even called for greater sex education for parents and children as a more effective tool for public officials to use to promote normative sexuality. Yet they all deplored what they saw as the hopelessness of public policies that criminalized sex acts between consenting adults in private.

In many ways, Alfred Kinsey's bestselling volumes on male and female sexuality in 1948 and 1953 sparked much of the postwar academic and legal interest in this subject.[81] First undertaken in the early 1940s, *Sexual Behavior and the Human Male* came out amid the postwar sex crime panic and circulated during the national debates about how to limit so-called sex deviates. Five years later, the researcher released a sequel dedicated to studying sexuality and the human female, which reached popular audiences, while states like California formulated policies on how to limit "perversion." In both volumes, Kinsey and his coauthors offered a startling array of statistics that contradicted many readers' preconceived notions about the prevalence of premarital sex, homosexuality, and even bestiality. They concluded, for example, that premarital sex and masturbation were widespread and that approximately 17 percent of men in rural areas had some kind of sexual contact with an animal.[82] In one of the most widely read portions of the books, they contended that approximately one-third of American men and 10 percent of women had had a homosexual encounter to the point of orgasm in their lifetimes.[83]

Although Kinsey and his coauthors often couched their study in turgid, academic prose, they criticized what they saw as the unnecessary handcuffing of scientific inquiry into sexuality in the United States. They particularly condemned "the custom and the law" that had placed "not immaterial restrictions" on previous studies of sex and rejected what they saw as the arbitrary hierarchies Americans had imposed on one another: "Nothing has done more to block the free investigation of sexual behavior than the almost universal acceptance, even among scientists, of certain aspects of that behavior as normal, and other aspects of that behavior as abnormal." According to Kinsey and his coauthors, this widespread tendency to arbitrarily mark some forms of consensual sex as "normal" and others as "deviant" meant that "subsequent generations" would widely condemn "the scientific quality of nineteenth century and early twentieth century scientists."[84]

Kinsey made subtle criticisms of the laws criminalizing sex in his books, but he made them more explicit in public appearances. When the California Assembly asked him to testify before its Special Subcommittee on Sex Crimes in 1949, Kinsey attacked what he saw as the hypocrisy of many state laws on the subject: "We find that 95 percent of the population has in actuality engaged in sexual activities which are contrary to the law. . . . If you and I don't like it, it doesn't alter the problem. . . . It is our judgment that there isn't more than 5 or 10 percent of the persons who are convicted under the law who are involved in behavior which is fundamentally different from behavior which is widespread in the population."[85] After the release of his book on sex and the human female, he spoke out against the teachers, psychologists, church leaders, and women's groups who had supported some of the most "extreme sex laws" in the state.[86]

Instead, Kinsey endorsed the creation of laws that decriminalized relations between consenting adults in private. Since so many Americans engaged in acts that violated local and state laws, he told the Special Subcommittee on Sex Crimes that they should focus their efforts on three types of offenders. First, he supported the notion that "society has the right and the obligation to protect itself and its individual members from forced relations." Second, he endorsed laws that protected younger children from "sexual activity forced on [them] by adults." And, to a lesser extent, he argued that society needed to protect itself from "nuisance offenders" like exhibitionists who committed sex acts repeatedly in public.[87] He paired this call for decriminalization with a broadening of most Americans' conceptions of sex education, endorsing instruction that covered the full range of human sexual behavior. In some cases, Kinsey employed language comparable to those of sex education's biggest proponents and argued that his research could help build stronger marriages.[88] In other instances, the famous researcher stepped outside the limited debate on the subject and argued that no education campaign could succeed if it focused on marriage alone. He warned in 1953 that "no balanced program for American youth can be confined to preparing them (only) for sexual relationship in marriage."[89]

Kinsey's findings made him a celebrity, but his ideas challenged many Americans' beliefs about the differences between "normal" and "abnormal" sexuality. San Francisco booksellers, for example, reported an upsurge in orders in advance of the publication of *Sexual Behavior in the Human Female* in 1953, and the *Chronicle* offered a tepid endorsement of Kinsey's work, calling it "something to be studied carefully . . . in the home, the church, and the court of law."[90] Several of the newspaper's readers, however, disapproved of the *Chronicle*'s endorsement and condemned Kinsey on religious and scientific grounds in letters to the editor. One writer criticized the media's coverage of the sex researcher, warning that all of the publicity "can do a great deal of harm" to "our youth."[91] Another writer called Kinsey's work "an insult to Christian womanhood" and demanded that public officials ban his books.[92]

Some San Franciscans supported the bestselling author, yet contrary to his statements, they largely defended him on the grounds that his work could help build stronger marriages. One woman wrote a letter to the *San Francisco Examiner* expressing her dismay that most people treated sex as "something to whisper about behind closed doors." She declared, "Too bad that there are not more Kinsey reports to expose the fear and guilt which has been instilled in many of our boys and girls, who grow up to become incompatible husbands and wives due to what was considered in the home an obnoxious topic—sex."[93] Another San Franciscan similarly ignored Kinsey's calls to think of sex as something other than either "normal" or "abnormal" and argued, "If the critical and pure minded will take time to investigate divorce records they will learn that a surprisingly big percentage of divorces is based on sex ignorance. Let us welcome more Kinsey reports to help us . . . solve humanity's hidden problems more intelligently and fearlessly."[94]

Kinsey, undoubtedly, represented a minority viewpoint when he spoke out against what he saw as the arbitrary and inhumane hierarchy at the heart of most sex laws in the United States. Nevertheless, his work inspired a variety of other writers to offer a limited critique of policing and the Straight State. Many writers followed Kinsey by highlighting the inherent problems in trying to police sex acts that took place out of public view. On occasion, these writers spoke of a fundamental "right" to privacy and warned of the unnecessary encroachment of the state into the personal affairs of its citizens. More often, however, they underscored the hypocrisy of criminalizing a small percentage of the population for acts committed by broad sections of the citizenry, and they underscored the impossibility of policing sex acts that took place behind closed doors. In almost every case, they stressed the importance of "privacy" as a part of their critique of the newly created sex crimes laws in states like California.

In the *University of Chicago Law Review* in 1949, for example, an anonymous writer reviewed the wide-ranging laws that criminalized sexual behavior between consenting adults in private. Writing just one year after the release of *Sexual Behavior in the Human Male*, the reviewer underscored the impracticality of criminalizing behavior that most Americans engaged in behind closed doors: "While an offense like nonmarital sodomy might itself impel a prosecution because of a genuinely outraged sense of decency, outsiders do not get a chance to observe another's sex conduct except accidentally or unless purposely violating the privacy sought by the participants."[95] Similarly, Morris Ploscowe, a New York City judge, used evidence from Kinsey's work to argue, "Adult homosexual behavior which occurs privately and which does not give rise to public scandal is presently not being punished by the law. It might be desirable to eliminate the legal prohibitions against adult homosexual behavior in private altogether."[96]

In the mid-1950s, the American Law Institute adopted many of the ideas of writers like Ploscowe when it formulated a "model penal code" for legislatures across the country. The group consisted of some of the nation's leading liberal legal theorists, and they encouraged states to decriminalize sex acts that did not involve minors, the use of force, or "public offense." They contended, "No harm to the secular community is involved in atypical (irregular) sex practice in private between consenting adult partners."[97] The ALI based its recommendations on a number of different criticisms of existing sex laws, including the ways in which they burdened police departments, the ways in which they deterred so-called sex deviates from seeking medical treatment, and the ways in which they encouraged blackmail. But most significantly, the ALI also argued that people had a fundamental right to privacy from unwarranted intrusions from the state: "There is the fundamental question of the protection to which every individual is entitled against state interference in his affairs when he is not hurting others."[98]

These kinds of statements, undoubtedly, represented the outer boundaries of acceptable critiques of sex and the law in the 1950s. Like Kinsey, the ALI faced significant criticism from other jurists and the general public. Chief Justice John Parker of the U.S. Federal Court of Appeals responded to early proposals to decriminalize private sex acts between adults by arguing that the legal system needed to "denounce" behaviors like homosexuality "in order that people might know that the state disapproves."[99]

Perhaps because of these criticisms, advocates for a "right to privacy" offered only limited challenges to the legal regime put in place after World War II, and they never directly confronted the hierarchy at the heart of the Straight State. Whereas Kinsey questioned the distinctions Americans made between "normal" and "abnormal" sex, most of the discussion of sex laws after he published his work focused on the effectiveness—instead of the ethics—of sex laws against consenting adults. The acceptance of this hierarchy was most apparent in the attention that writers like the ALI paid to the most disciplinary elements of public policy. They rarely questioned the distinction jurists made between marital heterosexuality and other forms of sexuality. Many of these writers highlighted what they saw as the unfair penalties associated with crimes like sodomy, but they never argued that homosexual relationships or premarital cohabitation represented a social good. Morris Ploscowe, for example, called extramarital sex a "lesser evil" and supported laws against "heterosexual and homosexual acts that outrage public decency."[100]

Because they at least publicly adhered to the social hierarchy that distinguished between marriage and all other relations, many writers who critiqued the criminal code also called for heteronormative sex education. According to the anonymous reviewer in the *University of Chicago Law Review*, "The powerful checks of home, school, church and social evaluation do not require as a supplement an unwieldly law enforcement apparatus."[101] Ploscowe similarly argued that police should cede their authority over sex acts between adults in private to agencies like "the schools, the churches [and] the family" because "propaganda, public education, and religious teaching may be far more effective in discouraging illicit sexual activity than legal sanctions."[102] Rather than calling for acceptance of something like homosexuality, writers like Ploscowe merely called for their eradication by other means.

The reliance of these writers on privacy largely engaged the Straight State on its own terms and reinforced the idea that public officials needed to drive some relationships into hiding. Calls for the decriminalization of behaviors like sodomy may have acknowledged some of the hypocrisy at the heart of a law enforcement approach to sexuality, but they never challenged the notion that these acts required concealment. The ALI in 1955, for instance, termed homosexuals who congregated in public a "nuisance" and called for their arrest for "offensively flaunting their deviance from general norms of behavior."[103] It did not dispute the fact that homosexuals or premarital cohabitators needed to conceal their actions, only that the state should not pursue them. In other words, even the most ardent argument in favor of privacy usually commented on the role of government, not the value of different forms of sexual expression.

By the mid-1950s, therefore, the Straight State had erected a growing number of incentives for Americans to adhere to marital heterosexuality and penalties for those who deviated from them. But those same policies also enabled a liberal critique of policing that focused on a sexual "right to privacy." That critique never actually challenged the hierarchy at the heart of the Straight State, with groups like ALI reinforcing the idea that heterosexuality and marriage represented important relationships that needed government support. Instead, they used some of the very language government officials used to promote their housing policies as a tool to challenge a third element of the Straight State. Even this limited critique garnered little support in the late 1940s and 1950s, but it would grow in popularity over time. By the mid-1960s, growing numbers of legal scholars and judges would recognize that Americans had a fundamental "right to privacy," and by the end of the 1970s, Americans across the political spectrum would invoke the term to justify multiple, competing points of view. In just a few decades, the right to privacy would move from an idea primarily used by a small number of liberal lawyers to a mainstream discourse that was almost impossible to avoid in discussions about sex and the law.

Those debates would emerge most sharply in a metropolitan region dramatically transformed by some of the policies described in this chapter. Federal housing subsidies not only would make bedroom privacy one of the basic expectations of the American middle class but also fueled one of the greatest sexual migrations of the twentieth century: postwar suburbanization. By making it easier for many Americans to buy new homes and restricting those benefits to white, married couples, federal housing officials remade the relationship between the metropolitan center and periphery. Newly empowered, millions of white, married couples bought new homes in newer suburbs, and their movement indirectly facilitated the meeting of growing numbers of lesbians, gay men, and other "single" people in older cities like San Francisco. Over the next two decades, these different communities would grow increasingly self-aware and politically engaged, and different notions of sexual privacy would lie at the heart of their sense of community and identity.

PART II

The Suburban Metropolis

Chapter 3

Building Better Bedrooms

For twenty years after World War II, public officials, private developers, and realtors made numerous promises about the new suburbs. Yet two marketing strategies were remarkably consistent: normative family life for whites and sexual privacy. Authorities at the Federal Housing Administration (FHA), for example, told consumers in 1954 to buy houses in "Desirable Neighborhoods" with sufficient "schools, churches, parks, and playgrounds," which meant "better living for the entire family." When it came to the houses themselves, government officials advocated that would-be homeowners watch for "Good Designs" that offered "privacy" and enough rooms to meet "family needs." Bankers at the U.S. Savings and Loan League similarly encouraged Americans to realize, "Most home-owning neighborhoods are comprised of people of similar social, economic and educational backgrounds," they declared. "This similarity of interests means a minimum of friction, and a maximum of opportunity for developing lasting . . . friendships, not only for parents, but for their children as well." One of the best parts of homeownership, the bankers continued, was the "freedom" it offered from "noise, prying eyes or 'big ears,' and complaints from janitors and landlords or other apartment dwellers." Bay Area real estate developer Joseph Eichler promised consumers multiple home designs, "each conceived with a different family in mind." Every option offered numerous amenities, including a "luxurious and secluded" master bedroom suite for parents interested in getting "away from the family."[1]

These dual promises of family-friendly living and sexual privacy helped trigger one of the most important sexual migrations in the history of the United States. During the long postwar marriage and baby booms, private developers and public officials in places like San Mateo and Santa Clara counties near San Francisco created entire neighborhoods for white parents and their children. In doing so, they transformed the "preventative agencies" many middle-class Americans deemed necessary for good childrearing into commodities designed to attract homebuyers. They clustered homes, schools, and churches in the residential parts of new suburbs, hoping to lure millions of new residents with the promise of wholesome, "family-friendly" living. This desire to create normative family life and sexual privacy also stoked sexual, racial, and class conflict as suburbanites excluded people and places that they deemed threatening. Municipal officials capped the number of bars in the suburbs and demolished encampments of transient agricultural laborers because they deemed them too queer or threatening. Government officials, private builders, and realtors, furthermore, excluded most people of color from new developments because they believed integration promoted friction and made it harder for white families to forge friendships with one another. These efforts proved enormously successful. In the two decades after World War II, millions of white, married, middle-class couples moved to new suburbs with the intention of raising their children.

From a fiscal point of view, however, they were too successful. The sheer concentration of families with children in the suburbs strained local schools and reshuffled the region's economy. As in other schools across the country, public education in San Mateo and Santa Clara counties suffered chronic classroom and teacher shortages well into the 1950s.[2] Faced with mounting costs, local officials pushed for rapid economic development to increase their city's tax base. Civic leaders in San Mateo and Santa Clara counties accelerated their efforts to attract industrial development amid the postwar school crisis, and they lured new businesses with a number of tools, including the promise that their workforce would find wholesome family environments. In time, this strategy worked. Bay Area suburbs like Sunnyvale and Palo Alto attracted lucrative defense-related employers like Lockheed-Martin and used the resultant revenue to abate the school crisis. The outward migration of married couples with children, therefore, not only shuffled the demographics of the metropolitan fringes but also provoked major shifts in regional economies.

Most of the actors who helped build the postwar suburbs believed that sexual privacy, in particular, reinforced normative family life. The believed that secluded bedrooms protected children from the erotic lives of their parents and freed couples to have sex without fear of intrusion from kids or neighbors. Millions of homebuyers, many motivated by memories of the wartime housing shortage, entered a new housing market that promised them sexual privacy, and the suburban housing boom helped popularize the notion that homeowners deserved the freedom to behave as they wished in their bedrooms. Yet the trend undermined marital heterosexuality as much as it reinforced it. Suburban privacy made it easier for people to have all kinds of sex, including ways that deviated from official norms. In many cases, this process had an unintended emancipatory effect. Suburban privacy, for example, allowed some people to experiment free of the "prying eyes" and "big ears" described by the U.S. Savings and Loan League. In other cases, it reinforced hierarchies within marriage. American law and custom since the late nineteenth century had protected husbands who beat or raped their wives because authorities considered marriage a "private domain," free of criminal scrutiny.[3] Low-density housing and private bedrooms give this ideal physical expression, secluding victims of domestic violence from the potentially helpful eyes and ears of their neighbors.

Suburbanization, therefore, was a key turning point in the history of sexuality, but it encompassed multiple trends. The suburban housing market commodified normative white family life and sexual privacy. The millions of people who moved to the postwar suburbs would form new sexual communities and, in time, develop their own sexual politics. Yet suburbanization also helped transform ideas about what constituted "normal" sex. Planners and developers spoke of privacy as a way of strengthening marriages and protecting children, but private spaces also freed suburban residents to have many kinds of sex, including consensual relations with others of the same sex. Furthermore, suburbanites experienced sexual privacy differently. While it liberated some to indulge previously forbidden desires, it also put many women in abusive relationships at greater risk. Neither inherently oppressive nor emancipatory, sexual privacy in the suburbs was Janus faced and defied easy categorization.

Marriage Boom, the State, and Housing

In the early twentieth century, the San Francisco Peninsula and South Bay boasted some of the most fertile fruit-growing lands in California. Farmers produced more apricots and strawberries than just about any other area in the nation, and the Santa Clara Valley was known as the "prune capital" of the world.[4] San Mateo and Santa Clara counties together had approximately

290,000 residents in 1940, and "agriculture" and "food processing" were the two largest categories of employment in the South Bay.[5] San Jose was the area's largest city with about 68,000 people, and several smaller towns like Sunnyvale, Palo Alto, and Redwood City dotted the rail line that tied the Peninsula and South Bay to San Francisco. According to a local historian, churches, saloons, and social clubs dominated the Santa Clara Valley's social life in the late nineteenth and early twentieth centuries, while farm owners often lived with their extended families under one roof.[6]

This agricultural economy attracted large numbers of transient workers who settled intermittently in the area. Some of them rented rooms in hotels in towns like Sunnyvale or Redwood City, while others lived in so-called hobo jungles, which were clusters of self-made shelters along the rail lines that snaked down from San Francisco. African Americans, Mexican Americans, and Filipinos made up a significant percentage of the farm workforce, but racial covenants enacted in the early twentieth century barred most of them from living near whites. Consequently, many multiracial communities erected informal settlements near the canneries and farms where their inhabitants often worked. According to one estimate, approximately 30 percent of Santa Clara County's residents lived on unincorporated land in 1940.[7]

In these autonomous communities, residents often lived outside of marriage, and their sexual relationships sometimes defied middle-class notions of respectability.[8] Men did much of the work in the area's agricultural economy, and many of the makeshift settlements along the rail lines were overwhelmingly transient and male. Workers often shared space, slept near one another, and enjoyed varying degrees of personal privacy. Some of their relations with one another were erotic, and inhabitants had sex in the most secluded place available to them. Richard McClure, a middle-class gay man, grew up in San Jose in the 1930s, and his first sexual experiences emerged out of this queer aspect of the agricultural economy. McClure first learned about anal sex when his friend witnessed two men having it in a train car in the city. He later recalled that before the war, "the standards were so low" in the area's "skid rows" and "seedier than seedy" bars that "no one criticized the gay people for coming in."[9]

The "queer domesticity" of these agricultural communities overlapped with a vice economy dependent on San Francisco. Late-night revelers, gamblers, and gay men frequently ventured down the Peninsula to drink and evade the stricter surveillance of the city. Sharp Park, a small fishing community on the Pacific coast, boasted a motel and bar named "Hazel's Inn" that sometimes attracted as many as 200 San Franciscans a night. Because of its remote location, the bar allowed men to dance with one another and sometimes drew a mixed, multiracial crowd.[10] Naval officer William Gaddis recalled one drunken, late-night outing down the Peninsula in one of his wartime letters. He and his friends took a trip to "Daily City [*sic*]" or, as he vaguely remembered, "it could have been Burlingame and I wouldn't have been the wiser" to evade the official bar curfew in the city. After a long drive, they "finally got to some shack" and passed through "broken down doors and bocci ball courts, etc." to drink beer and dance in what he called a "first-class dump."[11]

Postwar suburbanization radically reshaped this landscape. White, married residents had long disliked these queer amusements amid the settlements of the more transient elements of the agricultural workforce.[12] After World War II, however, an upsurge in marriages, a deepening housing shortage, and federal mortgage policies friendly to sprawling housing developments for white, middle-class married couples meant not only profits to local boosters but also the construction of new communities that marginalized the vices of both the city and the countryside. In the fifteen years after World War II, public officials, business leaders, realtors, and private developers worked together to build dozens of new subdivisions that they deemed beneficial to normative childrearing. In doing so, they commodified homes, schools, and churches and triggered a wave of white, middle-class, married migrants to the postwar suburbs. In doing so, the ambitious city builders of the Peninsula and South Bay would try to eliminate many of the transient labor camps and queer bars on the outskirts of their expanding communities.

These local boosters responded, in part, to forces beyond their immediate control. Although suburbs predated the postwar era, an uptick in marriages and births combined with the housing shortage in the 1940s to prompt government and business leaders to search for new ways to build homes. Following World War II, the United States went through the largest marriage and baby booms of its history, and this shift remade the San Francisco Bay Area in a particularly dramatic fashion. In 1948, the U.S. Department of Commerce reported that the marriage rate had outstripped population growth in the San Francisco–Oakland metropolitan region in the previous seven years by 41 percent.[13] And in 1950, the Bay Area Council, a regional chamber of commerce, crowed that the nine-county Bay Area alone boasted a birth rate that exceeded that of twenty-one states and the District of Columbia.[14] This high marriage and birth rate—combined with a decline in home construction during the Great Depression—created a massive demand for housing. Most returning veterans and their spouses expected to rent or own a home of their own, and the massive spike in marriages after the war aggravated the housing shortage in cities like San Francisco. Expert observers like the California Real Estate Association noted the relationship between the aggregate increase in marriages and a rise in demand for housing, observing in 1947, "This sudden increase in family units [has] caused additional demand for living space in congested areas."[15]

The expanding demand for housing caused Congress to increase the government's subsidies for home loans. Postwar mortgage insurance through the FHA and Veterans Administration (VA) made it easier for Americans to buy new homes and encouraged them to migrate away from older cities. These mortgages were, of course, not available to everyone. Government officials limited access to them based on their sexuality, race, and gender. Yet their policies were generous enough to give millions of white heterosexual men greater access to capital with which to buy a home and created a mass market for the private real estate industry. In many cases, government support made it cheaper to buy than to rent a home. Between the initial creation of the FHA and 1972, the percentage of homeowners living in the United States jumped from 44 percent to 63 percent.[16] From 1945 to 1966, the FHA and VA insured one out of every two houses in California, and in the first four years after World War II, 65 percent of new homes around San Francisco came just from loans guaranteed by the VA.[17]

This support for homeownership overlapped with two other federal policies that supported suburbanization. First, both the FHA and VA favored mortgages for the construction of owner-occupied single-family homes rather than for apartment buildings or other forms of consolidated living. Across the United States, in the first five years after the war, FHA-insured single-family loans exceeded those for multifamily dwellings by four to one, and between 1950 and 1960, that margin grew to seven to one.[18] In the Bay Area, owner-occupied, single-family homes made up 80 percent of all new housing built in the region. Second, federally supported loans favored new residences on the outskirts of metropolitan areas. This push to the urban fringe accompanied a massive highway building campaign, which, by providing automobile commuters easier access to downtown commercial districts, provided yet another federally supported incentive for decentralization. Nationwide, approximately 80 percent of all new home construction after the war occurred outside older cities. In 1951, University of California economist Sherman Maisel estimated that although 60 percent of the Bay Area's population resided in either San Francisco or Oakland, 83 percent of all new residential construction after the war took place outside the urban core.[19]

The upsurge in marriages and the state's support for mortgages, in turn, caused city officials, realtors, and private developers to build scores of new communities for middle-class white families with children. Developers and realtors hoped to profit from new home sales, while public officials hoped to build their tax base. Both parts of these city-building "growth machines" saw middle-class families with children as ideal consumers and citizens. In 1956, the Sunnyvale Chamber of Commerce told local residents, "No matter how large this city becomes, it is understood that the basic social unit is the family and Sunnyvale's guiding hand must aid and protect it."[20] The builders of San Jose's "Tropicana Village" subdivision, meanwhile, told would-be buyers that they had designed houses "with the dreams of young families in mind."[21]

In order to attract these consumers, residential architects and urban planners designed a physical landscape specifically to accommodate middle-class, married couples with children. When architects and developers built new subdivisions, they created commodities that spoke not to a single, individual family but to the broad audience of white, middle-class couples that made up the suburban real estate market. They hoped to find buyers for homes immediately after their construction and to facilitate the future resale of those residences. Public officials and private developers, therefore, built neighborhoods with the intention of helping residents forge social connections with one another. In this way, they turned the preventative agencies celebrated by many Americans—the home, the school, and the church—into commodities that would anchor area property values.

At the heart of their vision lay the detached single-family home. Americans had long seen these residences as signs of economic mobility, social independence, and healthy family living. Reinforcing federal preferences for low-density, detached dwellings, city planners used their zoning power to set aside large portions of their districts uniquely for their construction and made it exceedingly difficult for most single people, low-income renters, queer residents, or people of color from living on the Peninsula or in the South Bay. Between 1950 and 1956, the combined municipalities of Santa

Clara County zoned almost 83 percent of available residential areas exclusively for low-density, owner-occupied housing.[22] Several smaller communities in the valley, including Los Altos Hills and Monte Sereno, prohibited the construction of duplexes and apartment complexes altogether. And when larger cities such as Sunnyvale, Santa Clara, or San Jose permitted denser developments, they frequently limited their construction and used them to shield nearby groups of single-family homes from potential nuisances, including freeways, low-income housing, business districts, or manufacturing areas.[23]

Before World War II, planners like Clarence Perry had idealized self-contained neighborhood units as incubators of family-centered communities. After the war, suburban builders replicated and improved upon the strategy pursued by developers west of San Francisco's Twin Peaks and imposed the ideas of theorists like Perry onto the orchards of the Peninsula and South Bay. Private builders and city officials pushed most auto traffic away from residential areas, insuring that small children would face fewer threats from speeding motorists. Moving from cul-de-sacs to loop streets to connector roads and freeways, planners on the Peninsula and in the South Bay put together a circulatory system that encouraged automobile drivers to avoid the heart of new subdivisions, surrounding neighborhoods with busy roads like moats.[24]

The areas carved out by these thoroughfares served as tools for city builders eager to stabilize local property values as well as planning units to plan services for married couples and their children. Federal officials, private builders, bankers, and realtors demanded the inclusion of "community facilities" in order to attract young parents as buyers, and no institution garnered their attention more than new schools. The FHA advised mortgage evaluators, "Where a school has acquired prestige in the community . . . it will usually . . . be conducive to the maintenance of the desirability of the entire area comprising the school district."[25] The National Association of Homebuilders concurred, "The presence of elementary schools is one of the greatest drawing cards in new residential development, for it is the family with children of school and pre-school age which forms a substantial part of the prospective home-owning market."[26]

Local officials in San Mateo and Santa Clara counties assessed the need for new classrooms, in part, based on the number of building permits issued in an area and the size of surrounding homes. Planners endeavored to provide sufficient schools in developing areas and tried to make them easily accessible to local residents. After single-family houses, schools represented the most carefully planned feature of suburban residential districts, and officials on the Peninsula and in the South Bay almost universally promised to place campuses within short distances of the home. Santa Clara County officials decreed in 1952 that no campus should lie more than a half-mile from any student's doorstep.[27] San Jose authorities, meanwhile, boasted in 1958 that "each neighborhood design is developed with the elementary school as its nucleus."[28]

This proximity between home and school indicated more than just the practical concern of easing students' movements to class. Postwar architects and educational builders explicitly viewed elementary schools as extensions of the home. They believed that kindergartens and early grades represented the first steps children would take into the larger world, and they tried to ease the transition from the private world of the parents to the realm of the public school. Editors at the building journal *American School and University* told education officials in 1950, "A child's first venture away from home should not be too great a contrast which may create aversions. The elementary school should be child scale, low and small, with intimate homelike atmosphere rather than monumental or institutional."[29] In order to blend in with the sprawling subdivisions that surrounded them, most campuses from the period featured low-rise, single-story structures and boasted amply manicured lawns.[30]

Although schools represented the most significant addition to any neighborhood, federal officials, private builders, and banks also advocated the inclusion of churches and parks as a means of maintaining local property values and strengthening family life. In its 1953 *Home Builders Manual*, the National Association of Home Builders contended, "The church is an important and necessary component of American community life. [It] can help to stabilize neighborhood desirability and value, and often is a deciding factor in helping a prospective buyer to choose his location."[31] William Claire, an urban planner from Los Angeles, told his professional colleagues a year later, "The planner . . . sees the church as a factor in the stabilization of land values, the increase in neighborhood solidarity and the fostering of community pride. He sees the church as a focal point for family activities and interests; religious education for children . . . and, finally, as a means [of reducing] juvenile delinquency, crime, divorce, [and] loose morals."[32]

Even as private and public city builders crafted communities to meet the needs of middle-class married couples and their children, they also marginalized people and spaces that they believed threatened normative family life. Most notably, they saw racial exclusion as a prerequisite for profitable housing sales and healthy white children. Throughout the 1950s and early 1960s, Bay Area civil rights groups regularly charged that individual builders or brokers refused to admit people of color to all-white subdivisions. A 1950 study undertaken by students at San Jose State College determined that South Bay realtors regularly steered homebuyers of color away from new subdivisions and that at least one local broker lost his license for introducing Filipinos to an all-white neighborhood.[33] A civil rights investigation of housing discrimination in the 1970s found that in the previous three decades, South Bay developers and realtors had pushed most residents of color in the area into a narrow strip of housing tracts, stretching along the Bayshore freeway from East Palo Alto on the Peninsula to San Jose's eastside.[34]

This systematic discrimination resulted, in part, from the belief that segregation produced stable white families. In a 1953 manual assembled under the direction of Bay Area developer David Bohannon, for instance, the National Association of Home Builders recommended that developers use "discrimination in the selection of his buyers in order to insure . . . that families who are forming a new neighborhood belong to compatible racial and social groups."[35] Looking back on his actions in the 1950s, real estate developer Dick Randall candidly told the Santa Clara Human Relations Commission in 1975 that he believed wholesome family living demanded racial and class segregation, and according to the civil rights group's final report, "It was [Randall's] opinion that to 'mix widely priced living units next to or within the same subdivision would be a disservice to the lower income purchaser, since the children would probably have difficulty adjusting to the affluence evidenced by the higher income families.' "[36]

The belief that neighborhood schools made healthy families further reinforced segregation in the local housing market. A study on "interracial prejudice" in 1950 noted that only one teacher of Mexican descent and not a single African American worked in San Jose's schools, and in the mid-1950s, the Mayfair Elementary School in San Jose boasted a 65 percent Mexican American enrollment, while the neighboring districts had almost exclusively Anglo-white student bodies.[37] As late as 1968, a report sponsored by the Santa Clara County Department of Education concluded that the segregation of students of color and discriminatory hiring policies toward nonwhite teachers characterized the entire postwar era. Looking at the entire South Bay, the school authorities noted the "high concentration of minority ethnic groups in neighborhoods afflicted by social blight" and asserted that schools in the county had hired only one teacher with a "Spanish surname" for every ninety-three students.[38]

Racial segregation accompanied the destruction of spaces that city officials and private developers believed threatened middle-class families, including most vestiges of the "queer domesticity" in the older, agricultural economy. In 1948, the American Public Health Association (APHA) advised city planners to eliminate hazards that might "exert socially undesirable influence on the residents, especially children and adolescents." These "hazards" included "gambling houses, bars, low-grade taverns and night clubs, and houses of prostitution." In order to deal with these problematic places, the APHA counseled planners to work closely with local police departments but, most significantly, to design communities in such a manner that "streets leading to schools and other facilities used daily by the residents" should be free of the gathering spots of "immoral people." In 1950, the organization declared, "Where taverns, bars, liquor stores, gambling places, houses of prostitution and other undesirable elements are concentrated and intermixed with residences they present unquestionable moral hazards to adolescents and young people and a disruptive influence on family life."[39]

Beginning in the late 1940s, San Mateo and Santa Clara County police began clearing out the so-called hobo jungles, burning workers' homes, and threatening them with arrest.[40] The state's recently enacted sex crime laws made this process easier, and city authorities justified their campaigns based on what they saw as physical threats to other residents. The Santa Clara police chief, for example, justified the sweeps to the local newspaper by alleging that "over 75 percent of the hoboes are ex-convicts, sex degenerates, petty thieves, and vagrants."[41] In 1956, San Mateo County sheriffs raided Hazel's Inn in Sharp Park, arrested almost ninety people for "perversion," and helped revoke the bar's liquor license. Although it had operated in the county since 1939, the area had recently suburbanized and authorities cited complaints from "people who live near the tavern" that the bar catered to "sexual deviates" as one of the catalysts for their raid.[42] In 1962, officials in Mountain View passed an ordinance forbidding the opening of a bar with telephones at patrons' tables, with the suburb's police chief alleging that it might become a "pickup place" for "homosexuals or prostitutes."[43] By the mid-1960s, Santa Clara boasted the lowest ratio of on-site liquor licenses per person of any county in the state.[44]

Figure 4. Sheriffs arrest patrons at Hazel's Inn in Sharp Park, California. Fang family *San Francisco Examiner* photograph archive negative files, BANC PIC 2006.029:132223.01.11—NEG, Box 1084. © Regents of the University of California, Bancroft Library, University of California, Berkeley.

Fifteen years after the war, therefore, suburbanization had dramatically transformed the Peninsula and South Bay. San Mateo and Santa Clara counties' population effectively quadrupled after the war, and over a million residents lived there in 1960.[45] These newcomers, however, did not reflect the demographics of the larger Bay Area. Arthur Gimmey, an economist at San Jose State, observed that nine out of ten homeowners living in Santa Clara County in 1958 had children, and their average family size generally exceeded the national average by a significant margin.[46] Between 1950 and 1960, the percentage of married people living in San Mateo and Santa Clara counties boomed by 20 percent, while the number of "single" people living in San Francisco doubled. The 1960 census reported that 253,697 married couples lived in the two suburban counties and that over 98 percent of them had their own household.[47] The new suburbs exhibited unprecedented ratios of exclusivity, outstripping even prewar "family" areas like San Francisco's Sunset District. At least nineteen census tracts in the San Jose Standard Metropolitan Area in 1960 had almost no single adults over the age of eighteen. These areas overlapped with the newest residential developments, and they reflected the federal government and real estate industry's investment in racial segregation. Over 97 percent of Santa Clara County's residents in 1960 were white, and according to the census that year, only 13 percent of them had a "Spanish surname."[48]

Newcomers to the Bay Area suburbs came from places near and far, and they sought houses to meet a need for more space, to shorten a commute, or to build equity. Their common identity as parents and their mutual desire to own a home, however, pulled them into a collective search with thousands of other would-be buyers who similarly sought an ideal place in which to raise their children. Even as federal financing gave married borrowers preferential treatment in their application for a mortgage, the search for a new house gave buyers a heightened sense of responsibility for the kind of community in which they would raise their children. Couples selected from a range of relatively similar residential options on the Peninsula or in the South Bay. Even as Santa Clara County's developers and realtors spent fortunes on advertising campaigns designed to attract buyers, at least 50 percent of the people who bought houses in the South Bay in 1958 reported that they had primarily shopped for a new residence by traveling from one cluster of new houses to another.[49]

In his memoir, *Blue Sky Dreams*, Baby Boomer David Beers reminisced about the almost daily tours his mother and father took through the newly assembled subdivisions of the South Bay. His book suggests that married couples associated homeownership with good parenting as much as any realtor or developer: "[My parents] had sat in folding chairs in the garage of a model home while a salesman showed them maps of streets yet to exist, the inked idea of something to be called Clarendon Manor. They had been given a choice of three floor plans, the three floor plans from which all dwellings in Clarendon Manor were to be fashioned." After selecting the outline of their future home and signing the requisite mortgage paperwork, Beers reported that his parents grew restless in anticipation of their upcoming move, and he fondly remembered childhood trips to his yet-to-be-built home: "Early on, my father would go from stake to yellow-ribboned stake, telling us where the kitchen would be, where the front door would go, which would be getting the most sun. Later, after the concrete foundation and plywood subflooring were in and the skeletons of the walls were up, we would wander through the materializing form of our home, already inhabiting with our imaginations its perfect potentiality."[50]

Purchasing a new home involved elaborate conversations among consumers about where to invest, and few issues appeared to add more value to a neighborhood than buyers' identification with the people who already lived there. In 1957 and 1958, Stanford psychology professor Lois Meek Stolz enlisted a team of researchers to interview parents in Palo Alto, and many of their subjects thought that suburban living would allow them to meet other people "like themselves." One man, for instance, told her that he and his wife had moved to the Peninsula in search of a "community spirit" because they believed that cities suffered from "heterogeneous," "mixed" populations. He marveled that his neighbors could "all have pretty much the same patterns of raising children that we have, and that's very good."[51] A former San Franciscan likewise explained his family's move to Palo Alto by saying, "We basically moved down here for the children, [and I] keep telling them they're happier down here, and I'm sure they're happier."[52]

Suburban residents interviewed by local newspapers almost universally commented on how much they appreciated their new neighbors. Their words reflected, in part, the promises of realtors and developers who pledged to help buyers find communities of people with similar backgrounds and consumer preferences. Marian Correia from San Jose told the *Examiner* in 1962, "I like the particular place where we live. I like our neighbors and we've made friends." Doug Hale of San Mateo marveled that although he grew up in Oakland, after he'd moved to the Peninsula, "I've met some wonderful people."[53] And New York transplant Virginia Alfinito told her local paper that "the people of Santa Clara are very friendly and good" and that she liked suburban living "mostly for our children's sake."[54]

Discussions about what made places good for families mirrored and reinforced similar discourses about so-called bad areas for married couples and their children. Although not all residents reacted in the same way, it is clear that many white suburban residents viewed even token racial integration as a fundamental problem. One African American father in Stolz's study declared, "It seems as though . . . in this particular neighborhood that if you're colored, you're supposed to be dumb and stupid." After he and his wife bought their new house, most of their white neighbors avoided them, and some of the children called his family "niggers" and "trash."[55]

Another African American resident told Stolz that although they got along better now, a white father next door had given his son a "fine whipping" and made him "stay in the back yard" after he found him playing with black children.[56]

By the early 1960s, therefore, the marriage boom, federal mortgage policies, and the plans of local city builders helped turn the farms of the Peninsula and the South Bay into exclusive "family friendly" suburbs. To do so, they commodified the preventative agencies—the homes, schools, and churches—and assessed the value of a neighborhood based on its ability to attract white, middle-class married couples. They also waged a kind of class, sexual, and racial conflict by excluding communities of color and marginalizing people they deemed too queer to live in the suburbs. Within just a few years, their efforts helped trigger the largest sexual migration in the Bay Area's history as over 700,000 people moved to San Mateo and Santa Clara counties after World War II. These new residents did not come from a single mold, but the mechanisms of suburb building ensured that they were overwhelmingly white, married, and middle class.

Bedroom Communities and Economic Development

This in-migration of married white couples led to a major shift in the Bay Area's economy. Population growth in San Mateo and Santa Clara counties took place amid the national redistribution of wealth and jobs to states like California. After World War II, many midwestern and northeastern manufacturers eager to escape unions or seeking lower taxes relocated to western and southern states. Booming defense industries, in particular, opened plants in an ascendant Sunbelt region that stretched from Virginia to the Pacific Coast.[57] Cities across the country scrambled to attract new employment and taxable businesses, and Bay Area boosters avidly participated in this competition. As they did so, they often envisioned building what historian Robert Self has called the "industrial garden," or an idealized community that harmoniously blended "big city" manufacturing with pastoral suburban landscapes of single-family homes.[58] But Peninsula and South Bay elites also pursued outside investment because they worried about building a different kind of city that they associated with a different kind of fertility: the bedroom community. The progressive concentration of married couples with children increasingly burdened local schools in San Mateo and Santa Clara counties. Consequently, local public officials and

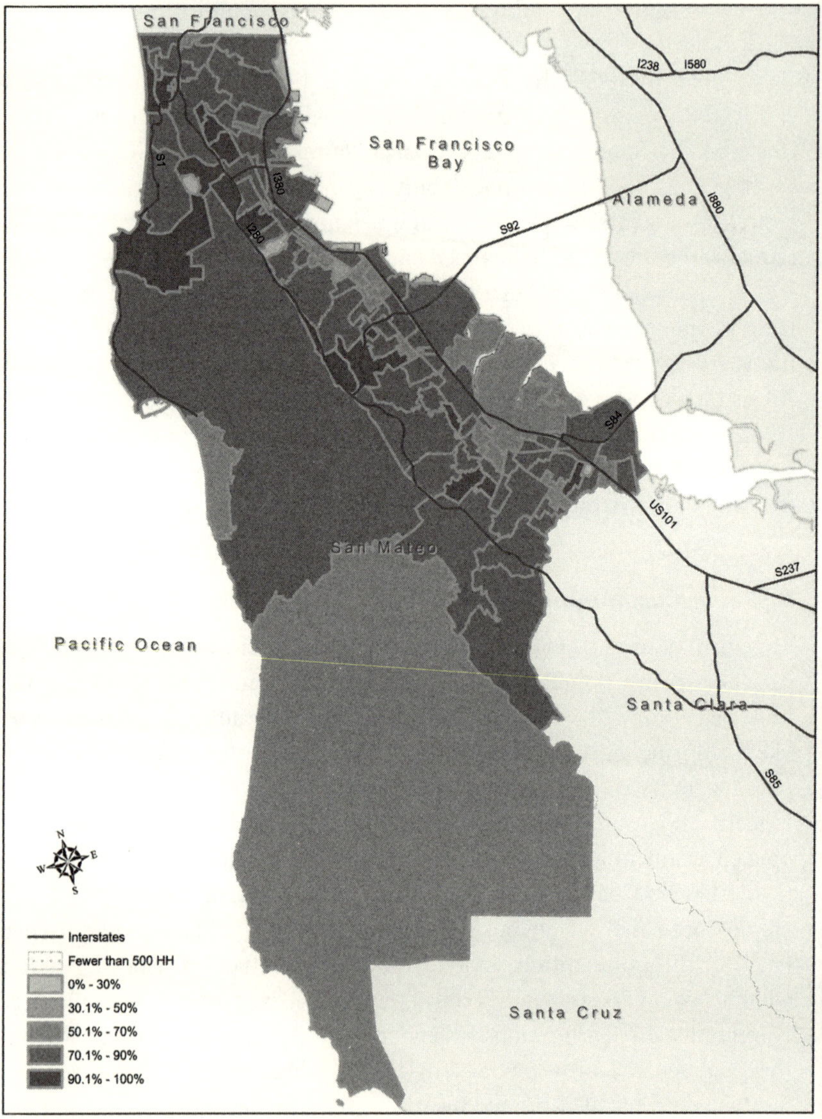

Map 4. Percentage of married couples with their own household in Santa Clara County by census tract, 1960. This map does not include information for tracts with fewer than 500 households. Center for Urban and Regional Analysis, Ohio State University.

Map 5. Percentage of married couples with their own household in San Francisco by census tract, 1960. This map does not include information for tracts with fewer than 500 households. Center for Urban and Regional Analysis, Ohio State University.

private business leaders argued that their suburbs could no longer afford to house middle-class residents with kids who worked elsewhere. Instead, they would need to attract their own economic bases in order to offset the growing costs of the Baby Boom. By the early 1960s, these elites had proven so successful that suburbs across the country tried to emulate the development strategies of the Peninsula and South Bay.[59]

This future as a model of Sunbelt growth was far from self-evident in San Mateo and Santa Clara counties in the 1940s, however. Local business elites had recruited defense-related manufacturing during World War II, but they still largely believed that industry in the region would continue to serve agricultural needs. But postwar suburbanization made them pursue more ambitious goals. As real estate agents sold cluster upon cluster of single-family homes on the Peninsula and in the South Bay, they helped shift the state's student population away from older urban centers and prompted the *San Jose Mercury* to reflect, "[Last year] subdivisions spread across the valley like a fast-growing ground cover in springtime. Every new batch of houses means more children to be educated in the district."[60] Whereas San Francisco's school enrollment stagnated in the postwar decades, Santa Clara County's student population grew from approximately 36,000 students in 1947 to almost 150,000 new pupils in 1960.[61] Although this enrollment boom paralleled the overall population growth of the area, young people under the age of eighteen made up a disproportionate percentage of the South Bay's residents. Similarly, San Mateo's student population outstripped general growth in this period, and although the county's population doubled over the course of the 1940s, the number of children living on the Peninsula tripled. By 1960, the number of people under eighteen living in San Mateo County exceeded the total population of the county before the war.[62]

Planners in the South Bay frequently assessed the number of school-age children in an area based on the number of local building permits issued in a community and the number of bedrooms in the surrounding homes. As the Baby Boom fueled the housing boom, therefore, the school districts of the Peninsula and South Bay underwent a subsequent classroom construction binge, and the soaring costs of education threatened to consume all of the suburbs' meager educational resources. In 1951, consultants for a district in San Mateo County observed pessimistically that "the diaper shortage of the forties has resulted in the elementary school shortage of the fifties, and will result in high school and college building problems for the foreseeable future."[63] Although San Mateo and Santa Clara counties' education authorities built many new schools after the war, classroom and teacher shortages loomed over the area for much of the Baby Boom. Throughout that period, observers reported on an educational system chronically deficient of resources. In 1956, the *Wall Street Journal* reported that 15 percent of all districts in Santa Clara Country had held "double sessions" in which students only attended school for half the day.[64] That same year, the *San Francisco Examiner* observed that education authorities in San Mateo had even resorted to asking churches for permission to host classes in their facilities.[65]

Unlike neighborhoods like San Francisco's West Side, individual suburbs could not rely on revenue generated from other parts of a larger city, and local officials resisted raising taxes on new residents' homes. In 1953, a report by the Urban Land Institute estimated that although it took approximately $204 a year to put a child through school in San Mateo County, residential property taxes that year yielded a mere $50 per house, and with most families sending more than one child to local public schools, the Peninsula suburbs faced an enormous budgetary deficit.[66] A 1955 study by independent consultants in Palo Alto concluded that, based on the current tax structure, a median-priced household in the city with a single child only paid for 44 percent of its share in school services, and that with larger families, the gap between property assessments and the cost of education grew.[67] In 1956, the *San Francisco Examiner* claimed that the Bay Area's largest city had, in effect, created San Mateo's educational problems when it had "made the Peninsula its bedroom," and James Tormey, an overwhelmed suburban school superintendent, observed, "We have a bedroom county and our problem essentially is that bedrooms are better producers of babies than they are of taxes."[68]

State aid provided some relief for struggling suburban school districts. In the first six years after World War II, the California legislature apportioned over $305 million for the construction of new schools in the state. Although public aid came in the form of loans, local districts only had to pay a small sum every year back to the state government, and after three decades, the legislature promised to forgive any outstanding debts. According to education consultants on the Peninsula, "In most cases, at the end of the 30-year period for which the State funds are granted, there will be a large amount still due; but, at that time, this remaining sum will be forgiven and no further payments to the State will be asked."[69] In order to ease the burden of growing suburban school districts, the California legislators essentially gave out over $300 million in loans, for which they largely did not expect repayment. This suburban subsidy lasted well into the 1960s, and a 1963 study by the University of California's Institute of Governmental Studies reported that "rapidly growing fringe districts" with "many children and little industrial or commercial property" were turning to "the state for additional loans for school housing after the early exhaustion of their own borrowing capacity."[70]

Although state aid defrayed some costs, officials in San Mateo and Santa Clara counties increasingly looked to industrial development in order to diversify their tax bases. Manufacturing plants and office complexes offered the potential to bring in revenues without sending more children to already strained suburban schools. The shortage was particularly acute on the Peninsula, where large hills and state parks limited the ability of local governments to reserve space for manufacturing centers. In 1953, consultants from the Urban Land Institute told the San Mateo County Planning Commission that "expansion of industrial plants has been far outstripped by residential building." They predicted that school costs would double by the end of the decade and that officials could ease these economic strains only through "a program of selective industrial development."[71] Similarly, with over 22 percent of the city's population under the age of eighteen, local planners in Palo Alto knew they faced an enormous budgetary shortfall, and in 1955, a group of private consultants warned the suburb's leadership that "the difference between what an average residence yields in school taxes, and the cost of educating the children from that household, must be made up by allocations from state tax funds, and by local taxes on non-residential property."[72]

A dramatic expansion of national spending on defense-related manufacturing in the 1950s helped them allay the ongoing school financial crisis. As early as 1951, the city of Sunnyvale pledged to pursue "balanced development" to avoid being a mere bedroom community. Even as legislators in Washington in this period rejected attempts to use federal funding explicitly for education, their willingness to spend liberally on Cold War weapons programs indirectly subsidized San Mateo and Santa Clara counties' classroom building programs. Between 1946 and 1965, the Defense Department consumed almost 62 percent of the federal government's total budget, and as several scholars have argued, this massive increase in spending allowed Sunbelt states such as California to attract manufacturers from the Northeast and Upper Midwest.[73] As early as 1948, private consultants in the South

Bay advised city leaders to target their efforts to attract new businesses in several key fields, including "ordinance and military equipment," "transportation equipment," and "scientific instruments." Their study took particular note of Santa Clara County's well-developed institutions of higher learning and concluded that the engineering schools at San Jose State, Santa Clara University, and, most notably, Stanford University could help the cities of the Peninsula and South Bay compete nationally for new industries.[74]

Over the course of the subsequent twelve years, Santa Clara County emerged as one of the nation's leading Cold War manufacturing centers. The armed forces' growing appetite for technology, such as satellites, missiles, and jets, fueled the growth of high-technology firms. Santa Clara County's boosters in this period successfully attracted an enormous number of military-related enterprises to defray the growing costs of public education. In 1956, for example, IBM built its West Coast headquarters on San Jose's south side, and in that same year, Lockheed opted to open its satellite and missile division in Sunnyvale.[75] By the early 1960s, Santa Clara County trailed only Los Angeles for projects funded by the Department of Defense in California. Between 1950 and 1963, military spending more than quadrupled manufacturing in the South Bay, with electronics construction increasing by 600 percent.[76]

This shift quickly garnered enthusiastic, yet misleading, media attention. The *San Francisco Chronicle* heralded the "industrial revolution" transforming the bedroom communities of the Peninsula, while *Business Week* marveled as the South Bay "discovers how it feels to be rich."[77] *Ladies' Home Journal* approvingly detailed the "cradle to college" pipeline of some of Santa Clara County's schools.[78] Lost in these success stories was not only the fact that suburban schools had faced an enormous fiscal crisis just a few years earlier but also that development had fallen unevenly across the region. The fragmented governance of San Mateo and Santa Clara counties meant that tax surpluses in some places did not necessarily flow across municipal boundaries. One city's gain was often another's loss, and the area's newfound industrial wealth did not cross the color line. Communities with the largest percentages of Latinos and African Americans received significantly less investment than their whiter counterparts. Residents in the predominantly black, bayside suburb of East Palo Alto, for example, protested their substandard schools and complained that they essentially had "no tax base to incorporate" in the 1960s. The San Mateo County auditor estimated in 1968 that households in East Palo Alto paid $200 more a year for schools than their wealthier, whiter counterparts.[79]

While economic development left some schools underfunded and overcrowded, most cites on the Peninsula and in the South Bay no longer worried about their status as bedroom communities by the 1960s. In fact, the suburban "industrial revolution" heralded by the newspapers meant that San Mateo and Santa Clara counties would soon outrun San Francisco for the title of the Bay Area's leading economic center. Once worried about crowded classrooms, the more affluent suburbs could now boast about their excellent schools and diversified tax base.

Sexual Privacy and Its Consequences

Public officials did not use the term "bedroom communities" by accident. Private bedrooms defined much of the housing built after the war. Suburbanization marked a key moment in the evolution of "sexual liberalism"—the belief that heterosexual pleasure led to personal happiness and matrimonial success—because realtors and developers marketed sexual privacy to a wide, middle-class audience.[80] Federal officials, of course, required private bedrooms in FHA- and VA-insured developments. But private developers, city officials, and individual homebuyers also believed sexual privacy contributed to happier marriages and stabilized property values. Although architects designed suburban houses with heterosexual married sex in mind, property owners used their homes for their own purposes. Just as liberals like Alfred Kinsey predicted, Americans with private bedrooms could break sexual taboos without facing the worst consequences of the Straight State. In this sense, suburbanization both "contained" sexuality by confining relations between middle-class married homeowners to bedrooms and "liberated" it by freeing them to stray from proscribed norms. Yet suburban privacy also had a darker side. Many Americans had long thought of conflicts within the home as a personal matter, outside the purview of the state. There is no way to know if domestic violence or marital rape increased in the 1950s, but the architecture and discourses around suburban privacy reinforced the notion that married couples sat apart from the wider society. Even as some elites worried about creating bedroom communities, therefore, suburban bedrooms witnessed many kinds of relations, including procreative marital sex, queer sex, and coercive violent sex.

Real estate developers' interest in sexual privacy stemmed, in part, from the beliefs of many postwar psychologists who believed that it built stronger families. Medical authorities from the era argued that exposing children to the sex lives of their parents damaged their psyches and that attempts to keep sex secret from children stressed parents' marriages. In 1950, the APHA pushed for the construction of larger homes with private bedrooms because, according to psychologist Paul Lamkau, "Crowding in bedrooms makes the sexual life of the parents very apparent to children who have not yet the maturity or capacity to understand this aspect of the living of their parents. . . . Parents are forced to make the sexual function furtive and guarded rather than fully satisfying as more likely would be if completed in the freedom of privacy."[81]

Nationally recognized architect Robert Woods Kennedy gave this ideal a concrete framework when he pushed the members of his profession to apply a "zoning scheme" to residential floor plans, grouping spaces by common usage and erecting walls between them. According to Kennedy, this clustering pattern broke up the house by degree of privacy, steering the circulation of outsiders away from areas reserved for "sleeping," "excreting," and "love making." "The increasing desire for privacy," declared Kennedy, "as one enters deeper and deeper into the family's activities, appears as a succession of barriers against sight and sound. In terms of privacy, the front door at one end, and the study, water closet, and connubial chamber at the other, are three worlds apart, separated by four distinct barriers. Each group of activities constitutes a little world of its own, cohesive and very distinct in atmosphere and character."[82] By dividing homes into "zones" defined by common usage, architects such as Kennedy not only discouraged couples from having sex outside the bedroom but also actively sanctioned them to have it within the "connubial chamber." Scaling their designs from bedroom to doorway, they ensconced straight couples behind a series of barriers that steered outsiders away from them, muffled sound, and limited their visibility.

From the late 1940s through the 1960s, public officials and builders on the Peninsula and in the South Bay almost universally promised that their homes afforded complete privacy to the places in which parents slept. These promises, in part, reflected requirements necessary to secure FHA and VA financing, but they also revealed developers' belief that consumers wanted sexual privacy. Palo Alto builders Stern and Price offered houses with "bedrooms set well back from the street for privacy." Santa Clara's Gavello Glen

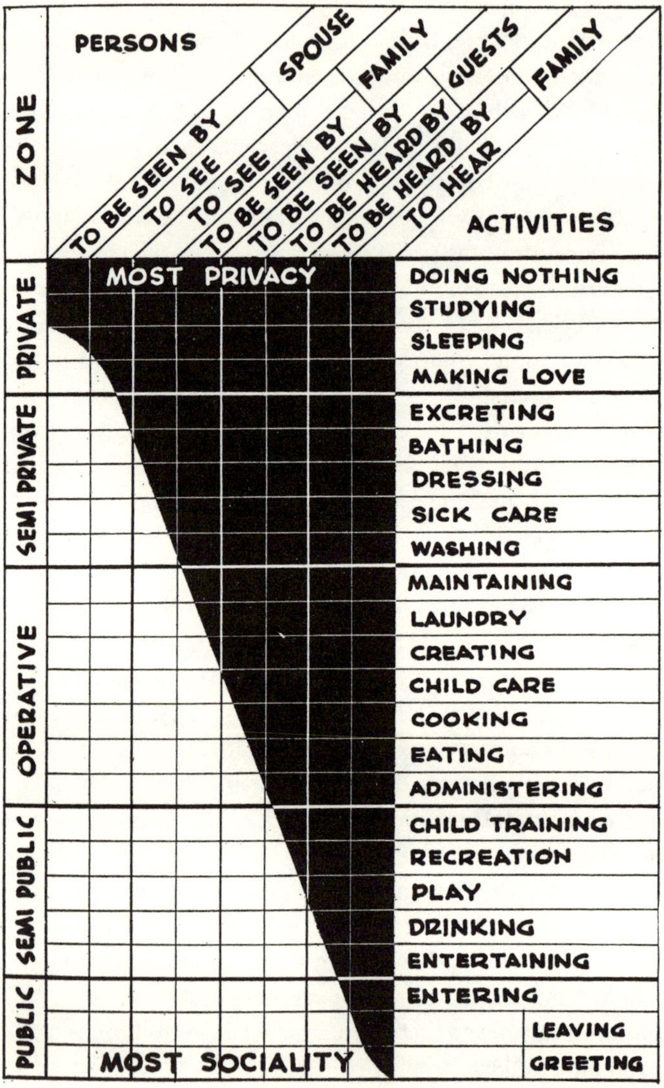

Figure 5. Privacy chart in *The Art of the House and Its Design* by Robert Woods Kennedy, 1953.

promised buyers that his subdivisions varied the lot orientation of each home and therefore "avoided the all-too-common practice of placing bedroom windows of neighboring houses opposite each other across a narrow side yard."[83] And Redwood City's John Funk designed houses with an "H"-shaped floor plan, separating sleeping spaces from living areas, providing "better sound insulation," and ensuring that parents' bedrooms looked out only onto secluded patios or backyards.[84]

This desire to give married couples personal privacy not only appeared in almost all residential development in the period but also served as a basic foundation for determining the size and location of all other rooms in the home. Floor plans of houses built in Santa Clara County invariably included the clustering of sleeping areas, with larger "master bedrooms" dwarfing those reserved for children. Suburban architects almost universally included several of these smaller spaces in their designs, implicitly acknowledging that couples with their own homes would have procreative sex, boosting population growth, and allowing the editors of *House and Home* to exclaim in 1954 that "the three bedroom [has] rapidly established itself as minimal for American families."[85] Cultural perceptions about the need to separate brothers and sisters during their sexual development further drove the physical expansion of the single-family home, with the APHA cautioning builders in 1950 that "children of different sexes, unless both are very young, should sleep in different rooms."[86] For the postwar real estate industry, larger families necessitated not only greater sleeping space but also more washing facilities, and as they added two or more showers to each home, household bathrooms joined bedrooms as one of the few places in postwar America where men, women, and their children commingled in states of undress. In 1954, the editors of *House and Home* advised developers to provide adequate heat since "the bathroom is the only place in the house where people traditionally run around naked," and "people want it warm when they get out of bed in the morning."[87]

Postwar architects envisioned, then, sharp distinctions between the "living" and "sleeping" zones of a postwar home, which reflected their belief in a middle-class gendered division of labor in each household. They designed kitchens, living rooms, and yards primarily to accommodate the perceived needs of Santa Clara County's stay-at-home mothers. Whereas they built bathrooms and bedrooms with the understanding that fathers would join their families to bathe, sleep, and have sex there, they built the rest of the house principally with the belief that mothers would cook, clean, and tend to their children. They also understood that much of middle-class women's social lives would take place within the home, hosting dinner parties, meeting with friends, or organizing PTA meetings. Living rooms and kitchens served as quasi-public spaces between the private worlds of the bedroom and the wider world beyond the home. Garages and yards often represented male space, with maintenance on house exteriors replicating the breadwinning that husbands allegedly did outside the home.[88]

As consumers entered the homebuying market, therefore, they found numerous discourses that connected sexual privacy to property values. But this emphasis on privacy in the home also accompanied new kinds of surveillance in public. In sharp contrast to the bedrooms and bathrooms that architects worked diligently to shield from prying eyes, builders designed suburban living rooms, kitchens, and backyards to help mothers watch their children. Although large glass doors, picture frame windows, and open space between kitchens and living rooms offered a variety of advantages to residents, postwar home designs served as a reminder that children faced numerous dangers, including sexual ones, and only vigilant parents could protect them. In 1954, South Bay builders Mackay and Associates told potential buyers, "Children are the major consideration in a four-bedroom house, so the architects planned the outdoors—like the indoors—as much for the kids as for the house-wife-mother. . . . The architects arranged glass walls and doorways in front of side yards so a mother could keep an eye on her children."[89]

Similarly, authorities stepped up their surveillance of other spaces for evidence of people violating sexual norms in the world beyond the home, particularly public restrooms. Principals at Buchser High and Wilson Intermediate Schools in Santa Clara, for example, set up "two way mirrors" in the boys' restrooms to ease surveillance of the spaces and to help instill "discipline."[90] In 1956 and 1959, Palo Alto police used "motion picture cameras" and "walkie-talkies" in high-tech "stakeouts" of the city's railroad station, and after watching the depot's men's room for ten days, they swept up dozens of local commuters, contending they had come there seeking gay sex.[91] And similarly, a ten-day vigil on a department store restroom in 1962 in Santa Clara allowed the city's law enforcement to arrest eight men "on homosexual charges."[92]

The seclusion of homes and the expansion of police surveillance, therefore, happened simultaneously, and the combination of the two made master bedrooms some of the only acceptable places to have sex in postwar

America. In this sense, bedrooms exemplified what a future generation of gay men and lesbians would call the "closet," the spatial expression of the wider society's repression and shame. Yet in the 1950s, it also had emancipatory meanings. Cordoned off and segregated from the rest of society, suburban homes also became sites of relative sexual freedom as middle-class homeowners—queer and straight—adapted their homes to serve their own sexual desires.[93]

Private sex, by definition, leaves few sources for historians to interpret. But some evidence exists that hints at the broader sexual lives of postwar suburbanites in San Mateo and Santa Clara counties. Many of Lois Meek Stolz's subjects told her researchers that they greatly valued the privacy their new homes afforded them, for example. One father shared that he wanted his young sons to realize that "their [bodies] are nothing to be made fun of" and that he appreciated the fact that they could walk to their bedrooms in the nude "like they were walking down Main Street" and "think nothing of it."[94] After moving out of his father's house, another Palo Alto resident similarly confessed, "We are very happy to be out in the country [Stanford Hills] with three acres of land around us, with an ability to walk around in the house completely naked if we feel like it, even though there's glass from floor to ceiling, we're far enough from the nearest house so that we are certain nobody is going to be out there to notice whether we have our underwear on."[95]

Although married people like this father made up the overwhelming majority of new suburban residents, most new homes offered a limited freedom to a smaller number of people interested in sex that varied from marital norms. Historian Lauren Jae Gutterman found several examples of married women who had sex with other women in their homes in the 1950s and 1960s, including in Santa Clara County. These women did not necessarily identify as "lesbians," but they engaged in sometimes lengthy affairs with lovers they met in their churches, neighborhoods, and workplaces. Their husbands often did not know about their wives' behaviors, and these women used the seclusion of their homes to keep their relationships secret. They often feared discovery by their families or neighbors, but they nevertheless used the privacy of their homes to their advantage. Gutterman argues that some women who experienced queer desires in the 1950s and 1960s surreptitiously turned their ostensibly "straight" homes into "lesbian spaces" while their husbands were away.[96]

The gendered and sexual meanings of suburban homes similarly shaped the erotic life of Richard Tooker, a gay man who moved to San Francisco

Figure 6. The home of Dr. Marvin Samuels in Sunnyvale, California. Fang family *San Francisco Examiner* photograph archive negative files, BANC PIC 2006.029:139218.04.01—NEG, box 1443. © Regents of the University of California, Bancroft Library, University of California, Berkeley.

in 1942. During the war, Tooker met a man in the city and later became friends with him and his wife. When the married couple moved to a new house on the Peninsula, Tooker occasionally visited and carried on an affair with the husband in secret. In a later interview, he alleged that the couple "had their difficulties" and the husband had told him that his wife was "freezing up on him" in the bedroom. Tooker, therefore, agreed to have sex with the man as an alternative to his unhappy marriage. "It just reached a point where he asked me to do him," Tooker recalled. "So I'd say the last four or five times that I went down there, we went out in the garage and I'd take care of him. She [the wife] was in the house with the children." Tooker and his friend never really spoke about the affair, but they ended it when the wife gossiped to him about a similar liaison between two men in their suburb. The police had allegedly caught one of the neighbors having sex with his brother-in-law. Tooker did not remember the details of the other affair, but he recalled that his friend soon broke off their meetings in the garage. "Well, we got out of that one, and I don't think she was ever the wiser."[97]

A few examples garnered from police and media sources offer even more hints at queer relationships taking place behind closed doors. In the mid-1960s local authorities arrested thirty-seven-year-old ophthalmologist Marvin Samuels for engaging in consensual sadomasochistic acts in his Sunnyvale home. The doctor used a "remodeled" room in the back of his house to whip men whom he had met in San Francisco. Authorities only learned of Samuel's sex life when an acclaimed director filmed some of his sessions and asked a Palo Alto camera shop to process it. The owner of the store notified the police, who then raided the ophthalmologist's house. After entering the premises, the authorities found what a local newspaper called "a weird assortment of whips and belts, straps and handcuffs in a rear room." Outside of the view of most of his neighbors and the police, the doctor had erected a heavy beam across part of his ceiling with dangling metal rings with which he handcuffed his partners.[98]

In 1955, Mountain View police arrested two male restaurant owners, Edward Goldstein and William Fromhold, for allegedly having sex with sailors from a nearby naval base and Los Gatos High School students. Both men were in their early forties, and although it is not clear how long they had lived together, court records reveal that at the time of their arrest, the defendants shared a secluded single-family detached home in the Los Altos hills.[99] The Santa Clara County district attorney tried them separately for multiple sex crimes, and according to a report issued to the Department of Corrections, Goldstein was a "homosexual for thirty years. For a long time he had many sailors from Moffett Field come to his home and he used them."[100] The prosecution alleged that one of those sailors had acted as a "procurer" for the restaurant owner, and on one occasion, he had brought a twenty-two-year-old unemployed cement mason over to Goldstein's house. Goldstein then took the cement mason into his bedroom and supposedly gave the man ten dollars for oral sex.[101] The prosecution's contention that Goldstein had "used" men in his home for "a long time" suggests that even the authorities believed that these acts could have continued uncontested indefinitely. Police only arrested Goldstein and Fromhold after stopping the car of three drunk, male Los Gatos High School students. After searching the vehicle, the police discovered a number of stolen items that the boys claimed they had taken from the defendants' house. The three students had allegedly gone to the Los Altos home to exchange sex for money, and while one of them was in the bedroom with Fromhold, the others pocketed a slide projector, several phonograph records, and a $175 set of silverware.[102]

Collectively, these stories hint at a sexual world in which suburban residents did not necessarily use their homes with the normative intent of their builders and reveal the ways that bedroom privacy both reinforced and undermined marital heterosexuality. Promising that homes strengthened marriages through privacy did not necessarily mean that suburbanites used the privacy afforded to them to have the kind of sex their neighbors, church, or the police would have found acceptable. Richard Tooker and his married friend carried on their clandestine affair with relative impunity. Suburbanites like Samuels, Fromhold, and Goldstein might have kept their sex lives secret from the police for years if their luck had not run out. These homeowners did not enjoy a legal right to privacy and yet they nevertheless used private homes to have consensual sex outside the law.

These relationships also reveal the ways in which postwar suburbanization helped commodify sex while stoking class differentiation. Homeownership gave many Americans the freedom to have various kinds of sex. People who lacked private bedrooms, meanwhile, faced greater scrutiny and persecution. Even as Richard Tooker, for example, had sex with his married friend on the Peninsula, local police raided Hazel's Inn and destroyed the so-called hobo jungles along the train tracks. The queer subculture that had characterized the prewar economy came under attack at the exact moment that homebuilders marketed houses with private bedrooms. The construction of middle-class bedrooms elevated the ideal of marital heterosexuality and, in an ironic twist, freed some to have queer extramarital sex. But this freedom also hinged on property ownership and notions of respectability that separated middle-class and wealthy Americans from poorer people who had more public kinds of sex.

If suburban privacy reinforced the idea that sex was an important part of marriage and unintentionally freed some people to have consensual queer relations, it also enabled some kinds of coercion. For almost a century, states like California had outlawed "wife beating" and rape, and in the 1950s, few Americans publicly defended violence within marriages. Yet since the mid-nineteenth century, authorities across the country often exempted married couples from laws against assault, and they justified their reluctance to interfere as a kind of respect for privacy in the home. Even when courts confronted egregious cases of domestic violence, they frequently refused to punish husbands who beat or raped their wives. Judges in these cases claimed that criminal penalties would unnecessarily bring the state into the home. Some even claimed that a successful prosecution for marital rape might expose the larger doings of the "marital bed chamber" to judicial review. Courts and the police often saw rape as something that happened "on the street" and not "in the home," and they therefore refused to even define coercive sex in marriage as violence. By the 1950s, many states, including California, offered separate "domestic relations" courts that handled violence within the home separate from the larger criminal system and often encouraged couples to reconcile rather than divorce.[103]

Suburbanization reinforced this norm in both practical and symbolic terms. The architectural emphasis on privacy made it more difficult for people outside the home to know about coercion and sex. The case of Fromhold and Goldstein, for example, provides some clues about the possibilities of violence in the suburbs. The police charged Fromhold and Goldstein not just with using their home to have sex with other adult men but also to sleep with high school–aged minors. There are, of course, important reasons to doubt the claims made by the police. Gay men frequently faced false accusations of pedophilia in postwar America, and the two men in this case faced scrutiny that no married couple would have faced. But it is also possible that police were not exaggerating in this case. The fact that they believed that the two men had conducted affairs with minors for a long time again suggests that private bedrooms could conceal many kinds of sex, including acts between adults and minors.[104]

The possible dangers of private homes were even more apparent in cases involving married women. Suburban houses not only physically concealed violent acts from potential witnesses but also symbolized the social and legal barriers that separated the family from the outside world. Both kinds of privacy emerged in a South Bay murder case after World War II. After Marge Talle married her husband Thomas in 1945, the couple settled near the South Bay town of Los Gatos and built a new home for themselves in the nearby hills. Court records reveal that Thomas Talle repeatedly hit his wife, and even though she reported her injuries to her friends and sought medical care for them, no one treated the violence she experienced as a crime. This abuse took place over the course of many years. In 1949, the authorities finally involved themselves in the Talle affair when Thomas drunkenly murdered his wife on the back patio of their home. None of the neighbors reported her killing, and the police arrested the abusive husband only after he turned himself in under the guidance of his attorney.[105]

These examples reveal that the history of bedroom privacy was not inherently normative, queer, emancipatory, or repressive. In fact, the near obsession that residential architects and public officials had with shielding bedrooms led to the construction of millions of figurative and literal "closets" in suburban homes, and no narrative can neatly summarize all of the possible uses of those spaces. Bedrooms represented one of the only socially acceptable and legal places in which people could have sex in the postwar era, and to the extent that seclusion made it easier for them to do so, residents of places like Santa Clara County used their homes for multiple erotic purposes. Even if public officials and residential architects stressed it for normative reasons, homeowners ultimately used their privacy to meet their own needs. Many suburban residents undoubtedly relished the designs of their new homes because they strengthened their marriages or brought their families newfound unity. But domestic privacy also led to sex that fell outside the law, including homosexual relationships between consenting adults and coercive acts like marital rape.

The marketing of sexual privacy and the actual lived experience of having a private bedroom would have a profound impact on many suburbanites' understandings of the state's relationship to sex in the 1960s and 1970s. But it only constituted one part of the ways that suburbanization transformed sexual liberalism. Even as it germinated the idea of a right to sexual privacy, the migration of hundreds of thousands of white, married couples with children to San Mateo and Santa Clara counties also spurred the growth of new normative sexual communities. The real estate market filtered residents based on their sexuality, race, and class, and marriage and parenting provided much of the social glue that united new suburbanites. Over the course of the 1950s and 1960s, the homes, schools, and churches of the Peninsula and South Bay witnessed the coming together of scores of new groups interested in marriage and childrearing. These communities offered friendship and advice to new mothers and fathers, but many of them grew politicized as they thought about the question of sex education. Newly exposed to psychological ideas promulgated by their church or the state and living in a figurative sea of children, many middle-class parents reasserted their desire to have sex taught in the schools.

Chapter 4

Normative Communities

Even as developers installed private bedrooms in new houses and homeowners used their newfound privacy to their own ends, suburban residents in the city of San Mateo vociferously debated sex's public dimensions. In 1951, Donald Nichols called for the resignation of his daughter's biology teacher, Ralph Steele, after he learned that Steele had taught his class about human reproduction, recommended sex education textbooks to his students, and answered students' questions about sex after class. Nichols's complaint divided the district, as some parents shared his alarm that Steele had offered "stimulative" material to young people while others defended the biology teacher. Bay Area newspapers closely followed the San Mateo controversy, and the county district attorney launched an official inquiry into the matter. After hearing Nichols's concerns, the district superintendent put together a committee to investigate the allegations and told Steele that he could no longer recommend sex education books to his students. The high school's board of trustees held an emergency meeting, and the board's chairman called some of the biology course "out of order for teenage children."[1]

The controversy, however, ended quickly. While the superintendent's committee recommended "common sense limitations" on sex education for high schoolers, it also agreed that the biology teacher's curriculum was the "correct one." Steele faced no further discipline, and the board of trustees promised that teachers would continue to offer "normal textbook material" on sex. As the dispute ended, the *San Francisco Call-Bulletin*'s editorial staff offered its readers important lessons in moderation: "The evasive 'hush hush' attitude, and that which would dismiss all restraint, delicacy, and moral considerations, are both in error," they declared. When it came to sex education, Americans needed moderation and "the parents . . . and the church, and the school, all can play an important role."[2]

Short-lived, the controversy in San Mateo nevertheless repeated itself in other postwar Bay Area suburbs. Again and again, parents, administrators, teachers, and clergy clashed over sex education, and these local battles resulted from the conflicting promises of the suburbs and the contradictory messages of the Straight State. Showdowns like the one between Steele and Nichols took place amid the mass migration of white, middle-class married couples with children to the Peninsula and South Bay. Many of these newcomers had benefited from government-subsidized mortgage programs and purchased homes with the expectation that local schools and churches would help them raise healthy families. Once in their new neighborhoods, many suburban residents participated in parenting groups through their local church or parent-teacher association (PTA).

These normative sexual communities formed at the exact moment when states like California launched sex education campaigns for new parents, teachers, and clergy. Lists of recommended films and textbooks—like the one Steele shared with his students—circulated widely at the grassroots level. Sex education experts, who often worked for the California Bureau of Parent Education or garnered some of their training thanks to the National Mental Health Act, found eager audiences in the postwar suburbs. Confronted with the Baby Boom, parents, teachers, and clergy debated and discussed the latest psychological theories about human sexual development and learned that heterosexuality was not inevitable. Adults needed to encourage it and watch for signs of homosexuality among the young. Americans married and had sex before World War II, obviously. But postwar parents grew increasingly comfortable attaching labels like "heterosexual," "homosexual," "healthy," and "maladjusted" to sexual desires and relationships.

In time, this knowledge would help many newly self-identified "straight" suburbanites differentiate themselves from "queer" people, but more immediately, it split normative communities. Postwar proponents of sex education had tried to balance their conviction in the power of psychology to help build healthier families with the concerns of people like Nichols that too much sexual knowledge encouraged youthful experimentation. Middle-class parents had long argued that sex education needed a balanced approach that included shared values in the home, school, and church. Government officials who supported sex education, therefore, stopped short of building a universal system of sex education in the public school system. Instead, they treated the issue as a voluntary public health campaign and knit together a coalition of PTAs and churches to encourage parents to speak to their children about so-called normal sexual development in the home. Their work increased public awareness of psychological ideas about sex, and even religious institutions that were skeptical of secular teachings, such as the Catholic Church, developed their own sex education programs to compete for families in the postwar suburbs.

The state's approach, however, contained important tensions that caused recurrent flareups in school districts such as San Mateo. Public authorities and medical experts convinced many Americans that sex education was a public necessity, essential to eradicating out-of-wedlock births, divorce, and sex deviations. This campaign could only truly work, they believed, if all adults understood the ways that children absorbed unconscious desires from their parents and spoke to their families about the importance of marriage. Yet the same authorities also argued that sex education was a private privilege. Acting from afar, state officials and psychologists empowered parents to see themselves as decisive agents in the sexual development of their children and made them even more resistant to what they saw as interference from outside the home. These messages further reinforced lessons taught in many parishes and congregations. As churches developed their own sex education curricula, some treated expansion of the subject in local schools as a threat to their autonomy.

These debates simmered at the local level for over two decades, and few participants spoke of a right to privacy. Most suburban residents, similar to the *Call-Bulletin* editorial staff, believed in a moderate balance between home, school, and church. Yet faith in the preventative agencies only lasted as long as people believed that children were receiving similar messages in all three institutions. During the 1950s and early 1960s, some suburban residents grew skeptical that all parents were offering sound sex education in the home, and therefore they demanded a greater role from the public schools. These residents increasingly clashed with others who saw teaching their children as their private privilege, and after the U.S. Supreme Court banned classroom prayer in 1962 and 1963, many parents protested attempts to teach sex without religion in public schools. Therefore, even though a majority of middle-class parents wanted to limit premarital sex, divorce, and sexual deviance, suburbanization and the expansion of sex education made it difficult for residents to agree on the methods needed to reach that goal.

Meeting Other Parents

In many ways, the sheer size of the baby boom and the concentration of middle-class, white parents in the suburbs helped ensure that sex education would generate acrimony in local schools. During the 1950s and early 1960s, hundreds of thousands of newcomers moved to San Mateo and Santa Clara counties and formed new normative sexual communities. In this period, the very uniformity of the postwar suburbs often facilitated new relationships. Childrearing and normative sexuality often served as a social glue that brought residents together, and PTAs and churches emerged as two particularly important communities of married people and parents. Yet the creation of these communities would also produce some of the rifts over sex education. Parenting groups often shared the goal of building so-called normal families but differed about how to reach that goal. Even as realtors and city builders promoted socially homogeneous neighborhoods as good for families, new suburban residents built their own communities among people they saw as their peers, and just as the housing market divided people based on class, race, sexuality, and lifestyle, the social market of the suburbs divided people into even more categories.

By 1960, nearly a million people lived in San Mateo and Santa Clara counties, and most of these residents had lived elsewhere a decade earlier. Untethered from friends and families in their old homes, these suburban migrants often eagerly sought connections with new neighbors. Unsurprisingly, parenting offered one of the most obvious ways of meeting people since residents were living in a figurative sea of young children. Many of the participants in Lois Meek Stolz's 1958 Palo Alto study, for example, mentioned meeting other parents because their kids went to school together. One father who had moved from San Francisco gushed about what he saw as the "congenial" nature of his new subdivision and how much he loved that he and his neighbors kept "up with each others' children."[3] Palo Altans like this father frequently noted the ways that they met other parents in groups like the Girl Scouts or a YMCA club called the "Indian Guides."[4]

Mothers played a particularly large role in these parenting groups. Women faced an upsurge in job-related discrimination after World War II, as employers fired female workers to turn positions over to returning veterans.[5] Furthermore, suburbanization itself encouraged married couples to adopt gender-specific divisions of labor within households. Planners divided new cities into "male" workplaces and "female" domestic zones, requiring residents to own an automobile to travel beyond the outer boundaries of most neighborhoods. Married women without cars frequently found themselves in "child-centered" districts built around pools of homes, schools, and churches. In 1960, San Mateo and Santa Clara counties boasted approximately 106,000 wives living in households where their husbands were the primary earners. These women made up most of the volunteers in suburban parent groups, and for many of them, their service constituted a rare opportunity to work outside the home. One of Stolz's Palo Altans remarked that her "community work" with other mothers had made her "notice that these women are much happier" than their counterparts "who spend all their time at home with their children."[6]

This division of labor, the Baby Boom, and the desire of many women to work outside their households led to an enormous upsurge in suburban PTA membership. Already one of the largest organizations dedicated to bringing "the home and school closer together," the group underwent a volunteer boom in the 1950s and early 1960s. In the postwar period, the number of women in the South Bay volunteering for the California Congress of Parents and Teachers ballooned, outgrowing its counterpart in San Francisco.[7] Whereas Santa Clara County's Sixth District listed 11,773 formal members in 1947, that number more than tripled by 1953; by the early 1960s, it more than doubled again, with the total number of volunteers reaching 71,775 by 1965. Although fathers occasionally contributed to local PTAs, female volunteers made up the vast majority of the organization. Records from the Sixth District in 1965 suggested that over 83 percent of all members were women.[8]

In some cases, this lopsided male to female ratio facilitated sexual relationships between women. Volunteering in a predominantly female group not only made it easier for lesbians to meet other women but also made it harder for hostile eyes to spot them. Barbara Kalish, a married PTA member from the Los Angeles area, for example, fell in love with a woman whom she met at a parent-teacher leadership conference in San Francisco in 1958. Not unlike the experiences of gay men and women during World War II, the sex-segregated spaces of parent-teacher associations created room for romantic relationships between women.[9] The experiences of lesbians like Kalish, however, were exceptional. PTA literature frequently acknowledged the difficulties faced by husbands and wives, but it also celebrated heterosexual marriages as the "most important" relationship in

Americans' lives, and middle-class married women made up the overwhelming majority of volunteers at the local level.[10]

PTA growth, however, reflected more than the concentration of married couples with children in specific parts of the postwar metropolis. Volunteers self-selected, sharing the organization's larger mission and seeking to meet people they deemed like themselves. PTA sources from the era cited "getting acquainted" as one of the main reasons for members to join the organization, and the new highways that crisscrossed the Peninsula and South Bay made it easier for them to come together.[11] Volunteers with cars overcame the atomization intrinsic to a low-density residential landscape, joining groups of likeminded individuals. While the National Congress of Parents and Teachers celebrated figurative "homes, schools, and churches," local volunteers came together in the literal homes, schools, and churches around them. This process of self-selection reinforced the distilling patterns at work in suburbanization. Although PTAs, like all communities, were never ideologically uniform, the fact that they were largely a self-selecting set of middle-class, married white women meant that members often shared similar values.[12]

This concentration of likeminded individuals, in turn, translated into a common parenting identity. Many PTA volunteers expressed relief at finding others with common problems and interests. When a graduate student at San Jose State University observed discussion groups in a nearby school district, she noted, "Parents realized that they were not facing their individual problems alone, but that all parents had something in common, and they learned from each other."[13] One mother told the Stolz interviewers that she had had a similar sense of self-awareness after a parent education course: "When you looked back to see the notes of the first discussion and compared the notes of the last one, you really could see the growth, although from day to day you were unconscious of it."[14]

Church growth in San Mateo and Santa Clara counties paralleled the PTA's phenomenal expansion. Across the United States, suburbanization prompted one of the largest church-building booms of the twentieth century. Polls suggested that religious observance in the United States peaked nationwide in the 1950s. But places like San Mateo and Santa Clara counties witnessed the arrival of hundreds of thousands of new residents who saw religion as essential to good childrearing. Some parents wanted their children raised in their specific faiths. Others felt no strong ties to a particular belief system but believed that religion itself constituted a necessary precursor to morality. One mother told Lois Meek Stolz's team, "I don't care what church it is, [but] I think they should have some belief in God and it helps them to be good."[15]

Newcomers with children offered churches the possibility of growing memberships, but established congregations in older cities faced painful dilemmas about expansion and relocation. As early as 1949, for example, members of the First Congregational Church in downtown San Jose observed, "San Jose and Santa Clara County have been growing in population at record breaking speed during the past ten years. . . . But as cities grow beyond 50,000, families move further and further from the center. Our younger families are following this centrifugal pattern—especially the new families that join us."[16] During the 1950s, Protestant groups such as the First Congregational Church took advantage of the shift in residential patterns and purchased land in the new subdivisions filling with married couples and young children. In the first decade after World War II, six of the twelve churches in Sunnyvale's downtown left for new locations on the city's periphery, and by 1962, eight Palo Alto congregations had relocated out of the suburb's center.[17]

The suburban boom similarly drew the attention of a group of nondenominational evangelicals, who formed their own church planting organization in 1953 in order to take advantage of the migration of normative families to the Peninsula and South Bay. In 1954, the *Christian Standard*, a weekly newspaper published in Ohio, proclaimed that in the Bay Area, "mile after mile of sections with new homes could be traveled without seeing a church" and that the recently created Northern California Evangelistic Association sought to channel resources to congregations eager to begin building programs.[18] Begun by a group of nondenominational Christian ministers affiliated with San Jose Bible College, the organization hired a full-time pastor in that same year to "plant new congregations" in "underchurched areas."[19]

Catholic, mainline Protestant, and evangelical clergy in San Mateo and Santa Clara counties employed multiple strategies to build new congregations. Patterning themselves after urban planners, many priests and pastors conducted surveys of area homeowners and collected demographic details on the community surrounding their churches. In his review of suburban church building, Catholic Bishop Josiah Chatham advised fellow clergymen to read the "society pages" of their local newspapers, advising them that "in wedding stories and similar accounts you can pick up clues to help you track down [nonobservant Catholics]."[20] The National Methodist Church's Commission on Membership and Evangelism counseled ministers to contact the relatives of current congregants and to reach out to families with whom they came in contact through weddings, funerals, and "other pastoral contacts."[21] Some of the more ambitious Protestant churches in the South Bay took out weekly advertisements in the *San Jose Mercury*'s Saturday religion section or rented space on billboards near the area's budding highway system.[22]

Knowing that they competed in a marketplace for churchgoers, Catholic, mainline Protestant, and evangelical clergy promised would-be adherents fellowship with communities of other likeminded married people with children. In 1959, the Protestant congregation-building magazine the *Methodist Story* advised its readers to "Make Your Church Family Conscious . . . and Lead Families into Worship."[23] In its "Invitation to Worship," the Congregationalist Ladera Community Church in Menlo Park offered prospective congregants a litany of photographs of men, women, and their children attending services together and told them, "The Ladera Community Church is a 'family of families,' seeking God and worshipping together in faith, freedom and fellowship. We welcome your visit and hope that you will feel that this is the church for you and your family."[24]

By the end of the 1950s, suburban priests and ministers had built an enormous collection of Christian "family-friendly" communities in the churches of the Peninsula and South Bay. In 1956, the National Council of Churches estimated that over 215,000 people in San Mateo and Santa Clara counties attended a Protestant or Catholic Church. The overwhelming majority of worshippers joined either a Catholic parish or mainline Protestant congregation, with just under 150,000 people reporting that they belonged to the former and just over 45,000 declaring they attended services at the latter. Although the survey conducted by the National Council of Churches ignored many nondenominational Christian groups, the census observed that just under 5 percent of the total attended evangelical or Pentecostal churches in the two counties.[25] In 1957, the *San Jose News* reported that Santa Clara County had over three hundred churches, and the executive director of the South Bay's Council of Churches declared that "60 to 75 per cent of the churches in the [area] erected new buildings or began plans for new structures in the past few years."[26] And in that same year, an association of ministers conducted a survey specifically of the churchgoing habits of Sunnyvale's residents, and they concluded that

Figure 7. New Woodside Road Methodist Church in Redwood City, California, 1954. Fang family *San Francisco Examiner* photograph archive negative files, BANC PIC 2006.029:132174.06.6—NEG, box 1081. © Regents of the University of California, Bancroft Library, University of California, Berkeley.

72 percent of families living in the Peninsula suburb attended services regularly.[27]

Yet these numbers concealed diversity among the religious communities in the Bay Area suburbs. Christians already differed in theology and tradition, but "church shopping" among residents encouraged segmentation even within religious groups. Clergy may have advertised their faiths to married couples with children, but they also offered an array of programs, events, and services to their followers. Congregants picked a church for many reasons, including religious faith, but they also did so because they liked a specific priest or minister, it was convenient to their homes, or their friends already attended services there. Like the PTAs, therefore, the many churches of the Peninsula and South Bay represented collections of likeminded individuals. In time, these different groups occupied different positions on social and political issues like sex education. But they initially grew out of the desire of tens of thousands of suburbanites to find others they deemed like themselves near their new homes. Once homeowners had passed through the filter of the real estate market itself, they then went through a second distillation process, as residents chose to join some communities but not others.

Secular Family Life Educators and the Middle Path

During the 1950s, secular experts published numerous texts about parenting and childrearing to meet the demand caused by the postwar Baby Boom. Population growth and the concentration of white married couples with children in the postwar suburbs, however, did more than increase the amount of sex education advice circulating at the grassroots level. It also magnified tensions within white middle-class normative sexual communities over the issue. Secular family experts and parenting groups like the PTA saw themselves as agents trying to find a reasonable middle between two unpleasant extremes. Sex education was important, they argued, because overly repressive parents and dirty "street" talk represented equally important dangers to children's "normal" sexual development. Yet the more some parents discussed the topic, the more it seemed fruitless to treat teaching children about sex purely as a voluntary issue. Although the home, school, and church needed to work together, it seemed to them that many mothers and fathers failed to the broach the topic or modeled unhealthy behaviors for their children. Family life experts themselves equivocated on this issue, simultaneously arguing that communities needed to tackle sex education together and that parents were uniquely qualified to address the subject with their children. By the early 1960s, sizable numbers of suburban residents broke this impasse and argued that public schools needed to take a larger role in combating promiscuity, divorce, and sexual deviance because sex education was too important to leave in the hands of "bad parents."

This politicization of sex education began with the expansion of sex education advice literature, and books by Benjamin Spock and Arnold Gesell were emblematic examples of popular postwar childrearing expertise. Written in 1946, Spock's *The Common Sense Book of Baby and Child Care* sold almost 8 million copies in its first decade of existence, and Gesell's series of books on developmental psychology routinely topped the nation's bestseller lists. Both authors emphasized the need for "balance" when teaching children about sex. Spock's work, in particular, included a ten-page summary of the era's leading psychological advice on sex education. "Sex education starts early whether you plan it or not," he warned. "A child begins his sex education as soon as he can sense how his mother and father get along with each other."[28] When children asked questions about sex, Spock warned parents to avoid answering fearfully: "The danger of scaring a sensitive child about sex is partly that you make him tense and apprehensive at the time, partly that you may destroy his or her ability to adjust to marriage later."[29] In a text coauthored with Frances Ilg, Gesell similarly argued, "The two extremes to be avoided are over protection through silence and evasion; and over reliance on excessively candid information."[30]

Authors like Spock, Gesell, and Ilg told mothers and fathers to pursue moderation in the education of their youth, but they rarely defined what the extremes of "silence" and "excessively candid information" looked like. Yet their vagueness about what exactly constituted an extreme did not stop them from including details about the problems children might face if their mothers or fathers failed to sufficiently moderate their approach. Homosexuality, for example, frequently came up as one possible consequence of poor parenting. Experts counseled readers not to worry about adolescents who carried "crushes" on peers of the same sex but encouraged them to speak to a doctor if their children did not grow out of this phase. Ralph Eckert, California's parent education consultant, published *Sex Attitudes in the Home* in 1956 and advised parents that boys and girls always move through a "homosexual" stage. Close friends of the same sex should never alarm parents, he promised, unless they thought their children "failed to move on from this phase into dating and normal heterosexual relationships during adolescence."[31]

If postwar advice manuals encouraged parents to pursue a middle path when it came to sex education, they also stressed the particular dangers that excessive mothering posed to young children. Although most of the writings of this largely male cohort of physicians, academics, and administrators used the gender-neutral term "parent," "mothers" most often bore the brunt of their analyses of mental illness. According to one representative example, "It is natural for parents, and for mothers especially, to express love and its normal accompaniment, protectiveness for their children. In an exaggerated form, however, overprotectiveness or oversolicitousness on the part of either parent, but particularly the mother, has been found to accompany some nervous conditions in children."[32]

Visions of bad childrearing like this one haunted the era's sex education advice literature, and authorities sent conflicting messages about parents' roles. Experts, such as Ralph Eckert, stressed the public necessity of teaching children wholesome attitudes about sex. Eckert complained that "the failure of even a few parents" exposed "other children to obscenity" and argued that sometimes a "good teacher" can help young people direct their "sex impulses towards marriage and normal, happy family life."[33] Therefore, experts sometimes encouraged supporters to work with community groups like PTAs and churches to implement sex education programs in schools.[34] Yet at the same time, these authorities also described sex education as a private privilege. Either out of conviction or pragmatism, experts framed telling children about marriage and reproduction as within the home as one of the primary honors of parenthood. According to Eckert, parents had the special "privilege" to give their children "an environment in which curiosity is encouraged, not feared," and "in which the satisfactions of marriage and family life are experienced and deserved." In this vision, teaching children about sex in the privacy of the home constituted one of the most satisfying parts of being a parent.[35]

As sex education texts circulated in the postwar suburbs, family life experts helped create an imagined community of dedicated, middle-class parents.[36] Readers often read the work of writers like Spock in their homes, but they read them knowing that millions of others like them had also purchased similar books. Authors frequently invoked this world, referencing the wider audience of good parents and the threats posed by bad parents. "Attitudes toward sex are too important to leave to chance or to other people's children," Eckert declared. "Our children need *our* guidance."[37] Parenting guides frequently spoke in the second person, addressing parents collectively, relating relevant anecdotes about different approaches to childrearing. With each example, they implicitly invoked a larger public of which the individual reader was only a part. When Spock rhetorically asked, "You may say, 'Why isn't it easier and less embarrassing to tell them about the stork?'" he did more than merely dismiss a common myth about childbirth. He also invoked what he saw as a "typical" question that many of his readers may have asked themselves. Each reader may have encountered it alone, but he or she could see a multitude of other Spock readers embedded in the question.

Many residents in suburbs like those of San Mateo and Santa Clara counties eagerly sought out this kind of advice. When Lois Meek Stolz led a team of researchers to interview dozens of Palo Alto residents about parenting, many respondents spoke about the ways in which authors like Spock had shifted their thinking. One woman declared that she had recently read *The Common Sense Book of Baby and Child Care* for the third time and that she "got a lot of enjoyment" out of it, while a second interviewee exclaimed, "I think [Spock]'s wonderful. I think his books are wonderful." Multiple interviewees also told Stolz's team that they looked for parenting tips in newspapers and magazines like *Ladies' Home Journal*.[38] These Palo Altans often declared that sex education was a parental responsibility, including one man who thought kids deserved to learn about sex so that they "understand what the other people are talking about instead of just going along with it."[39] One father felt so much anxiety over the issue that he annoyed Stolz's team by pestering them for advice on how to bring up the topic with his kids.[40] His wife, meanwhile, confessed that she felt a certain dread about speaking to her daughter about sex but felt the need to do it because "everyone's doing it."[41]

While the nation's family life experts spoke about sex education as an abstraction, suburbanites like this couple saw it in practical terms. Parents worried about how to specifically address the issue with their families, and they made numerous unspoken, daily choices related to sexual privacy at home. Several of Stolz's interviewees, for example, mentioned rules forbidding children from going in the parents' bedroom without permission and decisions about whether or not to leave bathroom doors open.[42] This difference between abstract sex education and the day-to-day lives of individual parents was particularly acute when it came to the subject of "bad parents." If national experts like Eckert wrote about the general dangers of poor childrearing, many of Stolz's interviewees spoke about specific people they saw as terrible role models. One father joked that he knew parents who felt so uncomfortable talking to their children about sex that "they just put it off until the kid was about 40 years old."[43] He spoke particularly harshly about neighbors whom he believed had taught their daughters to feel "shame" about their bodies.[44]

Practical questions about how to speak to children about sex and anxiety about bad parents helped make sex education one of the central concerns of San Mateo and Santa Clara county PTAs. No group championed the issue more than the PTA in the 1950s, and many of the group's volunteers shared experts' preference for "moderate" approaches to the topic. Articles in the *California Parent-Teacher*, like "Do You Answer Their Questions?" by William Plute, frequently decried unwholesome sex in magazines

Figure 8. Volunteers attend a workshop on parent education in Davis, California, 1955. Photograph is from a report published by the California Bureau of Adult Education and California Congress of Parents and Teachers about a conference at the University of California, Davis.

while pushing parents to avoid "a campaign of silence in hopes the child will 'learn when old enough.'"[45] At the same time, PTA books, magazines, and pamphlets invariably mentioned the importance of cooperation between the home, school, and church. In 1948, the Sunnyvale PTA even marked its thirtieth anniversary with a public performance featuring tableaus of the four "cornerstones" of the organization: "the school, the church, the home, and the community."[46]

The PTA shared many of the goals of writers like Benjamin Spock, but the group's overwhelmingly female membership also forged a complicated relationship with the predominantly male childrearing experts. The tendency of many authorities to ascribe sexual "maladjustment" to "smothering" mothers, in part, allowed historian Ruth Feldstein to sarcastically call "mom-bashing" a "national pastime" in postwar America.[47] Yet the gendered discourses that unfairly singled out mothers as possible threats to their children also empowered volunteers in maternalist groups like the PTA.[48] If bad mothers represented a crisis worthy of government intervention, then state administrators and healthy experts contended that women needed to participate in the solution. During the postwar period, the predominantly female California PTA served as the chief supporter of the sex education for parents and students.[49]

During the 1950s and early 1960s, the same highways that allowed for the congregation of new suburban parenting groups also facilitated the circulation of knowledge about sex and family. Mental health and education authorities, including Eckert, regularly came to these venues to speak on the merits of better marriages.[50] This transportation network also allowed for individual representatives of district, council, and local PTAs to attend conferences, meet fellow parents in other regions, and interview school administrators in distant districts.[51] In 1950 alone, the South Bay's PTAs attended a conference on "Home School Relationships" at nearby Stanford University and sent a representative to Santa Barbara to participate in a workshop on parent education run by Ralph Eckert. PTA volunteers in the South Bay used the information they garnered from these varying institutes to sponsor ten lectures on "Responsible Parenthood," concluding that "as an outgrowth of the classes, a guidance clinic seems assured for Santa Clara County."[52]

PTAs ardently supported "parent education" campaigns involving discussions of sex in the home, school, and church, and the number of programs in the South Bay proliferated rapidly during the 1950s. In 1951, the County Board of Education began recording the issuance of credentials to teachers specializing in parent or family life education, and between 1951 and 1953, it documented the arrival of twenty such instructors in local schools.[53] By 1956, the Sixth District reported that sixteen of its units possessed parent education study groups.[54] A year later, the Fremont Union High School District in the Santa Clara County suburb of Sunnyvale sponsored thirteen programs on child development at a Lutheran church, including meetings on "Sex Education," "Positive Family Relations," and "Human Beginnings."[55] By 1958, several South Bay school districts appointed former PTA members as special coordinators for their parent education classes.[56] And in the late 1950s, when Campbell Union High School implemented a comprehensive parent education program, it literally blurred the lines between home and school. Administrators took the unusual step of designating the individual living rooms in which study groups met as "official" extensions of the district and encouraging mothers to visit the model dining room in its home economics department on campus.[57]

These programs signaled the gradual expansion of scientific expertise about so-called normal sexuality at the grassroots level in the 1950s and early 1960s. The upsurge in parent education after the war helped instill the idea that "straightness" took effort and that not all forms of sexual expression were ideal. PTAs, therefore, not only were normative sexual communities thanks to the relative homogeneity of their members but also because they often came together to learn how to create better marriages and "normal" children. PTA volunteers did not merely passively absorb the ideas of the nation's parenting experts. They actively sought their advice, attending lectures, enrolling in classes, buying magazines, reading books, and viewing films. Together, these acts revealed an increasingly self-aware middle-class public of concerned parents who intended to use the latest scientific ideas to raise healthy, sexually "normal" kids.

This community, however, grew increasingly restless during the 1950s. The voluntary nature of parent education raised a contradiction in the minds of many suburbanites. Government officials in Sacramento and local districts repeatedly encouraged mothers and fathers to act as good role models for their children in the privacy of their homes. However, their emphasis on the dangers of failing to provide such an education raised the possibility of teachers circumventing parents and providing it directly to their students in schools. Voluntary participation in parent education, after all, did nothing for the children whose parents neglected to attend meetings or read the latest book on childrearing.

The decision to mobilize parents on behalf of family life education, therefore, carried within it contradictory impulses. Voluntary participation in parenting programs on sex created a growing number of voters who believed that only universal, mandatory sex education in schools could instill mental health and build future strong marriages. The more that members of groups like the PTA read about child developmental psychology, the more it seemed that they needed to convince others to require sex education in schools. State authorities both empowered individual parents and suggested that others had somehow failed to speak to their children in sufficient depth on the subject. The image of an unduly lax or repressive parent dogged almost all discussions of sex education in the 1950s and motivated activists in groups like the PTA to renew their efforts.

Religious Sex Education

The expansion of secular sex education for parents in the 1950s and early 1960s sparked a minor revolution among religious groups. Some churches, particularly mainline Protestant ones, allied themselves with PTAs, offering nonsectarian programs on sex alongside religious ones that fit their traditions. Other churches, including most Catholic and evangelical groups, responded to secular drives for sex education by creating their own programs. Viewed together, these initiatives revealed the growing consensus in support of sex education in the Bay Area suburbs. But the circulation of competing religious and secular sexual discourses also heightened tension within suburban communities. While some liberal churches supported sex education in public schools, others argued that classroom teaching on the subject might encourage experimentation or rob parents of the privilege to speak to their children on their own schedule. Even as groups like the PTA debated the merits of classroom-based sex education, many churches opposed the issue, and like secular groups, they framed their views as "moderate" alternatives to "extremes." Catholic and evangelical Protestant writers often wanted to sidestep "explicit" discussions of sex, but they also conceded that parents, teachers, and clergy needed to avoid total silence.

These debates grew, in part, thanks to increased clerical dedication to psychology in the 1950s. Although far from universal, many mainline Protestant and some Catholic churches adopted sex education programs for adults and children that drew upon secular expertise. As ministers and priests worked to make their congregations stand out in the intense competition for congregants of the postwar suburbs, they sometimes looked to secular family experts for new programs to offer would-be members. These clergy responded to writers like Benjamin Spock by adapting their ideas to meet their own needs.[58] Consequently, the 1950s witnessed a revolution in marital counseling programs, church sex education for adults and children, and literature that melded secular ideas about the family with older religious ideas on the subject.

This process required the expansion of academic institutions and networks. By 1960, 80 percent of Protestant seminaries, including the San Francisco Theological Seminary, offered courses on psychology, and a 1955 report found that approximately four thousand pastors across the country had received some kind of training on the subject. In the mid-1950s, the National Council of Churches created a "Department of Pastoral Services," which oversaw counseling programs and offered scholarships for ministers interested in pursuing advanced degrees in psychology.[59] Catholics adapted psychology at a slower rate, with many church leaders skeptical of what they saw as the field's preoccupation with sex. Yet in 1947, a group of

Catholic psychologists formed their own professional organization, and during the 1950s, several Catholic universities, including the University of San Francisco, began offering courses in psychology and degrees in marital counseling. The founding of religious academic journals in the 1950s, such as *Pastoral Psychology* and the *Guild of Catholic Psychiatry Newsletter*, further testified to the growing interest of ministers and priests in the field of mental health.[60]

These institutions disseminated psychological ideas about human sexual development, including homosexuality, and allowed clergy to blend scientific ideas with religious traditions.[61] Between 1955 and 1958, *Pastoral Psychology* carried at least six features on homosexuality, while Catholic journals like the *Priest* and *Homiletic and Pastoral Review* also published articles on the subject.[62] Many of these pieces presented clergy with the theory popular among psychologists that homosexuality originated in a stalled stage of adolescent development. Doctor Alfred Gross, for example, explained in *Pastoral Psychology* that people went through a "homosexual age" in adolescence but "the male homosexual may be regarded as one whose psychosexual development has been arrested on the level where he gets his chief gratification from men."[63]

The notion that homosexuality resulted from deep-rooted processes perplexed many ministers and priests. If erotic attachments to people of the same sex came from processes outside an individual's control, how could churches prohibit it? *Pastoral Psychology* carried a regular advice column entitled "The Consultation Clinic," in which ministers across the country solicited help on how to deal with congregants they suspected of homosexuality. These letters revealed a growing belief that homosexuality represented an innate condition—instead of a set of behaviors—and a search for possible tools to address it. One pastor, for example, asked for guidance on how to address two women in his church who appeared to have an "unnatural affection" for one another. He related that the women held hands and that one of them appeared more "mannish" than the other. The writer wondered if attraction could exist between two women, and if so, what was the "wise way" to "enter the situation?"[64] Another minister asked for help with a young man who had a reputation as a "sissy" and who had recently confessed to engaging in "homosexual practices." The pastor's dilemma, however, lay in his congregant's desire to marry a woman even though "he is aroused by seeing a good-looking man walk down the street." He, therefore, asked for "comments that would at least help me understand the situation of young men like this, and consequently put me in a better position to be of some possible help to him."[65]

Pastoral Psychology had a largely Protestant audience, but Catholic journals discussed the issue at length as well, and they revealed a similar educational process about the nature of homosexuality. John Cavanagh in the *Guild of Catholic Psychiatrists Bulletin*, for example, argued that "the clergymen, especially in his role as confessor and canon lawyer, should have a clear, sound knowledge of the subject." Like their Protestant counterparts, writers like Cavanagh presumed that their readers had little to no knowledge about the topic, and they almost always made sure to define the term "homosexual." Cavanagh described it as "not a disease *per se* but . . . the symptom of a neurosis or personality disorder. In homosexuality there is a deviation of the sex desire away from its proper heterosexual object to a sexual object of the self-sex."[66]

Many clergy solved the question of how to react to the seemingly deep-rooted nature of homosexuality by insisting that the condition needed a "cure." In 1962, *Parents* magazine reported, "Ministers are being taught . . . to recognize individuals who are deeply disturbed by sexual problems and who should be referred to qualified marriage counselors or psychiatrists."[67] Despite little evidence of an effective treatment, clergy often referred people who felt homoerotic desires to psychotherapists. A theologian responded to the minister worried about the young man intent on marrying a woman by recommending that all homosexuals get analytic treatment. The trouble, the professor alleged, lay in the fact that not all homosexuals were capable of reform: "Where there is any degree of interest to change . . . the chances are excellent. To the extent that there has been bondage of the inner will, the chances are very slight."[68]

Religious thinkers may have acknowledged a secular voice on this issue, but they also saw parallels with churches' longstanding interest in the question of chastity. Homoerotic urges may have originated unconsciously, but nevertheless, individuals still decided whether or not to act on them. In cases where therapists failed to "cure" patients of their homosexuality, they could always help them adjust to their condition. According to a writer in the Catholic journal *Priest*, "Although the homosexual may not think that sexual abstinence is possible for him, nevertheless it is. . . . There are many living proofs of heterosexual abstinence. Therefore, the homosexual cannot be permitted to continue his practices."[69]

This search for a cure caused religious writers to debate practical ways to address homosexuality, particularly when it came to the question of marriage. Clergy often wondered if they should encourage people experiencing same-sex desire to marry, and they pondered the fluidity of sexuality. If homosexuality represented a static condition, then it presented a narrow set of solutions. But if a person was attracted to both sexes, then the problem was more complex. Seward Hiltner, a theology professor writing in *Pastoral Psychology*, claimed that friends should never encourage a "fixed" homosexual to wed and that he even knew of "ministers who have married, knowing they have an exclusively homosexual pattern." Those unions allegedly ended in disaster, but Hiltner offered a different conclusion for people who did not feel an exclusive sexual desire for people of the same sex: "With a youngish person, not yet fixed in his homosexual patterns . . . I think the possibilities of actual transformation should actually be explored."[70]

Analyses of unconscious drives and the nature of human responsibility like this one represented an important cause of the expansion of religious sex education in the 1950s and early 1960s. Yet, regardless of their stance on psychology, many clergy responded to secular campaigns to educate parents and young people about it. The spread of discourses about sex was hardly universal, yet the surge in interest in the issue prompted *Parents* magazine to call the many religious commentaries on the subject akin to "a doctrinal revolution."[71] In 1955, the Methodist church advised youth leaders to provide "early sex education" in its guide *Home and Church Working Together*, and a few years later, it issued an official "marriage manual" for engaged couples.[72] A concern that outsiders might think their church regarded "sex as a regrettable and unmentionable necessity" prompted Presbyterians to issue guidelines about marital education in 1962.[73] During the 1950s, Catholic dioceses across the country launched new marriage preparation and counseling programs. Even some evangelical Christians, who moved more slowly on the issue, responded to secular calls for greater instruction on sex. In the early 1950s, the *Christian Standard* published an ongoing series entitled "Church and Home United" that addressed family life education.[74]

A particular fear of divorce spurred some of this religious sex education. Many Protestants and Catholics saw marriage manuals, parenting classes, and counseling sessions as a way of forestalling breakups. In this regard, their writings frequently echoed the concerns of secular writers that most

Americans needed their help to prevent "sexual maladjustment," divorce, and juvenile delinquency. The Methodist *Pastor's Manual for Premarital Counseling*, for instance, complained that many couples "know almost nothing about how religion can enrich marriage, about a family spending plan, about marriage law, about child spacing and sex education, and very little about many other matters that pertain to a successful home."[75] During the 1950s, Catholic archdioceses launched "Cana" and "Pre-Cana" programs to help young and old couples build strong marriages. Pre-Cana programs included education about married life before couples officially committed to one another, and they covered Catholic teachings about family life, communication between husband and wife, and sex. Cana groups built upon the lessons learned in these earlier sessions, bringing together married couples dedicated to Catholic family life. According to one estimate, three-quarters of archdioceses nationwide, including the Archdiocese of San Francisco, offered pre-Cana and Cana programs by 1950.[76]

Religious authorities across denominational divides, therefore, built a consensus around using sex education to promote marriage, and despite differences about issues like birth control, they also shared a belief that teachings on the issue required "moderation." Protestant and Catholic writers repeatedly stressed that sex educators, whether parents, teachers, or clergy, needed to avoid extremes. Sue Leong, a master's student at the mainline San Francisco Theological Seminary, declared, "Whatever parents do, sex education should not be overemphasized but be an integral part of the general parental responsibility to help the child understand the natural birth process."[77] This search for balance also permeated Catholic writings on the issue. According to Bernard Pisani, many Americans saw sex as "shameful" or a "necessary evil," and he warned readers that this "puritanical" point of view could ruin their marriages. Yet he also denounced what he saw as the "opposite extreme," which viewed sex as an "indulgence" with "no limits or responsibilities."[78]

This consensus about moderation, however, led religious groups to different conclusions regarding public schools. For many mainline Protestants, classroom-based sex education meant reinforcing lessons learned in church and home, balancing the strengths of the preventative agencies. The National Council of Churches in the 1950s and early 1960s endorsed teaching the subject in schools, provided students' parents supported it.[79] At the same time, many Catholic authorities saw classroom instruction as a threat to the moderation necessary for good sex education. Catholic Anna Rock, for example, pushed back against secular experts like Kirkendall and Eckert who wanted more straightforward explanations of reproduction and marriage. In her article "How Not to Give Sex Instruction to Children," she insisted that the best kind of education was "informal and not formal; implicit and not explicit." Parents, in particular, helped their children by keeping their answers to questions about sex short and to the point. "Excessive" explanations could give young people ideas and lead to experimentation. "If you tell [your child] about temptations," she warned, "you may be the cause of the very difficulty you're trying to avoid."[80] Writers like Rock inverted the logic that formal sex education from parent or teacher represented a reasonable "middle path," arguing that pressure to teach it might plant the seeds of sin in young people's minds.

This argument framed opposition to sex education in schools, in particular, as a moderate point of view. Part of what made it "reasonable" was a belief that pairing religion with sexuality ensured good morality. The Catholic Bishops of the United States denounced sex education in the public schools in the "strongest possible terms" in 1950 because "such information must be given individually." They declared, "Sex is more than a biological function. It can be . . . properly appreciated only within a religious . . . context."[81] The San Francisco Archdiocese, which oversaw parishes in the city and suburbs, insisted that schools did not need to teach the subject because church authorities already addressed it. At a conference in 1950, Diocesan official Thomas Bowe denied that the church had a "hush hush attitude towards sex education" and declared, "It is just as important (for a child) to know about sex as to know how to walk or how to eat." But he questioned whether public school teachers, "many of whom are not family people," could instill the necessary "willpower" in children to resist temptation.[82]

Few evangelical writers expressed enthusiasm for the issue of sex education, yet the topic resounded so much in religious circles in the 1950s that several writers addressed it in books and periodicals like the *Christian Standard*. Although evangelicals did not speak with one voice on the issue, several of them argued that all sex education needed to derive from the Bible. In 1959, L. Nelson Bell argued that weak parents had "transmitted a laxness of attitude to sex" to their children, which left them "sex obsessed." According to Bell, "The best course on sex education in the world is to be found within the pages of Scripture. . . . That which is good and that which is evil is made abundantly clear." Therefore, he proposed religious instruction in public schools akin to hot lunch programs for poor children, so that "teachers could address the spiritual as well as physical health of young people."[83]

Evangelical writers, like Catholics, did not call for silence on the subject of sex. Instead, they insisted that divorcing religion from sex upset the proper balance between home, school, and church, and pairing sex education with biblical teachings represented a "moderate" response to the issue. William Orr, for example, dismissed what he saw as the "hush-hush" attitude of bygone eras and the "brutally frank approach" used by some teachers: "Surely," he declared in the evangelical *Moody Monthly*, "there must be a happy medium between these two extremes—and there is. It's found in the Bible." God's commandments to marry and reproduce, paired with His prohibitions against adultery and fornication, provided young people with the necessary context for the sexual "temptations" faced by modern youth.[84]

For many San Mateo and Santa Clara county residents, therefore, religious teachings tempered the frankness of a purely secular form of sex education, and many supported Christian instruction in classrooms or "released-time" initiatives. Although many Peninsula and South Bay churches built schools in the 1950s, the vast majority of residents enrolled their children in the public education system. Nationwide, 79 percent of Americans told Gallup pollsters in 1962 that they approved of "religious observances" in public schools.[85] Authorities in San Mateo and Santa Clara counties not only allowed for school prayer but also permitted pupils to leave their classrooms once a week to attend hourlong courses at a church or synagogue of their choosing. From World War II through the mid-1960s, the Santa Clara County Council of Churches supported released-time education. Most residents saw schools and churches as mutually reinforcing "character-building" institutions, and the lines between religious and secular education often blurred.[86]

The debates about sex education, therefore, also raised questions about the role of religion in public life. As church leaders expanded their own campaigns, they sharpened the lines in the growing debate over whether or not schools should teach sex education. For many Catholics, in particular, "moderation" on the issue meant keeping communication about sex simple and out of secular classrooms. The expansion of religious discussions about the issue in the 1950s and early 1960s, consequently, not only caused psychological ideas about hetero- and homosexuality to reach a wider audience but also meant that the stakes for many religious suburbanites grew larger as they worried about the implications of "mass instruction" in public schools. Even as many groups like the PTA called for classroom-based sex education to combat the evils of "bad parents" and "street talk," churches launched their own campaigns to keep the issue out of public education.

Conflict in the Schools

Although many PTA volunteers and churchgoers championed sex education for parents and children, many of their neighbors cared less about the issue. The fact that texts on sex and parenting traveled in wider circles after World War II did not necessarily mean universal enthusiasm for them. A national poll conducted in the mid-1950s found that over three-quarters of teenagers in the United States had never spoken to their parents about sex.[87] In contrast to the women who cited their favorite childrearing guides, several of Stolz's interviewees expressed discomfort or hostility to the issue. One woman confessed that she did not know about sex until she married and that she had dressed in a literal "closet" as a child instead of in front of her sister. She nevertheless asserted, "I don't think it hurt me not knowing all of those things."[88] A father in the study called most childrearing advice "downright trash.[89]

This apathy and hostility about speaking to children about sex and marriage set the stage for a series of confrontations over whether or not schools should address those topics. PTAs and church parenting groups represented self-selecting sets of residents who grew increasingly invested in expanding sex education in their communities. At the root of their efforts lay the contradiction in much of the postwar sex education literature. If promiscuity, teen pregnancy, "sexual deviance," and divorce allegedly resulted from a lack of sex education, then how could voters leave the topic to the whims of parents? Notions about "bad" mothers and fathers stalked discussions on the topic in the postwar period, and those fears motivated volunteers to push for its inclusion in schools. In their eyes, only the near-universal reach of public education could diminish the threat of ignorance, and as a result, parents clashed over the role of schools again and again.

The fight in San Mateo in 1951 over Ralph Steele's biology class, for example, began with parents' enthusiasm over the issue. Ralph Eckert reported that every PTA in San Mateo County had hosted viewings of the latest sex education films approved by the state, and in 1949, several teachers on the Peninsula integrated the movies into their classes "with parental blessing."[90] Donald Nichols initially complained to school officials in private in 1950, and in response, parent groups in the district hosted a new round of forums on sex education for concerned residents. But the meeting failed to assuage some parents' concerns, and in February 1951, Nichols told sympathetic journalists about the sex education class and gave Steele's syllabus to San Mateo District Attorney Louis Dematteis.[91]

Although Bay Area newspapers published eye-catching headlines such as "Sex Syllabus Starts Furor at High School," the controversy actually demonstrated that many parents possessed a deep ambivalence—rather than outright hostility—toward sex education in schools. Whereas in the immediate aftermath of the press inquiries into the matter, San Mateo authorities, including Dematteis, investigated Steele's class, the biology teacher ultimately retained his position, and County Superintendent James Tormey only deemed him deserving of a light reprimand. Even Nichols, the parent most incensed by Steele's actions, made a point to declare that he did not oppose *all* sex education. He claimed that he only objected to the degree of "emphasis" his daughter's biology teacher gave the matter. When a group of other San Mateo parents rejected a plan to dismantle sex education in the high school, Nichols called his campaign a "failure."[92]

In the wake of the intense press scrutiny of their district, San Mateo administrators issued vague and contradictory information about their actions after the controversy, and it is unclear whether they integrated new material into the school's biology classes or retained old lessons taught prior to Steele's actions. Nevertheless, administrators' assurances that "common sense" would guide the interests of the curriculum committee, that they would only teach "normal textbook material," and that they would not "yield to the demands of any pressure group for or against instruction in this field" suggest that teachers continued to give limited lectures on human sexuality to high school seniors even after Nichols's complaints.[93] The controversy, therefore, revealed the contradictory impulses most Bay Area residents expressed toward the subject of sex education in schools. In the wake of the controversy, parents, administrators, and journalists struggled to reach some sort of middle ground. Superintendent James Tormey subsequently told a local newspaper that "common sense dictates a conservative approach (to sex education), taking into consideration differences of opinion in the community."[94]

Local school boards continued to debate the merits of sex education throughout the 1950s and early 1960s, but two broader shifts deepened the rift over the issue. First, courts liberalized the rules governing sexually explicit commerce. In a pair of cases in 1957, the U.S. Supreme Court ruled that the First Amendment did not protect "obscene" speech, yet officials needed to prove that material had appealed to a person's "prurient interest" as determined by "the average person applying contemporary community standards" before arresting people on obscenity charges. The decisions upheld laws governing the sale and distribution of pornography but also required authorities to define slippery terms like "average" and "community" before pursuing a conviction. They, therefore, effectively liberalized the rules governing pornography. Without clear criteria, authorities faced stiffer burdens to prosecute vendors for obscenity.

These standards sparked considerable concern in the South Bay and reignited the already tender issue of classroom-based sex education. In 1960, Santa Clara County District Attorney Louis Bergna attempted to organize a boycott of stores that sold what he called "smut," but his campaign produced mixed results. The prosecutor framed himself as a "moderate" who disapproved of "the government controlling" what people read in private. But in speeches to numerous PTAs and women's groups, he declared, "I'm very concerned with what your children—and mine—are going to see, hear and read about. Everyone . . . is being bombarded with sex today and it's bound to affect moral values."[95] Santa Clarans expressed mixed enthusiasm for his campaign. A mother wrote an open letter in the *Santa Clara Journal* asking local store owners to stop selling what she called "mental garbage."[96] At the same time, the *Journal* editorialized against the campaign because it would let loose "hundreds, if not thousands, of self-appointed censors" who would make decisions about "what publications are obscene and what stores are to be boycotted."[97]

Most important, the perceived threat of pornography revived the debate about sex education in the public schools. Asked her thoughts about Hollywood entertainment, a Santa Clara mother answered that although "there's nothing wrong with sex," she felt uncomfortable taking her daughter to the movies because they improperly focused on it. She further claimed that "schools overplay sex" and that they aggravated an already "unhealthy" situation. By contrast, another mother told the *Journal* that she did not want to hide knowledge from her children and that because some entertainment had racy content, "we would even like to have sex education with movies and that sort of thing taught in school."[98]

At the same time, the federal courts and local parents began to delineate stronger boundaries between religious and secular education. Several rulings on religion and education aggravated tensions between voters over how to best balance the interests of homes, schools, and churches. In 1962, the U.S. Supreme Court decided in *Engel v. Vitale* that the nation's schools could not allow prayer in their classrooms, including nondenominational invocations or ones that allowed students to opt out of participation.[99] A year later, federal justice reaffirmed its policy on religion and public education by ruling that school administrators could not require students to undertake daily Bible readings.[100] Together, these court decisions limited the religious instruction teachers could impart to students and further secularized the nation's public schools. In 1963, the Board of Trustees at the Jefferson High School in Santa Clara attempted to comply with the Supreme Court's rulings by denying a group of Methodists the right to meet in its classrooms, and they ended the practice of using district school buses to transport pupils to area churches for religious instruction.[101]

When, in 1962, a local newspaper asked people in downtown Santa Clara whether or not educators should teach children about the Bible, the respondents failed to reach a clear consensus on the subject. Whereas one retired resident told the *Santa Clara Journal* that he believed Bible "instruction would teach children to believe in the law when they're small," several other people indicated that, although they favored the practice, they opposed imposition of religious doctrine on their neighbors. Faith was a private matter best left to the discretion of individual families. Carla Henderson, an employee at the Peninsula Mortgage Company, contended that although "teaching the Bible has not hurt civilization so far . . . I believe it up to the discretion of the parents whether the Bible should be taught in public schools."[102]

By the early 1960s, these new rules on obscenity and classroom prayer upset the already precarious balance between home, school, and church. Many residents believed that the liberalized laws on pornography made children more vulnerable to dangers from the "street" and argued that schools needed sex education more than ever before. Yet quite a few parents also saw the prayer bans as dangerous threats to religion's role as a guarantor of youthful morality. Without Christian teachings in the classroom, they believed, any discussion of sex would lead students to experiment. If sex education divided voters throughout the 1950s, their differences appeared starker and starker by the early 1960s.

These competing visions about parenting, religion, and education spilled out into the open in the South Bay suburb of Santa Clara in 1962. The controversy began in early in February, when Alberta Rennert, the parent education chairwoman from the city's PTA, enlisted other residents to push the local high school to include sex education in its curricula. Rennert justified classroom-based teachings on the subject by declaring, "They'll learn better there than in the street."[103] When confronted with the argument that the home should bear the sole responsibility of teaching young people about sex, she responded with considerable skepticism. "This would be fine," she told the newspaper, "if most parents did something. But they don't, many of them until it's too late. And it's much harder to undo a wrong impression than plant the right one."[104]

Rennert spent months calling on the Santa Clara Unified School District to take up the issue, and her campaign initially generated significant enthusiasm among area residents. Over a hundred parents attended her panel entitled "Sane Sex Knowledge" in February, and the suburb's weekly newspaper endorsed her efforts with a bold editorial succinctly titled, "Sex Education—Yes."[105] At the end of February, the district's council PTA unanimously voted to support Rennert's campaign, and a few weeks later, she joked that the volume of inquiries from eager parents threatened to overwhelm her. With their support, she planned a forum in which a panel of experts from nearby San Lorenzo would talk about their experiences with family life education, and afterward, residents would vote on whether to bring it to Santa Clara.[106]

In the following months, letters flooded the *Journal*'s editorial page, with support for Rennert primarily coming from residents who viewed family life education as an extension rather than a contradiction of their roles as parents. One mother wrote a letter arguing that schools could buttress the work of parents. "Thanks to Mrs. Rennert and her committee," wrote Laura Smith, a self-described mother of two, "I was impressed and it made me realize that we need this kind of education. . . . Isn't the purpose of the school to educate the child? Why not educate the WHOLE child?" Rather than seeing classroom teachers in adversarial roles, parents such as Smith tended to see schools as supplements to sex education primarily administered by them in the home. Even though the two appeared to advance differing childrearing styles, with one seeming to underscore the significance of her sons' personal development and the other appearing to advocate a need for greater discipline, they both saw schools as extensions of their work as parents.[107]

Many Santa Clarans, however, responded negatively to Rennert's assertion that area residents were failing to adequately raise their children, and their objections to her proposal took two significant forms. First, several residents wrote to the editor claiming that a school-based program would undermine private work done in the home rather than supplement it. Mr. and Mrs. William Kelly, for example, contended, "We share [Rennert's] concern for the children who are getting sex education in the street. . . . Rather than relieve the parents [however] of this responsibility perhaps the parent educator committee, as its name implies, could aid the parents and help them overcome whatever difficulties they may have in talking to their children on this subject."[108] Rather than cede control over sex education to teachers, residents like the Kellys proposed a revitalization of the current system, in which some schools spoke directly to parents about childrearing and marriage.

If many letter writers expressed concern over what they saw as an attempt to eclipse the home, others complained about the increasing marginalization of churches. The scandal unfolding in Santa Clara occurred amid growing restrictions imposed by state and federal courts on religious instruction in schools, and many local mothers and fathers saw Alberta Rennert's campaign within the context of the increasing secularization of public education. "One cannot preach morality and practice immorality," noted R. H. Beecher in a letter to the editor. "We must follow the teachings of God if we hope to teach sex right! A school system which will not allow the teachings of God to be taught, how can they teach sex in the right light?"[109]

As the date of Rennert's districtwide forum approached, the suburb's mood soured considerably. Although many supported sex education, the notion that schools would undermine the work of the home and the church shadowed the campaign well into the spring of 1962. District Superintendent Wendell Huxtable, possibly conscious of earlier flareups over the issue, remained remarkably quiet on the subject. Although he promised residents that he would keep an open mind, he argued that sex education should "best be left to the parents."[110] In late March, the guest speakers from San Lorenzo scheduled to appear at Rennert's districtwide forum on family life education told the *Journal* that they feared stirring controversy in Santa Clara, and they requested a formal invitation from Huxtable before they would appear in his district.[111] Even after the superintendent acquiesced, the panel endured several unexplained delays and did not actually come together until the near end of the academic year on May 14.[112]

This postponement gave Rennert's opposition time to prepare for a confrontation. The forum planned by the committee working for family life education effectively brought two competing forms of suburban social organization into direct conflict with one another. The council PTA, working within the defined boundaries of the school district, ultimately clashed with area churches whose more porous boundaries allowed them to absorb members from across the county. Although no single congregation or parish singlehandedly outnumbered Rennert and her allies, the prolonged newspaper coverage of the issue gave several religious groups the opportunity to pool their opposition. When the lecturers from San Lorenzo finally spoke in Santa Clara High School, approximately 250 people appeared to hear them speak, including over a hundred residents whose children attended classes in neighboring districts or religious academies. Furious, Rennert charged that the parents of parochial school students had stacked the audience, and when they voted three to one to prohibit her family life education program, she attempted to bar their ballots.[113]

The *Santa Clara Journal* later alleged that church groups, both in and out of the suburb, organized to oppose her campaign, and the fact that several parents peppered the guest speakers from San Lorenzo with questions about religion supported its contention.[114] Even with Rennert's adjustment of the vote tally, however, the bid for family life education narrowly lost. Angry that her supporters did not turn out in greater numbers, she resigned her position with the PTA a few weeks later, and shortly thereafter, the organization most dedicated to "bringing the home and school closer together" told a reporter that all discussion of sex instruction would be off limits for the foreseeable future.[115]

From beginning to end, the controversy in Santa Clara lasted approximately five months, but it illuminated many of the forces at work at the grassroots level on the Peninsula and in the South Bay. Since the early twentieth century, many middle-class parents, clergy, psychological experts, and educators had valued a moral order that brought together the home, school, and church to teach children about sex, and in many ways, postwar suburbanization represented the culmination of that order. Parents flocked to PTA meetings to learn about sexual development, religious groups across the denominational divide offered sex and marital education, and public schools included prayer and released-time programs. In this sense, all sides agreed about the importance of normative family life, the desirability of some kind of sex education, and the need to "balance" the roles of the home, school, and church.

Yet the dissemination of postwar secular and religious texts also made another kind of consensus nearly impossible to reach. Residents had long disagreed on the correct balance between homes, schools, and churches and on what constituted "moderate" sex education, but the 1950s and early 1960s witnessed heightened anxiety over the issue. Parent education may have seemed like a reasonable compromise to many voters in the wake of World War II, but as mothers like Rennert increasingly saw sex education as a public health issue, volunteers in San Mateo and Santa Clara counties pushed to have the issue taught in their children's classrooms. While many of Rennert's supporters saw the strengthening of the schools as the only way to universalize normative behaviors like marriage, her opponents worried that secular education would overpower the teachings of parents and churches. These concerns became particularly acute as state and national courts placed restrictions on school prayer and released-time programs.

Rennert's opponents may have won in 1962, but their victory did not end debate in the Bay Area suburbs. Just four days before Rennert's final forum, several women's clubs across the freeway in San Jose hosted a meeting on sex education with a panel of local educators, ministers, and physicians. Noted only briefly within the inner pages of a daily newspaper, the juxtaposition of this largely unheralded event with the headline-snagging controversy in Santa Clara suggests that even in the face of growing opposition, family life education continued to garner significant support at the grassroots.[116] In just a few years, many of the Baby Boomers would enter high school, ushering in a new era of concern about premarital sex, sexual "deviance," and drug use.

Chapter 5

Policing and Redeveloping the Queer City

San Francisco officials in the 1950s and early 1960s looked out at what they saw as a crisis in the city's economic and moral order. For almost two decades, suburban rivals had built prosperous communities of middle-class, white married couples and lured industries, with their large tax resources, to the Peninsula and South Bay. This outward migration had transformed the city's economy and demographics, sparking dire predictions about San Francisco's future. A 1963 federally funded report by the Arthur Little consulting firm issued a stark warning to the mayor and Board of Supervisors about shifts under way in the city: "San Francisco," the consultants cautioned, "finds itself faced with a situation where middle-income families of all races are deserting the City for the amenities of suburban life." Those families represented the "cornerstone of society," and new residents with more varied sexual relationships were slowly replacing them: "The family . . . is leaving San Francisco, to be replaced by unrelated individuals—the widow or widower, the bachelor (temporary as well as perennial), [and] the working girl."[1] A year later, Arthur Little, Inc. counseled the mayor and Board of Supervisors that the city should work to maintain its current level of "middle-income families with children" in order to avoid further decay and that urban renewal constituted one of the most effective means of achieving that goal.[2]

Little and San Francisco's political leaders were observing two consequences of suburban growth. First, while the Peninsula and the South Bay drew increasing numbers of middle-class white, married couples with children, many people left out of the suburban housing market took up residence in the central city. Numerous people experiencing same-sex desires, in particular, settled in urban centers such as San Francisco, and like their suburban counterparts, they too formed communities of likeminded people. Second, the city encountered mounting economic problems. Like urban areas around the country, San Francisco lost population and investment in the postwar period. At the time of Little's report, city leaders believed they were facing the possibility of a dire fiscal crisis.

These two trends produced multiple reactions that ultimately reinforced the Straight State. For those experiencing same-sex desires, the growing number of self-identified gay people in San Francisco represented an opportunity, not a crisis. But many other San Franciscans saw prostitution and "vice" in the Western Addition, pornography in the Tenderloin, and gay bars near downtown as threats to their families and property values. At the same time, economic and political leaders stressed the importance of attracting investment downtown. As San Francisco gained a reputation for sexual deviance and "sleaze," these elites found it harder to attract the same kinds of investments enjoyed by their rivals on the Peninsula.

San Francisco's political leaders consequently used the tools at their disposal to try to solve these dilemmas. Beginning in the mid-1950s, public officials worked with state and federal authorities to police queer spaces, penalize people who deviated from heterosexual norms, and rebuild the city to make it more competitive with the suburbs. City and state authorities launched police sweeps of public places and sought to close gay bars, in part, because they worried about the threat sex and the streets posed to children. Housing reformers tore down residential hotels and tenements with little bedroom privacy, hoping that the eliminating "slum-like" buildings would drive sex back indoors and attract middle-class white married couples back to the city. Ultimately, their efforts largely failed to accomplish these goals. San Francisco later emerged as a key hub for queer life and politics in the United States. Yet the combined use of police and urban redevelopment demonstrates both the ways that suburbanization shaped sexual communities and the city and the ways in which the Straight State evolved to deal with the growing visibility of queer people in the city.

The Changing City

As public officials and private developers encouraged the outward migration of white, married couples to new suburbs after World War II, San Francisco's sexual and racial demographics shifted. Discrimination in suburban and city housing markets in the 1950s helped concentrate large numbers of unmarried residents, low-income workers, and people of color near the urban core. No single variable necessarily united these residents, yet many of them nevertheless lived in relationships outside heterosexual marriage. Some of them self-identified as gay men and lesbians, but many others lived with others not related to them by blood, marriage, or adoption and engaged in a variety of sexual relationships that did not neatly fall into a single category. Over time, the sexual variance in these neighborhoods helped produce different communities and gave rise to commercial institutions, like bars, that catered not only to downtown residents but also to people from the suburbs who commuted into the city for sex. By the mid-1950s, the bars and cruising areas in city parks and streets gave rise to an increasingly self-aware "queer public," whose members, if not completely united, saw themselves as a part of overlapping urban subcultures.

This shift unfolded, in part, thanks to major changes in the Bay Area's housing markets. San Francisco lost more than 35,000 residents between 1950 and 1960, and the census found over 24,000 fewer married couples and almost 90,000 fewer white people in the city at the end of that period. Meanwhile, the percentage of people classified by the census as "Negro" and "other races" rose to just under a fifth of the population.[3] This transformation appeared even more dramatic at the neighborhood level. Whereas numerous census tracts west of the Twin Peaks had many married couples, seventeen tracts near downtown had at least 70 percent of residents living with someone not related to them by blood, marriage, or adoption.[4] At the same time, nine census tracts, including Chinatown and the Western Addition, had "nonwhite" populations that exceeded 70 percent.[5]

Housing discrimination explains some of these numbers. Civil rights activists repeatedly complained that landlords in all-white neighborhoods refused to lease to renters of color. During the 1950s and early 1960s, groups like the Urban League and NAACP pushed the San Francisco Board of Supervisors to adopt fair housing laws with little success.[6] Urban neighborhoods also frequently included internal divisions based on marital status, and daily newspapers included advertisements for apartments that called for "single" or "married" tenants. These forms of discrimination paralleled and reinforced one another, and as a result, many neighborhoods with high percentages of unmarried residents also had significant numbers of nonwhite people.[7]

Discrimination based on sexuality and race hurt gay San Franciscans of color most acutely. Tom Redmon, an African American man, lived in the city in the early 1950s, for example, and he later recalled that he and his

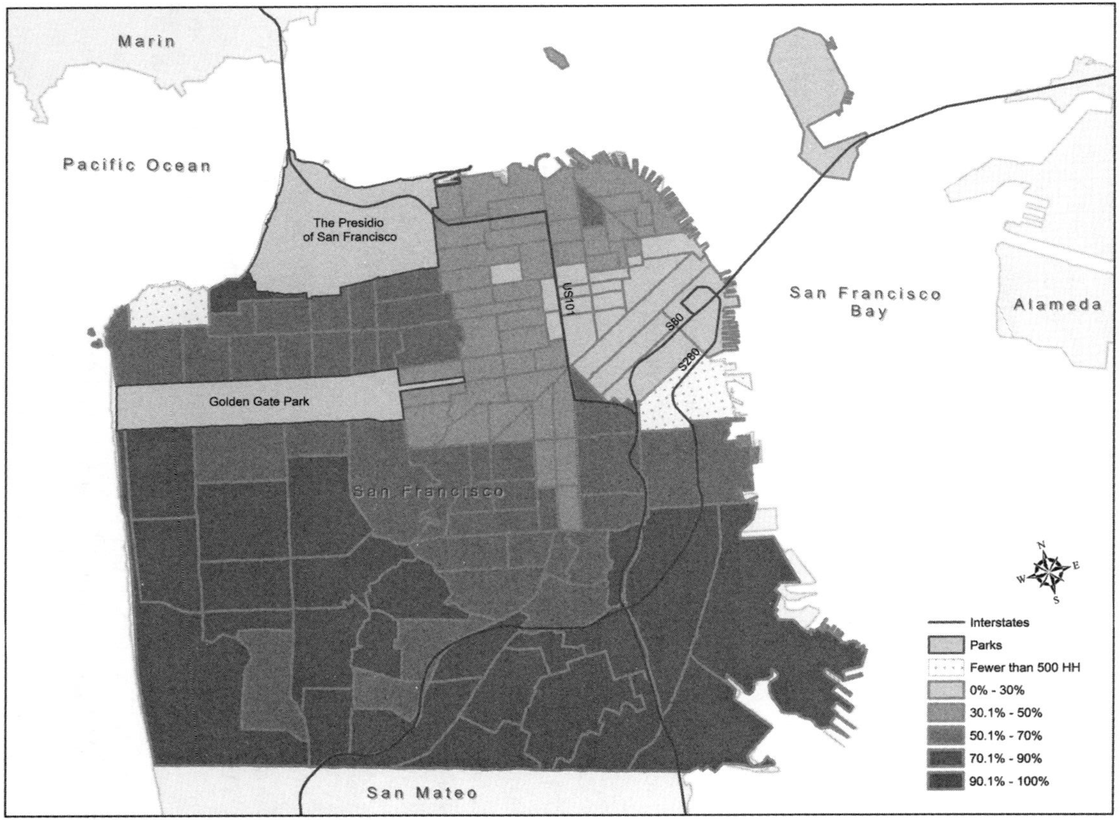

Map 6. Percentage of married couples with their own household in San Mateo County by census tract, 1960. This map does not include information for tracts with fewer than 500 households. Center for Urban and Regional Analysis, Ohio State University.

male partner "couldn't just live anywhere and everywhere." Facing persecution for both their race and sexual orientation, the two men lived temporarily in the YMCA before finding more permanent lodging in the bohemian districts near downtown. At one point, they rented an apartment from a former brothel madam and lived in some of the mixed-race census tracts that abutted Chinatown.[8]

Residential hotels near downtown occupied the lowest rungs of the city's housing market and often served as occupancies of last resort for many San Franciscans. Largely built to accommodate an industrial and maritime workforce in the late nineteenth century, these lodging houses offered tenants temporary and permanent rates, and they frequently served as one of the first sources of shelter for many newcomers to the city. According to a survey conducted at the beginning of the Depression, San Francisco boasted just under 65,000 hotel rooms, or one for every ten people in the city. Approximately 66 percent of those spaces catered to people who lived there on a more or less permanent basis, and at least half of that figure—roughly 25,000 rooms—provided shelter to the transient and day laborers in the lowest tier of the urban workforce.[9] Moreover, in a housing market largely segmented by sexuality, class, and race, these hotels represented some of the only accommodations available to single low-income residents of color. A study of San Francisco's "Manilatown" found that as Filipino workers passed through the city on their way to the farms of California's central valley, many of them found permanent homes in North Beach lodging houses on Jackson and Kearny streets. At its height, over ten thousand residents, "mostly Filipino bachelors," lived in the area.[10]

These hotels fostered unique social arrangements different from those in the single-family homes of San Mateo and Santa Clara counties. Hotel residents made up a low-income demographic similar to the Peninsula's "hobo jungles," but San Francisco had been a much larger hub in the early twentieth-century economy, and therefore, it hosted an even larger share of transient workers.[11] Inhabitants included self-identified gay men and lesbians, but they also consisted of residents involved in a variety of other erotic and social attachments that deviated from middle-class notions of respectability. Hotels often housed single mothers, male "drifters," unattached laborers, sex workers, and all-female households. They found shelter in these low-rent tenements both because of sexual, racial, and gender discrimination in the city's housing market and because few of them could afford to live elsewhere. This combination of discrimination, unemployment, and low wages pooled a racially diverse group of residents who lived outside the parameters of middle-class "respectable" marriage in San Francisco's low-cost hotels.[12]

Just as significantly, hotel residents enjoyed little to no privacy. In contrast to the seclusion that suburban home builders afforded married couples' bedrooms, hotel owners charged rates dependent on tenants' willingness to share space with other people. The price of lodging in these buildings varied considerably based on the privacy they offered residents. On one end of the scale, owners offered tenants enclosed rooms, soundproof walls, and private bathrooms. On the other end, they included mere cubicles separated by chicken wire, shared toilets, or mattresses laid out on the open floor. Historian Paul Groth observed, "The higher the price, the greater the privacy. The lower the price, the more one lived in a group."[13]

Whether in hotels or in more established neighborhoods, people in search of a diverse array of same-sex relationships remade San Francisco. As many gay residents who lived there in the 1950s recalled, almost any urban space where strangers congregated also served as a possible site for a pickup or sexual encounter. Parks, streets, the waterfront, beaches, public restrooms, and even department stores all became potential cruising areas in which queer men and, to a lesser extent, women found one another. According to longtime San Francisco resident Gerald Fabian, "There was a lot of cruising in and out of the parks, in the bushes and in the tearooms [bathrooms] and what have you."[14]

Many hotels, cafeterias, and bars that catered to transient maritime workers frequently doubled as sites for pickups and sexual encounters. The migratory nature of San Francisco's seafaring labor force facilitated the growth of an illicit subculture that allowed men passing through the city to engage in homoerotic acts but did not compel them to define their sexuality as "queer" or "gay." According to historian Allan Berubé, "Along the waterfronts in port cities were complex sexual cultures that incorporated . . . erotic arrangements between men, often with the threat of danger and violence." By the 1950s, Berubé added, "what might have been described as the early gay bars and nightlife in San Francisco might be more appropriately be called the homosexual aspects of waterfront culture."[15]

This erotic subculture catered to more than just the sailors, dock workers, and naval personnel who passed through the city; it also served a variety of men interested in same-sex encounters from across the metropolis. In

1955, for example, the San Francisco police complained that "many homosexuals, particularly during Saturday and Sunday mornings, from midnight on cruise the downtown areas in their autos attempting to pick up young servicemen or young civilian men."[16] Gerald Fabian recalled, "There were some hotels that were very popular [for meeting men] and . . . there was a cafeteria that was incredibly sleazy on Third Street that was just notorious because it was right, it was right where all the jitneys [cabs] would line up to take sailors back to Hunter's Point."[17]

For similar reasons, the commercial district near Powell Street emerged as a secondary, more upscale hub for gay life in the city. Just as the transient nature of work on the waterfront pulled groups of semi-anonymous strangers in and out of San Francisco, the city's shopping center drew visitors from across the region. The coming and going of consumers facilitated the meeting of largely middle-class gay men and lesbians and enabled a variety of queer encounters relatively free of official surveillance. Nob Hill resident Steve Tonkovish told an interviewer in the mid-1990s that "Union Square . . . [in the 1950s] was the one place where people went to get picked up,"[18] and Reba Hudson recalled that The Claridge, a cafe on nearby Maiden Lane, attracted wealthy lesbians, including "all the bisexual married women," who went there after they shopped downtown.[19]

Few places, however, played a more instrumental role in the development of San Francisco's queer public life than bars.[20] The high concentration of single adults living in San Francisco produced demand for a nightlife that catered to both hetero- and homosexual sex. According to the Department of Alcoholic Beverage Control, 792 bars operated in San Francisco in 1964, and separately, 231 of its restaurants advertised themselves in the phone book as "cocktail lounges, taverns or nightclubs."[21] Based on the 1960 census, this number gave the city a ratio of one public drinking place for every 717 people living in San Francisco and one for every 515 residents of legal drinking age. Although San Francisco had twice the population of Santa Clara County, it had over ten times as many bars as its suburban counterpart.[22]

These bars catered to a variety of groups, but many of them attracted unmarried people, including queer San Franciscans and poorer residents who made their homes in low-income hotels. Within the city, the census tracts with the highest percentage of unmarried people also had the largest number of public drinking places.[23] A study by the Department of City Planning in 1955 noted that apartments downtown "contain a large number of single-person households—roommates and apartment sharers. The proportion of such single-person households in San Francisco . . . is much higher than that of the Bay Area as a whole. . . . This large proportion has boosted the number of entertainment, restaurant and hotel facilities in and around the downtown."[24] Sociologist Sherri Cavan similarly found in the mid-1960s that the census tracts with the highest concentrations of bars in the city also contained higher proportions of unmarried residents, and she noted that several clusters of bars depended upon nearby "apartment houses, resident clubs, and hotels that cater to a relatively permanent clientele."[25]

Based on her research in the early 1960s, sociologist Nancy Achilles estimated that at least thirty-seven of the city's bars specifically catered to consumers in search of same-sex relationships.[26] Although businesses patronized by gay men and lesbians appeared in a variety of neighborhoods, clusters of queer liquor-selling establishments emerged near one another after the repeal of Prohibition along the city's waterfront, on the base of Telegraph Hill near North Beach and Chinatown, and in the central city Tenderloin District.[27] These businesses frequently drew customers from a variety of overlapping communities, including San Franciscans, tourists from across the country, suburban commuters, and sailors and military personnel temporarily living in the city.[28] Speaking about the popular Black Cat drag café, Gerald Fabian later remembered, "Well, it was a bar in which artists hung out . . . and it was a cross section of people from North Beach and . . . longshoremen and workers and dock workers and people from the Embarcadero, because it was in that area where those people often stayed; they stayed in those hotels around there."[29] Telegraph Hill resident Reba Hudson remembered that "working-class dykes" and "Peninsula type lesbians" all patronized places in North Beach because "they offered the only real girls' bars in San Francisco."[30]

Over the course of the long postwar period, these bars helped bring together an increasingly self-aware queer public, and they stood as a crucial counterpart to the new homes, schools, and churches dotting the residential landscapes of the Peninsula and South Bay. During the 1950s and early 1960s, gay men, lesbians, and bisexual and transgender people forged communities defined by their common transgressive sexual and gender identities. The proliferation of queer bars after World War II gave rise to a sense of common purpose among their patrons. Bar patrons did not necessarily always see one another as part of a singular community, but their presence in a shared space and their mutual concerns about the police often created a feeling of solidarity among them. In time, these common experiences would politicize many lesbian, gay, bisexual, and transgender (LGBT) people, and as historian Nan Alamilla Boyd notes, "The pockets of queer association and camaraderie that existed in bars and taverns" set the stage for later activism.[31]

Similar to suburban homes, schools, and churches, the shape and location of these businesses signaled to patrons who belonged and who did not. Unlike other establishments, however, bars that catered to LGBT patrons faced the possibility of arrest or harassment. The managers of these businesses, therefore, minimized their visibility to antagonistic authorities or outsiders. Bar owner Charlotte Coleman recalled choosing a semi-deserted spot for her business on the Embarcadero after a realtor showed her another more prominent commercial space downtown. In a later interview, she reflected on the alternative spot by explaining, "Here were all these kids with their mothers with their strollers going to the theater, and I thought I can't open a gay bar on this street (laughs). Because, you know, in those days, like my first one was down in the produce district where nobody was around, you know . . . so nobody would notice the gay people coming and going too much."[32] Similarly, sociologists Donald Webster Cory and Sherri Cavan each noted that the gay bars they visited in San Francisco frequently made it difficult for outsiders to find them, with one appearing at the top of a long flight of stairs and another merely presenting an unmarked, windowless façade to the street.[33]

Although San Francisco's bar culture helped many men and women develop a sense of a common gay or lesbian community, sexual identities remained fluid for others. Unlike a home mortgage, the purchase of a drink in a nightclub required no paperwork or serious financial investment. Unlike membership in a church or school group, bar patrons did not require fellow customers to give their names or check to see if they gave false ones. These businesses both gave some people a sense of solidarity with their fellow bargoers, therefore, and allowed anonymous visitors to come and go as they pleased. This fluidity offered patrons the possibility of straddling the sexual line between queer and straight identities. Bargoers could drink or sleep with openly gay, lesbian, bisexual, or transgender people, but they could also live married lives in the suburbs. They could define themselves as "gay" or as "homosexuals," or they could ignore the categories altogether.

Furthermore, bar life blended with the more fluid sexual publics that flourished in the city's streets, parks, and waterfront. For those unable to afford going to a bar or too young to buy a drink, these spaces allowed for socializing and sex. In the 1950s, working-class and poor residents in San Francisco used the streets, parks, and waterfront for heterosexual and homosexual encounters, and the very openness of these venues allowed a mixed-class cross section of men to seek queer sex without requiring them to define themselves publicly as "gay" or "bisexual." Although city streets and parks exposed would-be sexual partners to hostile surveillance, they also represented one of the few spaces that allowed sexual encounters between people of different classes, ages, and races.

Homophiles in the Postwar Metropolis

If the city allowed a heterogeneous population of people to meet for sex, postwar suburbanization also enabled the creation of a middle-class form of gay socializing and politics. In the early 1950s, a small group of self-identified gay men and lesbians organized two "homophile" societies, the Mattachine Society and the Daughters of Bilitis (DOB), which were dedicated to supporting civil rights for homosexuals. Numerous scholars have explored the history of the homophiles, documenting their origins, goals, and scope. Both groups began, in part, as responses to the crackdown on homosexuality after World War II, and although the Mattachine Society originated in Los Angeles, it joined the DOB in San Francisco in the mid-1950s. In the subsequent decade, homophiles pursued many goals, including educating the public about homosexuality, helping gay men and lesbians to meet one another safely, and changing the state's sex laws. Although San Francisco boasted some of the earliest groups, later chapters opened in cities across the country, including Denver and Chicago, and the homophiles reached a much wider audience through their newsletters and magazines.[34] However, scholars have yet to situate the homophiles in the context of postwar metropolitan growth. Just as middle-class married couples joined neighborhood associations, parent-teacher associations (PTAs), or churches, homophile organizations came together in a city transformed by suburbanization. They, too, represented communities of likeminded people, and like their suburban counterparts, the homophiles promoted their own form of sex education that tolerated homosexuality and the right to privacy.

Members of these groups were not necessarily affluent, but many were wealthy enough to opt to specifically live in San Francisco.[35] They made this decision, however, among a limited number of choices. Many homophiles lived in San Francisco not because the city offered a self-evidently more tolerant place to live but because suburbanization's strengthening of normative sexuality made it the best of a limited number of alternatives. Del Martin, one of the DOB's founding members, for example, grew up in San Francisco but briefly moved to the suburbs after she married a man. While living in the suburbs, she fell in love with another woman and divorced her husband. She later met her long-term partner Phyllis Lyon during a stint in Seattle, and the two women subsequently moved to San Francisco as a couple.[36] Although their 1972 semi-autobiographical *Lesbian/Woman* offers few specific dates, Martin and Lyon boast in the book that they owned a home together in San Francisco, and even if they had bought the house in the 1960s, real estate discrimination would have made a similar purchase by two women almost impossible in the suburbs. Moreover, the couple had few alternatives to living in the city if they hoped to socialize with other lesbians. "Above all," Martin and Lyon recalled, "we needed a sense of community with others like ourselves."[37]

Not all homophiles, however, lived in San Francisco. Some lived in the suburbs, and their commutes into the city make it clear that being openly gay was easier in some parts of the metropolis than in others. Although some homophiles resided on the Peninsula and in the South Bay, the Mattachine Society and Daughters of Bilitis never hosted events there. DOB records from 1963 listed approximately forty-five active members in the group's San Francisco chapter, including nine with addresses in San Mateo and Santa Clara counties.[38] A similar record of roughly 100 Mattachine correspondents from across the country included at least five people from the Peninsula and South Bay.[39] Although they lived in the suburbs, Mattachine and DOB supporters almost always commuted to the city for events. In 1962, an automobile-less woman in Redwood City wrote Phyllis Lyon and Del Martin and asked if they knew anyone on the Peninsula who could drive her to their meetings in San Francisco.[40]

This woman's letter highlights the significant "sifting" process at play in the postwar Bay Area. The slow growth of the Mattachine Society and DOB reflected the belief of many gay men and lesbians that they could find others "like themselves" in San Francisco, even if they lived in the suburbs. Both the DOB and Mattachine Society held small meetings, including "Koffee Klatches" and "Gab 'n Javas," in the privacy of members' homes in San Francisco and hosted social events at restaurants in places such as North

Beach.[41] One reader of the DOB's newsletter, the *Ladder*, wrote that she drove from San Jose to San Francisco to attend these events because she believed "there are so many problems we must face, and it seems that an organization such as this would be of the utmost help to us."[42]

During the 1950s and early 1960s, the homophiles assembled numerous panels on the legal, religious, and medical aspects of homosexuality and solicited the public to join them. These events brought together official members but also invited people experiencing gay desires to learn about the homophiles without necessarily exposing themselves to hostile scrutiny. The DOB and Mattachine Society advertised these panels as "educational" events, and not unlike an innocuous visit to a gay bar for a drink, they offered visitors from across the metropolis a pretext for attendance other than sex.[43] They offered similar justifications for subscriptions to their publications. The editors of homophiles' newsletters and magazines repeatedly insisted that their organizations were not just made up of homosexuals but rather "people interested in the sex problem, especially those of the homosexual."[44]

If the urban location of these events reflected the changes affecting cities and suburbs, their topics also signaled the homophiles' participation in the wider postwar circulation of sexual knowledge. The Mattachine Society and DOB both touted education as one of their key goals, and they hoped to teach gay men and lesbians that they deserved full equality in American life and politics.[45] Even as suburban PTAs and churches brought new residents together around marriage and parenting, the DOB and Mattachine Society created new communities dedicated to discussing sexuality with gay men, lesbians, or others eager to learn about same-sex desire. The Daughters of Bilitis, for example, promised to help lesbians "adjust to society in all its social, civic, and economic implications."[46] Messages about the normalcy of homosexuality often lay at the heart of these campaigns. The Mattachine Society in 1956 denied that gay people were "perverted" and insisted, "The fact is that most homosexuals can and do lead productive lives."[47]

Both groups created libraries of recent texts on sexuality and offered "seminars on sex education" in order to communicate these ideas.[48] In 1957, the Daughters of Bilitis invited a San Francisco parent education specialist to speak to the group and to answer questions from the audience. Since some DOB members had children, the organization created a forum entitled "Raising Children in a Deviant Relationship." Despite the title, the forum concluded that many kinds of parents could raise healthy families.[49]

Looking back on this panel fifteen years later, Martin and Lyon recalled that DOB members learned that "love and security in the home overshadow almost all other factors in determining the emotional stability" and that if parents love their children, they would "turn out to be normal and well adjusted."[50]

Whereas many advocates for sex education in the home, school, and church believed increased knowledge on the subject might help parents avert "deviance" in their children, homophiles sought to persuade Americans that homosexuality did not threaten families. The Mattachine Society and DOB closely followed the research of Alfred Kinsey until his death in 1956, and they touted his findings that homosexuality was relatively common in the United States. Hoping to change scientific attitudes about same-sex relationships, homophiles pushed members to volunteer for studies conducted by some of California's leading researchers and compiled their own case histories modeled after Kinsey's work.[51] They even invited prominent researchers from the Langley Porter Clinic who specialized in "sex deviation" to speak at their functions.[52]

Homophiles contacted leading sex educators because they hoped to liberalize many Americans' attitudes toward same-sex relationships. In 1955, the Mattachine Society published "An Open Letter to Mr. and Mrs. America," calling on mothers and fathers to educate themselves about homosexuality. The writers of the letter declared that parents often react with hostility when they discover that their "sons and daughters . . . may not develop strong heterosexual desires" and warned that Americans had mistakenly defined one set of relationships "as 'normal' to the exclusion of everything else." Learning about the commonality of homosexuality, the Mattachine Society alleged, parents could help their children achieve "self-acceptance."[53]

Perhaps no message resounded more strongly among homophile literature than conceptualizations of the "right to privacy." Rhetoric about privacy appealed to homophiles because it dovetailed with their efforts to present homosexuality in a nonthreatening manner and because it offered them an opportunity to reach potential liberal allies.[54] When the American Law Institute (ALI) drafted its "Model Penal Code" in the 1950s, the editors of the *Mattachine Review* placed Judge Learned Hand, one of the ALI's key members, on their cover. Karl Bowman, one of California's leading researchers on "sex deviance," believed that homosexuality was a kind of mental illness. Nevertheless, the *Mattachine Review* reprinted Bowman's arguments about privacy: "There should be changes made in sex laws of various states, Dr. Bowman stated, including those laws that make married couples liable to felony or misdemeanor [charges] for indulging in deviate sex acts, even when practiced in private, without harm, and with mutual consent."[55]

These arguments, however, also highlighted homophiles' limited ability to advocate for change. Proponents of privacy frequently rested their arguments on a call for restraint from the wider society, and those pleas for tolerance frequently left other inequities untouched. Tolerance did not necessarily mean equality or even fairness. Potential allies like Bowman distinguished between private sex acts committed by "married couples" with those of other people, and his belief in a right to privacy for consenting adults did not mean he endorsed homosexuality. The homophiles, who themselves often met in private or semi-private spaces like people's homes, navigated a difficult social landscape when it came to talking about the police. The right to privacy did not protect public sex, and these early gay rights activists condemned such actions in the name of respectability. When the police arrested twenty-three men looking for sex in the Palo Alto train station, the Mattachine Society criticized the arrestees for failing to conform to social norms: "Seeking understanding of and promoting education on the homosexual problem is one thing; affronting standards of public decency is another."[56]

Homophiles reinforced some notions of "public decency," therefore, even as they sought to reshape the debate about homosexuality through education and the law. Although San Francisco's Mattachine Society and DOB included only a few dozen official members apiece, their advocacy demonstrated an important shift in the metropolis. Even as many married couples self-selected and found one another in a church or parent group, many middle-class gay men and lesbians formed their own social organizations composed of "likeminded" individuals. The history of the homophiles further demonstrates that some gay men and lesbians sought to bend the debates about sex education to their own ends. Rather than supporting discourses that equated "normalcy" exclusively with heterosexuality and marriage, the DOB and Mattachine Society argued that homosexuality, if not entirely "normal," should nevertheless be abided by the wider society. Their calls for tolerance challenged parents, teachers, and clergy to accept children experiencing same-sex desire and pushed for larger legal reforms that guaranteed all Americans a right to privacy. Their arguments found only a narrow audience in the 1950s, yet the homophile societies laid some of the groundwork for the popularization of notions about privacy in subsequent decades.

Public Outrage and the Urban Crisis

If the homophiles saw the growing concentration of unmarried people in San Francisco as an opportunity, many other residents worried about what they saw as the growing visibility of "sleaze" in the city. Their concerns echoed ideas expressed in the postwar sex panic, yet many San Franciscans also now worried about what they saw as the sexual dimensions of an entrenched urban crisis. These residents did not fret about homosexuality in isolation. Instead, they connected queer sexuality to other changes connected to the changing demographics of the city. For many white parents in particular, gay bars in North Beach, street walkers in the Western Addition and South of Market, pornography near downtown, and teen drug use all symbolized a deterioration in the city's fortunes. San Francisco's business leaders, meanwhile, believed the growing visibility of certain kinds of nonmarital sexuality near downtown hurt their chances to attract outside investment. These economic elites looked longingly at their suburban neighbors to the south who had attracted strong tax bases thanks, in part, to their abilities to convince firms that they offered "family-friendly" environments. Over time, anxieties at both the grassroots and elite levels crept into local politics, as different candidates for higher office blamed one another for the city's ills. These political debates and the larger concerns that birthed them motivated a police crackdown and redevelopment of San Francisco's downtown.

For most of the 1950s and early 1960s, middle-class parent groups in the city, like the PTA, offered sex education programs just like their suburban counterparts. Unlike suburban PTAs or churches, however, middle-class white parents in San Francisco confronted significantly more visible prostitution, gay nightlife, and adult bookstores. Local newspapers in this era offered alarming stories about the growth of sex workers in the Western Addition and gay bars near downtown. For many residents, the changing cityscape appeared to signal the triumph of "back alley" morality, including sexual deviance. The triumph of sex education on the "street," of course, also allegedly revealed the failures of the institutions most responsible for the training of youth. Throughout the 1950s and early 1960s, many San

Franciscans complained about what they saw as the failure of the home, school, and church to work together. Although they may have shared a similar worldview and organizational affiliations as their suburban counterparts, many middle-class parents in the city saw sexual deviance and juvenile delinquency as a more immediate threat to their well-being.

In May 1954, the *San Francisco Chronicle* told its readers that juvenile delinquency in the city had increased "both in volume and degree." The cause of the upsurge, it reported, came from a rash of "broken homes" characterized by divorce and marital separation in the predominantly black Fillmore neighborhood and largely Latino Mission District.[57] Just a month later, the *Examiner* complained in an editorial of the "unwholesome condition in San Francisco" and objected to the dangers gay men and lesbians posed to young people. "The condition," the newspaper exclaimed, "is marked by the increase of homosexuals in the parks, public gathering places and certain taverns in the city. It is a bad situation. . . . Even worse, these deviates multiply by recruiting teenagers. . . . Now we need action."[58]

Parent groups in San Francisco held meetings related to sex education, but they also worked to stop gay cruising or to close gay bars. Few events spurred public outrage more than the 1954 arrest of two teenage girls at Tommy's Place, a North Beach lesbian bar. The case touched on the overlapping anxieties among many white parents in the city, as the police alleged that homosexual employees sold beer to the minors and introduced them to Jesse Winston, an African American man, who sold them marijuana and Benzedrine. Local journalists alleged that Winston, Grace Miller, and Joyce Van de Meer, the owners of Tommy's Place, ran a "vice academy," corrupting innocent white teenage girls with drug addiction, alcohol, and "sex perversion."[59] The city's newspapers followed the prosecution of Winston, Miller, and Van de Meer with great enthusiasm and avidly told the story as a case of pernicious adults willfully enabling youthful misconduct. The *Examiner* played up the class and racial dynamics of the encounter that one of the teenagers who testified about her time at Tommy's Place wore a "blue sports jacket pulled over her sweater" and "might have been the girl next door—or your own daughter."[60]

Although the police failed to convict the bar's owner for selling alcohol to minors, the case mobilized parent groups across the city. Just a few days after the arrests, San Francisco School Superintendent Harold Clish made an unscheduled speech before the executive board of the city's PTAs, pushing the organization to demand that state authorities revoke the North

Beach bar's liquor license.[61] The PTA then joined the city's district attorney and police chief to call for "the suppression of such establishments."[62] PTA units subsequently sent letters to the state government demanding a revocation of the bar's license, and members sat in the audience as the state asked the two teenage girls to testify about their ability to buy liquor and narcotics in the North Beach lesbian bar.[63] According to one volunteer who witnessed the proceedings, "As a mother, to me the child's story was sickening. To think that a child . . . could be induced to frequent these kinds of places and find it exciting. I have no daughters, but if this youngster were my child I would just die of shame."[64]

In the years after the raid on Tommy's Place, newspapers published numerous examples of outraged residents worried about the "degenerates" and "sleaze" visible on city streets. A letter written by a man to the *San Francisco Examiner* in September 1955 proclaimed, "I do not appreciate being stopped on the San Francisco streets by men every time I walk out the door. The solution to this problem is long overdue. . . . This is fast becoming a nuisance to every young man and child alike."[65] Just three months later, a mother told the *Examiner* that her "children were not allowed to go into the park" because of the large number of "sex degenerates" there.[66] In 1958, a group of mothers from the Visitacion Valley neighborhood demanded that city authorities step up their surveillance of the "queer characters" who regularly "lurked" in McLaren Park, and police detective Kevin Conroy told newspaper reporters, "Public parks, especially those near schools, often act as a magnet for 'queer characters.' "[67] Fearful of an attack on her children, one mother in 1959 suggested that public officials raze the trees and bushes in the city's parks in order to protect young people because "in cities of this size where all types of people congregate, sex degenerates are more numerous."[68] In 1962, PTA mothers lobbied merchants on Polk Street to push out gay men who loitered outside their stores.[69]

This anxiety about homosexuality overlapped with other anxieties, including the spread of prostitution and vice to "family-friendly" neighborhoods. During the 1950s and early 1960s, civil rights groups tried to open all-white areas to African American homeowners and renters, and numerous white residents resisted integration either by organizing to discourage black migration or fleeing the city altogether.[70] Segregationist whites feared many things, but many of them specifically worried about interracial sex and that black residents would transform their neighborhoods into vice districts.[71] The *Chronicle* in this era even launched multiple series on African American crime because its readers were "privately expressing alarm" about the issue and included a photo of black children playing in an alley with one article. The media's disproportionate focus on African Americans and vice eventually prompted a group of black ministers to formally protest the police's tolerance for white patrons in brothels near Fillmore Street. Pastor D. Manning Jackson wrote a scathing letter to the *Chronicle* decrying the way that a recent profile "deliberately bypassed the more decent element of our people and sought out the pariahs, the wretches, the dope addicts, the prostitutes, the criminals and boozers."[72]

Anxiety about the spread of the "street" also fueled criticism of the failure of the city's preventative agencies. Whereas suburban churches grew in record numbers in the 1950s, many city residents ascribed the changes in urban neighborhoods to the failure of local religious groups. "When we put God out of our homes and schools," asserted one letter in the *San Francisco Examiner* in 1957, "and replace the Bible . . . with the filth that is being put out in production-line fashion, how can we expect our children to do other than ape their elders?"[73] Another writer contended that delinquency stemmed from inadequate "love and security" and that "the church can provide these things and much more."[74] Many San Franciscans similarly faulted city schools, with newspaper readers attributing what they saw as an upsurge in juvenile delinquency to teachers' failure to emphasize "character building" and "respect for human life and property."[75] In 1958, a judge for the city's juvenile court told the Board of Supervisors, "The churches and schools must take positive, aggressive action against juvenile delinquency instead of the passive attitude that many now exhibit."[76]

For many residents, gay men in parks and bars, an apparent rise in "juvenile delinquency," prostitution in the Western Addition, and theaters that showed "immoral pictures" meant that the city no longer welcomed white married couples with children. San Francisco represented one of the only places on the West Coast to lose people in the 1950s, and newspapers repeatedly reported on a yawning "family gap" between city and suburb. As early as 1955, the *San Francisco Examiner* reported with alarm that the city's marriage rate had dropped to its lowest point since 1941.[77] When census takers at the end of the decade published their report on the divergent population trends within the postwar metropolis, journalists, government officials, and businessmen attributed San Francisco's population dip to the apparent desire of white middle-class couples to live in the suburbs.

" 'Let's face it,' said one real estate man in that same year, 'we are already at the stage where many people don't think San Francisco is a good place to bring up a family.' "[78]

This belief that white middle-class married couples with children were leaving the city particularly alarmed San Francisco's political and economic elites. As its port gradually declined in importance and it slowly gained significance as a banking and commercial center, the city's leadership increasingly grew hostile to their home's reputation as a "wide open town." One private consultant promised city officials a sunny economic future if they could erase San Francisco's reputation for sleaze: "There was apparently a time when San Francisco was proud of its vice. . . . Now the city has matured, [and] it is rapidly becoming a financial capital and convention city."[79] In 1959, the *Examiner* editorialized that although San Francisco's many bars and nightclubs helped it attract tourists and conventiongoers, too many of them gave the urban center an unsavory reputation.[80]

These elites increasingly looked to the suburbs for models of economic and population growth. In 1956, private consultants told journalists that the city needed a redevelopment plan to compete with its rivals on the Peninsula and in the South Bay. "If this isn't done soon," they warned, "the population will continue to spread out and business will go with it to the suburbs."[81] The probusiness San Francisco Planning and Housing Association called for a massive urban renewal program, lamenting that "most growth has taken place in the suburbs." Association members looked longingly at their rivals down the Peninsula and declared, "The centers of older cities are being abandoned by people; a substantial portion of the retail business has shifted from the central retail business districts to the suburbs. Industry, too, is on the move seeking the plant and parking space afforded by the suburban areas."[82]

City officials observed that many of the characteristics that made neighborhoods unattractive to middle-class, married couples also pushed businesses away. A report about the South of Market area near downtown declared that the neighborhood left "much to be desired" from the business point of view: "Narrow alleys, an almost total lack of off-street parking and loading space, the scattering of residential buildings, children playing in the streets, and homeless men stumbling in the gutters, contribute to an industrial environment so poor that many industries have left the city for greener pastures across the Bay or down the Peninsula."[83] According to a wholesaler who owned property in South of Market, "The riff-raff winos and bums make the entire area undesirable. . . . We would be better off to have a general office on the Peninsula with perhaps a downtown display and sales office."[84]

The police's inability to drive out "sex deviates" similarly crept steadily into local politics as a part of these larger discussions about the city's problems. George Christopher won the mayoralty in 1956, in part, based on his promise to "clean up San Francisco." A Republican, prominent businessman, and member of the Board of Supervisors, Christopher declared his intention to run for mayor soon after the Tommy's Place affair. Although he and his wife did not have children themselves, Christopher never missed an opportunity to stage publicity shots with young people, and he allegedly hung a picture of orphans above his desk.[85] In December 1955, he promised to reform the police and that "San Francisco [would] remain a closed town."[86]

When Christopher ran for reelection in 1959, his opponent, tax assessor Russ Wolden, made sexuality an explicit campaign issue and told a radio program a month before voters cast their ballots, "I say San Francisco is not a closed town. And it is not a clean town!"[87] In a follow-up investigation, the *San Francisco Progress* appeared to substantiate Wolden's claims by alleging that the city, under the Christopher administration, had become "the national headquarters for sex deviates in the United States." In its front-page article, the *Progress* underscored the gap between San Francisco and its suburbs: "The number of sex deviates in this city has soared by the thousands . . . while other communities in this area have virtually eliminated them."[88] In subsequent weeks, Wolden enlisted parent groups to support his campaign, sending direct mailings to PTA members and church groups in the city.[89]

The mayor's response that "in a blind drive for office my opponent has degraded our city" demonstrated that hostility to queer residents crossed the political spectrum.[90] Christopher not only termed his opponent's allegation a "smear" but also launched a competing rumor that Wolden secretly aspired to make San Francisco an "open town" for vice interests with ties to the tourism industry.[91] Meanwhile, the *Progress*'s assertion that Christopher had allowed "sex deviation" to flourish in San Francisco "while other communities in this area have virtually eliminated them" suggested that the apparent differences between city and suburb had spurred pressure on the local government to crack down on visibly queer residents.

Figure 9. George Christopher campaigns for mayor, 1955. San Francisco History Center, San Francisco Public Library.

Confronting the Sexuality of the Street

San Francisco's changing demographics thus sparked anxiety at the grassroots and elite levels, and the city's business and political leadership soon tried to solve the crisis. Like urban elites across the country, San Francisco authorities in the 1950s launched a wave of police repression to close bars that catered to prostitutes or homosexuals and to push people they deemed undesirable off the streets. At the same time, they used federal funds to redevelop neighborhoods near downtown. Urban renewal offered public officials like Mayor George Christopher the chance to help San Francisco compete with its suburban neighbors, and they used policy tools similar to their counterparts on the Peninsula and in the South Bay. Even as police raided gay bars, authorities tore down the hotels that housed many of the city's transient, unmarried residents; tore apart the predominantly black Western Addition; and built new homes with bedroom privacy designed to attract middle-class white married couples. These strategies ultimately failed to reverse the demographic revolutions set in motion by suburbanization. Nevertheless, they encouraged people to conceal potentially deviant relationships and reinforced the notion that sex needed to take place in private. Policing and redevelopment thus reinforced the Straight State even as they failed to reverse the urban crisis, offering incentives and penalties for people to conform to heterosexual marriage.

As they formulated their goals, public authorities specifically focused on the relationship between the "home" and the "street." Bars, in particular, stood out to them as spaces in which deviant subcultures, including homosexuals, transmitted threatening behaviors to the wider public. Health, planning, and policing experts across the country in the 1950s largely agreed that the concentration of vice-related businesses in central cities aggravated juvenile delinquency and encouraged "sex deviates" to gather in urban neighborhoods.[92] Former San Francisco District Attorney and California Attorney General Edmund Brown contended that an uneven distribution of liquor licenses created competition and compelled many owners to break the law in order to make money. "The marginal operator," he contended, "is often encouraged to engage in illicit activities, such as bookmaking, narcotics, [or] prostitution."[93]

Closing an "excess" of bars served as one strategy for cleaning up the "street," but city officials also turned their attention to people in urban spaces like parks and alleys. Many mental health and law enforcement authorities in the 1950s viewed forms of social deviance, such as homosexuality and juvenile delinquency, as learned behaviors. They alleged that if these activities went uncontested, they attracted other so-called deviants and allowed illicit subcultures to flourish. In a casebook distributed to police officers across the country in the late 1950s, criminologist James Melvin Reinhardt alleged that the increasing visibility of gay communities in major cities did not justify a parallel growth in tolerance of them because "the statistical chances that one's own brother or son may become a homosexual increases with the number of homosexuals in the community."[94] Authorities like Reinhardt applied this logic not only to homosexuals but also to a host of potential threats to normative families, including drug "peddlers" and juvenile delinquents. Law enforcement officials, therefore, aggressively policed areas in which children congregated and frequently employed the state's sweeping "vagrancy" laws to detain "any person who loiters about any school or public place at or near which children attend or normally congregate."[95]

Bar raids and surveillance of public spaces helped officials limit the potential dangers of the "street," but redevelopers also helped reinforce the idea that sex properly belonged in private in the home. Middle-class reformers, intent upon explaining what they saw as deviant behavior among the poor, frequently cited the ways that small apartments exposed small children to adult activities, such as sex, or subjected residents of all ages to the personal lives of their neighbors. This lack of privacy, in their estimation, threatened the normal psychological development of young people and left older ones unable to forge healthy connections with others. Urban planning professor Charles Abrams alleged in 1959, "Living in a single room deprives the parent of the opportunity for family discipline and drives the child into the street where he seeks his own associations."[96] Urban officials, therefore, saw "slum-like" tenements as threats to the sexual order of the city and looked to replace them with homes that offered families a greater degree of privacy.

This obsession with private bedrooms among planners irritated urban critic Jane Jacobs, who argued that Americans could think about privacy in more complex ways. Jacobs certainly did not see herself as a defender of gay people or public sex. In fact, in her 1961 opus *The Death and Life of Great American Cities*, she criticized the "perverts" that dwelled in some city parks.[97] However, she also critiqued the notion that privacy, including sexual privacy, meant walling people off from one another: "Architectural and planning literature deals with privacy in terms of windows, overlooks, and sight lines. . . . This is simple-minded," she complained. "Window privacy is the easiest commodity in the world to get. You just pull down the shades or adjust the blinds." Real privacy, Jacobs argued, depended on mutual respect between neighbors. She may have seen homosexuality as a part of the urban crisis and a problem just like the planners she critiqued. Yet she also reminded Americans that privacy was more than a question of design. A good neighbor, she contended, "combines a feeling of good will with a feeling of no personal responsibility over our affairs." Privacy, she wrote, came from the willingness of people to respect the boundaries around others' personal lives.[98]

Jacobs's book offered a firsthand account of the concerns many midcentury planners had with private bedrooms, but it came too late to make a difference in San Francisco. By the mid-1950s, San Francisco residents had already decided that what they saw as the sexual disorder near downtown needed eradication. In 1954, neighborhood business and homeowner groups, including several west of the Twin Peaks, held a meeting calling for a united front against what they saw as the problems afflicting the areas around downtown.[99] San Francisco Assemblyman Caspar Weinberger led a statewide investigation of California's liquor licensing laws that same year. His inquiry began due to corruption in the licensing system in Southern California, and Weinberger broadened his committee's focus to include the question of whether or not the "overconcentration" of urban bars attracted criminal elements. To deal with the crime it associated with bars, Weinberger's subcommittee created a new Department of Alcoholic Beverage Control (ABC), with a broad mandate to revoke the liquor licenses of businesses that served as "a resort for narcotics peddlers or addicts, prostitutes, panderers or sex deviates."[100]

The creation of the ABC offered San Francisco officials new tools for reinforcing sexual norms, and in January 1955, members of the new state agency worked with the city police to build stronger cases against businesses that catered to homosexuals. The legislature's revisions of the Alcoholic Beverage Control Act gave law enforcement authorities broad powers to revoke businesses' licenses, and in the spring of 1955, state and local law enforcement conducted sweeping raids of places visited by queer patrons.[101] In March of that year, authorities in Sacramento appointed Frank Fullenwider, a lawyer who made his career prosecuting organized crime in Los Angeles, liquor director for Northern California. Fullenwider, who lived in the Peninsula suburb of Atherton, pledged to cooperate closely with San Francisco's police to close bars that catered to "prostitutes or homosexuals" and enlisted local newspapers to support the state's efforts.[102]

State employees like Fullenwider found an ally in city hall when George Christopher won the mayor's office. Just after entering office in February 1956, he pushed undercover vice units to conduct independent investigations of organized crime and illegal bars, directed district captains to conduct surveys of conditions in their jurisdictions, and created an intelligence unit that gathered broad information about sex-related businesses and gambling in San Francisco.[103] A few weeks later, he met with Fullenwider, requested more law enforcement aid from Sacramento, and pledged closer cooperation between city police and the ABC.[104]

In a strategy that foreshadowed later redevelopment, officials sought to thin the number of bars in designated "problem areas" and stepped up police surveillance of public places. In September 1955, San Francisco Police Chief George Healy told the *Examiner* of his intention to block the issuance of new liquor licenses in the "neon belt of Turk, Mason and Eddy Streets,"[105] and shortly after Christopher's inauguration in 1956, the ABC singled out the Tenderloin, North Beach, Chinatown, and the South of Market districts for special attention.[106] In each case, they worked to limit bars through the denial of new permits and stringent enforcement of code violations. From 1955 through 1957, the ABC reported that it had either suspended or revoked sixty-two liquor licenses in the Tenderloin District alone.[107] In 1957, Fullenwider met with San Francisco School District Superintendent Harold Spears and, at the education chief's request, promised to specifically deny a liquor license to any establishment within 200 feet of a city school.[108]

The ABC and Christopher administration not only limited liquor licenses in parts of the city but also deployed out-of-uniform officers to monitor parks, schools, and bars. Their reliance on undercover investigations allowed them to develop a parasitic relationship with San Francisco's illicit nightlife. Strangers streamed in and out of the city, and the police hoped to use the same anonymity that allowed a patron to enter a gay bar or to solicit sex in a park relatively safely to their own advantage. Chief Ahern announced in 1956 that his department would increase its surveillance of parks and playgrounds after dark and that it would break up groups of three or more teenagers who congregated in the street after 8 p.m.[109] A year later, the Christopher administration launched "Operation S," an initiative designed to "saturate" high crime areas with plainclothes police officers late at night. Between August and October of that year, police arrested 209 people for behaving "suspiciously," and beginning in 1959, they compiled "interrogation cards" for "suspicious persons" whom they stopped but did not officially arrest.[110]

Operation S's detectives frequently detained residents for transgressive gender or sexual behavior, including a local high school teacher for having sex in a Golden Gate Park restroom in 1957 and three women college students for wearing slacks in a bar in 1959.[111] When the *Saturday Evening Review* profiled San Francisco's "S Squad" in 1962, its reporter, Dean Jennings, cheerily detailed the arrest of a man in the Tenderloin for wearing women's clothing and noted that the arresting officers complained that "the town's full of homos lately, most of them from back east."[112]

"Operation S" also notably increased police harassment of nonwhite residents and interracial couples, eliciting protests from civil rights groups. In 1956, a fifteen-year-old African American boy contended that a policeman beat him "without provocation" for loitering on a playground in the predominantly black Potrero District. A few years later, a white woman complained to the American Civil Liberties Union (ACLU) that the police in North Beach had repeatedly harassed her and her black boyfriend.[113] In 1958, the *San Francisco Chronicle* reported that 55 percent of the 2,500 vagrancy arrests in the city in the previous year involved African Americans. Meanwhile, the ACLU alleged that the San Francisco police committed "lawless enforcement of the law" by effectively kidnapping civilians they suspected of drug use or soliciting sex in a public place, fingerprinting them, and then releasing them without a charge.[114]

These strategies complemented officials' larger goal to use urban renewal to "clean up" the city by spatially isolating sexual and racial minorities. Business elites had called for redevelopment after World War II, but their efforts lagged until the election of George Christopher, and the mayor looked to the federal government to meet his goal. In the same year that the California legislature created the Department of Alcoholic Beverage Control to police bars, Congress passed a law that enabled cities to use federal financing to redevelop, rehabilitate, or conserve neighborhoods in need on behalf of normative family life. This new legislation implicitly addressed juvenile delinquency and sexual deviancy by requiring cities to develop a "workable program" to replace slums and blight "with well-organized residential neighborhoods of decent homes and suitable living environment for adequate family life."[115]

Not unlike Federal Housing Administration (FHA) guidelines that privileged married borrowers, federal redevelopment programs reinforced sexual norms. Government guidelines required that local redevelopment agencies offer "families" forced out of their homes by renewal projects $200 to assist with moving costs, but they did not require any payments for "single people" similarly displaced. Since the government defined "families" as "two or more persons living together related by blood, marriage, or adoption," the federal government essentially incentivized city redevelopment authorities to push out unmarried people without children.[116] These guidelines further allowed the redevelopment agency to deny responsibility for relocating "transient" residents, or people who had not lived at their address for longer than ninety days.[117]

Christopher's decision to appoint Justin Herman, a former head of the San Francisco Office of the Housing and Home Financing Agency, to replace Weinberger set the stage for urban renewal in the city. In the late 1940s and early 1950s, San Francisco planners had formulated plans to tear down "slum-like" tenements with insufficient privacy in neighborhoods like the Western Addition and South of Market districts. At the same time, they hoped to use undeveloped land in Diamond Heights to build housing that might attract white middle-class married couples back to the city.[118] Shortly after assuming control of the San Francisco Redevelopment Agency (SFRA), Herman launched three new redevelopment projects on the Waterfront, South of Market, and Hunters Point. Although term limits forced Christopher out of City Hall in 1964, many of the plans formulated during his mayoralty later came to fruition under Herman. During his tenure at the SFRA, the amount of office space in downtown San Francisco doubled, and the number of low-income hotels in the city plummeted.[119]

The push for urban renewal under Christopher and Herman included many objectives, including easing the city's transition to a white-collar economy.[120] Yet competition with the suburbs also motivated the SFRA to tear down housing that attracted large numbers of transient workers living in "queer domesticity" and to build homes that they believed attracted white married, middle-class residents. San Francisco's authorities almost always targeted areas frequented by large numbers of unmarried adults. In their preliminary evaluations of the Western Addition district, the Redevelopment Agency declared that 2,100 "single people" and 2,680 "families" lived in the neighborhood. In 1952, the renewal authority noted that 30 percent of the families in the Western Addition moved every year, and it helped justify rebuilding it "to the fact that the area serves to a great degree as a reception area for many residents when they first come to San Francisco until better housing can be located."[121] In the wake of the disastrous 1960 census that revealed San Francisco's declining population, Arthur D. Little, Inc. counseled the mayor and Board of Supervisors to maintain the city's current level of "middle-income families with children" in order to avoid further decay of its central core and to use urban renewal to achieve that goal.[122]

Therefore, even as the Christopher administration deployed the police to sweep San Francisco's parks, streets, and bars, the SFRA pushed construction projects to neighborhoods populated by large numbers of single people of all races and both straight and queer communities of color. In 1958, the redevelopment agency bought up residential tracts in the predominantly black Western Addition neighborhood, and a year later, when the agency could not negotiate prices with owners fast enough, it used its powers of eminent domain to seize properties in the district.[123] In 1961, Palo Alto–based Eichler Homes broke ground on 122 apartments in the area, and two years later, the *San Francisco Examiner* reported that Herman and his allies had cleared close to seven hundred buildings there.[124] By the end of 1960, these projects had displaced over four thousand people, 20 percent of whom were "single" and almost 70 percent of whom were "nonwhite."[125]

A second, larger renewal initiative in the area in 1965 pushed out another 13,500 people, including many of those evicted by the first round of demolition in 1959. A study undertaken by the SFRA before the start of this project noted that its new target area included 63 percent of the African Americans living in the district and 76 percent of the Asian Americans. These groups made up the vast majority of the "families" evicted from the redevelopment zone, and the study noted that the much smaller number of white residents in the neighborhood was overwhelmingly unmarried and elderly. According to the report, 86 percent of the whites in the second redevelopment area were "single," and at least a third of them were over the age of sixty.[126]

Most of San Francisco's elites understood that the city's days as a shipping hub had ended, and they paired plans to expand the central business district with redevelopment of the port facilities along the Embarcadero. In 1959, the *Examiner* reported that demand for space downtown had put an end to the infamous "Barbary Coast" red-light district along Pacific Avenue between Montgomery and Kearny streets, as private developers bought up bars and strip clubs in "San Francisco's notorious sinkhole" and replaced them with showrooms for expensive household goods.[127] In that same year, Christopher and the Port Authority announced a dramatic renovation of the city's waterfront north of Market Street. As the harbor declined as a transportation hub, the mayor and his allies turned the area over to real estate developers in the 1960s who built "a unified complex of hotels, convention halls, sidewalk cafes, office buildings and other nonmaritime facilities" along the Embarcadero from the Ferry Building to the Marina District.[128]

Even as private firms bought up real estate near the waterfront, the city seized land at the base of Market Street in order to put together its "Golden Gateway" redevelopment project. Under Herman's direction, the SFRA hoped to ease the eastward expansion of the Montgomery Street central business district, and it planned to pair the Embarcadero Center, a combined office and hotel complex, with new luxury apartments on the edge of the Bay. The agency began acquiring sites in the area at the end of 1959, and in the following year, it invited proposals from architectural firms for skyscrapers in the redevelopment site. By 1963, the *Examiner* reported that the SFRA had cleared ninety-four buildings in the Golden Gateway Redevelopment Area. These construction projects displaced approximately 200 single men but only forced out two dozen "families" from the waterfront district.[129] A few years later, the redevelopment agency continued its push to expand the central business district south of Market Street. As early as 1958, with city approval, private developers began purchasing old hotels in the area, evicting their tenants, and putting up new office buildings in their place.[130]

A few years after Christopher left office, the SFRA greatly magnified this redevelopment downtown. Its plans for the South of Market area encompassed an 87-acre parcel of land between Market and Folsom streets, and they anchored scores of new office buildings with a convention center and hotel complex. Although the agency chose the site for its proximity to the Montgomery Street central business district, it also designated the area for demolition in order to displace the high number of poor, single men who lived there. As one executive later told the *San Francisco Examiner*, "You certainly can't expect us to put up a 50 million dollar building in an area where dirty old men will be going around exposing themselves to our secretaries."[131] A study of the South of Market area by the SFRA in the mid-1960s concluded that 94 percent of the residents in the area were unmarried and that 57 percent of them made less than $5,000 a year. Although the same study concluded that over 90 percent of the people living in the overall neighborhood were white, the smaller section marked for demolition by the SFRA included a majority of the area's residents of color.[132]

At each step, the SFRA not only targeted areas largely populated by the unmarried and nonwhites but also specifically tore down low-income hotels. Public officials had discouraged the construction of new residential hotels since World War II, and by the late 1950s, they turned their attention to eradicating the longstanding homes of some of San Francisco's poorest residents.[133] The eradication of these residences accompanied the larger state-sponsored project to eliminate spaces such as queer bars. As early as 1956, officials at the SFRA called for the power to "acquire and raze, one at a time, the ancient hotels and flophouses" in the South of Market district.[134] The expansion of the central business district razed several residential hotels, including the "Terminal Hotel" on the Embarcadero and the "Portuguese Hotel" on Clay Street. The redevelopment project directly forced out at least one gay bar, and by remaking the waterfront, it had helped deprive the remaining queer businesses in North Beach a substantial portion of their customer base.[135]

The redevelopment agency, meanwhile, assembled houses and apartments that it believed would appeal to white, middle-class married couples. In 1960, the *Examiner* promised that the SFRA in the Western Addition had "laid down conditions assuring that the apartments will appeal to families with children. There'll be good-sized rooms, play areas, landscaping, open spaces and similar amenities."[136] Most notably, the development of Diamond Heights unfolded rapidly in the early 1960s. Having successfully won the lawsuits that had mired its construction plans since the mid-1950s, the SFRA began selling lots for the building of single-family homes, apartments, and townhouses in 1961. In that same year, the agency awarded the Peninsula-based Eichler homes the winning bid for 216 sites in Diamond Heights, and it auctioned off three spaces for churches in the hilly neighborhood.[137]

Working in tandem, the upsurge in policing and redevelopment levied new penalties for San Franciscans who lived outside of marriage, particularly poorer residents in the city's residential hotels. Yet the two strategies proved only marginally effective at achieving their larger goals. In 1959, the *San Francisco Examiner* reported that "Operation S" had effectively lowered the local crime rate, and a year later, at the end of Christopher's first term, it celebrated that at least half of the city's gay bars faced the threat of losing their licenses.[138] In 1961, in the largest raid of the Christopher era, the police arrested 103 patrons at the Tay-Bush Inn, a bar near the downtown financial district. These raids, however, failed to limit the number or visibility of the city's queer commerce. In 1965, San Francisco boasted as many gay bars as it had in 1960. Even though many residents resented their openly queer neighbors, the Christopher administration's policing strategy proved insufficient to wipe out San Francisco's gay, lesbian, bisexual, and transgender-related businesses. In 1963, the Mattachine Society derided the mayor's strategy, calling the efforts of the ABC and city detectives "a game of musical chairs."[139]

The aggressive police tactics motivated gay bar owners, the ACLU, and civil rights groups to contest the city's policies in court. The revelations that undercover detectives had solicited payoffs from gay bars in exchange for protection further damaged the Christopher administration's credibility. In 1960, a grand jury indicted seven detectives for extorting bribes from bar owners in the Tenderloin and along the Waterfront. The so-called gayola scandal that year not only underscored the inability of the Christopher administration to enforce its crackdown across the city but also suggested that relying on undercover officers worked against the overall goal of trying to close gay bars. This strategy empowered corrupt detectives who then solicited kickbacks, effectively shielding queer businesses from prosecution.[140]

At the same time, the SFRA's demolitions created a housing crisis for the poor. Most people forced out of the residential hotels around downtown also confronted discrimination in the Bay Area's wider real estate markets. Federal officials later condemned the redevelopment agency for its particularly lax assistance to people displaced by renewal projects. A review of the SFRA's work in the Western Addition District by the federal Comptroller General's Office (CGO) in 1959 concluded that local authorities had failed to assist families displaced by redevelopment to find adequate housing. CGO officials reported that the SFRA had given inaccurate statements about the relocations of people in the Western Addition, and it contended that substantial families pushed out of the area had relocated into nearby, substandard buildings.[141]

A year later, the Bay Area Council concluded that nonwhite residents pushed out of the district frequently relocated to areas very close to their old homes, with at least half of them staying within the Western Addition.

The regional business group noted that over 80 percent of all people pushed out by redevelopment in the Western Addition paid more for their apartments following their displacement and that unmarried people, particularly the elderly, disproportionately bore the brunt of these increases. The group's study concluded that whereas "single" people in the district had paid approximately 19 percent of their incomes for rent before renewal, they spent on average over half of their yearly pay for shelter after their relocation.[142]

Despite lawsuits brought by tenant groups, the SFRA went ahead with demolition. The agency's unwillingness to replace the low-cost hotels and apartments left a growing pool of largely unmarried and nonwhite residents in the city without shelter. If restrictions on suburban housing had pushed the renters at the bottom of the Bay Area's housing market into older cities, redevelopment further concentrated them in specific neighborhoods. In 1963, an assessment provided by the SFRA's own consulting firm pointed out the growing gap between San Francisco's population and its housing supply. "Undoubtedly, there is a strong general demand for low rent housing for single persons in San Francisco. The 1960 census shows there were about 124,400 primary individuals (those living alone or with non-relatives) in the city. . . . On the other hand the supply of low rent units has been diminishing."[143] The report later noted that the contraction of low-cost apartments alongside the upsurge in demand of unmarried people, particularly from the young and elderly, was pushing up rents among the few remaining residential hotels in the city. When landlords raised the rents in the Tenderloin near downtown, many of the city's residents most in need of low-income housing suddenly found themselves unable to afford their units.[144]

These difficulties reveal the metropolitan dimensions of the problem for city officials. Despite Christopher's efforts, many middle-class married couples had already left the city. Suburbs' ability to restrict sex- and alcohol-related businesses incentivized entrepreneurs in older urban neighborhoods to open bars, nightclubs, brothels, or pornographic movie theaters that catered to people from the entire metropolis. No purely local strategy could reverse a decades-long trend set in motion by the redistribution of resources by the federal government and by suburban zoning. No local effort ultimately could transform San Francisco into anything resembling the "family-friendly" communities of the Peninsula and South Bay.

By the end of the 1960s, the housing shortage in the neighborhoods around downtown represented the most significant consequence of San Francisco's decade-long redevelopment processes. A 1969 study conducted by a liberal advocacy group blamed the SFRA for all but completely eliminating affordable rentals in the city. It concluded, "San Francisco's housing crisis is not an accident" because "the city's own public actions, which should have ameliorated the problems have instead greatly exacerbated the crisis."[145] The authors declared that the SFRA had destroyed five thousand more low-income units than it had produced and that affordable apartments in San Francisco had a vacancy rate of zero percent. Despite the SFRA's assurances that tenants could find housing if they looked for it, the task force alleged that the vacancy rate for residential hotels was actually lower than that for individual apartments in the rental market. "Constant pressure on the poor, the elderly, racial minorities has not dispersed San Francisco's 'unwanted citizens' to other communities," they declared. "Its effect has been rather to force overcrowding in previously viable areas and create situations in which it is in the economic interests of owners to charge high rents and not maintain rents."[146]

Although the police had failed to substantially stem the number of gay bars in San Francisco, the combination of their crackdown with the physical remaking of large portions of the urban core pushed queer sites farther into the city. By the end of the 1960s, gay bars relocated to neighborhoods in the central part of San Francisco, and their move to new areas reflected a growing class divide. On one hand, a number of queer, "dive" bars followed many of the people displaced by urban renewal projects and opened in the increasingly crowded Tenderloin District. On the other hand, a number of businesses set up shop just up the hill from the Tenderloin in the area that would eventually become the "Castro District." As early as 1963, gay bars, such as the Missouri Mule, opened on the upper end of Market Street as many of the older Irish Catholic residents moved out to the suburbs. By the mid-1960s, the two neighborhoods stretched less than a mile from one another along Market Street but represented two divergent branches of queer life in San Francisco.

This class divide would play out in subsequent debates over gay rights in the city. As poorer residents, who sometimes engaged in sex work and deviated from family norms, increasingly migrated to the Tenderloin District in the Central City, growing numbers of gay professionals pushed for the repeal of California's sodomy laws and for a universal "right to privacy."

Although, in theory, this right protected all people, it largely benefited gay residents who most closely conformed to middle-class gender and sexual norms. "Privacy" not only required tolerance from people who had trouble seeing queer people as their equals but also required a place to live. As the housing crisis in San Francisco deepened and gay politics took on an increasingly organized form, therefore, "privacy" emerged as a contested discourse that closely followed class lines among queer residents.

PART III

The Era of Sexual Privacy

Chapter 6

Gay Privacy Politics

Dianne Feinstein's address to the Society for Individual Rights (SIR) in May 1971 elicited both hope and anxiety from the audience. President of the San Francisco Board of Supervisors, Feinstein spoke to city's largest gay organization in an effort to invigorate her run for mayor that year. As she campaigned, Feinstein staked out a middle ground on homosexuality that she hoped would attract gay voters without alienating the rest of the electorate. She promised that, if elected, she would protect "the private morality of San Franciscans." Yet she also condemned pornography, prostitution, and "homosexual cruising" because they "de-sensitized" young people to sex and made "mainstream" acceptance of gay relationships more difficult. Feinstein's words reassured many SIR members who wanted a candidate that supported decriminalizing private consensual sex between adults, including homosexual ones, but her speech also split the larger queer community. After her remarks, some middle-class, largely white, and gender-conforming gay men, in particular, complained about San Franciscans who sold sex for a living or dressed in drag. One male columnist in the *Bay Area Reporter* who wore women's clothes "on occasion" nevertheless criticized queens who made "silly public displays" and encouraged readers to "do something for (as Diane called it) the Main Stream [*sic*]." Another man wrote a scathing letter to the *Reporter* two weeks later, deploring "swishy queens," "Tenderloin prostitutes," and "undesirable little shits who carry on in public."[1]

Queer migrants to San Francisco in the 1960s found a city devastated by suburbanization and increasingly segmented by race, marital status, class, and gender identity. Housing markets concentrated lesbian, gay, bisexual, and transgender (LGBT) people in urban centers, but they also divided them. Middle-class whites who largely adhered to gender norms enjoyed a privileged standing in the city's real estate market, regardless of their marital status. They selected from a relatively large number of apartment options, and they often could afford homes with relatively private bedrooms. By contrast, housing and employment discrimination frequently confined poorer queer residents, including many people of color, to the city's growing red-light district. Drag queens, young runaways, transgender people, and most other people who could not conform to middle-class notions of respectability often lived in crowded residential hotels or on the streets of the Tenderloin. Unlike wealthier gay residents, these San Franciscans sometimes engaged in sex work and even lacked shelter altogether.

These divisions surfaced in the late 1960s and early 1970s when liberals like Feinstein and federal and state courts gradually recognized a sexual "right to privacy" for all Americans. Gay activists in cities such as San Francisco used arguments about sexual privacy to successfully challenge some of the most repressive elements of the postwar Straight State. Judges and policymakers limited the ability of police or employers to arrest or dismiss people for sex that took place behind closed doors. Yet privacy also foreclosed more radical challenges. Activists who used it succeeded in part because they engaged the Straight State on its own terms, which had made bedroom privacy a basic expectation of the nation's middle class. For more than a decade, liberal organizations such as the American Law Institute had argued that police could not enforce restrictions on sex behind closed doors. These arguments appealed to straight-identified elites in the 1960s who supported reforming but not overturning the sexual order. Gay activists in this era always paired calls for privacy with larger demands for respect, and they never spoke about it alone. Yet elites like Feinstein who controlled the levers of power defined the discourse narrowly. In their view, the right to privacy limited the state's ability to police citizens' sexuality, but it did not affirm homosexual relationships as equal to heterosexual ones.

Consequently, arguments about privacy split LGBT communities along class, gender, and ideological lines. Poorer and gender-variant activists in places like the Tenderloin often agreed with the need for a right to privacy in principle, but they clashed with their middle-class counterparts over its importance. Since many of them lacked private bedrooms or positions in the official labor market, they frequently argued that privacy did little to end queer poverty. Without better housing or employment, the principle failed to bring services or resources to the red-light district. At the same time, other activists, including those in the Committee for Homosexual Freedom (CHF), argued that privacy stopped short of true liberation. Without public recognition of gay or queer equality, they argued, people still needed to conceal relationships that differed from accepted norms. Appropriating the middle-class moral geography of the city, these radicals argued that the "street" was a fundamentally democratic space and that the nation's "homes, schools, and churches" only reinforced sexual hierarchies and shame. Lesbian feminists, in particular, critiqued the ways that privacy reinforced the notion that the home existed outside the purview of the government. They argued that women often struggled to access public resources and faced violence within the home precisely because they allegedly lived in a "private" realm free of the state and market.

By the early 1970s, therefore, many activists felt ambivalent about the right to privacy. Many celebrated the willingness of some policymakers, voters, and judges to decriminalize homosexuality. However, many also saw "privacy" as an extension of the "closet." Too often, they claimed, liberals like Feinstein shared the views of conservatives that same-sex relationships needed to be hidden. Many activists pushed back against this double standard by insisting that queer people needed to speak openly about their sexual relationships, just like other Americans. By the early 1970s, LGBT residents increasingly paired calls for the protections of the "right to privacy" with the need to "come out of the closet." Yet divisions among queer people never completely vanished. Privacy offered middle-class gay men and lesbians too attractive an opportunity to ignore, but compromises with officials like Feinstein guaranteed a reformation of the existing order, not a revolution, and left poorer or nonconforming citizens on the margins.

Privacy and the Divided Housing Market

Differences among queer activists about the "right to privacy" emerged, in part, thanks to the class stratification of LGBT residents in San Francisco. During the 1960s, cities across the country emerged as hubs for queer life, and tens of thousands of people experiencing homoerotic desires transformed urban neighborhoods decimated by suburbanization and redevelopment. Metropolitan growth had pulled many married, white residents away from the areas north and west of San Francisco's downtown, in particular, and during the 1960s, many middle-class, white gay men replaced some of the long-time inhabitants of those neighborhoods. At the same time, redevelopment helped turn the Tenderloin into the city's most notorious red-light district, largely inhabited by queer runaways, transgender people, and senior citizens. No issue highlighted the differences between these neighborhoods more than privacy. Even as activists cast legal and political arguments about the issue, San Francisco's housing market offered residents varying degrees of residential seclusion and personal space. While many middle-class gay men and lesbians enjoyed relative privacy, Tenderloin inhabitants often shared bedrooms, slept on the street, or lived in studios with decrepit, thin walls.

This stratification occurred thanks to the rising number of self-identified gay men, lesbians, and bisexual and transgender people living in the city. Similar to World War II, the Vietnam War's escalation in the mid-1960s sparked migrations to urban centers, particularly the Bay Area. The architects of the draft designed psychiatric evaluations to exclude men they suspected of homosexuality, and although they obviously never actually excluded all gay men, the conscription process prompted many soldiers to later self-identify as "gay."[2] After induction, military personnel risked discovery and, thanks to the Bay Area's role as an embarkation point for Vietnam, many soldiers and sailors discharged from the armed forces stayed in San Francisco. One study estimated that all branches of the military discharged approximately two to three thousand personnel per year for homosexuality nationwide in the 1960s.[3] It's not clear how many queer soldiers and sailors stayed in San Francisco in particular, but given the fact that many service personnel moved to California after World War II—gay or otherwise—it is likely that the war caused significant numbers of gay men and lesbians to move to the Bay Area in the 1960s.

Even as the military discharged men experiencing queer desires in San Francisco, the national media helped bring more LGBT people to major cities. In the mid-1960s, mainstream magazines published numerous exposés of gay life in the United States, and all of them invariably stressed their urban nature. A writer in *Life* declared that homosexuality "exists all over the U.S. . . . but it is most evident in New York, Chicago, Los Angeles, San Francisco, New Orleans and Miami."[4] *Time* agreed, calling homosexuality "more in evidence in the U.S. than ever before" and a "highly visible presence in cities," including San Francisco, which *Time* called the "capital of the gay world."[5] Most of these articles portrayed homosexuality as an illness and stereotyped gay life, yet many readers experiencing queer desires around the country nevertheless read them and opted to move to places like San Francisco.[6] Census data further hinted at the ways in which queer newcomers transformed San Francisco. Between 1960 and 1970, the federal government recorded a 13 percent drop in the number of "husband-wife households" in San Francisco, and fewer than 50 percent of households in the city included "married couples in 1970."[7]

Queer newcomers, therefore, entered a real estate market upended by suburban growth, and their housing prospects often hinged on their race, class, and ability to conform to middle-class gender norms. Landlords, realtors, and homeowners frequently looked at a pool of renters and buyers who were disproportionately poor, black, and unmarried. Between 1960 and 1970, San Francisco's white population fell by 10 percent while the number of "families"—which the census defined as people tied by "blood, marriage, or adoption"—fell by twenty thousand.[8] In this context, employed white men who generally adhered to gender norms, including unmarried ones, sat near the top of San Francisco's rental and real estate hierarchies in the late 1960s. If it meant a steady income or maintaining the city's many color lines, many owners and landlords looked the other way if two white men wanted to share a home.[9]

This process was most visible in the Eureka Valley district west of downtown. Over the course of the 1950s and 1960s, the area near Market and Castro streets lost many of its predominantly working-class, white married couples to the suburbs. Mary Ragison O'Shea, a former Eureka Valley resident, recalled that during the 1950s and 1960s, most of her friends, family, and neighbors took advantage of the G.I. Bill and moved to the suburbs. "My sisters, as they got married," she recalled, "they all followed. It was what was happening, and . . . everybody was buying homes."[10] Sharon Johnson, another former resident, similarly remembered that she and her husband moved to the Peninsula in 1966 because she believed that the suburbs offered a better community for young families: "As a young married person with our first child . . . there was no way to live in San Francisco."[11]

In the late 1960s and early 1970s, many white gay professionals slowly replaced long-time residents like Johnson and invested in San Francisco's aging Victorians. Obviously not all gay men renovated old homes, yet enough of them did so to prompt a writer in the gay magazine *Vector* to brag that "real estate people in this area . . . know that when two queens buy a new home it's going to be done up just right."[12] A cohort of white gay men encountered a Eureka Valley real estate market in flux, as suburbanization caused many current residents to worry about an influx of

African Americans from the nearby Western Addition.[13] Beginning in the mid- to late 1960s, therefore, Eureka Valley banks often lent money to white gay men seeking to fix up housing in the area while realtors near the intersection of Castro and Market streets carried advertisements for rentals in the district in magazines directed at middle-class white gay men.[14]

This did not mean that gay residents faced no discrimination. Gay professionals, no matter their race, in fact, confronted prejudice largely unknown to their straight counterparts. Biased lending made it more difficult for openly gay men and lesbians to buy homes, and by the 1970s, one of the most important characteristics of gay neighborhoods was the high proportion of renters.[15] More dramatically, gay people faced hostility from older residents. The influx of gay men into Eureka Valley led to panic selling and retaliatory violence reminiscent of the animosity that whites directed at new black residents in the 1950s and 1960s. One anxious Eureka Valley resident saw the neighborhood change and told his wife, "Our house is for sale! We're selling this house. I don't want our kids raised here anymore."[16] In 1961, three local teenagers beat a gay man and killed him by pushing him under a moving trolley.[17]

Just as redevelopers could not stop the outward migration of married, white couples to the suburbs, older residents could not halt the influx of gay professionals to their neighborhood. The first gay bar opened in the area in 1963, and as urban renewal remade the waterfront, large numbers of gay men flocked to Eureka Valley. Between 1960 and 1970, the number of "husband-wife" households in the census tracts near Castro and Market streets declined by a thousand, dipping from over 50 percent of occupied units in the area to just over a third of them.[18] Although the area remained largely white in the 1960s, the number of residents with college degrees doubled, moving from under 20 percent to almost 40 percent by 1970.[19]

By the 1970s, the area—now renamed "the Castro"—was one of the best-known middle-class gay neighborhoods in San Francisco, but it was just one relatively affluent district among many. Middle-class gay men and lesbians lived throughout the city, not just in one neighborhood. The 1970 census reported at least fifty-one tracts in San Francisco in which over 20 percent of the inhabitants lived with people not related to them by blood, marriage, or adoption, and these tracts cut a wide crescent around the financial district. They included the Castro but also gentrifying areas like the Haight-Ashbury and Hayes Valley and traditionally wealthy neighborhoods like Russian Hill, Pacific Heights, and Nob Hill. Gay periodicals advertised rentals in many of these areas, and a map of "places where gays gather" in the late 1960s and early 1970s put together by urbanist Manual Castells highlighted businesses across San Francisco.[20] Activist Gale Whittington remembered that many gay men in the 1960s referred to Nob Hill as "Snob Hill," and although redevelopment had disrupted queer life in North Beach, gay periodicals celebrated the "return" of the neighborhood's nightlife near the end of the decade.[21]

The history of many white, middle-class queer women, in particular, underscores the importance of looking beyond just the boundaries of the Castro. Many lesbians, including Daughters of Bilitis (DOB) cofounder Del Martin, had previously been married, and in some cases, they were the primary caretakers of their children. A survey conducted by the DOB in the early 1970s found that about one-third of its members had children.[22] As a result, a significant number of the group's members lived discrete lives in areas traditionally associated with married couples and their families. Although it is difficult to find traces of all of these women in the historical record, a small sample of addresses in the DOB newsletter reveals that several members lived away from downtown. Some were divorced or widowed, and the telephone directory listed them at addresses that they had once shared with their husbands. Some of the group's monthly coffee klatches, or "Gab 'n Javas," took place west of the Twin Peaks.[23]

At the same time, many younger queer women lived and socialized in areas closer to downtown. Most lesbian bars, like their male counterparts, migrated away from the waterfront after urban renewal and settled in neighborhoods west of downtown.[24] Like Eureka Valley, the Haight-Ashbury District lost many white, married residents to the suburbs, and during the 1960s, large numbers of young people rented apartments in the Victorians surrounding Golden Gate Park. The best known of those migrants were the hippies who celebrated the Summer of Love in 1967, and the counterculture attracted significant numbers of queer men and women.[25]

Middle-class to affluent gay men and lesbians may have lived in different places in San Francisco in the late 1960s and early 1970s, but in almost every area, they enjoyed relatively high amounts of privacy. No urban apartment rivaled suburban homes in terms of the seclusion it offered inhabitants, yet middle-class and affluent city dwellers nevertheless enjoyed varying degrees of personal space unknown to their poorer counterparts. *Vector*'s classifieds often contained few words, but many of them promised would-be renters "complete privacy."[26] Apartments in San Francisco's affluent neighborhoods often predated Federal Housing Administration (FHA) guidelines, yet they often offered tenants secluded bathrooms and bedrooms, which were once the privilege of the well-to-do of the early twentieth century.[27]

Even more important, apartment builders across the country underwent a minor revolution in soundproofing and acoustical design in the 1960s. In 1964, the FHA began including "noise control" recommendations in its "Minimum Property Standards" for multifamily housing and funded research on wall and floor insulation.[28] Architectural magazines from the era claimed that developers who concentrated on acoustical privacy had an important advantage over their competitors in the real estate market.[29] Even builders renovating older homes focused on privacy. Historic buildings offered less flexibility than newer ones, yet like suburban developers, rehabilitation manuals recommended grouping bedrooms near one another for "privacy and quiet." One guide encouraged owners to keep one bedroom wall free from windows to increase privacy and to add closets between rooms for insulation.[30] Federal guidelines on rehabilitation in 1968 conceded that owners often could not redo an entire structure, but they nevertheless recommended, "A degree of privacy shall be provided commensurate with suitable living conditions by means of the proper location of exterior openings . . . and by the interior arrangement of rooms."[31]

This level of seclusion, although far from absolute, distinguished most middle-class dwellings from almost all Tenderloin residences. Suburbanization and urban renewal helped turn San Francisco's red-light district into one of the poorest neighborhoods in the city, and in the mid-1960s, growing numbers of low-income queer and transgender residents made their homes there.[32] Although the area remained largely white, the number of people of color in the Tenderloin increased substantially between 1960 and 1970, and many of residents lived in old hotels or slept in the neighborhood's alleys and sidewalks.[33] A study of the district in the 1970s remarked that the area had "become the dumping ground for those displaced by urban renewal in the Western Addition and Yerba Buena." A slate of teenage "runaways," "draft dodgers," and poor people pushed out of other neighborhoods by rising housing prices had poured into the Tenderloin and "rented the old resort hotels, now infested with rats, piled high with garbage, ventilated by broken windows and plagued with faulty plumbing."[34]

Figure 10. Young people gather on the street in the Tenderloin, 1969. San Francisco History Center, San Francisco Public Library.

Commercial sex flourished in this neighborhood. The Tenderloin had served as a vice district since the nineteenth century, but urban renewal reshaped and expanded its sexual economy in a number of crucial ways. When the San Francisco Redevelopment Agency remade the waterfront, it pushed many working-class bars deeper into the city. By the early 1960s, the Tenderloin had emerged as one of the only remaining neighborhoods in San Francisco with a high concentration of low-end dives and nightclubs.[35] These bars supported many kinds of erotic commerce, which along with the drug trade provided some of the only stable employment for many residents. Activists working in the neighborhood in 1967 estimated that in the fourteen-block area encompassing Ellis, Market, Leavenworth, and Powell streets, 14 percent of all people between the ages of twelve and twenty-eight sold sex to make a living.[36]

Patrons of these businesses came from across the metropolis. The area's proximity to a newly created highway exit reoriented the city's queer businesses away from the waterfront. In 1966, the *San Francisco Chronicle* suggested that the district's high number of hotels and proximity to the freeway had changed the nature of how prostitutes plied their trade: "The girls, searching for clients, no longer simply walk the streets. They stand in the doorways of hotels and cafes, and solicit auto drivers who stop for red lights."[37] The completion of the interstate at the base of Market Street, in particular, gave suburban consumers easy access to the neighborhood. A study of pornography in San Francisco in 1970 reported that adult movie theaters structured film showings around the schedules of downtown commuters, and it concluded that the most frequent patrons of sexually explicit cinemas, bookstores, and arcades were male, married, white-collar professionals between the ages of twenty-six and forty-five.[38]

This concentrated zone of sex and poverty drew significant attention from law enforcement authorities. In 1965, the police temporarily closed down the Chukker Club, a bar that attracted black and white patrons and was popular with a large number of transgender people, sex workers, and drag queens. In one night, authorities forced out two hundred patrons and arrested fifty-six of them for disorderly conduct and for "impersonating women."[39] In 1966, the police swept through the neighborhood detaining more than a hundred sex workers, including several transgender residents.[40] These raids, however, only hinted at the level of police involvement in the neighborhood. As historian Susan Stryker has demonstrated, during the 1960s, San Francisco police not only used extralegal violence to control people living in the red-light district, but some of them also extorted sex workers and collected payments in exchange for providing safety.[41]

Yet perhaps the most salient characteristic of the Tenderloin was the relative lack of bedroom privacy available to most residents. Rental discrimination helped crowd apartments and residential hotels in the district. Census takers in 1970 found that the area had one of the highest ratios of people per room in the city.[42] Amanda St. James, a longtime Tenderloin resident, remembered transgender sex workers sharing rooms with one another in the hotels along Turk Street in the 1960s to save money. “We had no other place to go,” she recalled. “Other hotels wouldn’t rent to queens.”[43] Another set of demographers, looking at the neighborhood in the 1970s, further observed a “sizable population of street and alley dwellers” whose homelessness made them largely invisible to the official census.[44]

Segregation by race, class, and gender variance in San Francisco’s housing market, therefore, not only meant that LGBT residents lived in different neighborhoods but also meant that they enjoyed varying degrees of privacy. Although all queer people faced discrimination, they often faced varying degrees of persecution, and those differences translated into unequal opportunities for resources like employment and shelter. Middle-class gay neighborhoods like the Castro and red-light districts like the Tenderloin emerged in tandem, both products of postwar housing policies, economic opportunity, and rental discrimination. Simultaneously, San Francisco residents enjoyed different levels of privacy. Like neighborhood amenities or parking, sound and visual insulation were commodities in city housing markets. While urban townhouses or apartments never rivaled suburban homes in terms of privacy, they nevertheless gave middle-class to affluent San Franciscans relative freedom to behave as they saw fit in their bedrooms. Many poorer residents, by contrast, enjoyed very little privacy at home or lacked places to live altogether.

Privacy, Sex, and the Law

The growth of places like the Tenderloin and the Castro unfolded amid an important legal and political shift around sex and the state. In the 1960s, state and federal courts supported the decriminalization of most kinds of consensual sex acts between adults, based on the idea that Americans possessed a right to privacy. Their rulings, however, did not signal a new era of equality for gay rights advocates. Instead, court decisions in the mid-1960s to early 1970s redefined the boundaries of the closet, permitting some acts behind closed doors even as judges affirmed the value of marriage. The courts effectively created a new legal middle ground that distinguished previously illegal but consensual acts like the possession of pornography or gay sex from coercive ones like rape but also drew a line between these acts and heterosexual marriage.

These legal reforms emerged, in part, thanks to the work of liberal lawyers in the 1950s and early 1960s. Since they had first pushed for the decriminalization of most private consensual sex acts between adults in 1955, groups like the American Law Institute (ALI) had slowly built a proreform consensus among attorneys on the political left. The American Civil Liberties Union (ACLU) emerged as one of the most notable advocates for a sexual right to privacy, particularly when it came to birth control and pornography. Like many members of the ALI, most lawyers at the ACLU equivocated on whether or not to include homosexuality in their work, and as late as 1965, the group failed to argue that private same-sex relationships needed the same protections as married heterosexual ones. Gay organizations, like the Daughters of Bilitis and the Mattachine Society, however, still saw the ACLU as an important ally. Throughout the late 1950s and early 1960s, gay men and lesbians frequently lobbied the civil liberties group to take on cases involving homosexuality and pushed for sodomy's decriminalization.[45]

Although ACLU lawyers initially avoided the question of gay rights, advocates for legal reform nevertheless felt optimistic in the early to mid-1960s. American lawyers looked on with great interest when British jurists issued a called for the decriminalization of all sex acts between consenting adults in private in 1957, and in 1961, Illinois became the first state to adopt the ALI's "Model Penal Code."[46] Furthermore, the U.S. Supreme Court hinted that it might consider the constitutionality of a right to privacy in 1961. The Court dismissed a case involving birth control that year on a technicality, but in a pathbreaking dissent, four justices endorsed conditional support for arguments legalizing contraceptives based on privacy.[47] These events emboldened liberals in the media. ACLU lawyer Harriet Pilpel called most of the nation's sex laws "archaic and inhumane" in *Harper's* in 1965 because they encroached "on the privacy of our bedrooms."[48] Even *Time* magazine conceded in 1966 that the "most telling argument" for repealing bans on queer sex "is that the present statutes are unenforceable as long as the homosexual acts are performed in private."[49]

Feminist claims about contraception and abortion similarly built support for legal reforms based around notions of "privacy." During the 1960s, a coalition of liberal doctors and women's rights activists fought to liberalize California's laws governing abortion. They laid out multiple arguments about why the state should eliminate prohibitions against the medical practice, including population control, the elimination of poverty, and women's rights to control their bodies. They also, however, frequently spoke about the "zone of personal privacy," which freed a woman to make choices about her body in consultation with her doctor free of government interference.[50] In 1966, San Francisco activists tested California's restrictive abortion laws with acts of civil disobedience. As she passed out handbills on the city streets about how to obtain an abortion, Patricia McGinnis declared, "The most gross invasion of privacy is the use of police surveillance to control what should be a private matter between a woman and her physician."[51]

These arguments set the stage for the success of privacy-related arguments in state and federal judiciaries in the second half of the 1960s. Most famously, the U.S. Supreme Court ruled in *Griswold v. Connecticut* that the Fourth and Fifth Amendments to the Constitution protected married couples from unlawful searches from states looking to deny them the use of birth control. The majority opinion in *Griswold* rhetorically asked, "Would we allow the police to search the sacred precincts of marital bedrooms for telltale signs of the use of contraceptives? The very idea is repulsive to the notions of privacy surrounding the marriage relationship."[52] The *Griswold* case set an important precedent for other rulings at the national and state levels that affirmed Americans' right to sexual privacy. In 1969, for example, the U.S. Supreme Court ruled that police could not arrest individuals for possessing pornography in their homes, and in that same year, the California Supreme Court ruled that the right to privacy protected homosexual schoolteachers.[53]

For groups like the ACLU, which helped file *Griswold*, these decisions represented remarkable achievements. Yet even as they won in state and federal courts, arguments about privacy still faced numerous obstacles. Laws against sodomy remained on the books in most states throughout the 1960s, and many officials insisted that governments needed to prescribe the sexual morality of their citizens.[54] Even judges who supported the right to privacy often interpreted it narrowly. Decriminalization did not mean that the courts or liberal advocates for privacy saw all sex equally. Privacy arguments affirmed the importance of marriage while denigrating most sex acts that took place outside of it.[55]

Evidence of the legal system's support for heterosexual marriage abounded in many of the major decisions of the era, which frequently focused narrowly on the role of the police. As evidenced in the Supreme Court's emphasis on the "marriage relationship" in *Griswold*, many rulings on privacy limited the state's power specifically because justices believed enforcing laws against contraceptives violated the higher law of marriage, not because they believed Americans had an unfettered right to use their bodies as they pleased. Just two years after *Griswold*, the Supreme Court used the right to privacy, in part, to overturn Virginia's ban on interracial unions, calling marriage "one of the 'basic civil rights of man,' fundamental to his existence and survival."[56] It took the Court seven years to decriminalize contraceptives for unmarried people, and in the case *Eisenstadt v. Baird*, several of the justices who wrote the majority opinion reaffirmed the importance of marriage. They argued that doctors and pharmacists might not know if patients were married, and therefore, laws prohibiting birth control for single people unintentionally discriminated against married people.[57]

Courts, therefore, distinguished between limiting the government and affirming homosexuality or pornography. The California Supreme Court, for example, declared in a ruling on gay teachers, "We do not, of course, hold that homosexuals must be permitted to teach in the public schools." Instead, the justices merely required that the State Board of Education prove that an individual was "unfit" to teach while not impairing his "right to live his private life."[58] In these examples, "privacy" extended the closet by separating relationships and acts expressed in secret from those that bore the state's approval. Unlike normative marriage, according to the courts, gay relationships or the use of pornography did not represent self-evident goods that deserved the wider protection of the state. They merely did not constitute problems so severe that they warranted an expansive police apparatus to monitor citizens behind closed doors.

Privacy, Sex, and Politics

These rulings around privacy occurred in a period of newly assertive gay and lesbian political action. San Francisco and New York City witnessed the biggest surges in activism, but the movement for gay rights exploded nationwide, particularly in urban areas. For almost a decade, authorities had tried to root out evidence of queer life in large and small cities. While police raids and redevelopment failed to keep white married couples in urban centers, they ultimately sparked organized resistance from LGBT people. In the mid-1960s, activists across the country slowly replaced the more cautious homophile organizations with newly assertive ones designed to more directly confront queer people's oppression. The founders of these groups drew inspiration, in part, from other social movements. Gay men and lesbians participated in the black freedom struggle, antiwar movement, and second-wave feminism, and even those who watched from afar hoped to use some combination of sit-ins, voting drives, lawsuits, boycotts, and marches to win rights for "the homosexual." By the end of the 1960s, gay men and lesbians challenged their marginalization in almost every arena of public life, including the workplace, housing, medicine, religion, the law, and electoral politics.[59]

This organizing unfolded at the same time as court decisions like *Griswold*, and numerous activists hoped to take advantage of the new protections seemingly offered by a sexual right to privacy. Organizations like the Mattachine Society had long supported reforms like the Model Penal Code, but the rising tide of support for privacy from liberals and the court decisions made them especially hopeful. Writers in the *Mattachine Review* optimistically predicted an end to "Victorian prudery" and that "case after case will test the legality of private acts among consenting adults."[60] In 1966, homophiles across the United States adopted a resolution declaring, "Laws against homosexual conduct between consenting adults in private should be removed from the criminal codes."[61]

This enthusiasm was not unfounded. Growing support for the right to privacy handed LGBT activists an important tool with which to combat the most oppressive elements of economic discrimination and the Straight State. Yet the histories of two San Francisco organizations illustrate both the power and limits of privacy as a discourse for social justice. The Council on Religion and the Homosexual (CRH) and the Society for Individual Rights (SIR) emerged at approximately the same time, shared many members, and pursued similar goals. Both grew out of the postwar migration of LGBT people to San Francisco and worked in a city reshaped by suburbanization. Both made legal arguments about sexual privacy and used the discourse to educate straight-identified audiences about the fundamental unfairness of discrimination against lesbians and gay men. Yet they also never spoke about privacy alone. The CRH and SIR saw their work as a part of a larger project to win same-sex relationships the respect that society bestowed on straight ones and to materially improve the lives of lesbians and gay men. However, they faced more difficulty in accomplishing these other projects than the ones that relied on privacy alone. Activists interested in changing the material conditions of queer people in San Francisco struggled to convince the wider public that they deserved affirmative gestures from the state. Whether sex education or housing or medical care, advocates for LGBT equality frequently faced stiff resistance to their attempts to create programs that went beyond the narrowest understanding of sexual privacy.

The first organization, the Council on Religion and the Homosexual, emerged out of an alliance between the homophile movement and liberal Protestants at one of the largest churches in San Francisco. The Glide Methodist Church was founded in the late nineteenth century in the Tenderloin, and in the 1950s, it had drawn close to one thousand people to Sunday services, most of whom were white, middle-class married couples with children. But suburbanization had decimated its congregation, and young queer people now literally slept on its doorstep. Urban congregations across the country faced problems similar to Glide, but the Tenderloin church possessed a unique philanthropic wing that allowed it to experiment with new kinds of social outreach. In the early 1960s, the Glide Foundation invited several young ministers from across the country to move to San Francisco and to find new ways to connect the church with the surrounding city. The black freedom struggle had inspired many of these pastors, and they hoped to make liberal Protestantism responsive to the needs of the urban poor, particularly young people.[62]

These ministers came to San Francisco as a part of a paternalistic mission to bring Christianity to young people living around downtown. Yet they soon found themselves radicalized. Reverend Ted McIlvenna, a former church marriage counselor, recalled that soon after he arrived in San Francisco, the Mattachine Society asked him to help a gay teenager beaten by the police in the Tenderloin. All the ministers found this abuse appalling, and the homophiles hoped that sympathetic clergy would give them partners capable of speaking to mainstream institutions free of sexual stigma.[63] In 1964, McIlvenna, Del Martin, Phyllis Lyon, and other ministers and homophiles organized a retreat outside San Francisco to discuss the church and homosexuality. The CRH grew out of this meeting, and the new organization promised to promote tolerance for gay men and lesbians and to start a "continuing dialogue" with churches about the broad "spectrum of human sexuality."[64] Whereas some of the ministers had once thought of themselves as missionaries reforming the city streets with Christian morality, by the mid-1960s, they considered themselves church reformers, rebuilding the church so that it spoke to needs of the people of the street. McIlvenna argued in 1965 that if Protestants seriously intended to follow Christ's teachings, they would need to "recognize" that the "originating impulse for urban Christianity must come from city persons" who will invigorate the church with their own "cultural expressions."[65]

The Society for Individual Rights similarly grew out of the changes in San Francisco in the 1960s, and it drew its early members from a pool of relatively middle-class, recent migrants to the city. Bill Beardemphl, a former New Yorker and chef, helped found the group in his Haight Ashbury home, which he owned with his partner John DeLeon. Bill Plath—another early member—was from Chicago, lived in the Western Addition, and managed a bar. Several important SIR members practiced law in San Francisco and worked on local cases related to racial equality and the War on Poverty. Their participation in these causes inspired many of them to build a social movement for gay equality—or what one member called "the matter of civil rights in relation to sexual orientation." SIR's members in the mid-1960s believed that a "great injustice had been done to all homosexuals," and they were optimistic that they could "change society" to promote the "dignity" of gay men and lesbians. They often participated in multiple other gay rights organizations, including the CRH, and even held early meetings at Glide.[66]

SIR profited enormously from the gay migration to San Francisco, boasting almost a thousand members in 1969, yet it also reflected the racial, class, and gender segmentation of LGBT people in the city.[67] Although members sometimes sympathized with the black freedom struggle and feminism, SIR was overwhelmingly white and male. Many of its leaders lived in gentrifying areas like the Castro or affluent neighborhoods like Pacific Heights, and the relatively well-off members enjoyed at least modest amounts of bedroom privacy. War on Poverty lawyer and SIR member Herb Donaldson recalled that, despite needing relatively high down payments, many of the men in the group owned their own homes.[68] Not long after SIR's founding, Beardemphl and DeLeon left the Haight-Ashbury and bought another house in the Castro District.[69] Dorr Jones, SIR's president in 1967, lived in a historic ten-room "estate" in Russian Hill.[70]

The early work of both the CRH and SIR owed a great deal to the changing legal and political climate around privacy. The CRH, for example, used the discourse after a particularly dramatic confrontation with the law in 1965. When the Council sponsored a dance and fundraiser that year, San Francisco police parked paddy wagons in front of the event and took photographs of guests attending it. Officers later entered the building over objections from homophile attorneys, arresting three people for allegedly obstructing justice.[71] Ministers on the Council hosted an angry press conference the next day, condemning the police actions as a violation of a "private" fundraiser. The CRH later issued a manifesto entitled *A Brief of Injustices*, which described the New Year's Eve fiasco and used it as the foundation for a larger plea for legal reform: "We believe that the law should sustain the right of each individual to engage in private sexual activity," the CRH declared. "Most sex laws are unjust, vague, unenforceable or unrealistic. Such laws serve best to open avenues for blackmail, police brutality, and the violation of civil rights."[72]

SIR provided legal counsel for the CRH in its complaint with the police, and it also spoke about privacy. The organization had a permanent legal committee that included lawyers who followed the courts' rulings closely.[73] SIR's founding statement, published in 1964, used language remarkably similar to *A Brief of Injustices*, declaring, "There should be an end to dismissals from our jobs; an end to police harassment, and the interference of the state with the sanctity of the individual within his home."[74] Writers in SIR's magazine similarly applauded the ACLU for applying privacy to cases involving homosexuality in 1966.[75]

SIR and the CRH never spoke about privacy alone, however. Both tied the idea to the larger question of sexual equality, insisting that the state could not deny citizens free speech, employment, or housing based on their personal lives. Unless society permitted people to have private lives free of government intrusion, they argued, no one could fully live up to their potential as human beings. The CRH argued in *A Brief of Injustices* that the right to assemble or work was "closely related" to the right to privacy since people unfairly made assumptions about what homosexuals did behind closed doors when they closed a bar or fired them. Those assumptions transformed both the accuser and the accused, damaging both: "The excessive concern of some Americans over what are essentially areas of personal expression in sexual behavior, exercised between adults in private, can result in our becoming a nation of professional snoopers and privacy invaders." As a result, Americans squandered public resources and wasted "potential contributions to the growth of our society."[76]

SIR's leadership used privacy to denounce what they saw as the double standard that public officials used to apply the law. All sexuality was public to some degree and homosexuals faced an unusually high bar to keep their relationships private, they argued. The wider society celebrated heterosexual relationships, particularly marriage. Gay couples, by contrast, needed to hide their love for one another. "We believe that sex is private and that it should be done in private. . . . But who determines what [else] should be committed only in private?" asked *Vector*'s editors in 1966. Police routinely arrested men for publicly displaying affection toward other men, including by "holding hands" and "standing close to one another." Heterosexual couples, by contrast, never faced prosecution for similar acts.[77]

Just as important, both groups believed in improving the material conditions of queer people in the city. The CRH, in particular, tried to improve life in the Tenderloin. Ministers from the Council opened a coffee shop in Glide and started a community center called "Hospitality House" downtown, which temporarily offered young people a place to sleep off the street.[78] The CRH also helped sponsor two new group homes for "runaways" in the city. When Tenderloin residents organized a Community Action Program for the War on Poverty, several CRH and SIR members joined their cause. The Council officially endorsed the Central City poverty program, which went on to bring mobile health clinics and other social services to the district.[79] These projects subsequently led to a revival at Glide. The church officially opened its doors to Tenderloin residents in 1965, and its ministers preached acceptance for gay men and lesbians. In just a few years, Glide became one of the most gay-friendly congregations in the country, and newspapers reported that when ministers spoke about sexual equality, "homosexuals packed the church, in drag and all," and by end of the decade, Glide once again boasted over a thousand regular congregants.[80]

In addition to its legal and political work, SIR saw itself as a community-building organization. Bars offered some of the only social outlets for queer people in the city in the mid-1960s, and California law forbade same-sex couples from dancing together. SIR created new spaces for gay men and lesbians to come together. In 1966, the Society moved out of Glide and opened a "community house project" around the corner downtown. This center offered a meeting place for gay men, in particular. SIR later used it to host dances, drag shows, and even musicals. Additionally, the group organized bowling nights, hiking trips, discussion groups, and a softball league.[81]

Within just a few years, CRH and SIR had accomplished a great deal, and some of their biggest successes lay in their ability to use the right to privacy to build alliances with predominantly straight institutions. They convinced the ACLU, including its San Francisco chapter, to defend private adult homosexual relationships in 1965.[82] Thanks to the support and advocacy of groups like the ACLU, eighteen states, including California, established commissions considering sex law reform by 1968.[83] In 1967, the Council convinced the Episcopal Diocese of San Francisco to endorse, among other things, the repeal of state laws against "any sex behavior between consenting adults in private" and a "broad sex education," including homosexuality for its congregants. That same year, a writer in the liberal religious journal *Social Action* professed that although he felt "indifference and hostility" toward homosexuals, he nevertheless believed that churches needed to pay more attention to their problems. After learning about the subject from the CRH, he pushed churches to combat stereotypes about gay men and lesbians that had "little if any relation to reality" and to promote the decriminalization of sex acts between consenting adults in private.[84]

When gay activists sought allies in the 1960s and early 1970s, however, they found more sympathetic ears when they spoke about legal reform than when they called for new policies on behalf of LGBT people. Although the CRH and SIR never spoke about "privacy" alone, predominantly straight organizations like the Episcopal Diocese or the ACLU continued to see homosexuality as an illness. They frequently supported gay rights groups primarily as a part of a larger principled stance against police abuse or employment discrimination in general. They did not necessarily support spending money on behalf of LGBT people or creating new programs to help them. Many of their own members criticized any action that appeared to affirm homosexuality. In 1967, for example, trustees at the most prominent Episcopal Church in San Francisco, Grace Cathedral, denounced the CRH and the wider Episcopal Diocese's support for decriminalizing private adult sexual conduct.[85]

No issue better illustrated this dilemma than efforts to ameliorate queer poverty. Social services initiated by gay rights groups in the Tenderloin were often limited and short-lived. While attendance at Glide remained high in the late 1960s and 1970s, conditions outside the church deteriorated. The

Tenderloin's War on Poverty program, which spun off the early work of the CRH, faced steep budget cuts within just a few years. Antipoverty projects across the nation faced similar problems, but the Central City program faced particularly serious difficulties. In 1968, California Governor Ronald Reagan singled it out for budget cuts because it supported "homosexuals and drug addicts."[86]

Hospitality House, by contrast, endured beyond the 1960s and even expanded to a nearby larger space. But like service agencies in other poor areas, it struggled to attract funding.[87] These difficulties primarily stemmed from the structural forces that had created the red-light district in the first place. Even the most beneficial soup kitchen, community center, or mobile medical unit could not overcome the concentrated queer poverty wrought by suburbanization and urban renewal. People cut off from employment or their families often had few other options than the Tenderloin's underground economy and crowded housing conditions. According to one report, Hospitality House struggled to provide food once a week to three thousand youth in the red-light district in 1970. These young people included "drag queens and lesbians" who were living on the streets because of conflicts with their families back home.[88]

Gay rights groups encountered similar problems around the issue of sex education. Throughout the 1960s, the CRH and SIR understood that young people were flocking to San Francisco, and many of them were queer teens who had fled hostile homes, schools, and churches. Both groups, therefore, tried to develop programs for LGBT youth. Council members argued that young people in the Tenderloin not only struggled to find food or housing but also labored to make sense of desires they felt for others of the same sex. This "confusion" about their identities aggravated their poverty since it often sparked conflicts with families who cut their children off financially and drove teenagers into the vice economy. Unlike most religious groups at the time, the CRH did not believe parents, teachers, or clergy should try to change their children's sexuality. Instead, the group argued that adults should accept and try to understand them. The Council denounced "situations where parents . . . disowned their children when they discovered they were homosexuals" and decried that fact that "when a homosexual's sexual orientation is exposed the result usually is instant and overwhelming social condemnation."[89]

Taboos about sex education in general and homosexuality in particular, however, handicapped SIR and the CRH's efforts. Gay men and lesbians faced accusations that they "seduced" or molested children, which left the CRH in a difficult position when it came to helping young people. In July 1965, Phyllis Lyon proposed that the CRH create a homosexual youth group under the direction of a minister and his wife, but an attorney in the Council protested that "sanctimonious people" would accuse them of "proselytizing and recruitment" of impressionable teenagers into the "homosexual lifestyle."[90] Lyon's partner Del Martin made the same plea a few years later to SIR but found little support for the idea. Fears that outsiders would accuse them of "seducing" young people prompted SIR to maintain a rigid adults-only admissions policy throughout the 1960s.[91] Don Lucas, who served in both SIR and the CRH, recalled visiting one of the church-sponsored coffee houses and going to "counsel with these young people to try to get them to go home. And that's when, of course, I'd find out a lot of them couldn't go home because they'd been kicked out."[92] In order to help ameliorate the situation, Lucas encouraged teenagers to bring their parents in to meet with him, "to get the parents to understand and accept their son for who he was."[93]

These improvised sessions about tolerance represented the outer boundaries of permissible sex education for SIR and the CRH. Lucas later confessed that even though he personally counseled individual teenagers about homosexuality, he believed that any group that advocated that kind of sex education risked dire consequences: "Legally it was doom to be associated with minors in any context. . . . It was a very dangerous area. All the attorneys would advise me constantly to be extremely careful in how I did it."[94] Minutes from council meetings revealed that as late as 1968, the group's members still struggled to find ways to help queer youth.[95]

Liberal advocacy for the right to privacy and court rulings like *Griswold*, therefore, opened some options while foreclosing others. Because groups such as the ACLU or the Supreme Court framed homosexuality, pornography, or extramarital sex as unworthy of criminalization but not as worthy as marriage, gay activists slowly gained support for the repeal of most sex laws but struggled to achieve wider goals. SIR and the CRH promoted tolerance for gay men and lesbians and a universal right to privacy. The CRH, in particular, dedicated itself to promoting dialogue among ministers, doctors, and parents about homosexuality before eventually disbanding in the late 1970s.[96] This strategy produced important results, including a growing acceptance of homosexuals among liberal churches and increasing support for legal reform. Yet, in a pattern that would repeat itself, activists struggled to win support for new policies and rights, like gay-friendly sex education, that might benefit queer people. In their first encounters with the right to privacy after *Griswold*, gay rights advocates discovered that although they faced an uphill battle to end discrimination, they confronted even steeper obstacles when they tried to create new programs.

Privacy and Conflict Within Queer Communities

In the late 1960s and early 1970s, two formerly parallel trends in LGBT activism collided over the issue of privacy. On one hand, a largely middle-class and white contingent of gay men and lesbians entered mainstream American politics. Most notably, gay liberals became key members of the Democratic Party. SIR helped pioneer this transition in San Francisco, convincing a growing number of local politicians to support their cause. On the other hand, new LGBT groups proliferated in the late 1960s and early 1970s. Many of these organizations identified with the more radical wings of second-wave feminism and antiwar movement and expressed skepticism about mainstream institutions.[97] Local manifestations of this kind of Gay Liberation in San Francisco included diverse groups, but they shared a fundamental distrust of any organizing strategy that overly relied on sexual privacy. Some of these radicals argued that "privacy" was merely another word for "shame." They reversed longstanding middle-class discourses about urban vice and called for queer people to "come out" and build a sexual democracy "in the streets." Others saw the discourse as insufficient for overcoming queer poverty. Activists in the Tenderloin, in particular, argued that having the right to have consensual sex in private did little for people who literally had no bedrooms. Many radicalized lesbians, meanwhile, argued that privacy only reinforced notions about the importance of the home that men used to oppress women. At the dawn of the 1970s, therefore, LGBT activists achieved some important victories, but they also fought one another over the meaning and nature of the right to privacy.

These conflicts surfaced, in part, thanks to SIR's arguments that gay people needed to organize and vote in their self-interest. This view assumed that lesbians and gay men shared more similarities than differences, and Society members believed that if they united, SIR could force elites in San Francisco to support their cause at the ballot box. They knew that elected officials believed supporting any notion of gay rights was risky, and thus they tried to use the growing number of self-identified gay men and lesbians in San Francisco to their advantage. In 1967, Society President Dorr Jones argued that "one possible and powerful solution to the daily problems we face in our private lives is the development of a strong political force."[98]

SIR, therefore, organized "candidates' nights" to push San Francisco politicians to support gay rights, and from the very outset, these campaign events dramatized the possibilities and limits of a privacy-based political strategy. Few politicians wanted to speak to the group in the mid-1960s, but SIR forced many of them to see gay voters as a united bloc that could swing elections. Over time, SIR won the support of State Assemblyman Willie Brown, Supervisor Jack Morrison, State Senator John Burton, and, most dramatically, Board of Supervisors President Dianne Feinstein.[99] Feinstein, a married Pacific Heights resident, had voted against a policy that would have forbidden ex-convicts from having homosexual relationships while she served on a parole board. When she ran for city supervisor in 1969, she nevertheless garnered SIR's support and the organization's leaders claimed that their members helped her win the election that fall.[100]

These politicians took important risks to support gay rights, but they also carefully parsed out a discursive middle ground built around privacy. Brown and Burton proved particularly sympathetic, and they proposed a bill in the California legislature decriminalizing all private sex acts between consenting adults in 1969.[101] Yet the Society's political allies also saw privacy as a double-edged issue that allowed them to advocate for gay rights even as they denied greater gay equality. Feinstein, for example, called herself a "centrist" in the 1970s, squeezed by the left and right, and when she campaigned for mayor, she carefully distinguished between "legitimate gay groups," which included middle-class organizations like SIR, and "gay cruising."[102] When John Burton spoke at a SIR meeting, he declared, "Unfortunately . . . [sexual] activity in parks and public toilets are the things people point to when you talk about reform." Therefore, he claimed, "Homosexuals must not only educate heterosexuals, but those within the community itself."[103]

These statements caused queer San Franciscans to vigorously debate how best to represent the "community." Elections and outreach required compromises with outsiders. Demands that employers and the state respect a person's privacy raised important questions about what exactly constituted a public act. Could one's appearance violate someone else's privacy? Did ending discrimination mean conforming to larger social norms? SIR's leaders often suggested that they spoke for a unified set of LGBT people,

Figure 11. Candidate Dianne Feinstein meets members of the Society for Individual Rights, 1971. Fang family *San Francisco Examiner* photograph archive negative files, BANC PIC 2006.029:141662.02.15—NEG, box 1564. © Regents of the University of California, Bancroft Library, University of California, Berkeley.

yet queer residents differed in terms of their class, gender, and ideology. SIR's membership, in particular, represented an important but hardly universal set of experiences. They hosted drag shows, yet they often conformed to gender norms in their day-to-day lives. Many of them were lawyers, doctors, or other professionals. And, most important, some of the group's wealthier members lived in the same neighborhoods as politicians like Feinstein, often enjoying significant amounts of privacy in their homes. Even as San Francisco's liberal establishment offered limited recognition to gay residents, therefore, SIR's members were most likely to win their acceptance.

In time, the willingness of middle-class gay men to compromise with elites like Feinstein aggravated preexisting divisions among LGBT people. SIR paired its political campaigns with outreach to parent groups, universities, and churches, and its members worked to appear nonthreatening, relying on their ability to conform to gender norms and middle-class standards of dress. Rick Stokes recalled that the group's education strategy "tried to meet people where they were," and in many ways, SIR's success rested on its ability to convince others that gay men and lesbians were fundamentally "normal" and good citizens.[104]

Underneath these campaigns lay the belief that prejudices against gay men and lesbians primarily resulted from false stereotypes, including ones about gender nonconformity and public sex, and that SIR could best advance gay rights by confronting those mistaken beliefs.[105] One woman articulated this view in the *Ladder*, arguing that most homosexuals "are indistinguishable from the heterosexuals around us."[106] Dorr Jones announced with satisfaction that when he spoke to church and university audiences, "many are astonished to see a man dressed in a business suit freely speaking about the problems society causes homosexuals. It destroys the 'appearance' stereotype many have held, along with other strange ideas about our living patterns."[107]

SIR members were not entirely wrong. Politicians like Feinstein and Burton believed that they could best justify supporting gay rights if they looked like they were helping otherwise "normal" people unfairly persecuted by society. Straight elites more often chose to work with gay men and lesbians they deemed most like themselves. When Mayor Joseph Alioto appointed representatives to San Francisco's "Committee on Crime" in 1970, an advisor recommended SIR member Herb Donaldson because he had "an excellent reputation in [the] gay community but looks 'straight' by appearance."[108]

The ability of activists like Donaldson to conform to the larger society's expectations of what middle-class men should look like thus allowed them to reach powerful allies. But SIR's emphasis on assimilation also ostracized other queer people. The organization's emphasis on the fundamental "normalcy" of gay men and lesbians rested, in part, on their class standing, and some queer people saw it as paternalism. Many of the Society's male members had worn women's clothes in stage performances, and the Society used drag shows as fundraisers. Yet many of them also felt uncomfortable expressing support for effeminate "queens," transgender people, or men who habitually dressed in drag.[109] One anonymous letter writer to *Vector* declared, "If the drag continues in the 'Tenderloin' and other public areas, I feel that the heterosexual community is going to bring *great* pressure on *all* of the homosexual community . . . I dislike being a fall guy for a group that shows very little inclination to contribute to the group or even to themselves."[110]

The Society confronted these dilemmas even as it faced challenges from other queer groups in the city. Although they did not reject the right to privacy altogether, many other activists in San Francisco called for bolder assaults on heterosexual privilege. Inspired by the New Left, groups like the Committee for Homosexual Freedom argued that queer people needed to challenge the larger society to accept them on their own terms. Rather than compromise with those who insisted that Americans experiencing same-sex desires ought to conceal their relationships, they argued that queer people needed to bring those relationships into the open. One woman insisted that her sexual desires were a crucial piece of her identity, not something that she should need to hide: "I'm not just a Lesbian in bed, I'm a Lesbian twenty-four hours a day. . . . This consciousness runs counter to the impressions of many liberal, urban people who maintain that Lesbianism is a private matter—'What you do in the bedroom is your business.'"[111] Members of the CHF, meanwhile, condemned groups like SIR for playing into the assimilationist expectations of liberals, sacrificing what they saw as the characteristics that made queer people unique: "All too many of our brothers SUCCEED in passing," they wrote. "They become straighter than straight."[112]

Groups like the CHF shared SIR's goal to decriminalize homosexuality, but they often criticized the larger organization for relying too heavily on the right to privacy. In 1969, San Francisco radicals argued that although Great Britain had long since decriminalized private sex acts between consenting adults, popular "abhorrence" for homosexuality in the country remained "firmly entrenched."[113] Changing those attitudes required queer people to bring their relationships into the open, forcing those around them to accept the notion that "gay is good." CHF activists asked, "Why shouldn't a homosexual be free to walk down the street hand and hand with his lover . . . [and] to declare publicly that he feels good and wants to share his happiness?" A gay man engaging in such behavior risked imprisonment or the loss of his job, but the CHF retorted, "If anything he should be promoted, because a man who is happy and fulfilled, who is not engaged in a constant game of lies, is a more efficient worker."[114]

Activists commonly evoked the image of two men or two women holding hands on the streets because they associated a progressive vision of sex with urban space. Groups like the CHF employed spatial metaphors that contrasted domestic inauthenticity with the freedom of the city. On one hand, they spoke about life in the "closet," a term that connoted repression and the denial of one's true self. Activists used the word to mean the compulsion to privacy. A writer in *Gay Sunshine* recalled facing disapproval of his sexuality while in college, and as a result, he "built higher and thicker walls around my soul and retreated deeper into my closet."[115] On the other hand, activists spoke about life in the "streets" to imply participation in a democratic sexual politics that publicly celebrated all relations between consenting adults. In contrast to middle-class sexual geographies that cast "streets" and "back alleys" as degraded spaces, the radicals used the terms to signify freedom and dignity. In 1969, the CHF described itself as "In the Streets for the Revolution" and declared, "The new world will be built by new people who are in the open, free of chains."[116]

With the "closet" and the "streets" representing "repression" and "freedom," respectively, radicals sometimes celebrated gender variance as symbols of an authentic queer identity. Since men who dressed in drag or transgender people could not necessarily pass in straight society, they seemingly represented breakaways from the repression of the closet.[117] Christopher Mitchell, a self-described "fairy," expressed enormous frustration in the *Gay San Francisco Free Press* with what she saw as a larger society and "repressed" gay activists who denied her the ability to express herself as she saw fit: "I'm pissed at every person who denies me . . . the freedom to speak, act, live, dress, and fuck as I want."[118]

Mitchell's anger hinted at fissures among queer activists along gender and class lines, as well as the ways in which political strategies that rested on privacy aggravated those divisions in the late 1960s and 1970s. Most lesbians, for example, supported the right to privacy and the decriminalization of homosexuality, but many of them also criticized what they saw as male preoccupations with the issue.[119] In 1966, Shirley Willer, the president of the DOB, declared that even though few women faced police harassment or "arrest for solicitation," most lesbians in San Francisco nevertheless supported the decriminalization of homosexuality. Yet few male activists, she complained, supported women's claims to "job security, career advancement, and family relationships." She argued, "I would guess that a preponderance of male homosexuals would believe their ultimate goal achieved if the laws relating to sodomy were removed and a male homosexual appointed chief of police." Because men in the movement seemed unconcerned by the problems specifically faced by women like low pay or childcare, many lesbians like Willer felt alienated from male-dominated organizations like SIR.[120]

In the early 1970s, this conflict between gay men and lesbians erupted into a public feud over women's role in the movement and privacy's salience. Across the country in this period, many lesbians moved away from male-dominated organizations and embraced what they saw as the radical possibilities of feminism. Writers like Sally Gearhart in the San Francisco magazine *Sisters* argued that while gay men and lesbians had much in common, notions about the meaning of private life oppressed women to an even greater extent than their male counterparts. "I am in revolt against the nuclear family—home, motherhood, and even apple pie—which tells me (as it does not tell any man) that the only choice I have is to marry and have children," she wrote.[121] Like many feminists, Gearhart singled out the private world of the "home" as a particularly oppressive place for women, and the possibility of violence within the family made many feminists particularly skeptical about any ideology that overly relied on privacy. "The privacy of the home supposedly protects a comfortable space in which intimate and affectionate relationships . . . become richer and deeper with each passing year," Del Martin declared in 1976. Yet because of domestic violence, "women may be less safe in their homes than they are in the streets."[122]

Similarly, as groups like SIR promoted the right to privacy, Tenderloin residents confronted housing shortages, and drag queens and transgender people, particularly those of color, faced the steepest challenges in their searches for places to live. Queer residents in the early 1970s organized around housing issues, and the actions of activists in the red-light district contrasted sharply with those of their middle-class counterparts. All of them supported the decriminalization of sex acts between consenting adults, but Tenderloin residents focused more on the need for social services, limiting redevelopment, and securing places to live. These San Franciscans differed from SIR's members not because they did not believe in the right to privacy but because they often literally lacked private bedrooms in which to have sex. A dozen drag queens drew attention to the housing shortage by picketing a residential hotel that evicted them in 1973. A flyer circulated by the demonstrators claimed that "just a year ago, eleven of the larger hotels would rent to Drag Queens, and now only one will, and it is filled to overflowing."[123]

Tenderloin activists argued that, rather than spending money on support for legal reform, money raised by the gay community should support housing and social services for the queer poor. Middle-class activists, in their view, focused on privacy and nondiscrimination because those issues most closely aligned with their own class interests. Gender-variant and poorer queer residents believed they would hardly benefit from any political strategy that thought about sexuality purely in personal terms. In the early 1970s, some activists assailed what they saw as an undue preoccupation with privacy and respectability in groups like SIR, prompting one "fairy" to exclaim, "I WANT ARMIES OF EYELASH QUEENS MARCHING ON BROOKS BROTHERS."[124]

SIR's members never reacted to these criticisms with one voice, but some of them called radical critiques of their work naive and dangerous. Perry George, a writer in *Vector*, dismissed groups like the CHF as "Gay Bolshevik Bab[ies]" and argued that radicals merely resented SIR's ability to secure gay rights "within the socio-legal structure of the existing establishment." He sarcastically declared, "I'm afraid that many of our 'Gayrev' brethren . . . only live and socialize in the depressed parts of town and don't get enough from money on their General Assistance Checks from the establishment supported public welfare . . . to engage in anything as 'unhip' as working for a living." In George's view, radicals' calls for greater confrontations with straight society were naive at best. "I would suggest to them," he spat, "that they drive or be driven from San Francisco to San Jose and see the new homes with TV antennas and rows of shiny cars repeated for over 50 miles . . . then tell me that an anticapitalistic revolution will get off the ground and be successful."[125]

The differences among queer communities burst into the open over Willie Brown's attempts to the repeal California's sodomy laws in the early 1970s. Although he proposed a reform bill every year starting in 1969, other legislators refused to support it, and Governor Reagan threatened to veto it. SIR members, meanwhile, had become adept at fundraising and voter mobilization. The organization drew financial support from the relatively affluent lawyers and bar owners in its membership and found allies among liberal donors in the city. Richard Hongisto, a SIR-backed candidate for county sheriff, told the *Chronicle*, "I've had personal fund-raising events thrown for me in Pacific Heights mansions with original Rembrandts hanging on the wall. I've frankly received contributions from the gay community running into four figures." After Dianne Feinstein's victory in 1969, SIR Political Chairman Jim Foster boasted that "the gay community is now willing to vote in a bloc."[126]

Foster's words rang somewhat hollow, however, when the Society organized a fundraiser for Brown and his consenting adults bill in 1972. SIR hoped to raise enough money to mobilize support for the issue across the state and to hire a full-time lobbyist to promote it in Sacramento. When donors arrived at the upscale downtown hotel, however, they confronted twenty to thirty demonstrators from the Tenderloin. The picketers hurled accusations at SIR's guests, including the claim that "SIR-domites have continually ignored the plight of working class gays as well as looking down their noses at street gays."[127] A leaflet circulated by the protesters declared, "SIR hosts $12 dinners while Gays go hungry—$12 would buy a week's food for a Tenderloin Gay."[128]

By the early 1970s, despite these protests, SIR's pursuit of a right to privacy paid dividends. In 1971, SIR convinced the Northern California Council of Churches and the San Francisco Catholic Archdiocese to support a citywide nondiscrimination ordinance for sexual orientation.[129] A year later, Feinstein helped make San Francisco one of the first cities in the country to pass a nondiscrimination ordinance protecting people working in the public sector or for businesses with city contracts regardless of gender or sexual orientation.[130] And in 1975, SIR supported Assemblyman Willie Brown in a successful bid to overturn California's laws prohibiting sodomy between consenting adults in private.[131]

Yet SIR's accomplishment left many challenges unaddressed and even reinforced some inequities. The decriminalization of homosexuality did not necessarily help spread the idea that "gay is good" and left Californians free to discriminate privately. The law that allowed lesbians and gay men to have sex behind closed doors did not make it easier to affirm homosexual relationships in public or to create new programs that acknowledge the specific needs of queer people. It also meant little to people who sold sex for a living or lacked literal bedrooms. SIR's work sometimes reinforced the notion that a "private" world existed in the home apart from the state. In the case of decriminalizing gay sex, this strategy worked. But as many feminists argued at the time, the discourse left many women vulnerable to rape, violence, and exploitation in the allegedly "private" domain of the home.

The history of SIR and other gay rights organizations in the late 1960s and early 1970s, therefore, reveals the possibilities and limits of a strategy built around privacy. The Society arguably represented one of the most productive gay rights groups in the 1960s, engineering changes in policing, limiting employers' ability to discriminate, and eventually ending the state's ban on sodomy. They did not succeed in every attempt to change laws, yet they achieved far more when they called for an end to discrimination than when they called for greater support from the state. SIR's reliance on privacy allowed it to forge alliances with powerful political figures like Dianne Feinstein while eschewing a larger economic agenda. Just as significantly, the Society's strategy aggravated preexisting tensions within San Francisco's queer communities. The group's emphasis on privacy not only avoided more demanding campaigns for social services but also encouraged middle-class gay men to try to reform drag queens, sex workers, transgender residents, and men who had public sex. Speaking about the right to privacy gave groups like SIR unprecedented access to political resources even as it encouraged them to distance themselves from other queer San Franciscans who were less able or willing to meet the expectations of large swathes of the American middle class.

Many gay professionals undoubtedly carried some of the prejudices of other Americans about gender norms and respectability. Yet the debates within SIR about privacy, poverty, and drag cannot be separated from the larger socioeconomic and political context of the era. During the 1960s, housing discrimination not only pushed queer people to different parts of San Francisco based on their income but also meant that they had varying experiences with privacy in their own homes. That same prejudice hampered gay rights advocates in the political arena as well. Activists never argued for the right to privacy alone, but city and state political leaders listened more readily to calls for the decriminalization of homosexuality than they did to calls for queer-friendly sex education, housing, or social services. If SIR warrants criticism for its narrow focus on assimilationist goals that excluded some queer San Franciscans, then officials like Ronald Reagan deserve even greater condemnation for denying poor people health care and housing.

In later years, gay organizations pushed for equality that went beyond the narrow parameters of the right to privacy. By the early 1970s, queer San Franciscans across the class and ideological spectrum embraced the CHF's call for gay men, lesbians, and bisexuals to "come out of the closet." Even SIR, which still advanced a pragmatic strategy built around education and compromise, insisted that gay men and lesbians needed to speak openly about their relationships just as their normative counterparts did. During the 1970s and 1980s, LGBT activists struggled to link calls for the decriminalization of homosexuality with the larger question of gay equality. Those policymakers and voters who recognized a right to privacy for gay men and lesbians rarely interpreted that right to mean that queer relationships equaled straight ones. In subsequent decades, therefore, LGBT activists labored to pair their calls for privacy with a broader campaign to convince others that homosexuality needed equal treatment under all aspects of the law.

Chapter 7

A Moderate Revolution

When the Gay Counseling Service spoke to students at San Francisco's Roosevelt Junior High in 1972, they set off a controversy that rippled across California. One Roosevelt parent complained about "gutter talk" in his child's school to columnist Guy Wright, who subsequently wrote several incendiary pieces on the incident in the *San Francisco Examiner*. "With a tight school budget," Wright cracked, "homosexual sex education is something I could be persuaded to do without." The California Board of Education investigated the talk following the *Examiner*'s revelations, while worried journalists contacted suburban officials to inquire if their schools invited similar speakers. Newspaper readers subsequently commented on Wright's work and raised the question of privacy. One gay writer criticized the columnist: "The primary message we gays wish to bring out is, 'Forget about what we do in bed and try to understand that less than 5 percent of our lives is spent there. Concentrate on the other 95 percent.'" Another reader invoked a different "right to privacy" when he criticized the Gay Counseling Service: "I am not starting a campaign against homosexuals—let them do their thing—but they don't belong in a school program on family."[1]

The Roosevelt story erupted amid the biggest shifts in sexual norms since World War II, and the subsequent scandal reveals important themes in the ways in which many Bay Area suburbanites tried to manage those shifts. Beginning in the late 1960s, Americans engaged in higher rates of premarital sex, used more contraception, married later, divorced in greater numbers, and loosened their attitudes toward previously stigmatized acts like buying pornography. New ideas about sex filtered out to the suburbs from countercultural enclaves in older cities like San Francisco, particularly among the young. Just as importantly, suburban areas "urbanized" themselves, growing more economically and residentially diverse. Though San Mateo and Santa Clara counties, which exceeded 1.5 million residents in 1970, remained disproportionately white, affluent, and married, these suburbs increasingly assumed characteristics that many had once associated with city life. Sex, in the form of adult bookstores and a youth counterculture, appeared more public in their neighborhoods. Young women pushed back against restrictive dress codes and sexual double standards. African American and Chicano residents, barred from the Peninsula and South Bay's better neighborhoods and schools, protested their marginalization. Rather than havens from city life, San Mateo and Santa Clara counties increasingly looked like extensions of it.

Sex education and the right to privacy emerged side by side as tools with which numerous suburbanites sought to understand and manage this revolution. For almost two decades, San Mateo and Santa Clara county residents had debated the merits of teaching sex in schools. The issue had divided many parents, even as they established a consensus on the importance of sex education in the home, school, and church. The demographic and cultural shifts in the 1960s broke this deadlock as national associations like the Sex Information and Education Council of the United States (SIECUS) allied with local parent groups to demand classroom-based instruction on the subject. These organizations strove to make sex education a required part of California's curricula and helped popularize notions about sexual privacy. Frequently criticizing what they saw as "archaic" and "ineffective" laws, groups like SIECUS, parent-teacher associations (PTAs), and many churches introduced suburban parents to legal arguments about privacy and sex.

Their work, however, did not usher in a new era of sexual equality, and the battles over sex education in the late 1960s reveal the ways in which the discourse of privacy could serve multiple political viewpoints. Sex education's proponents, first and foremost, wanted to strengthen heterosexual marriage and manage social upheaval. They helped reform the ways in which the state regulated sexuality, even as they reinforced the hierarchy between marital sexuality and other kinds of relationships. By the end of the 1960s, thanks in part to SIECUS, the PTA, and their religious allies, most Americans saw private sex acts between consenting adults outside of marriage in a new middle ground. In this new system, pornography or homosexuality no longer merited criminal prosecution, but they also did not represent social goods, like marriage, that were worthy of the state's support. Bay Area residents like the newspaper reader who insisted in 1972 that Americans should let homosexuals "do their thing" put this hierarchy into words, and ideas about sex education lay at the heart of it. Many Americans supported sex education specifically because they believed it offered a more effective mechanism for regulating the behavior of youth, and like Guy Wright's reader, they often believed gay people "don't belong in a school program on family." They viewed it as a middle path that veered from what they saw as the failed disciplinary measures of the past and total sexual freedom.

Just as important, suburban residents treated the right to privacy as a flexible discourse. Like the parallel debate about how to balance the needs of the "home, school, and church," voters meant different things when they spoke of privacy. Some of them echoed the gay letter writer who wanted Americans to "forget about what we do in bed." These Americans invoked privacy to promote sexual tolerance and to repeal laws that penalized consensual sex between adults. Other voters used it to breathe new life into repression of the postwar era. Disturbed by the sexual revolution, they argued that pornography or homosexual relationships violated their own "right to privacy." Those who used the discourse of privacy in this way often wanted the state to take greater repressive measures and to penalize people who violated sexual norms. Even the foot soldiers in an emergent New Right spoke about privacy as they waged a war against obscenity and sex education in schools. As school-based sex education became a new tool to manage the public dimensions of acceptable sexual conduct, many conservative parents argued that instruction on sex and marriage violated their own "right" to teach their own traditions in their homes and churches. By the end of the 1960s, suburbanites across the political spectrum used privacy as a discourse to different ends.

The spread of sex education and sexual privacy did not mark the death of sexual liberalism, therefore. Instead, they refashioned and breathed new life into the idea. Unlike most gay activists in San Francisco, suburban residents tended to see heterosexuality and marriage as superior to other kinds of relationships. For many liberals and moderates, in fact, sex education offered a tool for producing better marriages. While many of them adopted greater tolerance for homosexuality, pornography, and premarital sex, they also insisted that Americans should conduct those acts discretely and out of public view. Like the letter writer who insisted that the Gay

Counseling Service be allowed to "do their thing" but "they did not belong in a school program on family," many Bay Area residents differentiated between toleration for consensual sex acts outside of marriage and relationships that the government should actively promote.

The Suburbanization of Drugs and Teen Sexuality

The scandal at Roosevelt Junior High, with its anxiety about social norms and condemnation of "gutter talk," resembled the panic surrounding the upheaval of World War II. Yet it also differed in several significant ways. For almost two decades, homebuilders had marketed suburbs as "family-friendly" spaces free from the dangers of the city. By the mid-1960s, however, many suburban residents witnessed changes in their communities that signaled declining fortunes. That newspaper reporters asked South Bay school superintendents if they too planned to invite homosexual speakers suggests that many suburban residents believed the line between city and suburb was blurring and that they worried about its demise. The increasing visibility of vices once associated primarily with San Francisco, including a teenage counterculture and pornography, sparked a panic among many people in San Mateo and Santa Clara counties.

The reason for this shift lay in the fact that the city and suburbs were fundamentally interconnected. In the two decades after World War II, San Francisco emerged as a center for a variety of sexual communities. Even as the Tenderloin became the region's premiere red-light district and the Castro became one of the nation's best-known middle-class gay neighborhoods, teenagers transformed the Haight-Ashbury District into a celebrated bohemian enclave. Young people from across the country flocked to the area near the Golden Gate Park panhandle to experiment with drugs and sex. Like the Castro, the Haight-Ashbury lost residents to suburbanization, and sexual migrants moved there as rents fell and housing opened up. Over 60 percent of residents in the neighborhood in 1970 were under thirty-five years old, while 40 percent of residents were under twenty-five years old. In both cases, the neighborhood's youth exceeded citywide averages by 5 to 10 percent.[2]

Although the Haight-Asbury was perhaps the best-known countercultural enclave in the United States in the 1960s, it exemplified larger, national trends. Los Angeles' Sunset Strip, New York's Greenwich Village, Atlanta's 14th Street, and Chicago's Old Town simultaneously emerged as neighborhoods that attracted disaffected middle-class youth. Newcomers to these areas often defined themselves in opposition to older generations, adopting more open attitudes about premarital sex and drug use that distinguished them from their parents.[3] Many countercultural migrants saw places like the Haight-Ashbury as havens from their hometowns and even defined their new homes in opposition to the suburbs. When the *San Jose Mercury* ran a feature-length story on the San Francisco neighborhood, an "older hippie" told the newspaper, "What's different about this scene . . . is the youth factor. They come here to find what's missing in San Jose, Redwood City, and Marin."[4]

Teenagers sometimes traveled great distances to live in these areas, but they also drew numerous local suburbanites. According to one survey, approximately 12 percent of the people living in the Haight-Ashbury in the late 1960s came from other parts of the Bay Area, and at least one-third of the "runaways" at a shelter in the district were of local origin.[5] Some of these teens joined the countercultural community on a more or less permanent basis, but others commuted in every week. Like suburban patrons of the city's gay bars, some young people traveled to the city but did not necessarily live there. Modern transit systems like the highways that connected the Peninsula to the urban core allowed people with cars to visit the Haight-Ashbury on a limited basis. In 1967, for example, a San Francisco police officer complained to a journalist that teenagers were having sex in Golden Gate Park, and he called many of them "'plastic hippies' . . . high schools kids that come over just on weekends."[6]

Illegal drugs helped draw many of these young people to the Haight-Ashbury, and over time, Bay Area teenagers brought drugs back home. According to one historian, suburban experiments with marijuana, LSD, and other drugs swelled out of bohemian vice districts in older urban centers in the late 1960s.[7] Teens involved in the counterculture similarly imported ideas about sex and relationships with them back to the suburbs. One Tenderloin prostitute told an alternative newspaper that before he started sex work, he used to "drive up to San Francisco from my suburbia home to attend . . . psychedelic Hippie dances."[8] Many teens in a Haight-Ashbury shelter reported that they saw no problem with sex outside marriage if the people involved loved one another. Although these specific young people may not have returned home, many of their counterparts did and brought liberalized ideas about sex with them. A sociologist studying the East Bay suburb of Pleasant Hill noted that many teens believed "sexual activity was no longer considered something to be saved until marriage" and that they celebrated sex as "fun."[9]

In addition to moving in and out of the city, Bay Area teenagers passed around underground newspapers that operated like homophile magazines or sex education materials of the PTAs. Texts like the *Berkeley Barb* and *San Francisco Free Press* circulated among young suburban residents, and as they spread, they brought with them both nontraditional ideas about sex and reminders that teens elsewhere were participating in a wider community of readers interested in those ideas. Some parents who saw the papers noted with alarm the ways in which they smuggled deviant ideas about sex into their communities. James Donati, for example, complained in the *Santa Clara Journal* about a teacher in his community who "loves to smoke pot" and a social worker "who placed an ad in the Berkeley Barb looking for a man."[10]

These countercultural ideas helped spark generational conflict in Santa Clara County, and young people specifically clashed with older residents over school dress codes. In 1968, more than a hundred teenagers packed a school board meeting in Sunnyvale and demanded the right for boys to wear long hair and for girls to wear mini skirts and pants. Fourteen young women purposefully wore slacks to Buchser High School in April 1969 to protest the district's skirt and dress-only policy for girls. Education officials issued numerous suspensions for these acts of civil disobedience, but they also saw the issue as an unwinnable fight. By the end of the 1960s, most schools in the South Bay liberalized their dress codes.[11]

These battles overlapped with civil rights struggles over educational boundaries, curricula, and discipline. Whereas San Francisco's black and Latino populations had increased considerably in the postwar decades, most suburban realtors, city officials, and homebuilders had confined non-white residents to housing developments east of U.S. Highway 101 and San Jose's Eastside. In the early 1960s, civil rights groups challenged the district zone boundaries that had ensured that most students of color attended a handful of schools on the Peninsula and in the South Bay.[12] In 1967, black and Asian American parent groups pushed education officials in San Mateo to admit dozens of students of color to previously all-white schools. Much to the dismay of many suburban residents, in 1969, federal judges compelled San Francisco to bus students across neighborhood boundaries to achieve racial integration, and a much-publicized report in Santa Clara County that same year recommended similar measures for the South Bay.

Although the South Bay never actually implemented a countywide desegregation plan, public officials and voters debated the topic well into the 1970s.[13]

Student activism over racial discrimination within schools further upset the South Bay's social order. In 1968, dozens of Mexican American students at Wilcox High in Santa Clara walked out of class and picketed school grounds over allegations that administrators punished Chicanos for violations more harshly than their Anglo counterparts. After their walkout, the protesters demanded fairer disciplinary procedures, the removal of prejudiced faculty, and new courses in Mexican American and black history. These protests over school boundaries, curricula, and discipline dovetailed with the concurrent fights over dress codes as Chicano teens demanded the right to wear berets in solidarity with Mexican American protesters outside the school.[14]

Even as many South Bay teenagers adopted countercultural ideas and campaigned against discrimination, adult businesses proliferated in the suburbs. The liberalization of the rules governing obscenity in the late 1960s allowed new adult bookstores, erotic movie theaters, and topless bars to open in Santa Clara County. Although San Francisco continued to offer the lion's share of the Bay Area's adult entertainment, the line between city and suburb blurred as Santa Clara County's population climbed in the 1960s. By 1970, almost a million people lived in the South Bay, and local entrepreneurs took advantage of liberalized obscenity laws to offer legal erotic commerce. Some of these businesses, like "Daly's Idle Hour Book Store," sold erotic fiction to office workers who commuted to San Jose's downtown and students at nearby San Jose State University.[15] Other adult businesses opened along one of the South Bay's main boulevards, El Camino Real. In the late 1960s, Charles Hammers opened an adult bookstore in a strip mall along the four-lane highway in Santa Clara, and the Cinema Theater in downtown Sunnyvale began showing adult films with titles like *The Sensuous Male.*[16]

Collectively, youthful rebellion and the growth of sex-related commerce combined to challenge many Californians' vision of suburban living and sparked anxiety reminiscent of the 1940s. Many South Bay residents complained about what they saw as San Francisco's degeneration and decay. Theodore Scott told his local newspaper that "the Hippies, Weirdos and Beatniks have about ruined the [city's] business district," and he argued that "the homosexuals parading about the Turk and Taylor district would shock most Santa Clarans."[17] Yet suburbanites also saw the lines between San Francisco and the South Bay blur. Just a few months after Scott complained about San Francisco, the *Santa Clara Journal* tartly observed that the counterculture had not only reached "the suburban ranch houses" of the hippies' parents but also had spread through their neighborhoods "by psychedelic advertising, psychedelic posters reproduced in mass magazines . . . and psychedelic jewelry."[18]

The new visibility of the counterculture and sex-related commerce in the suburbs caused a vigorous public debate about how to slow what many Americans saw as social decay. Like the 1940s, many authorities fingered parents as the principal cause of the problems. *Time* magazine alleged in 1968 that despite evidence of widespread recreational pot smoking, "the discovery that their own kids are smoking marijuana still leaves most parents incredulous."[19] Confronted with the sexual revolution in 1969, a writer in the *New York Times* argued, "Most American parents fail to do an adequate job in sex education." In order to close the generation gap, he advised mothers and fathers to speak to rebellious children about how sex can "contribute to a loving and lasting marriage."[20]

Concerned residents in the South Bay demanded that public officials limit the sexual revolution. In 1967, the city of Santa Clara closed a dance hall after parents alleged that its owners allowed teenagers to engage in a "love-in" during a concert by The Doors.[21] Two years later, Santa Clarans tried to defund a public library because they believed it promoted teenage rebellion. In 1967, the South Bay county library system opened a youth-oriented branch in the Franklin Mall in effort to reach "dropouts and others who . . . would not be likely to visit a traditional library." Approximately 500 teenagers visited the branch in 1969, but older residents complained to the police that the so-called Underground Library encouraged student protests, "abusive language," and drug use.[22]

At the same time, church leaders and parents flooded planning meetings to close or prevent the opening of adult businesses. In 1968, Santa Clara residents protested a request from the owners of the "Banana Ranch" bar when they asked for a permit allowing topless dancers on their premises.[23] A year later, a Catholic priest and several parents in Mountain View contested their city council's decision to approve the construction of a bar with dancing off El Camino Real. Reverend Leonard Rose of St. Althanasius Church objected to the new business since a parochial school lay less than a mile away, and he told council members that its arrival did not "lie in the best interests of people living in the area."[24] Mary Martindale, a nearby storeowner, voiced concern "for the welfare of children and teen-agers in the neighborhood" by declaring, "Certainly the majority of residents would not benefit or have need of this type of neighborhood business."[25]

Sex Education and the Moral Order

This anxiety in places like Santa Clara sparked a national search for tools to preserve the existing moral order, and subsequent discussions about managing the sexual revolution popularized two ideas about sex, citizens, and the state. First, many secular and religious family life experts argued that education offered a better strategy for encouraging marriage and "responsible" sexual behavior than policing. Writers in journals like *Pastoral Psychology* or members of the American Social Health Association pointed to rising rates of premarital sex as evidence that schools needed to do more to teach the young about "normal" family life. Second, many of these same experts paired their arguments for sex education with calls for the "right to privacy." They contended that policing had largely failed to stop the spread of pornography or "sexual deviance," in particular, and they claimed that education offered a more effective strategy for managing social problems.

No organization better exemplified this philosophy than the Sex Information and Education Council of the United States (SIECUS). Lester Kirkendall and Planned Parenthood Director Mary Calderone founded the Council in 1964 in an attempt to promote sex education in the nation's schools and as a clearinghouse for information on the subject. Early board members included family life experts like Kirkendall and Evelyn Mills Duvall, several Catholic thinkers, William Genné from the National Council of Churches' Commission on Marriage and Family Life, and the head of the American Association of Marriage Counselors. The Council's leadership, furthermore, included not only Calderone, the former head of Planned Parenthood, but also Harriet Pilpel, an ACLU lawyer from the *Griswold* case.[26]

SIECUS saw itself as a champion of free and open discussions about sex in an otherwise repressive society. Council members promoted research on the topic, and they believed that speaking about sex as a natural part of human life could liberate many repressed Americans.[27] SIECUS leaders saw classroom-based sex education as just one part of their mission, yet in the 1960s and early 1970s, they were best known for their advocacy on the issue. They helped schools across the country develop curricula on sex and family life and provided resources to local groups interested in implementing programs in their communities. One of SIECUS's most important victories came in 1966 when it convinced federal education officials to provide schools with funding to develop new programs.[28]

SIECUS's leadership included veteran experts on sex education, but despite their deep roots in the issue, they subtly reframed their understanding of the relationship between parents, clergy, and teachers. For most of the twentieth century, sex educators had called for an alliance between home, school, and church. Though they still spoke about the importance of homes and churches, they now privileged schools as places where students could learn the "facts" of sex and relationships. Clergy and parents, by contrast, could teach young people about their own individual moral traditions. Instead of a unified "home, school, and church" that reinforced similar values, they singled out schools' ability to teach students "scientific" information that they could then use to make their own decisions about relationships. Homes and churches, in this view, offered more individualized instruction that provided related, but separate, functions in the moral universe of sex education. While teachers equipped students with "facts" and taught them decision-making skills, their parents and clergy provided them with nuanced understandings of their place in the world to help them make important life choices. According to one SIECUS pamphlet, "It is clear that sex education is not a task for any one institution alone. Only as each contributes . . . its *unique* strength can one hope for a broadly balanced, societally-based-and-supported sex education program."[29]

Pronouncements like this reinforced sex educators' longstanding skepticism about voluntary programs for parents and churchgoers. Amid the sexual revolution, SIECUS members lobbed bolder warnings about what they saw as the dangers of "bad" parents and clergy. In 1968, Mary Calderone praised churches and families who took sex education seriously but lamented that "most parents are surprisingly ignorant of a good many of the basic facts of human sexuality" and that religious programs were often "sporadic and inadequate."[30] She and her allies believed that homes, churches, and schools had different roles to play in young people's lives, but they also wrote in an era in which the courts had curtailed religious teachings in classrooms. Whereas public school teachers in the 1940s could pair lectures on reproduction with Bible readings, rulings like *Engel v. Vitale* made those lesson plans harder to justify.[31]

Figure 12. SIECUS president Mary Calderone gives an interview at a San Francisco hotel, 1966. Fang family *San Francisco Examiner* photograph archive negative files, BANC PIC 2006.029:139863.01.3—NEG, box 1476. © Regents of the University of California, Bancroft Library, University of California, Berkeley.

While SIECUS members saw schools as places for students to gain "objective" evidence about sex, they also viewed them as forums where young people could discuss their own attitudes toward relationships. Many of them responded to the upheaval of the 1960s by acknowledging that Americans held different beliefs about sex and family life. According to textbook writer James McCary, "There are individual human differences which extend into every aspect of life, including expression of sexuality; and any valid program of sex education must take into account these differences."[32] Changing gender roles, in particular, motivated sex educators to broaden their definition of family. Lester Kirkendall and Roger Libby looked at men with long hair, women wearing pants, and working mothers, and they called "building an understanding of changing sex roles" one of the key goals of sex and family life education.[33] Consequently, SIECUS members pushed teachers to build their classes around discussions that allowed young people to ask questions and to make their own choices about relationships based on scientific evidence. One writer asked in 1968, "How can children intelligently and rationally discuss relationships with others and 'right' and 'wrong' acts without being aware of what they themselves hold as value?"[34]

This emphasis on discussion dovetailed with SIECUS's arguments about the right to privacy. In their view, teachers, like legislators, should not compel Americans to adhere to a single, universal moral standard. Echoing Alfred Kinsey in the late 1940s, McCary condemned the hypocrisy of the nation's sex laws, but unlike the late sexologist, he framed many of his objections in terms of citizens' right to privacy: "The extent," he declared, "to which some of our present laws are at odds with reality is evidenced by the fact that in certain states a married couple can . . . be arrested and convicted for any sexual behavior, conducted in the privacy of their bedroom, that goes beyond the insertion of the penis in the vagina."[35]

These new ideas about morality's relativity and the importance of privacy, however, did not mean sex educators saw all relationships equally. Instead, they advocated for a "middle ground" that distinguished between excessively repressive and libertine views of sexuality. Sex educators criticized what they saw as "prudish" or "ostrich-like" attitudes toward sex. But they also dismissed the notion that individuals had complete freedom to use their bodies as they saw fit. Mary Calderone justified SIECUS's founding by condemning both "those who think sex is simply for fun" and "those who think it is so holy one should never have it."[36] James McCary criticized the "thou shalt not" school of sex education, which "treats sexuality as a gift from God that is to be used solely for procreation," and the "sexual anarchy" approach "which would grant unrestrained license" to individuals in search of gratification.[37]

Historians have often painted SIECUS as a bridge between an older, more "prudish" understanding of sexuality and an allegedly more liberated future.[38] Yet the discussion system promoted by writers like McCary coexisted with the longstanding disciplinary tendencies in most sex education. Although they allegedly did not want to dictate value judgments to their students, instructors often saw their mission as an attempt to explain "normal" and "abnormal" behavior to their students. Thus, even as sex educators disseminated ideas about the right to privacy, they also stressed the public obligations of Americans to have sex "responsibly." "We need to deal more effectively with the growing tendency of modern youth to consider their sexual behavior as solely a personal and private matter," declared one writer in 1969. "Democratic individualism and permissiveness may lead to greater freedom and simple human decency, or to irresponsibility with society holding the bag."[39]

These sex educators, therefore, did not oppose sexual hierarchies. Instead, they crafted a new one based on a simultaneous celebration of marriage and a new middle ground that tolerated private sex acts between consenting adults. In their view, homosexuality, like masturbation and the viewing of pornography, warranted decriminalization, but it also did not merit official sanction. Guided by the "right to privacy," sex educators in the late 1960s espoused tolerance for gay relationships but emphatically distinguished them from heteronormative ones.

In some cases, sex educators made this distinction explicit. James Moore, a SIECUS member, frequently explored the nature of "abnormal" sexual behavior. He declared, "One of the greatest advantages of heterosexuality is marriage and the knowledge that one is loved according to a stable model of affection within a socially acceptable and legitimate relationship."[40] Moore alleged that gay men and lesbians could never develop these unions because they disrupted the traditional gendered division of household labor, suffered from emotional "narcissism," and tended to see their partners purely as sexual fantasies rather than real people.[41] Calderone declared that "apparent increases in homosexuality," unwed pregnant teens, "effective means of contraception," and pornography had helped stir "confusion" about sex, and therefore, Americans needed a group like SIECUS for guidance.[42]

More often, however, sex educators spoke about homosexuality reluctantly. Sometimes their writings implicitly contrasted the more normative elements of curricula, particularly marriage, with lists of "deviant" practices, which often included same-sex relationships. Calderone, for example, warned in 1966 that "the act of sexual intercourse is of great significance in itself. It is part of the most important relationship we know, that between a man and a woman who choose each other as husband and wife."[43] By contrast, she recommended that for high school seniors, "Due attention be paid to alcoholism, drug addiction, promiscuity, venereal diseases, broken homes, homosexuality . . . the techniques of dating and courtship and 'the whole panorama of marriage.'"[44] By framing sex as part of the "most important relationship" between husbands and wives and including homosexuality alongside divorce and "drug addiction," Calderone reinforced the normative impulses in the "new" sex education.

Sex educators, furthermore, avidly participated in a wider discussion during the War on Poverty about the supposed differences between the behaviors of middle-class whites and poorer African Americans. In 1965, Democratic Senator Daniel Patrick Moynihan released a report that explained black poverty as the result of "matriarchal households" and called for new policies that would encourage African American men to marry the mothers of their children.[45] This highly controversial statement relied on newly popular notions about a "culture of poverty" in which low-income people allegedly passed along negative character traits to their children that eroded their work ethic, including sexual promiscuity and laziness. Many adherents of the "culture of poverty" thesis saw themselves as liberal advocates of the poor, but their conclusions often ignored evidence that contradicted their preexisting beliefs. They overlooked, for example, "promiscuity" and laziness among wealthier groups, choosing to believe that low-income Americans were more prone to both characteristics. Furthermore, they paid relatively little attention to the structural barriers like real estate discrimination or inadequately funded schools that kept many African Americans from climbing the economic ladder.

The "culture of poverty" thesis nevertheless garnered many adherents in the 1960s, and SIECUS's engagement with the issue further demonstrated the ways its members thought about privacy as a part of a larger social hierarchy between "normal" and "deviant" sex. Like the slum reformers of the New Deal and postwar eras, Council experts understood "promiscuity" among poor people as the result of inadequate bedroom privacy and sex education. Boone Hammond and Joyce Lardner argued in a 1970 SIECUS manual that "gross lack of privacy" forced "slum dwellers" to engage in sex acts in places within the full view of children. To break this cycle, Hammond and Lardner called for greater sex education, improved housing, and social services and justified funneling these resources to the poor by reaffirming what they saw as the fundamental differences between more affluent whites and black "slum dwellers." "Because of the importance assigned to sex in this environment, one finds a more permissive attitude than in the middle class."[46] With greater privacy and education, however, Hammond and Lardner suggested that African Americans and the poor more generally might adopt more restrained attitudes toward sex that would help lift them out of poverty.[47]

SIECUS thus offered a complex mixture of progressive rhetoric and the reinforcement of a sexual hierarchy that treated consensual adult relationships unequally. The Council came together right as places like Santa Clara County underwent important social changes, including a newly visible youth counterculture and legalized pornography. Many of those aspects of the sexual revolution precisely represented the kind of hedonistic "extreme" that SIECUS members wanted to contain. They promoted sex education specifically because they believed it offered a more effective way to promote marriage than legal repression. Relative to the bar raids of George Christopher's San Francisco or the California Commission of Credentials' investigations, the Council's attitudes undoubtedly represented a liberalization of attitudes toward sex. However, their celebration of marriage and denigration of so-called deviant practices like homosexuality represented more than mere leftovers from an earlier era. By pairing sex education with the "right to privacy," SIECUS liberalized attitudes toward some relationships even as it introduced new disciplinary tools to preserve parts of the old moral order.

Churches Split on Sex Education and the Right to Privacy

Religious audiences met SIECUS's "new morality" with mixed reactions, and the Council's ideas helped reshuffle the relationship between churches. Worshippers in places like Santa Clara County had long differed on sex education, but the sexual revolution brought some churches closer together while driving others part. Many mainline Protestants and Catholics, most notably, found common ground. After the Second Vatican Council in the early 1960s, the Catholic Church dropped its opposition to classroom-based sex education and supported the issue during the sexual revolution. Court decisions like *Griswold* and outreach from groups like the Council on Religion and the Homosexual, meanwhile, introduced many Protestants and Catholics to the right to privacy. Even some evangelicals in this era offered tepid support for sex education and privacy.

Yet Christian proponents of sex education and privacy also met with stiff opposition. Many churches argued that sex education without religion only encouraged youthful experimentation and that laws needed to enforce biblical rules. Numerous conservative evangelicals and Catholics objected to what they saw as the secularization of public schools in the wake of the *Vitale* decision. Sex education in the nation's classrooms, in their view, violated the prerogatives of the church and the home, and they mobilized to roll back new school curricula and to stop the decriminalization of things like pornography.

This split began, in part, thanks to the creation of SIECUS. The Council included prominent clergy on its governing board, and secular experts like Lester Kirkendall wrote numerous articles for religious publications like *Pastoral Psychology*.[48] Like the PTA, mainline Protestants had spent decades encouraging pastors to integrate sex education into their youth and parenting programs. Major denominations like the Presbyterian Church, U.S.A. and the United Methodist Church held national conferences on sex and family life in the early to mid-1960s, and by the end of the decade, their work appeared to have borne fruit. A study commissioned by the National Council of Churches in 1968 examined eight major Protestant groups and concluded that earlier criticisms of Christians' silence about sex needed to be "greatly revised." The report found that all eight denominations under investigation had incorporated sex education into their youth and parenting programs, and some of them even planned to broaden their initiatives.[49] Most mainline discussions of the issue focused on work performed by churches, but Protestant leaders also supported teaching it in schools.[50]

Catholics, too, worked with SIECUS, but the Second Vatican Council of the early 1960s provided an even greater impetus for the Church to drop its longstanding opposition to sex education in schools. Between 1962 and 1965, leaders in Rome issued a series of reforms, including a vernacular mass and a new willingness to accept other faiths' understandings of salvation. These reforms sparked an important debate about the Church's teachings about birth control. In 1966, a commission assembled by the Vatican formally recommended limited support for Catholics to use contraceptives. Although Pope Paul VI reaffirmed the Church's traditional teachings on family planning in 1968, the gap between the bishops' report and his statement made many American Catholic leaders reluctant to speak out against birth control. The National Council of Catholic Bishops avoided the issue for two years before issuing an ambiguous statement that made their views on contraceptives even more unclear.[51]

This ambivalence and the reforms surrounding Vatican II fueled a rebellion among lay Catholics about the Church's teachings on sex. A 1967 survey found that almost three-quarters of American Catholics wanted the Church to change its stance on birth control.[52] Periodicals from the mid-1960s confirmed that suburbanization, with its expansion of automobile transit, had reinforced the tendency of churches to be communities of like-minded believers, particularly when it came to sex. One study found that Catholics in the 1960s often "shopped around," looking for a priest who might give them "at least temporary permission to use the Pill."[53] Priests also faced even greater challenges thanks to the very marriage and family life programs that they had organized after World War II. For almost two decades, Catholic leaders in pre-Cana conferences and the Christian Family Movement had encouraged the laity to see marital sex as a sign of God's grace. By the early 1960s, those teachings further undermined the authority of celibate priests. Over the course of the decade, American clergy complained that their commitment to chastity made them appear out of touch with the experiences of everyday people.[54]

Vatican reforms and this restlessness among the laity prompted growing enthusiasm for school-based sex education among many Catholics. The Church's relaxation of some longstanding prohibitions and the sexual revolution prompted many Catholics to see sex education as a tool for supporting marriage and normative family life. Even as trends in sexual behavior between Catholics and non-Catholics converged in the 1960s, churches across the denominational divide adopted similar strategies to promote what they deemed "moral behavior." In 1968, the National Council of Catholic Bishops called for greater teaching on the subject in American schools. Citing the Second Vatican Council, they affirmed the "value and necessity of wisely planned education of children of human sexuality."[55] In that same year, *America* issued a tepid endorsement of SIECUS's attempts to teach young people about responsible sexuality, and Catholic groups worked with other religious leaders to promote sex education in the schools.[56]

As they gradually accepted classroom-based sex education, Protestants and Catholics grappled with the Supreme Court's rulings on school prayer. Since decisions like *Vitale* required schools to adopt what one Catholic writer called "religious neutrality," in the eyes of many religious thinkers, teachers needed to pair "knowledge of facts about biology" with context about the importance of religion in the learning of sexual values.[57] Protestant and Catholic writers, therefore, adopted stances similar to leading secular writers on the topic. In their view, schools, homes, and churches complemented one another, but they now played different roles in the moral universe of young people.

The U.S. Catholic Conference Family Life Bureau joined the National Council of Churches' Committee on Marriage and Family and the Synagogue Council of America Committee on Family to publish an *Interfaith Statement on Sex Education* in 1968. In this text, the ecumenical group called for teachers, parents, and religious leaders to play different but complementary roles—"each in own role and competence"—in the sex education of youth. The statement affirmed the value of teachers because they "can integrate sound sexual information and attitudes with the total education" but pushed religious leaders to instruct students "in the light of their [specific] religious heritage."[58] Similarly, the 1968 report by the National Council of Churches found that many denominations believed "schools are better equipped than churches to deal with the physiology and biology of sex." By contrast, it concluded that "churches and Christian homes" had "distinctive opportunities," which separated them from schools, including giving students a "frame of reference" about sex "at its deepest and most meaningful level."[59]

The acceptance of sex education among religious groups paralleled their newfound support for the right to privacy. In the minds of many religious writers, legal prohibitions against pornography, premarital sex, and homosexuality had failed to stop the sexual revolution. They consequently often spoke about sex education as an alternative to more coercive methods. Protestant Richard Hettlinger, for example, argued in 1966 that "unofficial, independent bodies" like churches needed to uphold "responsible sexual behavior." But religious groups should have no power to compel or punish people who do not conform to their ideas about sin. Instead, they needed to allow people the freedom to make their own decisions. Consequently, Hettlinger opposed laws that did not focus on "offenses in which criminal force is used, or in which children or the mentally defective are subject to abuse, or in which sexual activity constitutes a public nuisance."[60]

Catholic writers rarely specifically spoke about the right to privacy, but they often shared Hettlinger's notion that coercive methods from the state did not work. Catholic writer Joseph Breig, for example, argued in 1966 that when it came to pornography, "every effort at censorship seems doomed to failure." Even if outright bans on obscenity could somehow stem the tide of sex-related commerce, Breig alleged that policing could only be a "stop-gap measure." Instead, he claimed, "What is really needed is really adequate education about sex."[61]

By the end of the decade, therefore, growing numbers of Catholics and Protestants supported the right to privacy and sex education in schools. The suddenness of Catholic enthusiasm for the issues seems less surprising when the two issues are viewed alongside one another. Like SIECUS, mainline Protestant and Catholic leaders turned to sex education not because they wanted to weaken marriage but because they wanted it strengthened. Schools, in their view, offered what growing numbers of Christian thinkers saw as a new front with which to stem the tide of sexual permissiveness. Conrad Baars, a Catholic doctor, claimed that "the increasing appearance in both men and women of personality features . . . typical of the opposite sex," the "breakdown in family life," and an "increase in homosexuality" had convinced him of the necessity of sex education in the nation's schools.[62]

Sex education in schools and the right to privacy, however, found a cooler reception among the nation's evangelicals. For many of these Christians, the two trends contradicted their understanding of the relationship between church and state. In particular, the Supreme Court's rulings on school prayer violated many evangelicals' belief that sex education needed a specific religious context. James Huffman, for example, writing in *Christianity Today* argued that SIECUS texts treated sex "in an unbiblical, relativistic point of view that the evangelical finds unsatisfactory."[63] In 1969, the National Association of Evangelicals (NAE) condemned sex education in public schools and petitioned Congress to reverse many of the nation's court rulings "involving pornographic literature."[64] The NAE and its allies drew a sharp line between themselves and Catholic and mainline Protestant thinkers on these subjects. Instead of seeing sex education as a program that brought homes, schools, and churches into greater cooperation, they saw it as a wedge that drove them apart.[65]

Their belief that schools needed religious teachings as much as homes and churches prompted the NAE to attempt to change the U.S. Constitution. In 1964, conservatives in Southern California led "Project Prayer," a drive to support an amendment making it easier for teachers to lead students in demonstrations of religious devotion.[66] Two years later, Illinois Senator Everett Dirksen tried to pass a similar amendment, declaring, "The Court has shut the door on school prayer. I'm here to open that door."[67] Neither amendment, however, passed. Most U.S. senators and representatives opposed them because the Court already allowed for voluntary expressions of faith from students and, therefore, protected the "private" traditions of schoolchildren. They primarily resisted changes to the Constitution that would have made prayer mandatory.[68]

Just as significantly, many evangelicals rejected the liberalization of laws governing issues like pornography as a break with biblical commandments. Several conservative Protestants argued that local, state, and federal policy needed to reinforce teachings found in the Bible. John Baird, for example, argued in the *Christian Standard* that while "no individual has a right to force his private views on another," the same could not be said about the state. In his view, government "is God's instrument for peace and order in society. As Christians, we struggle to bring the laws of the state into harmony with the revealed will of God."[69]

Evangelicals did not speak about these issues with one voice, however. Some evangelical writers tepidly supported sex education in schools and the right to privacy. Like more liberal thinkers, they claimed instruction in schools and churches better addressed immorality than legal prohibitions. The president of the NAE, Rufus Jones, claimed in 1969, "The answer to pornography is revival—not legislation."[70] Just a few months later, B. L. Smith in *Christianity Today* condemned homosexuality but suggested that private acts involving adults " 'is not the concern of criminal law.' "[71] James Huffman critiqued SIECUS for its religious neutrality, but he nevertheless described their work as "wholesome" and encouraged his fellow evangelicals to work with secular educators to develop suitable sex education programs for their communities.[72]

Jones, Huffman, and Smith represented a minority of evangelicals, but their words demonstrated the growing appeal of education and privacy as tools for regulating sex. Although many religious writers liberalized their attitudes in the 1960s, the hierarchy that elevated marital heterosexuality above all other relationships remained largely untouched. The fact that even writers in Billy Graham's *Christianity Today* found common ground with mainline Protestants seems less surprising in light of the fundamentally conservative nature of sex education and the right to privacy. Religious writers who endorsed the latter often did so in the name of the former.

More important, conservative evangelicals and Catholics also spoke of privacy to justify stricter punishment for acts like the sale of pornography. George Steiner, writing in *U.S. Catholic* magazine, argued that pornography moved sex "more and more into the public domain" and degraded the act by exposing something that should remain in the home. "The new pornographers," according to Steiner, "subvert . . . privacy. They take away the words that were of the night and shout them over the rooftops."[73] A writer in *Catholic Digest* similarly used privacy to help explain how he wanted to stop explicit materials from coming to his house: "Lacking my invitation," he declared, "you could not enter my house unless you had a warrant. The mailbox, being a part of my home, should come under the same constitutional protection. And if I determine a given piece of mail obscene . . . I have a parental right to keep it from being sent to me or my child."[74]

These stories highlighted a number of important trends among religious writers in the 1960s and early 1970s. First and foremost, "privacy" offered a flexible discourse that suited multiple purposes. While many Protestants and Catholics saw sex education as a substitute for laws governing sexual conduct, others used similar language to justify more repressive legal measures. Some churches used "privacy" to limit the power of the state to criminalize sexual behavior of citizens, while many religious conservatives employed the same language to call for an expansion of the government's police powers. This shared language also reveals yet another common element between the opposing sides in these debates. Almost all churches in the country supported heterosexual norms and wanted marriage strengthened. Even the most liberal religious supporter of the right to privacy and sex education did so as a way to reinforce marital traditions and to teach young people "responsibility." While Protestant and Catholic churches aligned along different axes, they always shared a common desire to keep large portions of the existing social order in place.

Sex Education and the Triumph of the Middle

These national conversations circulated at the local level and helped birth grassroots activism in favor of sex education in schools and the "right to privacy." Organizations like the PTA, which had championed sex education for decades, consolidated their efforts in the mid-1960s and pushed local officials to adopt new curricula in the issue. Working amid the generational conflict of the late 1960s, volunteers successfully convinced schools in San Mateo and Santa Clara counties to teach sex and family life education. Their work, in many ways, paralleled the discussions by groups like the National Council of Churches and SIECUS, and South Bay groups shared many of the same values of these larger organizations. However, they also experienced privacy on a more personal level. Instead of a legal abstraction, privacy played a key role in the lived experience of most suburban residents. Homeowners experienced seclusion as a commodity when they entered the real estate market, and after their purchase, they lived in spaces that divided bedrooms from the more public areas of the house. Liberated from snooping in-laws, nosy neighbors, and—to a lesser extent—curious children, many Peninsula and South Bay residents saw privacy as a fundamental part of their day-to-day lives. Even as suburban activists pushed through sex education programs in their local schools, they also experienced the perceived virtues of bedroom privacy in their actual homes.

Throughout the 1960s, PTAs continued to offer courses on sex education and family life for interested mothers in the homes, schools, and churches of San Mateo and Santa Clara counties. Some of these meetings literally took place within a few dozen feet of the hosts' private bedrooms, but by the mid-1960s, enthusiasm for the topic forced PTAs to move meetings to larger venues. Pat Hardel, a PTA leader in the city of Santa Clara, told the local newspaper that popular demand for classes with titles like "What to Tell Them?" and "When to Tell Them?" had forced her to exceed her allotted time. "We're only supposed to be there for an hour and a half," she declared, "but we haven't gotten out in under two hours yet. I keep telling them the janitor has to mop, but it doesn't do much good."[75]

Suburban interest in sex education produced a new organization to promote the issue in the public schools. In 1964—the same year that SIECUS was founded—a coalition of parents, clergy, and academics created the Family Life Education Association (FLEA) to promote classroom-based instruction on sex. This new organization sprang out of the longstanding parenting networks operating in the postwar suburbs, and it brought together the South Bay's leading religious and middle-class women's organizations. Helen Hansen, the executive secretary of the local Catholic Social Services, formed the group alongside Dorothy Dyer, a family life educator from Palo Alto. Both women had children, were active in groups like the PTA, and had volunteered in formal parent education programs in the South Bay.[76] Hansen justified the new organization because she believed that the South Bay's incredible postwar growth had exposed the weaknesses of voluntary parent education and counseling services. She later recalled, "With all these tract homes being built and the county's population doubling in ten years, our professional staff knew there would never be enough counselors to meet the needs of all the people who had family problems."[77]

Hansen and Dyer united approximately twenty local groups interested in teaching young people about marriage and sex. These included academic experts from nearby San Jose State University, Planned Parenthood, the Catholic Archdiocese, the Council of Churches, and the PTA. In 1964 and 1965, FLEA brought in experts, such as SIECUS president-to-be Wallace Fulton, to coordinate the different programs in the county and offered an eight-part training course for volunteers interested in learning about family life education. In May 1965, the *Santa Clara Journal* reported that in the previous two years, approximately 3,000 people had participated in some sort of study class or discussion group on the topic in the South Bay.[78] Hansen recalled that "people came from all over. They were school people and PTAers. They were mainly just people interested in helping to preserve and strengthen family units." She called them "a grass roots movement of people who were concerned about the family and who saw all these problems of modern society."[79]

Like SIECUS, Santa Clara County volunteers believed that schools needed to finally play a more decisive role in teaching young people about sex. FLEA members, which included numerous religious and parent groups, shared the views of experts like Mary Calderone that homes and churches had a role to play in sex education, but schools could best provide the "objective" science that students needed. At a 1964 conference at St. Martin's Church in Sunnyvale, Dorothy Dyer argued that "courses in family life training should be ranked in importance with those in science. While the ideal means of gaining self-identity is through the family, if this fails, it becomes the responsibility of the community to offer supplementary training."[80] When the California PTA issued a new call for sex and family life education in the state's public schools, the group acknowledged "the primary responsibility of the home in the matter of sex education" but also claimed that schools should "impart scientific information" to students.[81]

In just a few years, FLEA and its allies slowly convinced public officials that schools needed to take on a greater share of sex education. In 1964, the Cupertino Board of Education put together a special committee of parents, teachers, and school officials to determine if educators should show films, such as *Human Growth and Development*, to their pupils.[82] Los Gatos High School began offering a six-week family life education program to its sophomores and a four-week course to its seniors that same year. The school's principal later told the *San Jose News*, "I think sex education should be taught in the home by parents, but it is not being taught there. . . . Students are getting their sex information from their peers. And they get as much misinformation from other students."[83] In 1966, advocates for greater classroom-based sex education convinced authorities in San Jose, the South Bay's biggest municipality, to encourage its schools to develop programs on the subject.[84]

These efforts in the schools paralleled reforms among religious groups. Early FLEA conferences included talks by a former minister and special panels led by church leaders on how to implement new programs suited to their religious traditions.[85] FLEA leaders worked with the San Francisco Archdiocese to revise curricula in Bay Area parochial schools. In 1967 and 1968, volunteers arranged meetings between secular family life educators and Catholic leaders to discuss sex-related curricula and helped the latter adopt ideas from the former to suit their own religious traditions.[86] An Archdiocesan advisory committee recommended in 1967 that "a curriculum of Family Life Education should be introduced in all parochial schools" and that they could use materials from the public education system as an "acceptable" foundation for their own Catholic program.[87]

Proponents of classroom-based sex education won their greatest victory when the California legislature required all schools in the state to offer courses on the subject in 1969. Grassroots support for the measure spiked in the latter half of the 1960s. In 1967, a group called the Citizens Committee for Family Life Education petitioned state officials to develop a model curriculum on the subject for districts across the state.[88] A year later, FLEA and its allies across the state convinced the legislature to pass Senate Bill-1 (SB-1), which required every school in California to offer a "study in health, including instruction in the principles and practices of individual, and community health." These guidelines opened the door for programs on sex and family life education in schools across the state. In anticipation of the passage of SB-1, officials in San Francisco launched a pilot program on the subject in 1967 and, noting that over 80 percent of residents favored the action, Santa Clara city schools adopted their own curriculum on the subject in 1968.[89]

The spread of family life education mirrored the gradual dissemination of ideas about sex, privacy, and the law. Local media, of course, covered Supreme Court decisions regarding pornography and birth control, but organizations like FLEA, the PTA, and sympathetic churches also circulated ideas about privacy at the grassroots level. Like the 1950s and early 1960s, these organizations brought together self-selecting groups of adherents, who often sought communities of likeminded individuals.[90] Most of the materials produced by SIECUS or the PTA focused primarily on the question of whether or not schools should shoulder more of the burden of sex education. Because they primarily dealt with students, these debates often skipped over the right to privacy, since minors did not qualify as "consenting adults." Nevertheless, many of the latest materials on sex and family life education included important, if subtle, references to a more tolerant understanding of sex and the law. The PTA, for example, recommended Lester Kirkendall and Elizabeth Ogg's *Sex and Society*, which criticized the nation's "antiquated laws" and asked parents to reconsider "punitive laws against homosexuals" and the "legal definitions of pornography."[91]

This newfound tolerance for sexual privacy hardly made FLEA and the PTA radicals. In an interview with the *San Jose News*, FLEA organizer Richard Sheehan explained, "We believe that the basic values of our society are taught in the family," and he argued that "heretofore there has been little concentrated effort in preparing individuals for the most important interpersonal relationship of their lives—marriage."[92] PTA articles regularly categorized strengthening the "family as the basic social unit" and helping young people develop "moral responsibility so that they understand their role in marriage" as some of the key goals in sex education.[93] San Jose's curriculum emphasized the reproductive process and the importance of marriage. Early units in its sex education program explained "the reproductive system" and culminated in instruction on "marriage . . . child care and human sexual needs." By contrast, students learned about social problems like "unwed mothers" and "homosexualism" alongside explanations of "venereal disease," "alcohol," and "drugs."[94] Furthermore, PTA literature occasionally used privacy as a rhetorical tool to limit sexual expression. Marjorie Holmes, for example, issued a "Plea for Privacy" in the *PTA Magazine*. "When sex blasts at us from loudspeakers," she complained, "the result is to deprive sex of its rightful role as the most fascinating relationship man can have with woman."[95]

Suburban residents' enthusiasm for "privacy," therefore, remained contingent and contested throughout the 1960s and early 1970s. SIECUS materials about sex education circulated in San Mateo and Santa Clara counties' homes, schools, and churches in the 1960s, and grassroots groups like FLEA won major victories at the state and local levels. Yet most suburban voters held even more traditional beliefs about sexuality than SIECUS's relatively conservative point of view. After the *Griswold* decision, many Peninsula and South Bay residents embraced the "right to privacy," but they used it in a flexible and contingent manner. They used similar language, but they often used it to justify different policies. Even as sex education's proponents persuaded school officials to adopt new curricula on the subject, growing numbers of suburban voters embraced privacy because it reinforced their own day-to-day experiences in their homes and because it offered them a flexible discourse that appeared neutral and natural to them.

Conservatives Claim the Right to Privacy

This ambivalence and the larger search for tools to contain the sexual revolution provide important context for the emergence of the New Right. Teenage premarital sex, drug use, gay rights activism, and the spread of adult entertainment spurred many conservatives to organize in the Bay Area suburbs in the 1960s. For these voters, sex education in schools looked just like the spread of pornography, and they associated groups like FLEA with more radical proponents of the sexual revolution. Many conservatives saw sex education and pornography interchangeably, and they mobilized to oppose both.

These voters, however, lost more often than they won. The rise of the New Right is best seen as an important grassroots insurgency whose failures at the ballot box reveal three important truths about politics in the 1960s. First, activists or parties that neglected to frame sexual issues in terms of "privacy" usually lost the argument. Though conservatives who contended that the state needed to enforce religious edicts found some sympathetic voters, they often lost campaigns that left out privacy's importance. Second, sex education inspired some New Right activists to organize, but it remained too popular for them to roll back. Instead, their fights over sex education reveal the popularity and flexibility of the right to privacy.

Conservatives worried about government expansion adopted the discourse themselves in a rearguard attempt to keep the issue out of schools. Third, the New Right's politics reveal a consensus among suburban voters about the importance of preserving heterosexual norms, particularly marriage. Conservatives and their opponents fought bitter battles over school prayer and sex education, but they shared a belief in the importance of marriage. They differed over how to best preserve the institution, but they agreed that it needed protection.

Several examples illustrate these trends. One case involves conservatives' attempts to restrict pornography in the immediate aftermath of the U.S. Supreme Court's liberalization of obscenity laws. In 1966, San Diego Republican Assemblyman Richard Barnes helped organize the California League Enlisting Action Now (CLEAN), which helped place Proposition 16 on the November ballot. If passed, the initiative would have allowed district attorneys to prosecute cases involving sexually explicit materials without having to prove that a text lacked "redeeming social importance." By placing the issue directly before the voters, CLEAN hoped to circumvent the legislature that included lawmakers with reservations about a law that contradicted the Supreme Court.[96] The proposal garnered support from conservative politicians and religious groups. Republican gubernatorial candidate Ronald Reagan championed it, and regional leaders of the NAE called it "a mandate for decency in our society."[97]

Many voters objected to what they saw as the proposition's violation of consumers' right to privacy. Indeed, though wide swathes of Californians in the 1960s voiced opposition to pornography, their concerns did not translate into broader support for conservative politics. In a poll before the referendum, over three-quarters of people in the state indicated that they favored more stringent restrictions on obscenity.[98] Nevertheless, large numbers of voters turned out to oppose Proposition 16. It eventually lost by a sizable margin, thanks to opposition from several prominent organizations in the state. San Francisco Methodist Bishop Harvey Tippett asserted that Proposition 16, with its broad powers, could possibility inhibit the distribution of Shakespeare and the Holy Bible.[99] The Northern California–Nevada Council of Churches called Proposition 16 "appalling" and a form of "sweeping censorship."[100] In the South Bay suburbs, the *Sunnyvale Register Leader* opposed the measure because it would allow "any crackpot to set himself up as a self-appointed censor. . . . Ideally, the answer to smut control lies not in legislating morality, but rather in raising the moral sights of society."[101]

This opposition did not mean that suburban voters had adopted libertarian attitudes toward obscenity. Instead, they saw the initiative as a violation of their privacy, even as they opposed pornography. In the wake of the Supreme Court's *Stanley* decision in 1969, the *San Jose Mercury* conducted an informal survey of people at the Valley Fair Shopping Center to see if they agreed with the ruling. Buzz Pulsifer, a salesman from San Jose, answered, "I'm against pornography but what a person does in his own home is his own business. If that's how they get their kicks, it's all right."[102] If they raised concerns at all, the *Mercury*'s respondents singled out exposure to children as the only reason why they might consider limiting sex-related commerce. But even these Santa Clarans drew a distinction between "adult entertainment" privately consumed and "public obscenity" that risked drawing the attention of young people. Linda Wright, a student from San Jose, declared, "People have the right to do and say what they want. But that stuff shouldn't be sold out on the streets where it can influence children."[103]

City officials responded to the ambivalence of voters like Wright by limiting adult entertainment rather than banning it. By the end of the 1960s, almost every city in Santa Clara County had adopted new rules regulating topless or nude entertainment. In February 1968, the city of Santa Clara required any business that sought to hire topless dancers or "go-go girls" to pay a $175 fee and mandated that they post a sign warning minors not to enter.[104] A year later, Campbell passed an ordinance banning semi-nude dancers, and in that same month, Palo Alto's city council tried to block the transfer of a bar's liquor license to a new owner on the grounds that it sanctioned nude shows.[105]

These regulations suggest that although anxiety about pornography did not necessarily translate into enthusiasm for the New Right, it did lead to a regulatory system built around a larger consensus dedicated to protecting privacy and middle-class notions of respectability. Rules governing obscenity did not outlaw it. Instead, they moved adult bookstores and topless bars to underpopulated districts away from downtowns and schools. Consumers who sought to purchase sex-related materials needed to seek them out. This process happened piecemeal at first, but it received the Supreme Court's approval in the 1970s. In *Young v. American Mini Theatres, Inc.*, a majority ruled that although the cities could not ban adult entertainment, they could dictate where it was located. The Court upheld a Detroit "dispersal ordinance" that required adult businesses to be separated from one another and

500 feet from any residential area.[106] Immediately after the ruling, San Jose and other South Bay cities adopted their own ordinances prohibiting "adult enterprises" from opening within 1,000 feet of schools, hotels, motels, bowling alleys, or other sex-related businesses.[107]

These rules appeared colorblind and class neutral, but they often forced erotic businesses to move from central locations "across the tracks" to low-income neighborhoods of color. As national groups like SIECUS explained the sexual behavior of the poor through the culture of poverty thesis, suburban authorities reinforced the association between poor people and taboo sexuality by pushing adult entertainment into low-income neighborhoods. Dispersal ordinances like the one adopted by San Jose and its neighbors, in fact, reinforced stigmas against pornography, racially integrated neighborhoods, and poverty all at once. Spatially proximate, the mixture of all three variables in a single area warned would-be homeowners and other businesses from investing in those neighborhoods, which, in turn, reinforced preexisting beliefs that racial integration brought poverty and "sleaze," that pornography was degenerate, and that poor people were more sexual than their richer counterparts. Even as conservative activists failed to bring back old rules governing sex-related commerce, therefore, city officials erected a new disciplinary system that used the imagined privacy of affluent residents as a justification for relocating adult entertainment to out-of-the-way, often poor, places.

These fights paralleled a second important example of conservatives struggling with the right to privacy involving sex education in schools. Controversy over the issue, of course, predated the 1960s, but the panic over youth culture, so-called deviant sex, and desegregation in the latter half of the decade renewed opposition to it. This opposition grew as groups like FLEA slowly convinced local officials to adopt sex education classes. Like the early 1950s, some of sex education's adversaries saw the issue through the lens of the Cold War. The John Birch Society, for example, launched a campaign against it because they believed it led to communism and destroyed Americans' "moral fiber." These Cold War concerns dovetailed with other anxiety about liberalism and the role of government. Conservatives who saw the War on Poverty as a steppingstone toward totalitarianism also frequently saw sex education as part of a larger piece in a government takeover of individual liberty. Virginia Schaffer, a city councilor in San Jose, for example, called her city's sex education program "unfair to taxpayers" and a "dangerous proposal" because "the city is getting into an area that rightfully belongs to the schools and the parents."[108]

Court school desegregation orders in the late 1960s dovetailed with this concern, and many conservatives saw busing and sex education as two interrelated phenomena. The largest foe of sex education in San Francisco, for example, was Mothers Support Neighborhood Schools, a group primarily organized to fight the desegregation plan that the city faced in 1968.[109] Many opponents of sex education in Santa Clara County similarly linked the two issues. Constance De Grey wrote a letter to the *Santa Clara Journal* to complain about the "protesting 'ethnic' parents" in her suburb. She complained that while Mexican Americans and African Americans "nitpick for incidents of 'bias,' the schools make headway in corrupting their children with a dangerously dingaling [*sic*] waste of time called 'Family Life.' "[110]

Just as importantly, many conservatives criticized the courts' ban on classroom prayer for divorcing sex education from religious teachings. As these opponents saw it, the secular nature of public education robbed parents of the privilege to teach their children in their own particular moral tradition. Marilyn Hillyer told the readers of the *West Valley Times*, "A 'God-loving' person finds it impossible to instruct sex matters without paralleling . . . the two subjects—God and sex. Our teachers cannot mention God without breaking the law."[111] SIECUS's advocacy for open-ended discussion in sex education courses particularly alarmed these voters. Although family life educators sought to instill a respect for marriage in their classrooms, some conservatives accused them of reaching children to make their "own value and moral judgments and to sit in analytical judgment . . . of parents."[112]

Conservatives organized for multiple reasons, but a shared skepticism about the reach of government united them. Proponents like the PTA almost never spoke about their cause as an expansion of government and merely described it as a "normal" or "necessary" health measure. Their adversaries, by contrast, tirelessly commented on the public dimensions of sex education. The Santa Clara County Citizens Action Committee Against Family Life Education, for example, described its members as "housewives, mothers, and taxpayers" and complained that "FLEA may be receiving federal funds for its promotion work."[113]

Framing sex education as a taxpayer issue allowed conservatives like Hillyer to explain their struggle as a fight for privacy. In the wake of the state law requiring districts to offer "health instruction," conservatives found a champion in State Senator John Schmitz who crusaded against sex education by calling it a violation of families' privacy. In May 1969, the Orange County Republican sponsored a bill allowing parents to look over materials used in their children's sex education courses and to withdraw them if they deemed it a violation of their religious traditions. A year later, he garnered enough support in the California Senate to pass a bill that he called "an anti-invasion of privacy bill," forbidding teachers from asking students questions that dealt with "parents' sex lives, or the family's morality or religion."[114]

Conservatives like Schmitz, however, lost more often than they won. Despite their work in the late 1960s and early 1970s, they largely failed to stop the expansion of the program. Their lack of success stemmed, in part, from many parents' belief that the issue offered them an opportunity to contain the sexual revolution. A grand jury investigation into sex education in Santa Clara County in 1969 absolved local schools of any wrongdoing and commended sex education for "contributing to the formation of effective, responsible parents by helping students understand basic concepts in child growth and development."[115] In 1970, a national Gallup poll found that 72 percent of Americans with children in public schools said they favored sex education in their children's classrooms, with only 22 percent saying that they opposed it.[116] That same year, the *Los Angeles Times* estimated that 25 to 50 percent of California's 1,200 school districts had "true sex education" programs and that the subject "had been introduced in schools in almost every part of the nation."[117] The California Department of Education reported two years later that only 5 percent of parents in the state had exercised their option to withdraw students from classes on sex.[118]

Sex education's popularity and conservatives' failure largely rested on a moderate consensus on the issue. Children were minors, and therefore, they did not possess the same right to privacy as adults. Many voters agreed that the threat of "bad parents" unable to teach their families about sexual responsibility outweighed any dangers from a sex education program. Furthermore, proponents of the topic often framed it as a renewal of the alliance between the nation's three leading supporters of families: the home, the school, and the church. National PTA President Elizabeth Hendryson accused conservatives in 1969 of failing to recognize that "many churches provide no sex education or that if they do they want reinforcement from the school. They also ignored the fact that many homes provide no sound sex education whatever and that many of these homes, like many churches, are eager for the schools to share this task."[119]

Conservatives, furthermore, failed to stop the spread of sex education because their own arguments about privacy limited their ability to make sweeping indictments of the new curricula. An anti–sex education group in San Mateo County, for example, sued the public schools, alleging that they had violated parents' right to privacy. Both the Superior Court of San Mateo County and the California Court of Appeals rejected the group's arguments, and the state Supreme Court refused to review the case in 1976. The Court of Appeals noted that rather than disrupting the relationship between the home, school, and church, the county's sex education program encouraged students to go to "their parents and religious advisors for specific instruction." More important, the court found that the Schmitz rule robbed the plaintiffs of their legal standing. In effect, by winning the privilege to withdraw their students from classes they did not like, conservative parents had lost the ability to challenge the larger system. "The program," the appeals court declared, "was in no way compulsory, and, therefore, we cannot see how the state . . . contravened the parents' right to privacy."[120]

Conservative opposition to sex education, like the movement against pornography, often failed to achieve its larger goals. But the New Right's stumbles reveal several principles about the emerging consensus about sex and the state in the 1960s. First, almost all sides in the debate about sex made appeals to privacy. The San Mateo lawsuit, for example, demonstrated that while conservatives argued that school-based sex education violated their privacy, the Court of Appeals reaffirmed the importance of privacy even as it rejected their claims. Second, the hardening lines between proponents and adversaries of sex education concealed the underlying consensus uniting them. Both sides wanted to reinforce marital heterosexuality. They differed primarily on the means to reach that goal. Many conservatives resented the absence of religion in the public schools, and some rejected the idea that Americans had a fundamental right to sexual privacy. But they shared much of their adversaries' belief that marriage needed strengthening. In effect, the debate about sex education revealed unity among many voters as much as it revealed polarization.

No case better illustrates these points than the 1973 California Board of Education fight over textbooks. Less than two weeks after the controversy over gay speakers in San Francisco, board member Eugene Ragle tried to bar James McCary's *Human Sexuality* from the state's list of recommended textbooks for being "too explicit." Ragle objected to McCary's work for allegedly encouraging students to experiment with sex and for describing "abnormal" behaviors like voyeurism, pornography, and homosexuality in great detail. But, most important, he and his supporters chafed at the book's sexual ethics. "'Sexual behavior,'" the *San Francisco Chronicle* explained, citing an offending passage in the text, "'should not be considered abnormal or perverted if . . . the behavior is not harmful to partners, it is carried out by adults who consent to it without any sort of force or threat being used against them, and it takes place out of sight and sound of unwilling observers.'"[121]

Other Board of Education members deliberated over Ragle's complaint, and they devised a solution that reaffirmed privacy's importance and the state's commitment to preserving normative heterosexuality. By a 7 to 1 vote, the group approved an expurgated version of *Human Sexuality* for use in California schools. A special censoring committee excised sections on impotency, "frigidity," sadism, and incest from the text, and the new version no longer offered a chapter that began with the words "Sex is Everywhere." Passages on homosexuality, promiscuity, prostitution, and pornography were "toned down," and the board added new ones on the "'spiritual' values of sex." Board member John Ford defended the new text to critics by applauding its claim that premarital sex "can carry much grief and disappointment." The book was not perfect, Ford claimed, but it "let students get their sex information in classrooms, not on the streets."[122]

Like the other two examples, the textbook fight illustrated the limited power of conservatives like Ragle while also reaffirming the importance of privacy as a mediating discourse over sexuality and the state's commitment to preserving sexual norms. While Ragle had tried to reject the textbook altogether, he alone voted against approving it. McCrary's statements about the importance of privacy remained in the final version. However, the board's revisions also illustrated the unequal application of the right to privacy among Californians. Similar to the discussions favored by national groups like SIECUS, the foregrounding of marriage in the text, the addition of a section on "spiritual values," and the elimination or toning down of topics like homosexuality demonstrated that sex educators did not see all relationships equally. Like the zoning ordinances that limited where adult businesses could locate, the expurgated textbooks illustrated the ways in which the state simultaneously affirmed the right to privacy and regulated access to sexual material. Limited enthusiasm for the New Right, therefore, did not necessarily translate into a more equal society. Sex education offered a new form of regulation, and even as more and more voters affirmed their belief in a "right to privacy," the hierarchy distinguishing marital heterosexuality from other kinds of relationships remained firmly in place.

Historians, therefore, should not see the popularity of the "right to privacy" in the late 1960s as an unequivocal triumph for a more liberal, open society. Privacy, instead, was a contested political discourse that produced multiple interpretations and justified more than one goal. In general, notions of sexual privacy made it difficult to justify legal prohibitions against sex acts involving consenting adults behind closed doors. But multiple interpretations of the notion proliferated in the late 1960s and 1970s, and voters yoked it to conservative ends as often as they did to progressive ones. Groups like the PTA applied it inconsistently, parsing the differences between issues like abortion, pornography, homosexuality, and masturbation. Privacy in one circumstance did not always extend to decriminalization or tolerance in another. Voters in the late 1960s and early 1970s often held contradictory feelings on sex and law, sometimes desiring greater laxity and regulation at the same time.

This ambivalence distinguished them from conservatives who lumped sex education and pornography together and opposed the "right to privacy." Conservatives frequently faced accusations of "censorship" or "repression," even as self-described moderates expanded government's role in the regulation of sexuality through the public schools. The fact that sex education triumphed at the same time that courts struck down many older rules governing sexual behaviors suggests that the state can discipline its citizens in multiple ways. It further demonstrates that some social movements defy easy categorization on the political "left" or "right." In the late 1960s, a moderate profamily movement emerged on the Peninsula and in the South Bay in simultaneous support of the "right to privacy" and sex education in the public schools. Its members often opposed self-described members of the New Right, even as they defended the importance of marriage and the naturalness of heterosexuality.

This support for normative ideas about sex and family laid the foundation for many self-described moderates to swing between the different sides in the subsequent "culture wars" of the late twentieth century. Uncomfortable with both a newly assertive Religious Right and Gay Liberation, these centrist voters looked for an in-between path between what they saw as two extremes. Even as sex education spread in California's public schools, many moderates embraced privacy as a middle ground. Intent upon preserving a sexual hierarchy that tolerated homosexuality but celebrated heterosexual marriage, these voters spoke about privacy as a way to distinguish themselves from both what they saw as the radical agenda of Gay Liberation and the repression of the Religious Right.

Chapter 8

Gay Rights, the Religious Right, and a Moderate Right to Privacy

Less than ten years after California's fights over sex education, the national media announced a new round of debates over sex and public life. In the mid-1970s, America's "culture wars" broke into the national spotlight. Between 1975 and 1980, media across the country narrated clashes between Gay Liberation and the Religious Right. *Newsweek* proclaimed 1976 the "Year of the Evangelical" and, a year later, highlighted the looming nationwide "Battle over Gay Rights." The *Nation* predicted a "Coming Struggle" over homosexuality in 1977, and *Time* announced that gays were "On the March." Beneath the headlines of crusading evangelicals and marching gays, however, these periodicals also hinted at an ambivalent centrist position on homosexuality. *Newsweek* framed the conflict as a perplexing dilemma for lawmakers: "How to protect the civil rights of homosexuals without suggesting approval of a practice that most Americans still consider deviant." *Time*, meanwhile, asserted that the "argument of homosexual militants is persuasive: no one should be harassed by the law, evicted from his apartment, or prevented from earning a living because of the private sex acts he happens to performs with . . . consenting adults." But the magazine also quickly noted, "It is one thing to remove legal discrimination against homosexuals. It is another to mandate approval."[1]

These stories reveal the ascendance of three of the most important political movements of the twentieth century: the largely white and middle-class wing of the gay rights movement, the Religious Right, and straight-identified moderates. All three represented outgrowths of the larger mid-century reordering of metropolitan space based around sexuality, race, class, and ideology. Three decades after World War II, gay activists primarily based in cities challenged the most repressive elements of the Straight State, and a newly visible Religious Right built around suburban churches rose to challenge them. Although San Francisco emerged as a national hub in the gay rights movement, a smaller fight for equality also took place in the suburbs. By the 1970s, openly gay ministers broke into the clerical ranks of several Protestant denominations, gay teachers challenged the policies that kept them out of classrooms, and gay activists demanded sex education in public schools that embraced homosexuality as a civil rights issue. At the same time, religious conservatives petitioned for the rollback of California's "consenting adults" sex law, banned same-sex marriage in the state, and tried to expel openly gay teachers from its classrooms.

This clash also mobilized straight-identified suburbanites who objected to what they saw as gay "militancy" and conservative "discrimination." These self-described moderates distinguished themselves from the two social movements by emphasizing their support for sexual privacy. Liberal activists had first used the term to decriminalize adult consensual sex out of public view in the 1940s, while family life educators later used it to carve out a middle ground between coercive acts such as rape and relationships they deemed socially beneficial such as marriage. During the pornography debates of the late 1960s, many suburban residents used privacy as a centrist discourse in order to support decriminalizing obscenity even as they called for sex education to contain it. When the conflicts over gay rights broke out less than a decade later, inhabitants of places such as Santa Clara County once again used privacy to carve out a moderate position between what they perceived as two political extremes. Support for sexual privacy seemed to them like common sense, accepting the inevitably of acts behind closed doors while also circumscribing public support for them. As a moderate strategy, it opened up a limited space for gay activists to erode some forms of discrimination, but it also foreclosed larger debates about respect and equality.

The right to privacy, however, was more than a centrist political position. It also represented a new moral order around which to reorganize metropolitan space and a common, if contested, discourse to explain citizens' relationship to the state. For decades, many Americans had spoken about the need for a unified "home, school, and church" to build "normal" families. After the sex education battles of the late 1960s, however, references to these institutions gradually declined. Privacy did not directly replace this older discourse, but it offered an increasingly popular way to understand the association of government, citizens, and public space. Like home, school, and church, the new moral order offered Americans a common vocabulary with multiple, competing interpretations. "Privacy," at times, meant the "right to be left alone" and allowed moderates to support nondiscrimination laws and the decriminalization of homosexuality. On other occasions, voters used it to restrict gay equality. "Privacy" in these moments represented attempts to breathe new life into the postwar "closet," as moderates and conservatives demanded that gay men and lesbians keep their "personal" lives out of public sight. At the same time, privacy signified a distinctly class-based understanding of the metropolis. Although its adherents often thought of it as a universal right, "privacy" required Americans to have bedrooms in which to have sex. It implicitly rested on the availability of appropriate housing, further stigmatizing homeless people, sex workers, the poor, and other marginalized groups whose erotic lives were lived more publicly.

Looking at privacy as a common discourse, therefore, destabilizes understandings of politics that divide Americans into neat "liberal" and "conservative" categories. Voters who spoke about sexual privacy not only shared a longstanding middle-class tendency to valorize the ideological middle but also used the discourse in ways that underscored the centrality of heterosexual norms to American politics. Few things united voters across the partisan spectrum in the 1970s more than the belief that heterosexuality was superior to homosexuality and that the state needed to protect that hierarchy. Sexual privacy not only gave many Americans a common language with which to speak about sex and the state but also gave them a seemingly neutral way to reaffirm the hierarchy between gay and straight relationships. Over time, this represented the most pernicious legacy of the right to privacy. Not unlike "colorblind" rhetoric from the same period, which affirmed the ideal of equal opportunity while also denying white privilege, "privacy" denied discrimination even as many Americans privileged heterosexuality and marriage. Although many residents in places like Santa Clara County rejected the rhetoric of the Religious Right, they nevertheless shared an underlying discomfort with gay relationships similar to that of self-identified conservatives. In the late twentieth century, both political parties embraced the term, offering rhetorical opposition to "intolerance" even as they supported discriminatory policies.

Reordering the Sexual Metropolis

The rise of the Religious Right, gay rights, and a moderate right to privacy stemmed, in part, from the reorganization of metropolitan regions like the Bay Area in the late 1960s and 1970s. San Francisco in this period emerged as a global financial leader, while Santa Clara County's defense-related economy evolved into one dedicated to producing computers for the civilian sector. These shifts, in turn, caused important transformations for the region's sexual communities. San Francisco's reinvigorated downtown attracted new white-collar workers, including many gay men and lesbians. These newcomers helped make the Castro District the center of a newly assertive middle-class gay politics. Santa Clara County's economy, meanwhile, diversified the South Bay's housing stock and differentiated newer suburbs from older ones. Apartments built to accommodate technology workers offered some middle-class gay men and lesbians safe places to live. Maturing suburbs like Palo Alto and Sunnyvale included many white middle-class families with children, but changing marital patterns, aging residents, and diversified housing also meant that they were a smaller share of the community than in previous decades. Newer suburbs like Saratoga and Morgan Hill, by contrast, attracted higher percentages of married, middle-class white couples with children. As Americans battled over the meaning of the sexual revolution, therefore, structural changes in metropolitan economies reorganized residents based on social characteristics like sexuality, class, and race.

San Francisco's economic transformation was most visible in the central business district near Montgomery Street. By the mid-1970s, the city ranked second only to New York among U.S. cities in international trade. This shift brought an influx of white-collar workers, including many middle-class white gay men and lesbians, as manufacturing jobs left the city in a wave of deindustrialization.[2] Many of San Francisco's newest gay residents who worked in the financial sector were relatively homogeneous by race and class. *Chronicle* reporter Randy Shilts described the new gay arrivals as primarily white and college educated, declaring, "It would have been harder to find a segment of the population more suited to fill the thousands of new jobs in the skyscraper corporate headquarters and tourist industries." Journalists like Shilts frequently portrayed migrants attracted to members of the same sex as upwardly mobile, and reporters like *Los Angeles Times* writer Herbert Gold almost reflexively equated "gay" with "relatively high spendable income."[3]

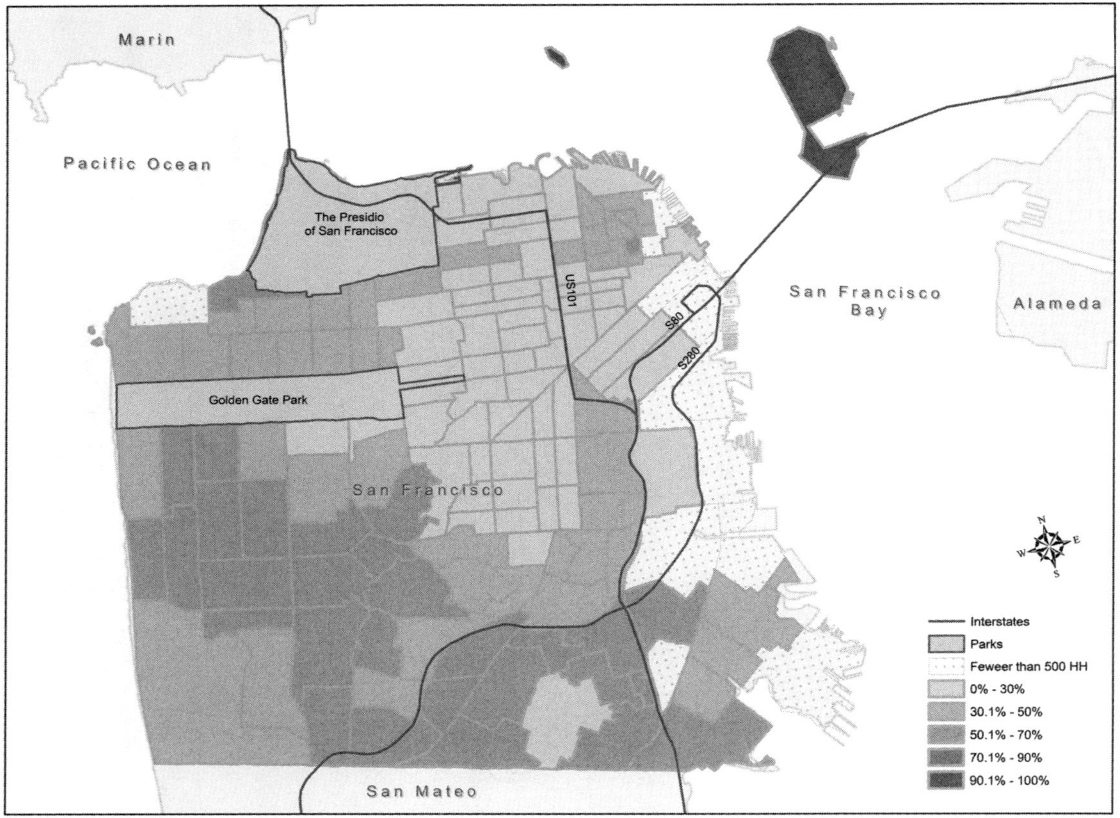

Map 7. Percentage of married couple families in San Francisco by census tract, 1980. This map does not include information for tracts with fewer than 500 households. Center for Urban and Regional Analysis, Ohio State University.

The newcomers described by Gold and Shilts dominated a metropolitan real estate market increasingly divided between haves and have nots. Urban renewal had paved the way for San Francisco's downtown renaissance, but it had also demolished portions of the city's housing. New office construction brought new white-collar workers to a city already suffering from residential shortages. In 1978, the U.S. Savings and Loan League awarded San Francisco the dubious title of city with the highest home prices in the country.[4] During the 1960s, many white, gay middle-class men had taken advantage of a housing hierarchy in which landlords and realtors favored them over most people of color, women, the poor, or gender-nonconforming residents. This preexisting dynamic exploded in the 1970s, as white gay professionals bought property and rented homes in previously predominantly black areas like Lower Haight Street and the Western Addition. Newspapers in the late 1970s recorded growing conflicts between these newcomers and poorer African Americans. The *San Francisco Chronicle* recounted, for example, a community meeting in 1979 in which a black woman accused her white gay neighbors of "taking over" the Western Addition: "I resent a pair of single white men who can earn more and spend $400 each for rent," she declared, "where a young black couple with a child—even a young white couple—can't afford that."[5]

These stories carried an important degree of truth since reporters for newspapers like the *Chronicle* were observing a sexual migration unfolding amid a long economic restructuring process. Many white gay professionals, like the one who asked, "Why the hell should this gem of a city be given over to welfare blacks?" relished their role in gentrification.[6] Yet these stories also concealed the complexity in urban neighborhoods. Heterosexuals also played an important role in gentrifying poorer areas, and not all gay people were white. Moreover, conflicts between white gay professionals and poorer communities of color resulted, in part, from the wider discrimination in the Bay Area's housing markets. Suburban homeowners and realtors had long discriminated against nonwhites and those living outside of marriage, and conflicts over gentrification often involved groups who faced persecution elsewhere in the metropolis. Ads for roommates in the gay press hinted at the ongoing discrimination in the suburbs and wealthier San Francisco neighborhoods. One Sunnyvale resident, for example, asked potential roommates to be "straight appearing" while a Russian Hill man noted he did not want to live with "Fems."[7]

More important, portrayals of "gays" as upwardly mobile glossed over important class and gender divisions among queer people in San Francisco. Upbeat stories about gay gentrification were often separate from accounts of deteriorating conditions in the red-light district. The Tenderloin continued to offer housing of last resort for people who could not find places to live elsewhere in the Bay Area, even as the bottom of the rental market grew even tighter. Between 1975 and 1981, redevelopers demolished or converted nineteen residential hotels in the Tenderloin, taking more than a thousand rooms off the market.[8] These projects occurred amid another influx of queer teenagers in the late 1970s. Smaller than the larger migration of white-collar gay men and lesbians, several hundred queer and gender-variant teenagers nevertheless moved to the Tenderloin mid-decade, prompting social workers to worry about yet another "crisis" in the red-light district.[9]

These housing shifts paralleled the diversification of the suburbs. In the late 1960s, manufacturing in Santa Clara County's aerospace, electronics, and defense industries boomed. The Vietnam War spurred demand for military-related goods, and between 1965 and 1968, South Bay employers with ties to the armed forces added 37,200 jobs to the area.[10] When the war ended, many of these firms produced electronics for civilian use, and during the 1970s, the Peninsula and South Bay—later renamed "Silicon Valley"—emerged as a world leader in tech manufacturing.[11]

This booming regional economy, in turn, propelled the diversification of the housing market. By the early 1970s, demand for single-family homes on the Peninsula and in the South Bay had slackened considerably.[12] In response, local builders erected apartments in record numbers. In the city of Mountain View between 1961 and 1974, 88 percent of all new residential construction consisted of multifamily housing, and the U.S. Department of Housing and Urban Development (HUD) reported in 1970 that "there has been a concentration [of rental units] in areas near employment centers in San Jose, Santa Clara, and Sunnyvale."[13]

Apartment construction in the South Bay not only reflected the region's booming economy but also responded to new ideas about sex and marriage. Young people's tendency to delay marriages and California's legalization of "no-fault" divorce in 1969 created a growing residential market of single people who did not want or could not afford to purchase their own home. HUD observed that the "most recently built units have been designed for that segment of the rental market without young children with restrictions placed upon occupancy to achieve that end."[14] An aggressive developer on the Peninsula advertised Sunnyvale condominiums by bluntly asking in a newspaper advertisement, "Where do you live if you're divorced?"[15]

Changes in family life included more than just easier divorces and delayed marriages, however. They also involved rising numbers of older "empty nesters" and childless couples. Many of the suburbs that stretched from San Mateo to west San Jose had once boasted almost exclusive numbers of married couples with kids, yet between 1970 and 1980 the kinds of households in those areas grew more diverse. This shift, in part, mirrored national trends toward smaller families but also reflected the aging of the suburbs and the growing trend toward multifamily housing. By the early 1970s, some of the postwar Baby Boom had grown up, and new apartment complexes in the area tended to attract unmarried people and childless couples. Between 1970 and 1980, the percentage of children under the age of eighteen living in San Mateo and Santa Clara counties dropped by almost 10 percent.[16] A 1970 survey of neighborhoods in Los Altos found that almost half of the residents indicated they no longer had children under the age of eighteen living with them. Just six years later, a second poll found that 58 percent of the households in the same city consisted exclusively of adults.[17]

These older suburbs differed from the newer, wealthier communities on the west and south sides of the county. Apartment construction primarily took place in the cities closest to the valley floor, such as Mountain View, San Jose, Santa Clara, and Sunnyvale, while the more exclusive suburbs in the area, including Saratoga, Los Altos Hills, and Los Gatos, vigorously enforced zoning regulations against multiunit housing. Between 1966 and 1970, developers further segmented the real estate market by limiting new construction in those towns to increasingly expensive single-family homes. In 1970, the County Planning Department reported that high housing costs had trickled into the rental market, with over half the landlords in the area raising their monthly rates. These trends meant not only that poor people could not find housing in most residential areas in the South Bay but also that rising prices were dividing wealthy neighborhoods on the periphery from middle-class ones near the center.[18]

These segmentations had important implications for family life in the South Bay. Although the number of married people dropped in every tract in Santa Clara County during the decade, the areas near town centers at

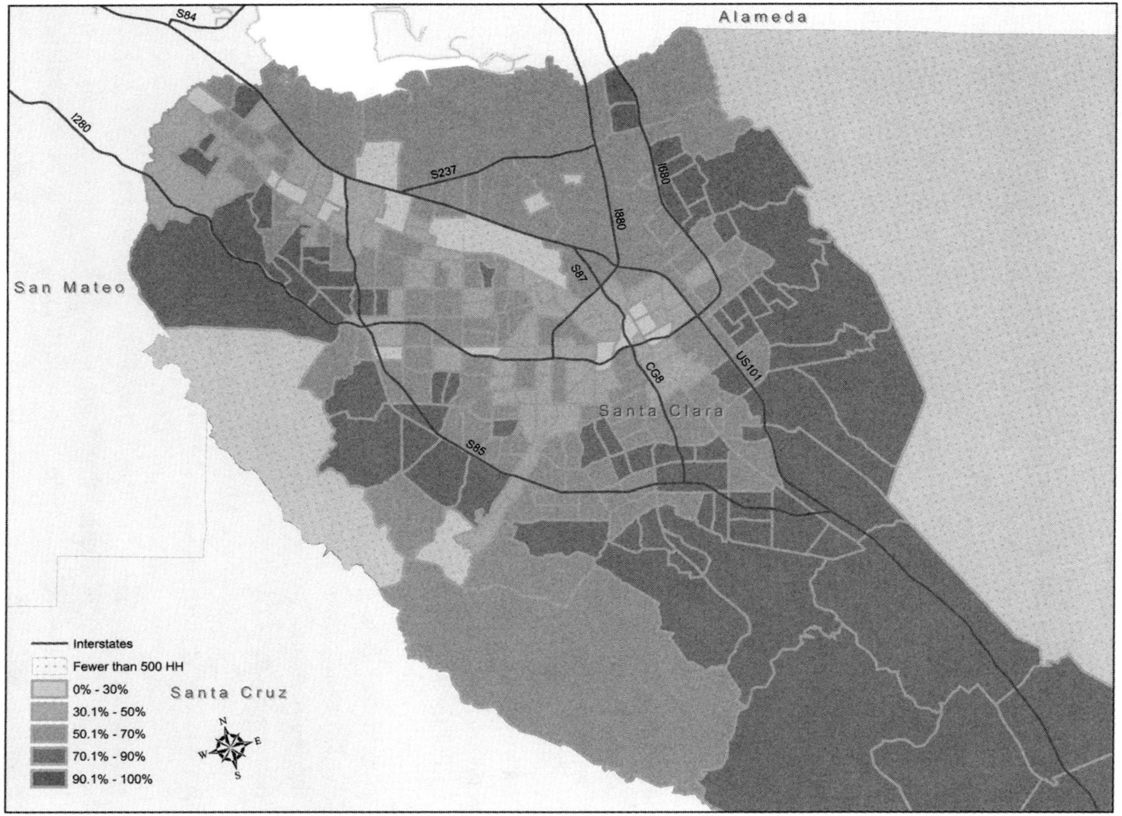

Map 8. Percentage of married couple families in Santa Clara County by census tract, 1980. This map does not include information for tracts with fewer than 500 households. Center for Urban and Regional Analysis, Ohio State University.

the northern end of the valley saw the largest declines. Many tracts between U.S. 101 and Interstate 280, in particular, had majorities of married couples in 1970 but saw the percentages of husband-wife families drop to almost a third of all households in 1980.[19] By contrast, over 85 percent of the adults living on Saratoga's Westside, on San Jose's southern tip, and in the fledgling suburbs near Morgan Hill were married in 1980.[20]

These differences among suburbs set the stage for an uptick in middle-class, white gay communities in San Mateo and Santa Clara counties. Although lesbians and gay men had always lived in the suburbs, discrimination and the high percentage of married couples with children living there had limited their numbers. Moreover, police surveillance and an almost complete lack of bars of any type meant that gay residents who lived in the area prior to 1970 had few available social outlets. Discrimination continued to shape the decisions of where lesbians and gay men lived in the 1970s. In 1974, the San Jose chapter of the National Organization for Women (NOW) objected to landlords who made comments like, "You two women been livin' together very long? Well, you know, I prefer a man and woman couple."[21] Population growth and the "multifamily housing" that came with it, however, created growing pockets of unmarried residents that included gay men and lesbians. According to one gay San Jose renter in 1977, "Many homosexuals manage to keep their 'gay life' invisible by living in large apartment complexes."[22]

Their growing presence in the South Bay spurred the creation of new commercial outlets for gay patrons. In almost every case, these businesses opened in economically marginal places in older suburbs near the northern end of the county. Between 1960 and 1979, over two dozen gay bars opened in Santa Clara County, although no more than eight of them existed at any given time.[23] Two of the South Bay's earliest gay bars, the Crystal Saloon and the Piedmont, opened in the red-light district near San Jose's downtown in the 1960s. As the South Bay sprawled in the subsequent decade, gay-friendly businesses appeared in strip malls and spaces convenient to the freeways. When Barbara Walters and Marsha Martinez opened a lesbian-friendly bookstore in a strip mall in San Jose in 1975, they reported encountering a few "hostile neighbors" but otherwise described their business as a success.[24] Jon Snell located his bar Club Desperado's near the highways in Campbell. Although he initially worried that the spot would hurt business, he later saw it as an advantage because "a lot of people did not want to be seen entering a gay bar. So, being out of the way, they could be anonymous."[25]

Businesses like Club Desperado's were islands for people experiencing same-sex desires in the larger sprawl of the Peninsula and South Bay. Just as other suburbanites had long "shopped" for churches and parenting groups, middle-class gay residents self-selected and joined communities of like-minded people. Looking back on the 1960s and 1970s, longtime Santa Clara County resident Wiggsy Sivertsen recalled that gay men and lesbians needed apartment parties, private meetings in living rooms, and visible commercial establishments like bars and bookstores in order to recognize themselves as a group: "I see our community as a series of tiny veins that spread out into the Santa Clara Valley. It's not like San Francisco," she noted, "where you can point to . . . the Castro, and say, this is where gay people live. For the most part, we gays in the South Bay live and work amongst heterosexuals so the sense of community in a geographic sense does not exist. Instead, we gather together at various places and events to support each other."[26]

Gay Activism in City and Suburb

These shifts in the Bay Area's economy, housing stock, and spatial organization set the stage for multiple forms of gay activism, particularly the large, white middle-class wing of the national gay rights movement. San Francisco, in particular, emerged in the 1970s as a national center for gay politics, while smaller groups of activists launched less-known campaigns for equality in the suburbs. In both places, advocates for gay rights struggled to craft a strategy that reconciled the private and public dimensions of sexuality. Whereas many activists had appealed for the right to privacy in the 1960s, most gay organizations used the term more carefully a decade later. Too often, privacy kept people attracted to others of the same sex from sharing their desires or relationships in public. Gay activists almost always argued that institutions such as mental health groups, schools, churches, and political groups needed to accept the participation of openly gay men and lesbians. Yet, at the same time, the largely white middle-class wing of the gay rights movement also understood that straight-identified people most often related to people they deemed like themselves. Consequently, some of the most successful activists in the 1970s paired calls for the acceptance of openly gay men and lesbians with assurances that most gay people were fundamentally normal and that private and public discrimination violated their privacy. As in moderate politics, the discourse of privacy cut many ways among gay activists.

During the 1970s, gay activists across the ideological spectrum increasingly expressed skepticism about privacy as a discourse for gay liberation. Phyllis Lyon and Del Martin, for example, recognized that many Americans treated "privacy" merely as a synonym for "tolerance," not "equality," and they argued, "We Lesbians are not seeking changes in the law that will only protect us in the 'privacy' of our bedrooms; we want our full citizenship with all its privileges and responsibilities."[27] Gay men and lesbians in this era frequently spoke about the need to "come out of the closet" to expand their claims for equality. Skepticism about privacy grew out of radical arguments in the 1960s, which had framed the "closet" as a repressive domestic place and the "street" as a sexually liberated space, and no event better embodied this ideal than the Gay Pride Parade. When they first planned the event in San Francisco in 1972, organizers argued that the parade expressed important political meanings. "The fact that homosexuals are marching in the streets in large numbers, unafraid and unashamed," they claimed, "forces heterosexuals to re-evaluate their attitudes." But it also helped "closet queens" join the movement since on-lookers might conclude that if "my brothers and sisters are marching in the streets and getting away with it, so can I."[28]

"Privacy" may have fallen out of favor as an organizing discourse for many gay activists, but some advocates found it easy to reconcile older ideas with new ones in campaigns for the repeal of sex laws and the passage of nondiscrimination ordinances. Both reforms relied on notions about privacy, as proponents of gay rights argued that the state should leave the sex lives of its citizens alone. If the government should do anything, these activists argued, it should protect workers' and consumers' abilities to operate in markets free of prejudice. That freedom, however, would never come about unless other Americans understood the discrimination faced by gay people. The largely white, middle-class wing of the movement, therefore, pushed people experiencing same-sex desires to identify themselves publicly so that their families, elected officials, and employers would connect their feelings about homosexuality with specific people.[29]

This combination of "privacy" and "coming out" worked particularly well when lesbians and gay men challenged medical experts' classification of same-sex desire as an illness in need of treatment. Many activists in San Francisco, in particular, rejected the notion that people feeling attracted to the same sex were "disordered," and in the late 1960s and 1970s, they used multiple strategies to challenge this view. When the American Psychiatric

Association (APA) came to San Francisco in 1970, activists disrupted the meeting by shouting, "Off the Couches and Into the Streets!"[30] In 1971, the Council on Religion and the Homosexual convinced the San Francisco Mental Health Association to oppose the criminalization of private, adult, consensual sex and to state that "homosexuality can no longer be equated only with sickness, but may properly be considered as a preference, or orientation for certain kinds of life styles."[31]

Similar pressure in other cities led the largest national group of mental health professionals to eventually change their treatment of homosexuality. In December 1973, the APA voted to reclassify homosexuality as a "disturbance" rather than a "disorder."[32] The change meant that psychiatrists only needed to treat same-sex desire as a problem if a patient asked for help. Their resolution on the subject further urged the decriminalization of private sex acts between consenting adults, reversing almost fifty years' worth of psychiatric and psychological thinking on the subject.

The APA's decision divided the profession, and many doctors continued to treat same-sex desires as a disorder well into the twenty-first century. The change, however, opened the door for gay teachers in particular to fight discrimination in the classroom. By the early 1970s, school districts across California operated in legal limbo when it came to homosexuality. The 1969 *Morrison* decision had directed administrators to tolerate teachers who had slept with members of the same sex in isolated incidents as long as they treated their "private" lives with discretion. This standard created a bind for gay teachers. Whereas most instructors did not need to conceal their out-of-work relationships, school employees in same-sex relationships faced the threat of termination. When it came to workplace violence and harassment, school workers found few alternatives to silence, since an official complaint could lead to dismissal.[33]

In 1975, a group of gay teachers led by Hank Wilson and Tom Ammiano challenged what they called the district's "ostrich-like" policies. They created a Gay Teachers Coalition (GTC) that year and lobbied the Board of Education to amend its policy of nondiscrimination to include "sexual orientation."[34] After several protests, the board reversed its position and reincluded "sexual orientation" in its nondiscrimination policy. Board member Eugene Hopp specifically supported the change because the APA no longer defined homosexuality as an "illness," and even the most conservative official endorsed the amendment because of an aversion to "discrimination."[35]

Activists also sparked conversations about sexuality among most of the nation's major churches. In the mid-1970s, many mainline Protestant denominations in the Bay Area had established caucuses or conferences dedicated to reforming their church's attitudes toward gay men and lesbians. The Northern California Conference of the United Church of Christ, for example, passed resolutions calling for the decriminalization of private adult consensual sex, nominated two openly gay men to its Board of Directors, and petitioned the national Congregationalist Synod to "address itself to employment discrimination based on sexual orientation or marital status within the denomination."[36] Gay Catholics, meanwhile, created a national organization called "Dignity," which sought to reconcile the Church's condemnation of homosexuality with the personal relationships of many of its members. Although the Archdiocese did not endorse the groups, a San Francisco Dignity chapter began meeting in a Mission District church in 1973, and San Jose Catholics formed their own South Bay chapter in 1977.[37] Gay men and lesbians alienated by conservative evangelicals found a haven in the newly created Metropolitan Community Churches (MCC). During the 1970s, this gay-friendly Pentecostal group included some of the fastest growing churches in the United States, and in 1973, 500 people built a congregation near the Castro District.[38]

Gay activists' emphasis on both coming out and privacy expressed itself most clearly in electoral politics. In 1975, at least one Republican and five Democratic political clubs operated in San Francisco. The Alice B. Toklas Club was the largest collection of gay Democrats, and it expanded the candidates' nights first held by the Society for Individual Rights (SIR) in the 1960s. The group endorsed politicians for public office, pushed California Democrats to adopt a gay rights plank, and pressured San Francisco officials to protect gay residents from violence and harassment.[39] The club met with relative success in Sacramento, helping to win passage of California's "consenting adults law" in 1975 and debate over an employment protections bill a year later.[40]

Even more dramatically, Harvey Milk paired notions of "coming out" and "privacy" to become the first openly gay man elected to the City Board of Supervisors. A small business owner and a recent transplant from New York, Milk favored an ideologically mixed set of policies. He supported lower taxes, a balanced budget, less spending on the Vietnam War, and more money for schools.[41] But his success largely grew out of his ability to articulate a political vision for a city transformed by suburbanization. Milk specifically spoke for the "new" San Francisco. As he saw it, his constituents were not "gentrifiers"; they were residents rebuilding the city from the ground up. "Who's buying the houses and using their own sweat and funds to restore them and make them liveable?" he asked in a speech. "The people who are doing this are . . . renovating the spirit of city as well." Milk argued that openly gay men and lesbians were part of the future of the Democratic Party since they were rapidly replacing residents "who can hardly wait to move to Marin or San Jose."[42] If openly gay residents could "stick together," they could confidently "ask for an end to police harassment and discrimination."[43]

Milk argued that openly gay men and lesbians could not succeed alone. Instead, they needed to see the transformation of cities such as San Francisco as an opportunity and ally themselves with other urban communities. "The typical American family with two cars and 2.2 kids doesn't live here anymore," he declared. "It hasn't for years. . . . The city is a city of singles and young married, the city of the retired and the poor, a city of many colors who speak in many tongues." Implicit in this call for "gays" to work with other parts of the city was the recognition that racial segregation, class segmentation, sexual exclusion, and gender differentiation gave neighborhoods their identities. But instead of building his career around challenging those boundaries, Milk campaigned for higher office by pledging to cooperate across them. Just a few years into his political career, his vision became a reality. San Francisco voters approved a plan to elect six of the eleven members of the Board of Supervisors through district, rather than citywide, elections. With a district carved out around the Castro, Milk easily sailed into office in 1977.[44]

While Milk's victory garnered national headlines, the gay rights movement also unfolded outside of urban centers. Small numbers of suburbanites also pushed for gay equality during the 1970s. These predominantly white activists were often recent migrants to the Peninsula and South Bay and frequently lived in the new apartments in places like Palo Alto, far from subdivisions populated by married couples with children. In the early 1970s, they banded together to try to make local institutions more accepting of same-sex relationships. However, the same economic transformations that expanded the suburban lesbian and gay communities also led to the segmentation of Peninsula and South Bay communities, which made their efforts more challenging than in the city. While the aging of the postwar suburbs meant that fewer residents had children, thus freeing them from worries that kids might be exposed to homosexuals on the street or in schools, newer suburbs with larger concentrations of white married couples expressed greater hostility to the gay rights movement. This ultimately meant that though few straight-identified Peninsula or South Bay residents celebrated gay rights, lesbians and gay men found greater tolerance in older communities than in newer ones.

No institution better exemplified the connections between activism and the suburbs' new economy than Stanford. The university educated much of the talent that helped later transform the area into "Silicon Valley."[45] As it grew in size and importance, Stanford attracted activists who opposed the Vietnam War, supported feminism, and advocated for gay rights. During the 1970s, it served as a gathering place for not only gay students but also lesbians and gay men from surrounding communities. For many of San Mateo and Santa Clara counties' gay residents, Stanford offered a rare safe space to meet others like themselves. Donna Hughes-Oldenberg, for example, joined a campus group of lesbians and gay men after separating from her husband, coming out as a lesbian, and moving in with four roommates in what she later joked "had to be the last farmhouse in Sunnyvale."[46]

Lesbian suburbanites like Hughes-Oldenberg played an instrumental role in changing other Peninsula and South Bay residents' ideas about homosexuality when they founded the Gay Community of Concern (GCC) in 1974. Created shortly after the APA's decision to reclassify homosexuality, the GCC helped gay residents find sympathetic mental health professionals and to create a crisis line for people experiencing trauma related to their sexual orientation.[47] The GCC also taught local social agencies to respond sympathetically to gay clients. When its members met with San Mateo Family Services, for example, they reported that the organization's leadership exhibited "some hostility" toward them but also "some receptivity." The GCC asked the agency to change its approach to community outreach by making it clear that gay people "come under the scope of 'family services.' "[48]

The GCC improved the lives of many gay residents and helped reform several mental health agencies, but it also paved the way for legal reforms in several suburbs. In its first year, the group reached out to almost four hundred community organizations, including San Jose Catholic Social Services, Palo Alto schools, and the Santa Clara Council of Churches. Gay activists then used these relationships to push for legal protections for gay men and lesbians at work. When suburban activists Frank Fitch and Boyce

Hinman helped organize a drive for a nondiscrimination ordinance in San Mateo County in 1974, they recruited "12 church denominational and community agencies" to support their cause.[49] When residents with connections to the GCC pressed the Palo Alto Board of Education to include "sexual orientation" in its nondiscrimination policy a year later, they solicited "mental health professionals, clergy, and various humanist supporters" to back their request.[50]

Organizers like Fitch and Hinman needed these alliances because, unlike San Francisco's political clubs, they did not have enough openly gay voters to swing elections, and Peninsula and South Bay officials expressed even more resistance to gay rights than their counterparts in the city. Consequently, activists in places like Palo Alto frequently paired appeals for gay and lesbian equality with respect for privacy. Palo Alto School Board member James Steele, for example, initially opposed hiring openly gay educators because they might use their classrooms to advocate for "their lifestyle."[51] Groups such as the GCC consequently stressed that ending discrimination against gay teachers represented an effort to respect everyone's privacy. GCC staff member Dick Hingson wrote a joint letter to the *Palo Alto Times* in support of protecting gay teachers because the board already forbade "any expression on sexual subjects in the classroom. This applies equally to gay and straight." Therefore, Hingson and his supporters claimed that passing a nondiscrimination ordinance would keep school officials from using "criteria unrelated in themselves to teaching ability" in their hiring decisions.[52]

These arguments proved remarkably successful, but the achievements of groups such as the GCC reveal both the possibilities and limits of suburban gay activism in the 1970s. Thanks to pressure from residents like Hingson, the Palo Alto Board of Education added "sexual orientation" to its nondiscrimination policy, and San Jose, the city of Palo Alto, Mountain View, and Cupertino passed laws protecting gay public workers. These ordinances placed several Santa Clara County suburbs in the vanguard of lesbian and gay rights policy in the mid-1970s. In these efforts, activists benefited from the small scale of municipal politics in the South Bay.[53] Suburban school boards and city councils did not need a massive show of force from gay voters for policymakers to adopt reforms because they only governed a relatively small area. However, metropolitan fragmentation also slowed progress. Whereas San Francisco's ordinance covered all of the residents in the county, the patchwork of laws in Santa Clara County left numerous cities free to legally discriminate. Indeed, these laws notwithstanding, private-sector employees and roughly a third of South Bay residents were left unprotected. This discrepancy, in part, reflected the changing demographics of the South Bay. All of the municipalities that passed nondiscrimination ordinances lay at the northern edge of Santa Clara County and had declining school populations. Western suburbs with high concentrations of married white, middle-class people with children such as Saratoga, by contrast, did not pass protective legislation.

At the same time, campaigns for nondiscrimination ordinances in both San Francisco and Santa Clara County suffered from the limits of reforms overly reliant on the "right to privacy." Most gay activists recognized that privacy limited them to appeals for tolerance from the straight majority. Rosalie Nichols, a South Bay writer and bookstore owner, echoed her counterparts in San Francisco when she declared that "toleration of our 'differences' is not enough" and that lesbians needed to "demand the recognition and respect that are our rightful due." But stiff resistance from police departments, public health offices, school boards, and other government agencies—combined with the reluctance of potential allies to stand up for radical changes—often forced activists like Nichols to downplay claims that "gay is good."

Diversity among cities and suburbs, therefore, helps explain some of the successes and limits of gay rights activism in the 1970s. Although suburban groups shared many of the same goals as middle-class activists in places like the Castro District, including a push for nondiscrimination laws and electing sympathetic leaders to public office, the scale of gay social movements varied across the Bay Area. The high concentration of openly gay men and women in San Francisco helped integrate them into the city's organized politics and gave them enough leverage at the ballot box to elect Harvey Milk and other politicians sympathetic to their cause. Suburban groups enjoyed more modest success thanks to the smaller scale of municipal elections in the South Bay and on the Peninsula. With the exception of San Jose, most cities had small electorates, which left city officials more vulnerable to petition drives and protests. But it also meant organizers in the South Bay needed to mount more numerous campaigns to change laws. Moreover, suburban governments often exhibited more hostility toward notions of gay rights than their counterparts in San Francisco, with residents in the newer southern and western suburbs offering more resistance than their neighbors in older suburbs.

Sexual Privacy and Straight-Identified Communities

While gays debated the "right to privacy," a similarly heated conversation occurred in self-identified straight communities about the meaning of the term. During the 1970s, professional sex educators, parent-teacher associations (PTAs), most mainline Protestant denominations, and, to a lesser extent, the Catholic Church accepted the idea that "consenting adults" should not go to jail or lose employment because of their sex lives. These institutions stopped short of accepting gay equality, however. Instead, they came to a consensus around the three-part sexual hierarchy first elaborated by groups like the Sex Information and Education Council of the United States (SIECUS) in the 1960s: society should encourage people to marry, the state should punish rape and other violent sex crimes, and the government should neither support nor condemn but tolerate private consensual adult relationships outside of marriage, including homosexual ones. Even though many institutions accepted this limited notion of sexual privacy, they still faced criticism from conservatives who insisted that the state should reflect divine rules about sex. Many evangelical Christians, in particular, saw the repeal of state laws banning gay sex or the enactment of nondiscrimination ordinances as violations of their privacy. Thus, many straight-identified people remained divided over issues of sexuality while invoking a similar discourse of privacy to support their viewpoint.

SIECUS had promoted ideas about privacy in the 1960s, but changes in the scientific and social consensus on the nature of sexuality reshaped sex educators' commitment to the idea. Medical experiments in the 1960s had allegedly revealed that adult sexual desires originated in a combination of genetics, very early childhood experiences, and hormones. Researchers initially hesitated to specify the exact origins of a person's sexual orientation, but over the course of the 1970s, they gradually moved away from Freudian ideas about role models.[54] At the same time, family experts responded to the call for sexual autonomy from the women's movement. Many feminists in the late 1960s rejected the longstanding notion that men had strong sexual urges while women desired "affection" or "romance." Writers like Shulamith Firestone and Anne Koendt called for women to experience sexual pleasure on equal footing with men and pushed back against Freudian theories about the passivity of female desire.[55] Activists paired these calls for sexual equality with broader claims about women's reproductive autonomy, denouncing restrictions on contraceptives, the criminalization of abortion, and the legitimation of rape.[56]

Together, the new tendency to ascribe sexuality to predetermined influences and feminist demands for sexual autonomy motivated a rethinking of sex education's goals. The environments in which postwar psychologists had once claimed that children unconsciously learned about sex now seemed less relevant since, as Mary Calderone declared, "by the age of five, one should recognize that a child comes to school with the primary part of his or her sex education completed and fixed."[57] Groups like SIECUS consequently celebrated what they now called the "new sex education" or "self-actualization," which involved helping Americans of all ages to seek personal fulfillment through consensual relationships with others. SIECUS issued a new set of goals in 1974, which called "sexual choice a fundamental human right." Individuals' ability to exercise that right required education so that they could develop a "personal ethical code" that allowed them to make "rational" decisions about their bodies.[58] According to this new position, when government no longer "coerced" people into abiding by a particular norm or another, sex education could empower individuals to select relationships in a growing marketplace of family models and "lifestyles."[59]

This empowerment, however, clashed with sex educators' tendency to limit the marketplace of acceptable ideas. Though SIECUS moved away from some of its more conservative positions on the primacy of marriage in the 1970s, its earlier ideas still defined the field. In particular, most family life educators from the period continued to treat heterosexual marriage as superior to other kinds of relationships, and no issue illustrated this pattern better than their treatment of homosexuality. With the new research about the early development of sexual attraction, family experts dropped the most stigmatizing references to homosexuality in their work. Yet a study of health textbooks in the mid-1970s complained that "almost without exception, the message of these texts seems to be that sex education is 'about' boys and girls growing up to be men and women who have monogamous marriage to produce babies, and that anything outside that pattern is 'abnormal.'" The study indicated that most of these materials barely mentioned same-sex relationships, citing a 113-page textbook in which only 2 percent of the content dealt with homosexuality.[60] These books offered no information about how people of the same sex derived physical pleasure from one another or if gay relationships carried the same interpersonal dynamics as heterosexual ones. One SIECUS writer complained that although many of his peers supported the view "that homosexual acts between consenting adults should not be proscribed by law," they still believed "homosexuality is not quite right."[61]

Bay Area gay activists witnessed the limits of the "new sex education" firsthand when they sought to change curricula in local schools in the mid-1970s. The San Francisco Board of Education considered changes to the city's program on sex and family life so that it reflected "gay lifestyles accurately" in 1977.[62] The move came in the wake of gay teachers' successful bid to force the board to add "sexual orientation" to its nondiscrimination policy. But the gay activists faced more resistance on the new subject. Public officials disliked the idea that schools might detail gay sex acts or equate homosexuality with heterosexuality, and they limited changes to the program to only the elimination of "stereotypes." Board of Education member Eugene Hopp told the *Examiner* that he firmly believed "derogatory language and harassment of gays should cease, 'but that's a long way from teaching elementary school children the benefits of homosexuality.' "[63]

These texts about family life moved among an increasingly divided parenting public. Numerous factors caused the National PTA, a longtime champion of sex education, to shed members after the mid-1960s. Shrinking birth rates reduced the number of parents with school-aged children, leaving PTAs with a smaller pool of potential volunteers. Their decline, however, also stemmed from changing gender norms. The PTA's vision of an order built around "home, school, and church" had relied heavily upon the work of middle-class married mothers, and during the 1970s, feminism and rising numbers of women workers in the paid labor force meant fewer mothers available to volunteer.[64] At the same time, PTAs split over school integration. Much to the dismay of liberal units in places like San Francisco, the California PTA endorsed an amendment to the U.S. Constitution banning "court ordered busing" to achieve "racial balance" in classrooms in 1974.[65] Suburban units later flooded the state organization's office with official resolutions calling racial integration between districts a violation of the PTA's mission to bring "into closer relation the home and school."[66]

This combination of declining birth rates, feminism, higher rates of women in the paid labor force, and controversy over topics like racial integration, therefore, drove PTA membership downward. Between 1963 and 1977, the number of dues-paying members fell by 50 percent nationwide. When the organization increased fees to cover the costs of this decline, it sparked an even greater exodus. After a dues hike in 1973, over 80,000 volunteers quit in California alone. In 1974, the organization canceled its monthly magazine the *National Parent-Teacher* thanks to its inability to cover the costs of publication.[67] Records from the South Bay's Sixth District reveal declining membership in the aging suburbs in the north end of the county. In the early 1970s, thirty-two PTA units worked in the city of Santa Clara. Between 1971 and 1972, nineteen of those units lost members, with several of them losing over a hundred people.[68]

Amid this decline, the National PTA and its California branch said very little about homosexuality. Parent-teacher magazines carried articles on sex education, yet they said next to nothing about gay rights or same-sex relationships. This omission, in part, reflected the new "middle ground" in which many Americans saw gay relationships. Like the textbooks of the era, this silence reflected the popular notion that the "right to privacy" protected homosexual acts but that same-sex couples did not equal heterosexual ones. PTAs often avoided appearing to "endorse" homosexuality by refusing to condemn or even mention it. In 1977, PTA President Grace Baisinger told the readers of *Parents* magazine that the nation "faced a crisis for families." She listed single-parent households, teenage pregnancy, and inadequate sex education in schools but made no mention of gay rights. Instead, she promised her readers that the PTA simply would "Focus on the Family."[69]

When the Gay Teachers Coalition pushed the San Francisco Board of Education to include more positive references to homosexuality in its family life program, parent groups resisted. In the mid-1970s, the city's PTA notably tolerated gay rights. The group did not protest when the Board of Education added "sexual orientation" to its nondiscrimination policy, and it even asked gay political groups in the city to support school bond issues.[70] But many of its volunteers also rejected amendments to the curriculum that suggested that children could choose homosexuality as a viable alternative to heterosexual marriage. The *Examiner* reported that the San Francisco PTA received numerous phone calls from parents protesting the decision to make the city's family life education program more gay affirming.[71]

Many mainline Protestants and Catholics similarly supported an individual's right to privacy from the state, but they also expressed ambivalence about the sexual boundaries that churches should impose on their members. One Protestant writer called it "unthinkable" that people might "lose jobs, be denied housing, and suffer police harassment" for "what happens in bedrooms."[72] Doctrinal teachings on homosexuality, however, caused serious internal debates among churches. Although most supported the right to privacy when it came to the law, they often disagreed over whether their faith should treat homosexual relationships as equal to heterosexual ones. Herbert Anderson, a Protestant theologian, observed in 1978 that, when it came to sex, Christians increasingly wanted ministers to help them "differentiate what is [just] legal from what is moral" and that "the matter of homosexuality will require special consideration by religious communities."[73]

This distinction between "morality" and "legality" split churches, as they increasingly differed over whether or not homosexuality warranted condemnation or acceptance. In the mid-1970s, gay-friendly Catholic groups like Dignity and liberal Protestant thinkers such Norman Pettinger called for their faiths to recognize homosexual relationships as signs of God's grace and love. Theological conservatives, meanwhile, rejected what they saw as the dismantling of the core tenets of their religion. Pope Paul VI bookended a ten- to twelve-year period of relative doctrinal liberalism in the Catholic Church with the "Declaration on Certain Questions of Sexual Ethics" in 1976. The document reaffirmed the Church's stance on premarital chastity and, despite policy changes in groups like the APA, singled out homosexual acts as "intrinsically disordered" and a "mortal sin."[74]

Many Mainline Protestants and Catholics, however, still embraced a consensus around the "right to privacy." Catholic writer Eugene Kennedy, for example, rejected "extreme positions" that either made homosexuals "outcasts from ordinary society" or "tell us that gay is good." Instead, he advocated for a "large middle ground" that "does not make homosexuality into a model way of life, but it at least permits the rest of the world to see and perhaps understand the living problems of homosexuals."[75] Protestant theologian William Muehl declared, "What is required is a firm reassertion of the time-honored distinction between toleration on one hand and approval on the other."[76]

Family life education in public schools and the right to privacy changed many mainline Protestants' and Catholics' ideas about sex and the state, but arguably the most important revolution on these issues came among evangelical Christians in the 1970s. Many religious conservatives withdrew from public schools altogether. The *Los Angeles Times* noted in 1978 that conservative churches were founding an average of two new schools a day across the country and three a week in California alone. The newspaper attributed this growth to a longstanding desire of some parents to give their children an education with "moral and religious dimensions" and more recent attempts by some whites to escape court-ordered busing in the public schools.[77] At the same time, small numbers of Christian parents withdrew their children from public education and opted to "homeschool" them. A *San Jose Mercury* article from the mid-1980s estimated that just over eighteen hundred families in California taught their kids at home and profiled Karen Genthrup, a South Bay mother who pulled her two sons out of the public education system in order to "teach them the Bible in depth."[78]

The numbers of church-schooled and homeschooled students remained relatively small in the 1970s, but their growth signaled both the splintering of the older imagined unity between parents, teachers, and clergy and evangelicals' embrace of privacy on their own terms. Secular sex education, the sexual revolution, and racial integration prompted many religious conservatives to launch their own biblically inspired programs on family life. Distrustful of public schools, these campaigns offered evangelical parents tools to teach their children about sex in accordance with their faith, free of the state's interference. James Dobson, author of the bestselling *Dare to Discipline*, emerged as the most well-known evangelical author, publishing numerous parenting guides in the 1970s. He argued that young people needed to hear "what the Bible teaches" because they were "bombarded with sexual messages that contradict what we believe." Public schools, in his view, had failed students because they refused to discuss "the morality of sex."[79]

Evangelicals like Dobson had launched sex education campaigns in the past, but the 1970s witnessed both greater skepticism about secular education and greater interest in psychological theories from the 1950s. Some churches in the postwar era had argued that the Bible offered the best manual on parenting. But in the 1970s, evangelical writers paired religious arguments with theories remarkably similar to the advice dispensed by Freudian-influenced childrearing experts in the postwar period. Southern Baptist writer John Howell, for example, borrowed liberally from both older family experts like Evelyn Mills Duvall and portions of the Bible. He counseled parents that children go through "stages of development" and that well before they "do any verbal teaching of the child, their own sexual attitudes will be communicated to him through their interaction with one another."[80]

Writers such as Howell celebrated parents' freedom to remove their children from public schools and relied on postwar theories about sexual development, but they expressed alarm about the ways the right to privacy had loosened the rules governing sex. Many conservative Christians argued that the state's laws reflected divine rules about appropriate human behavior.[81] Deviating from those tenets meant potential chaos not only for an individual but also for the larger society. Dobson best articulated this point of view when he decried what he called the destruction of "traditional family relationships." God, he contended, "created the family and the principles which make it work. And if we deviate from His plan to substitute our puny schemes, we will witness (I believe) the disintegration of everything of value and meaning."[82]

Not all evangelical parenting texts from the era, however, treated the state as direct extensions of the church. Many of them offered contradictory advice that paired rhetorical support for individual choice with absolutist claims about the divine rules of sex. Not unlike secular parenting experts in the same period, evangelical sex educators often stressed preparing young people to develop their own value systems. Experts like Henry Hollis frequently cited the need to do away with "Puritanical" views and that churches had a responsibility to tell their members that "sex is God's good gift to be celebrated and responsibly expressed."[83] This pairing of celebration with responsibility defined many evangelical books on the subject. Young people were free to develop their own values systems, but they also needed to learn that God did not view all beliefs equally.[84] Christian parenting experts particularly struggled to reconcile their psychological beliefs that same-sex desires originated in early childhood traumas with their religious views that people should choose to follow biblical teachings about sex. James Dobson, for example, called homosexuality "an abnormal desire that reflects deep problems."[85] But he also criticized "the person who chooses that way of life in defiance of God."[86]

Dobson's distinction not only reveals the difficulties of reconciling a psychological theory that homosexuality was an innate "disorder" with a religious view that expected people to "choose" relationships in accordance with the Bible. It also suggests that some evangelical writers in the 1970s formulated their own "middle path" when it came to talking about same-sex desires. Conservative Christian parenting experts encouraged their readers to "love the sinner but hate the sin," and they even sometimes paired the right to privacy with biblical condemnations of same-sex relationships. John Drakeford acknowledged in *A Christian View of Homosexuality* that "the church must recognize that homosexuals, too, have been unfairly treated in the past. Most of the laws and practices which discriminate against homosexuals are obviously unfair." But he also argued, "This does not mean that we have to accept the practice of homosexuality any more than we have to accept any other sinful practice."[87]

Sex and the Suburban Religious Marketplace

These discussions about sex, faith, and the state did not play out in a vacuum. Christian parenting experts wrote amid one of the most dramatic religious transformations of the twentieth century. In the 1970s, mainline Protestant and Catholic churches shed members in record numbers, while evangelical congregations exploded. This process, in part, reflected divides over the meaning of the sexual revolution, as worshippers voted with their feet by joining more conservative churches or abandoning religion altogether. In the South Bay, questions about homosexuality and privacy's meaning upset the religious marketplace that church builders had erected in the postwar suburbs. As conflicts about sex grew closer to home, Santa Clara County churches made difficult decisions about whether or not to officially welcome a gay-friendly church in their midst. The debates around the issue in the mid-1970s drew into sharp relief the differences between churches that at least nominally accepted that gay men and lesbians had a right to privacy and those that did not.

One could see these changes with merely a cursory look at media coverage of religion in the 1970s. As early as 1968, the *San Jose Mercury-News* noted a "New Religious Awakening" in the South Bay. The newspaper reported that Protestant church attendance seemed to follow population shifts and that in "the West Valley's rapidly growing suburban areas, church strength is gaining."[88] Conservative Protestant congregations grew at astonishing rates in the subsequent decade. San Jose's Calvary Community Church, for example, expanded from 365 members in 1970 to almost five thousand a decade later. Kenny Foreman founded a new church in the South Bay in 1965 and built a congregation of three thousand people by 1980.[89] When Minister Marvin Rickard joined the Los Gatos Christian Church (LGCC) in 1959, it had only eighty-three members, but by the early 1980s, it boasted over five thousand.[90]

These churches owed much of their growth to their pastors' ability to navigate the South Bay's religious market. Enterprising ministers frequently patterned their churches after popular shopping malls, locating them near busy freeways, using billboards to attract motorists, and advertising on Christian television and radio networks. These strategies paralleled efforts by gay businesses to advertise and to locate off the interstates, and they highlight important similarities between gay and evangelical Christian groups. Like the gay communities described by Wiggsy Sivertsen, conservative congregations in the 1970s stretched out across the area around the South Bay like a series of "veins" and "arteries" centered on central churches.[91]

Congregants joined new churches for many reasons, including religious faith. But concerns about normative family life and a desire to participate in communities of likeminded people also fueled the growth of conservative evangelical churches. Evangelical pastors in the 1970s frequently marketed their congregations as a means of strengthening ties between husbands, wives, and their children. One San Jose minister observed in 1980 that South Bay worshippers were increasingly "moving towards independent churches, big super churches, where people come as families, where the churches attempt to minister to the whole family."[92] These conservative "big super churches" often advertised that they offered congregants marital counseling, Christian sex education, and parenting seminars.[93] They further promised would-be members communities bound by relative ideological, sexual, class, and racial homogeneity. In an influential book on congregation building, Donald McGavran told ambitious ministers in 1970 that if they wanted to boost membership, they needed to respect the "undeniable fact" that "people like to become Christians without crossing racial, linguistic, or class barriers."[94] Although it is unclear if South Bay ministers specifically read McGavran's work, they used similar approaches to build congregations. The LGCC's Marvin Rickard believed that social heterogeneity bred strife within the church, and he therefore attempted to build a congregation of people with similar backgrounds. In his memoir *Let It Grow*, he advised other pastors, "When a church is stratified economically, ethnically or racially, all others feel a little less than welcome."[95]

The LGCC, of course, was not the first church to encourage homogeneous communities; many mainline Protestants and Catholics had previously pursued similar strategies in the South Bay. But Rickard's success underscores the ways in which the new "megachurches" reinforced stratification in the suburbs. By using the personal relationships of his congregants to invite new members, he built a community of "likeminded" people without necessarily having to evangelize in predominantly African American or Latino neighborhoods.[96]

The phenomenal gains of churches like Rickard's largely came at the expense of mainline Protestants and Catholics. A Gallup poll, for example, found that the Catholic Church lost 18 percent of its members between 1962 and 1975, while a separate survey concluded that the number of Methodists, Congregationalists, and Episcopalians dropped by 15 percent between 1970 and 1985.[97] Methodist District Superintendent Arthur Schuck told the *San Jose Mercury News* in 1968, "It's a change from the 1950s, when there was a greater enthusiasm for the church as an established spiritual center."[98]

Schuck's nostalgia for the postwar period highlights the ways in which church membership often reflected the communities around them. Protestants and Catholics had built numerous congregations and parishes in the 1940s and 1950s in subdivisions filled with newly married couples with children. However, as Santa Clara County evolved into a "postsuburban" landscape with both aging suburbs and newer ones with high concentrations of married couples with children, churches in older areas lost members. Church planners across the country noted similar phenomena. In a study of mainline Protestant churches near Albany, New York, Douglas Walrath observed that in areas along the interstate highway system, where "housing has been purchased by younger middle-aged couples with children," congregations expanded or stabilized. Congregations unable to follow this trend faced declining memberships.[99] The Santa Clara Methodist Church faced this exact problem in 1966 when it borrowed heavily to build a new sanctuary. The congregation anticipated growth for the foreseeable future, but when the Baby Boom slowed and fewer couples with kids moved to the surrounding area, attendance dropped and it faced financial ruin.[100]

Yet the shift in religious affiliation also stemmed from the era's sexual politics. Sociologist Dean Hoge noted in 1979 that people who reported the strongest religious affiliations proclaimed having deep opposition to "premarital sex, extramarital sex, homosexuality, abortion, divorce, and pornography."[101] While most Americans had adopted more liberal views on those subjects in the 1970s, they also tended to abandon religion altogether and left mainline Protestants competing for a shrinking pool of worshippers. "The value shift," Hoge concluded, "seems to conduce people to no church participation at all, not to participation in liberal churches."[102] As moderate churches shifted incrementally on issues such as gay rights, they not only failed to attract new members but also shed conservatives who frequently sought churches who shared their beliefs. Looking back on the 1970s, the *San Jose Mercury* reported in 1980, "Abortion, homosexuality, the role of women, and Scripture were the big issues on the American religious scene during the decade, and they took a toll among the 'mainline' denominations."[103]

These debates about religion and homosexuality and the changing membership of many Christian denominations set the stage for a fight over gay rights in the Santa Clara County Council of Churches in 1975. During the 1970s, the South Bay's largest organization of mainline Protestants watched uneasily as evangelical ministers built increasingly larger congregations. Conservative churches organized the Greater San Jose Association of Evangelicals (GSJAE) in 1974, a rival group that pledged greater cooperation among conservative churches on "moral issues," and the Council of Churches' leadership greeted it tepidly.[104] At the same time, a group of South Bay Christians founded a local branch of the gay-friendly Metropolitan Community Church.[105]

The wider religious debates about homosexuality broke apart the South Bay's Council of Churches when the MCC tried to join the group in 1974. The Council's leadership agonized over the question for almost a year, and its Board of Directors only approved the MCC's petition in December 1975 after conceding that their constitution required them to accept any applicant who "believes in the divinity of Jesus Christ."[106] This justification proved insufficient for many of the group's more conservative members who demanded a new vote to expel the gay-friendly congregation. Several ministers in this faction alleged that accepting the MCC constituted an endorsement of homosexuality.

Their complaints led the Council to schedule a new referendum on the issue and prompted a countywide discussion about gay rights and the church. Throughout these debates, partisans on all sides of the issue framed their positions as "moderate" and gestured toward the right to privacy. Many of the MCC's opponents often distinguished between homosexual individuals whom they claimed to love regardless of sin and public "endorsement" of homosexuality. The Blossom Hill Baptist Church's leadership conceded in a letter that they wanted to help "homosexuals and all others involved with problems for which society is often irresponsible, insensitive, and cruel." But they rejected the notion that "the gay lifestyle is an acceptable alternative to heterosexuality."[107] Joy Wilson of San Jose's First United Church criticized the Council for what she described as its "sanction" of homosexuality. Yet she also insisted that her letter was "not an attempt to condemn persons" but rather opposition to "what we consider a harmful way of life."[108]

While the MCC's opponents distinguished their views from extreme forms of "discrimination," its supporters drew a similar line between "tolerance" and "acceptance." Many letters written to the Council stressed the New Testament's admonition for Christians to "love their neighbors." Henry Wagner dissented from his church's criticism of the MCC, and he protested what he saw as his fellow Presbyterians' failure to recognize that "Jesus Christ expressed the love of God in word and deed and became a brother to all kinds of sinful men." But as indicated by his reference to "sinful men," Wagner's letter of support left the notion that homosexuality was a problem untouched, framing his support for the MCC as a matter of charity instead of equal treatment.[109]

When the Council revoted on the issue, allies of the gay-friendly congregation won by an almost two-to-one margin, but the group's final resolution insisted that the decision "should not be construed as condoning homosexuality."[110] President Fred Hillier told the *San Francisco Chronicle* that he worried about the "future of the group" because he thought acceptance of the MCC gave "people a distorted picture." Executive Director Kenneth Bell, meanwhile, asked the "homosexual community" to "not to push too hard" after the vote to preserve unity.[111] Nevertheless, the Council's decision alienated many of its conservative members. Between 1975 and 1976, seven churches left the group and several more announced that they planned to cut their donations to the Council. Bell privately worried about the financial viability of his organization and bitterly told a lesbian who aspired to become a Presbyterian minister, "You don't make all the gains in 24 hours, or even two months, and there needs to be some wisdom."[112]

Religious groups, therefore, increasingly split over the question of gay rights in the 1970s. As some mainline Protestants and Catholics edged toward tolerance of homosexuality, many evangelical churches denounced them and gained members. While the new megachurches included only a fraction of the South Bay's total population, they represented a new social and political phenomenon at the dawn of the culture wars. Reinforcing tendencies already at play in suburban development, these congregations represented distilled communities of likeminded believers. Though groups like the Council of Churches fought internal battles over homosexuality, as Bell's comments made clear, these divisions did not neatly map onto a clear liberal-conservative division. With the notable exception of the MCC, most South Bay churches spoke about tolerance even as they reinforced a distinction between the value of gay and straight relationships.

San Jose's Gay Pride and the Briggs Initiative

By the mid-1970s, many of the dominant pieces of the late twentieth-century culture wars were in place. After the California legislature passed the consenting adults law in 1975, conservative churches in Santa Clara County joined a statewide network called the Concerned Citizens Coalition to try to repeal it. The Coalition and its later iteration—the "Family Lobby"—tried to place the issue on the ballot in 1975 and 1976, failing both times.[113] Conservatives in the legislature crushed a statewide nondiscrimination law championed by gay organizations and banned same-sex marriage for the first time in the state's history.[114] Gay organizations, meanwhile, worked to secure protections based on sexual orientation at the local and state levels. Shortly after winning office, Harvey Milk ushered a more comprehensive nondiscrimination ordinance through the San Francisco Board of Supervisors. The new regulation made it illegal for private employers, landlords, homeowners, or the operators of public accommodations such as restaurants to discriminate based on sexual orientation.[115]

As these battles transpired, politicians at the local and national levels expressed sympathy for gay rights, even as they distanced themselves from "endorsements" of homosexuality. City Supervisor Dianne Feinstein supported San Francisco's 1978 broadened nondiscrimination code because it covered "basics" like employment. But she promised to "move for repeal" if gay employees used the law to go to work in drag or to move into neighborhoods with families who lacked a "depth of understanding."[116] Meanwhile, presidential candidate and Southern Baptist Jimmy Carter claimed that the "Bible teaches against homosexuality," and "I do believe in the teachings of the Bible." But he also supported laws against discrimination because he did not think "it's right to single out homosexuals for special abuse or harassment."[117] The larger public seemed to support this middle ground. A survey taken in 1977 found that only 17 percent of Californians thought that gay men and lesbians should be "approved of by society and allowed to live their own homosexual lifestyles," and 43 percent of people polled replied that they should be "tolerated, but only if they don't show their way of life."[118] The same survey, meanwhile, found that 59 percent of Californians opposed same-sex marriage and a narrow majority favored banning gay teachers.[119]

These straight-identified centrists, who tolerated but did not approve of homosexuality, dominated most discussions of a national campaign against gay rights in 1977. That year, conservative activist Anita Bryant successfully fought for the repeal of a nondiscrimination ordinance in Dade County, Florida. In Miami and its suburbs, she called homosexuality a "sin" and alleged that the county ordinance attempted to "legitimize a lifestyle that is both perverse and dangerous."[120] Bryant won the fight in South Florida, in part thanks to her appeals to local churches where get out the vote drives were "waged with evangelical fervor."[121] The conservative singer subsequently launched similar drives in midsized cities like St. Paul, Minnesota, and Wichita, Kansas, in which she united conservative churches with straight-identified moderates who believed nondiscrimination laws gave homosexuals license to do as they wished.

Bryant's campaigns drew national attention, including in the Bay Area suburbs. The *San Jose Mercury* ran numerous forums in which local residents expressed both dismay and excitement at the coming "culture war." Sonia Bailey from Morgan Hill, for example, celebrated Bryant because Americans had a "God-given responsibility to protect our children from the harmful exposure of pornography, homosexuals, and all the other garbage."[122] Gay rights groups in the South Bay expressed mixed feelings, with some worried that even though local residents allegedly "have more of an open mind" than Floridians, "a gay rights issue has not been tested in San Jose or Santa Clara County."[123] The *Mercury*, meanwhile, editorialized that "most Americans are willing to accept homosexuality as a fact of life, but they are not willing to grant it social approval." At issue, according to the newspapers' editors, was the question of privacy: "Stripped to its essence, it is probably accurate to say most Americans want gays to stay in the closet."[124]

After Bryant's successes in 1977, two local examples underscored the ways in which many straight-identified South Bay residents used privacy to alternately restrict and support gay rights. The first broke out when the San Jose City Council designated a week in June 1978 as "Gay Pride Week." Approximately forty to fifty conservative churches phoned elected officials and circulated petitions demanding that they rescind the proclamation. Pride Week's adversaries denounced the plan for numerous reasons, including biblical injunctions against homosexuality, but they often framed their opposition in terms of privacy. The city council's decision, according to the protesters, represented their government's affirmation of behaviors of which they disapproved. This differed from "discrimination" because an officially designated "Pride Week" violated their right not to endorse homosexuality. Ed Adams from San Jose's Foxworthy Baptist Church declared, "We don't take pride in gay activity, and we don't think the council should condone such activity. We aren't trying to put people down, but the council is rubbing our noses in it."[125]

The city council subsequently renamed the celebration "Gay Human Rights Week." Opponents, however, rejected the change in wording and won over many other South Bay residents. When nine hundred people showed up at a city council meeting to protest any gay rights declaration, Councilman David Runyon said, "The City Council should not be involved in an issue favoring any sexual orientation group."[126] When conservatives like Runyon threatened to recall the officials who supported the proclamation, would-be candidates for city council criticized the measure for violating other citizens' privacy. Council candidate Jerry Estruth claimed, "My feeling is that it's not the legitimate function of government to sanction human sexual behavior. The government is already intruding in too many facets of life."[127]

Gay organizations, including the local MCC, turned out to support both measures, but they ultimately failed. Facing a tight election, the city council rescinded its support for "Gay Human Rights Week" by a five-to-two vote. Garza, one of the legislators who switched sides, read a prepared statement to explain his changing views after the meeting: "There has been an overwhelming consensus," he claimed, "that the Council should not involve itself in identifying either positively or negatively with the personal lifestyle of any of its citizens."[128]

Privacy again came to the fore just a few months later when South Bay voters considered Proposition 6, a proposed ban on gay teachers. State Senator John Briggs from suburban Orange County near Los Angeles sponsored the measure. If passed, the so-called Briggs Initiative would have required California school administrators to remove any teacher "who engages in public homosexual activity and/or public homosexual conduct direct at, or likely to the attention of schoolchildren or other school employees." As he campaigned for Proposition 6, Briggs portrayed the wider gay rights movement as a violation of the privacy of California's citizens. In October 1978, he tried to draw attention to what he saw as the "excesses" of homosexuality by holding a press conference near a gay Halloween celebration in San Francisco. On another occasion, he declared, "I don't think the average person in San Francisco shares the views of the gays. People are just sick and tired of them flaunting it."[129]

Although he claimed to speak for San Franciscans, Briggs frequently condemned the city and campaigned as a specifically "suburban" candidate." The state senator and Proposition 6 drew most of their support from large conservative churches in places like Santa Clara County. Conservative South Bay pastors expressed support for a ban on gay teachers as early as 1977, and in October 1978, Briggs spoke at the North Valley Baptist Church in Santa Clara to promote Proposition 6.[130] As he campaigned, the state senator from Orange County highlighted what he saw as the moral causes of the urban crisis. On one occasion, he even called San Francisco "the moral garbage dump of homosexuality in this country" and declared, "It's time to get rid of those people who want to lead an openly immoral life and expect a 21-gun salute every time they go past."[131]

Briggs's insistence that the gay rights movement violated other Californians' privacy drew a calculated response from figures like Harvey Milk, who also used privacy to support his position. Milk and his allies simultaneously pushed lesbians and gay men to organize politically while telling the rest of the electorate that conservatives—not homosexuals—violated people's privacy. The Castro supervisor argued in 1978 that gay men and lesbians could fight the Briggs Initiative by being open about their sexuality. "You must come out to your parents," he declared. "I know that it is hard and will hurt them but think about how they will hurt you in the voting booth! Come out to your relatives. I know that is hard and will upset them, but think about how that will upset you in the voting booth . . . come out to your friends, if indeed they are your friends . . . come out to your co-workers."[132] At the same time, Milk argued that Briggs and his supporters were trying to use the law to impose their "private" morality on everyone else. At a debate with the Orange County state senator, Milk told his opponent, "Go to church and preach your religion, but don't legislate it. You want to legalize and constitutionalize bigotry, and I say no."[133]

The San Francisco supervisor had a point. Although Briggs sometimes framed his initiative as a tool to protect Californians' privacy, he and his

Figure 13. State Senator John Briggs speaks to reporters outside San Francisco's city hall, while protesters picket on sidewalk, 1978. Fang family *San Francisco Examiner* photograph archive negative files, BANC PIC 2006.029:144863.03.33—NEG, box 1734. © Regents of the University of California, Bancroft Library, University of California, Berkeley.

supporters also defended it with the language of "morality." Most notably, they relied on biblical arguments against homosexuality that connected the secular law of the state with the divine commandments of the Bible. San Jose's Jan Swanson, for example, wrote to the *San Jose Mercury*, "The Bible . . . says there will be no homosexuals in Heaven. If [God] doesn't want them in Heaven, then I don't want them teaching my kids."[134]

Conservative Christians had made similar arguments in other campaigns, including the debates about San Jose's Pride Week. But Proposition 6's supporters faced an uphill battle. Unlike the gay pride debate, many Santa Clara County residents saw Briggs as an opportunist trying to impose his religious views on others, and his alliances with conservative churches did not help his cause. Similarly, many mainline Protestant and some Catholic leaders saw Proposition 6 as an attempt by evangelicals to impose their values on the state's legal system. When Briggs made an early trip to Santa Clara County to campaign for a ban on gay teachers, ministers from the

Council of Churches invaded a private meeting to protest what they described as a violation of "civil rights."[135] C. Kilmer Myers, Episcopal bishop of California, warned, "We have been [too] 'nice' to the fundamentalists. . . . This political farce operating under the cloak of a distorted Christianity could lead to fascism American-style."[136]

Myers's invocation of "fundamentalists" and "fascism" highlighted the ways in which opponents of the Briggs Initiative increasingly focused on constitutional questions and voters' dislike of conservative Christians rather than on sexual equality. Unlike gay activists who framed the issue as a matter of "rights," many suburban voters spoke about privacy in a manner that allowed them to oppose Proposition 6 without appearing to endorse homosexuality. In an interview with a local newspaper, John Kelly, a priest from the Peninsula, justified his opposition to the measure because "it doesn't do away with homosexuality. [But] it sets up a dangerous form of policing individual lives in a frightening way."[137] Frank Gells of Half Moon Bay similarly wrote, "Prop 6 must be viewed as a blatant attempt to create a climate of fear in the schools. . . . It has little to do with homosexuality and a lot to do with freedom of speech and teachers' rights."[138]

Although it is unclear how a ban on gay teachers "has little to do with homosexuality," Gells's letter reveals how some voters could oppose both the Religious Right and gay rights. By the fall of 1978, every major newspaper in the state opposed the Briggs Initiative, and several of California's leading political figures came out against it. In every case, they voiced their opposition as a stand for privacy rather than support for gay rights. The *San Francisco Examiner*, for example, editorialized, "The prevailing . . . attitude in the straight community is to accept those of the homosexual persuasion as long as they indulge their bent in private. . . . [The Briggs Initiative] would trample on the rights of many citizens whose public conduct gives no cause for offense and whose private conduct is not public business. It will not solve the 'problem' of the homosexual teacher to whatever arguable extent a problem exists."[139] Governor Jerry Brown spoke out against Proposition 6 by declaring that "the right to privacy is a very important protection, and I think it ought to be very vigorously enforced at all levels."[140] Former governor Ronald Reagan alleged that the proposal had "the potential of infringing on basic rights of privacy" and declared, "Proposition 6 is not needed to protect our children."[141]

By the fall of 1978, therefore, a moderate bipartisan majority opposed Briggs and Proposition 6. When Californians voted on 7 November 1978, they overwhelmingly rejected it. Approximately 3.9 million voters, or 58 percent of the total, opposed Proposition 6, while only 2.8 million, or 42 percent of the total, supported it.[142] Every major metropolitan area turned it down, including Briggs's home district in Orange County. San Franciscans rejected it by a three-to-one margin, while voters in Santa Clara County defeated it by a narrower margin, with 53 percent of South Bay voters opposing it.[143]

San Jose's Pride Week and the Briggs Initiative represent just two examples of the ways in which metropolitan development and the consensus around privacy shaped the nascent culture wars over gay rights. But if the debates over the Briggs Initiative and San Jose's Pride Week reflected the changing sexual communities of the post-1960s metropolis, they also illustrated the changing discourses of the political center. As fewer Americans referenced a unity between home, school, and church, privacy ascended as a newer discourse with which to explain the state's relationship to sex and its citizens. As with the earlier moral order, Americans spoke about privacy in multiple and contradictory ways. Its flexibility and seeming neutrality made it attractive to voters and politicians alike. Although most news coverage of the culture wars highlighted the voices of the Religious Right and gay rights advocates, implicit in these stories was the presence of an ambivalent center. These Americans often occupied private bedrooms themselves, sympathized with the nation's creed of equality and opportunity, and firmly believed in normative family life. Neither conservative nor liberal, privacy offered self-identified straight moderates a vocabulary to distance themselves from what they saw as the intolerance of someone such as Briggs even as they disliked homosexuality.

Epilogue

Seeking the Highest Meaning

In June 2015, a majority of the U.S. Supreme Court decided to legalize same-sex marriage across the country, and as Justice Anthony Kennedy read the opinion that struck down the last state bans on the practice, he emphasized marriage's public and private dimensions. Marriage, Kennedy argued, was a "public institution" and a "keystone of the social order." Weddings not only committed two people to one another but also committed "society" to giving the couple "symbolic recognition and material benefits to nourish and protect their union." The elimination of state bans on same-sex marriages finally gave same-sex couples the same recognition and benefits as heterosexual ones, including the right to inherit wealth, to adopt children together, and to visit sick spouses in the hospital. Yet even as he acknowledged the government's longstanding support for marriage, Kennedy also described the institution as something that existed apart from the world of public policy and economics. "No union is more profound than marriage," he wrote, "for it embodies the highest ideals of love, fidelity, and devotion." Laws against same-sex marriage, Kennedy argued, denied same-sex couples the ability to "aspire to the transcendent purposes of marriage and seek fulfillment in its highest meaning."[1]

The Court's decision sparked "jubilation" in most of San Francisco. Celebrants gathered outside Harvey Milk's former Castro District camera store, and the Reverend Cecil Williams from the Glide Memorial Church married two women near City Hall. Local reporters found numerous San Franciscans and visitors from other parts of the world who echoed the sentiments in Kennedy's decision. Nicole Mazar, a Homeland Security employee, exclaimed, "For the first time in my life, I felt like I was normal, and I've never felt that," while participants in the annual Pride March two days later chanted, "Love wins!" on Market Street.[2] Some San Franciscans were cautiously optimistic, however. Activist Monica Francis Helms spoke at a more sober Trans Pride rally near the Castro: "The right we got today was the right to marry," she declared. "That's wonderful, but if you can't put food on your table, it doesn't do much good."[3]

South Bay residents, meanwhile, displayed an even more diverse array of responses to the ruling. A small but joyful group celebrated the decision outside of San Jose's City Hall, and longtime gay activist Ken Yeager described the rally as a moment where "love won" over "the voices of hatred and intolerance."[4] At the same time, San Jose pastor Dick Bernal announced that his 12,000-member Christian Jubilee Center would not perform same-sex weddings, and one of his congregants told the local news, "Churches should have the right to do what they want to do outside the bounds of government."[5] Yet even suburbanites who respected the Court's ruling used similar language about individual freedom and privacy to criticize opponents of same-sex marriage. In a letter to the *San Jose Mercury News*, Nan Zender told conservatives that if they did not like same-sex marriages, they have "every right to decide not to enter one." But their beliefs "should not have any bearing on the decisions that other people . . . make."[6]

Kennedy's opinion and the diverse reactions of these Bay Area residents are the latest chapter of the history of the culture wars told in this book. The gay rights movement and the widespread acceptance of privacy as a popular discourse in the 1960s and 1970s eroded some of the worst elements of the Straight State in the late twentieth century. But the postwar policy regime's legacy shaped debates about lesbian, gay, bisexual, and transgender (LGBT) rights well into the twenty-first century. In the nearly four decades that stretched between the Briggs Initiative and the 2015 U.S. Supreme Court ruling on marriage, the "culture wars" over homosexuality moved close to the center of American politics. The nation's voters repeatedly reexamined the question of LGBT rights in conflicts over AIDS policy, gays in the military, hate crimes legislation, school bullying, employment discrimination, and other issues.

During these debates, many Americans argued that LGBT claims to equality constituted demands for special rights and violated the right of others not to support their lifestyle. The military's "don't ask, don't tell" policy from 1993 to 2011 formalized privacy's less egalitarian meanings, requiring LGBT service personnel to hide their relationships while recognizing the relationships of personnel who appeared to be straight. Throughout these debates, few people acknowledged that the government has long offered married couples benefits that it has denied to the unmarried or that LGBT activists were responding to a long history of "special rights" conferred on straight-identified people. Beginning in 2012, slim majorities of Americans supported same-sex marriage based on the notion that the state should not interfere in the personal lives of its citizens.[7] Yet only 19 percent of all high schools in the United States in the same era provided curricula or materials that are LGBT inclusive, and even the most progressive school districts have largely steered clear of affirming homosexuality as equal to heterosexuality, focusing primarily on preventing disease and disrupting stereotypes.[8]

It is unlikely that the fight over same-sex marriage will be the final clash over LGBT equality, and as scholars and the wider public consider new conflicts, this book offers three important conclusions about politics, the metropolis, and the state. Building a more egalitarian society requires grappling with the complex legacy of the Straight State and acknowledging the contradictions within the postwar heteronormative legal regime. The U.S. Supreme Court's recognition of same-sex marriage undeniably represents an enormous shift from the government's treatment of homosexuality after World War II. Yet the contemporary history of same-sex marriage, including the Court's 2015 ruling, is as much a legacy of the Straight State as a repudiation of it. Vast majorities of the public came to accept privacy as a guiding principle in the debates over homosexuality in part because the Straight State itself had promoted it. During the 1960s and 1970s, many straight-identified people embraced the right to privacy because they saw it as a middle path between what they saw as the repressiveness of the Religious Right and the openness of the gay rights movement. In doing so, they helped reform the nation's sexual order even as they opposed more radical changes. Scholars and the public thus need to consider the continuities as well as the breaks between the present and the past, and each of the following conclusions attempts to connect recent history with the long postwar period that lasted approximately from 1945 to 1978.

First, consensus matters as much as polarization in U.S. politics. Much of the recent political history has tended to bifurcate voters into left and right camps.[9] Americans have split over many issues, and historians have rightfully investigated the origins of those divisions. The gay rights movement and Religious Right, for instance, are two of the most important social movements of the late twentieth and early twenty-first centuries, and no historian could claim to study the culture wars without acknowledging their significance. Yet exclusively focusing on social movements can erase the ideology of the large numbers of Americans who have identified as "moderates." They too have a history, and they have played an essential role in numerous policy debates, including disputes over gay rights. Rather than treating these centrists as static parties waiting for activists to change their minds, historians can interrogate their views as part of a long tradition of ideological moderation in American politics.

The late twentieth and early twenty-first centuries were not a period of conservative triumph or gay equality. Instead, a majority of voters and politicians in both major parties supported tolerance for gay men and lesbians at the same time that they insisted that marital heterosexuality was a superior set of relationships. Those tendencies coexisted and paved the way for the recent lurches in the debates over same-sex marriage. In 2017, 62 percent of Americans reported that they supported same-sex marriage. This figure was a dramatic change from 2004 when an almost identical percentage of respondents said that they opposed legalizing the practice.[10] Yet almost half of Americans in 2017 also reported that they supported a business owner's right to deny service to same-sex couples out of personal conviction. Similarly, half of Americans that year believed that transgender people should use the bathroom that corresponds to their birth gender.[11] These statistics suggest that many Americans hold competing and contradictory values on LGBT equality, and in most cases, they have framed the issue as a question of privacy. In the case of the bathroom controversy, elected officials and voters have alternatively described the debate as one where transgender people deserve the right to privately use the bathroom of their choice versus one where cis-gendered people deserve the right to privately use bathrooms without the presence of trans people.

Exploring moderation as a coherent ideology does not deny polarization's relevance in American politics, but it pushes scholars to draw different conclusions about issues like LGBT rights. Moderation is a conservative political tradition with a small "c." Self-described moderates or centrists have tended to view large changes of any kind with skepticism, and their politics differ from those of the New Right. For better or worse, many white, middle-class voters have supported incremental reforms but have resisted revolutions. In this context, scholars need to parse the differences between notions of tolerance and equality. For most of the late twentieth and early twenty-first centuries, many self-identified straight people saw the rhetoric of the Religious Right as harsh and discriminatory. Yet many of these same Americans also rejected the idea that gay relationships deserved equal treatment to heterosexual ones. The fact that many Americans can simultaneously support same-sex couples' right to marry and businesses' right to discriminate against same-sex couples suggests that moderation continues to define many popular opinions on this subject.

Moderation's small-"c" conservative tendencies have put particular pressure on social movements. The tendency of straight-identified moderates to demand that proponents for LGBT rights not violate their privacy has incentivized some gay men and lesbians to distance themselves from others who do not conform to middle-class notions of respectability. Same-sex marriage's success in the courts and in popular opinion, in particular, has stemmed from advocates' ability to convince the wider public that gay couples who wanted to marry were fundamentally "normal" and that their desire to marry violated no one's privacy. Lawyers hoping to overturn bans on same-sex marriages searched for candidates who would garner sympathy from straight-identified judges and voters.[12] Freedom to Marry, one of the nation's largest organizations dedicated to marriage equality, made its case to the wider public with testimonials on their website from a largely white, middle-class cohort of same-sex couples. Jamie Cunningham and Courtney Seals, for example, described themselves on the site as "just a normal couple living our normal lives with our normal family."[13] Advocates for marriage equality may have needed to frame their arguments in this way in order to overturn discriminatory laws. Yet political strategies designed to win rights for "normal" people inevitably divide most middle-class lesbians and gay men from others less able to assimilate to mainstream ideas about sexual propriety, including the queer poor and most transgender people.[14]

Second, discriminatory public policies and private actions after World War II transformed metropolises across the country, creating new sexual communities and politics.[15] In the late twentieth century, segments of the largely white, middle-class wing of the gay rights movement integrated themselves into urban political coalitions, and city leaders around the nation frequently celebrated the presence of openly gay men and lesbians. Mayor Gavin Newsom's 2004 decision to break California law by marrying same-sex couples again underscored San Francisco's reputation as a gay mecca. Yet the Bay Area's central city was merely one large star in a constellation of LGBT-friendly urban centers in the United States. In the early twenty-first century, Atlanta boasted an openly gay city councilwoman, Houston elected a lesbian mayor, and the U.S. congressional district around Madison, Wisconsin, sent two consecutive gay representatives to Washington.[16] These political milestones overlapped with attempts by city leaders to attract affluent gay men and lesbians as a part of an economic development strategy. Beginning with Richard Florida's bestselling *The Rise of the Creative Class*, public officials and business elites across the country associated relatively wealthy white gay residents with rising property values and a successful technology sector. Hoping to emulate the wealth of places such as San Francisco, Boston, and Austin, many twenty-first-century city planners reversed the postwar trend of trying to expel openly gay people and tried to create "tolerant" climates that they believed would produce urban renaissances.[17]

At the same time, conservative suburban churchgoers became key parts of the Republican coalition. Even as LGBT people helped remake older cities, housing developers and local governments continued to concentrate high numbers of white, married people with children in the outer suburbs, which in turn set the stage for the creation of new "family-friendly" churches. Evangelical planners have often singled out new subdivisions as ideal places to start congregations.[18] Since the 1970s, many Asian American, Latino, and African American ministers have also built sizable evangelical churches, and some predominantly white congregations have recently grown more welcoming of people of color. Yet in 2014, eight out of ten churchgoers attended services at a place in which at least 80 percent of the worshippers were from a single racial or ethnic group, and most of the large churches affiliated with conservative causes have grown near predominantly white suburbs.[19] Many of these congregations have mixed biblical opposition to homosexuality with psychological theories about sexuality from the postwar era. After some pollsters attributed George W. Bush's 2004 reelection to support from conservative "values voters," many journalists again focused on the nation's "megachurches" and reported on pastors who argued that people unconsciously learned homosexuality from negative role models from their youth.[20]

These communities with high concentrations of white, middle-class married couples with children, however, cannot stand in for all suburbs. Demographic shifts outside of urban centers since the 1970s have created multiple sexual communities beyond the middle-class gay neighborhoods and megachurches highlighted in most popular understandings of the culture wars. Conservative congregations have often struggled as nearby neighborhoods have aged or undergone racial transitions. By the early 2000s, many churches that had once supported the Briggs Initiative had folded, relocated, or dwindled in membership.[21] Meanwhile, economic growth in places such as Santa Clara County has fueled population booms and diversified the housing stock. Postsuburban landscapes across the United States since the 1970s have featured diverse sexual communities and, consequently, many kinds of sexual politics. These have included openly gay men and lesbians, divorced people, empty nesters, straight singles, and married couples with children. This sexual diversity has accompanied significant shifts in the racial makeup of suburbs as well. Although segregation continues to define most twenty-first-century neighborhoods, many previously all-white suburbs in Santa Clara County have witnessed significant racial turnover. Asian Americans, for example, make up almost two-thirds of the population of the South Bay city of Cupertino.[22]

These diverse sexual communities represent an important legacy of discriminatory public policies and private actions, but the Straight State's support for sexual privacy has played an equally important role in the recent culture wars. In the early twenty-first century, over 80 percent of Americans said that they supported a right to privacy in the bedroom.[23] At the same time, however, realtors, developers, renters, and homebuyers largely treated private bedrooms as commodities available only to those who can afford them. Recent popular culture has often celebrated the garish master bedrooms of new suburban homes, and many parents have welcomed physical insulation from their children. Real estate magazines such as *Sunset*, which caters toward a West Coast audience, have encouraged home remodelers to "find privacy" in their master bedrooms and to "keep the sleeping area away from gathering spots."[24]

Meanwhile, housing costs in major cities have made it difficult for many urban residents to achieve the "buffer zones" celebrated by real estate magazines. Although courts have guaranteed Americans a constitutional right to sexual privacy in the home, the ability to exercise that right has depended on access to appropriate housing. A 2017 study of San Franciscans found that 38 percent of adults in the city lived with roommates or their parents.[25] In that same year, federal officials estimated that approximately 7,500 people lived on San Francisco's streets and recent studies suggest that approximately 29 percent of the city's homeless population is lesbian, gay, bisexual, transgender, or queer. Although the region's poorest people live in the central city, rising housing costs have also created pockets of homelessness in the Bay Area suburbs reminiscent of the "hobo jungles" destroyed by municipal officials after World War II.[26]

Third, historians should see the culture wars over LGBT rights as contests over public policies, not just values. World War II represented a crucial moment when federal, state, and local policymakers took a particular interest in eliminating homosexuality and promoting heterosexual norms, particularly marriage. Beginning in the 1970s, LGBT activists challenged many of the policies erected in the postwar era, but government officials in the late twentieth century created new ones that advantaged straight-identified people. The 1996 Defense of Marriage Act, for example, gave heterosexual married couples rights around health care, housing, inheritance, and taxes denied to same-sex couples. In other cases, public officials resisted repealing discriminatory laws or enacting new protections for LGBT people because they argued that nondiscrimination laws constitute "special rights" for queer people rather than equality. Even after the legalization of same-sex marriage, approximately 50 percent of LGBT people in the United States in 2018 risked legal termination from their job if their employer disliked their sexual orientation or gender identity.[27]

The tendency of many straight-identified people to view claims about LGBT equality as demands for "special rights" played a particularly important role in the debates over same-sex marriage. During the 1990s and early 2000s, advocates for the legalization of same-sex marriage frequently spoke of the institution's public and private dimensions. They often simultaneously claimed that they sought to protect the personal lives of gay men and lesbians from unfair state regulation and to give same-sex couples access to the same legal, economic, and policy benefits that heterosexual couples enjoyed.[28] Yet for many straight-identified conservatives and moderates, these references to taxes and legal rights contradicted their understanding of marriage as a personal relationship bound by love and religious faith. After a wave of states, including California, passed constitutional bans on same-sex marriages, groups such as Freedom to Marry conducted studies to determine how they could avoid future defeats at the ballot box. According to the *Atlantic*, "In survey after survey, researchers would ask people what marriage meant to them—not gay marriage, but marriage itself. And the answers were always the same: love and commitment." But when the researchers asked, "Why do you think gay people want to get married?" respondents gave different answers: "They want rights and benefits. They're trying to make a political point. They don't understand what marriage is about."[29]

Consequently, some gay rights organizations began to emphasize the personal aspects of their relationships. In the wake of their findings, Freedom to Marry and its allies launched new campaigns that stressed the "personal" dimensions of marriage. Whereas commercials supportive of same-sex marriage had once featured judges talking about "rights," they now showed "committed, long-term gay couples doing the same things that married couples do," such as "mowing the lawn, helping an elderly neighbor, and talking about their hopes and dreams." These arguments helped turn the tide of public opinion, and in 2012, gay rights groups—now redubbed supporters of "marriage equality"—won popular campaigns in Maine, Minnesota, Maryland, and Washington.[30]

In academic writing and the popular imagination, the right to privacy has often represented a kind of "negative liberty" or a freedom from government interference.[31] But the history of same-sex marriage also suggests another important conclusion about the state and the right to sexual privacy. When gay rights advocates successfully reframed their cause as a "private" right, they won greater popular support. Whereas groups such as Freedom to Marry once underscored the economic and political rights same-sex couples lost due to their inability to legally marry, they later emphasized marriage's personal dimension to win wider acceptance for their cause. In doing so, however, they helped expand the role of government. The Supreme Court's decisions effectively increased the numbers of licenses issued at courthouses and city halls, even as supporters of marriage equality frequently argued that the government should not decide who should wed and who should not. The campaign for same-sex marriage, therefore, helped conceal the state's role in the sex lives of its citizens even as it helped expand it. One of the most important lessons of the battles over same-sex marriage is that sexual social movements have needed to speak about privacy even when they have expanded the scope of government. As advocates for same-sex marriage spoke about economic and political rights less and less, they contributed to the wider belief of most Americans that marriage fundamentally has very little to do with the state.

This camouflaging of the state's role in marriage further obscures the institution's redistributive elements. Even as many federal and state officials fought to ban same-sex marriages, a bipartisan coalition in Congress allocated $750 million for marriage education and parenting programs. Some of these initiatives targeted the poor, but the federal government also bankrolled premarital education, marriage enrichment, and divorce prevention programs for Americans regardless of their income.[32] Generally speaking, married couples in the early twenty-first century paid lower taxes than their single counterparts, and challenges to bans on same-sex marriage often hinged on questions about the fairness of gay couples paying higher taxes.[33] A system that taxes same-sex and heterosexual relationships at the same rates is clearly fairer than a system that treats them differently. But these cases also revealed the ways that the government treats married and unmarried people differently, regardless of sexual orientation. Americans living outside of marriage face higher penalties on retirement benefits, lower Social Security payments, stiffer health insurance premiums, and more obstacles to securing a mortgage.[34] When Justice Kennedy ruled that bans on same-sex marriage denied gay couples "equal protection" and therefore violated the Fifth and Fourteenth Amendments, he neglected to comment on the 50 percent of unmarried American adults who were unaffected by the decision. These citizens, of differing sexual orientations, would continue to pay many of the costs incurred by same-sex couples before the Supreme Court legalized same-sex marriage.[35]

This means that the most important question in U.S. political history might not be how have the "left" and "right" won particular elections but rather which government policies have Americans labeled "public," which ones do they consider "private," and who has the power to apply those labels? One of the most important exercises of power in early twenty-first-century politics has been the ability of one group or another to determine what constitutes "government action" and what merely represents a "normal" effect of the free market or individual initiative. Many social conservatives, for example, have long criticized sex education in the public schools as an unwarranted expansion of state power and a violation of their "privacy." Classroom-based sex education, however, has long garnered popular support from parents who have wanted schools to teach their children about sexual responsibility and the importance of marriage.[36] Similarly, LGBT people are considerably more likely to lack permanent housing, but when the Chicago and Houston Housing Authorities built their first developments for queer and transgender senior citizens in 2015, some local residents rejected what they saw as a "public subsidy."[37] Labeling a policy "public" has often contributed to its unpopularity, while longstanding government support for much of the American middle class has frequently gone without comment.

When Justice Anthony Kennedy read the Supreme Court's majority opinion in 2015, his words marked a conclusion and an extension of the policies and attitudes of the postwar era. Few people in 1955 would have believed that sixty years later, the nation would formally recognize relationships between two men or two women. This fact reveals a clear contrast between the postwar era and the present. Yet the ruling and debates around it also highlighted less obvious legacies from the past. The Straight State helped shape how Americans understood the relationship between government and sexuality, where and when people could openly express their sexuality, and whose relationships deserved public celebration and support. Not everyone framed their arguments in terms of privacy in the early twenty-first century, yet the term continued to dominate the debates about sex, family, and the law.

Privacy does not need to be synonymous with shame, however. If people can acknowledge that all sexual relationships have public dimensions, they can also allow others to define themselves in a manner of their choosing. Giving someone privacy can mean respecting that person's right to sexual self-determination, and consensual relationships between adults do not need to be ranked in a social order. The problem in the culture wars has been that numerous Americans have benefited from a sexual hierarchy even as they have denied its existence. Many straight-identified Americans have seen their relationships publicly celebrated and supported by the government while simultaneously insisting that their sex lives are entirely private and that queer people should hide their sexuality. Many social conservatives have subscribed to this worldview, but so too have many self-described moderates, who have both rejected discrimination and elevated heterosexual marriage above all other forms of intimacy. This too is a consequence of the Straight State, and the extension of marriage rights to same-sex couples cannot overcome this legacy alone. Acknowledging the true scope of past discrimination offers one possible path to a more egalitarian future.

Notes

Introduction

1. Eugene Robinson, "A Wild Debate—Briggs vs. Milk," *San Francisco Chronicle*, 12 October 1978; "Doyle McManus, "Prop. 6 Will 'Draw a Moral Line'—Briggs," *Los Angeles Times*, 31 October 1978; Harvey Milk, "Where Do We Go from Here?" *Bay Area Reporter*, 9 November 1978. For the best-known account of the Milk-Briggs debates, see Randy Shilts, *The Mayor of Castro Street: The Life and Times of Harvey Milk* (New York: St. Martin's, 1982); *The Times of Harvey Milk*, directed by Robert Epstein and Richard Schmiechen (San Francisco: Black Sand Productions, 1984).

2. "Briggs' Wild Rumors About Gay Teachers in the City," *San Francisco Examiner*, 3 October 1978; U.S. Bureau of the Census, *1980 Census of Population: Number of Inhabitants, California*, vol. 1, chap. 1, chap. A, pt. 6 (Washington, DC: Government Printing Office, 1982)

3. "Gallup Poll on Homosexuality," *San Francisco Examiner*, 24 July 1977.

4. Bay Area Committee Against the Briggs Initiative, *Stop Briggs: Protect Your Rights* (San Francisco: Gay, Lesbian, Bisexual, and Transgender Historical Society of Northern California, n.d.).

5. Larry Peterson, "Sexual Role Models Key Issue at GG Prop. 6 Debate," *Register*, 3 November 1978.

6. J. E. S. Tyson, letter, *San Jose Mercury*, 4 November 1978.

7. "Prop 6 Vote to Mark Milestone in Homosexual Controversy," *Orange County Register*, 27 October 1978; John Gallagher and Chris Bull, *Perfect Enemies: The Religious Right, the Gay Movement, and the Politics of the 1990s* (New York: Crown, 1996).

8. Evelyn Nieves, "Gay Rights Groups Map Common Agenda," *Washington Post*, 17 January 2005.

9. Richard Stevenson, "Winning While Losing," *New York Times*, 15 July 2004.

10. Trudy Ring, "Fewer Americans Say Being Gay Is a Sin," *Advocate*, 11 January 2013, accessed 3 July 2015, http://www.advocate.com/politics/religion/2013/01/11/fewer-americans-say-being-gay-sin; Harris Interactive, "Americans Favor Safety over Privacy, Though Majority Recognize Need for Balance," 5 August 2014, accessed 20 September 2014, http://www.harrisinteractive.com/NewsRoom/HarrisPolls/tabid/447/ctl/ReadCustom%20Default/mid/1508/ArticleId/1479/Default.aspx. Many gay rights activists stressed the public dimensions of marriage, including access to health care and Social Security benefits. But large organizations like Marriage Equality frequently used language about marriage's private dimensions, such as love and affection, to make their case to the wider public. Molly Ball, "How Gay Marriage

Became a Constitutional Right," *Atlantic*, 1 July 2015, accessed 3 July 2015, http://www.theatlantic.com/politics/archive/2015/07/gay-marriage-supreme-court-politics-activism/397052/.

11. *Obergefell v. Hodges*, 135 S. Ct. 2584 (2015).

12. For the policing of sexuality before World War II, see George Chauncey, *Gay New York: Gender, Urban Culture, and the Making of the Gay Word, 1890–1940* (New York: Basic Books, 1994); Nayan Shah, *Contagious Divides: Epidemics and Race in San Francisco's Chinatown* (Berkeley: University of California Press, 2001); Helen Lefkowitz Horowitz, *Rereading Sex: Battles over Sexual Knowledge and Suppression in Nineteenth Century America* (New York: Knopf, 2002).

13. Quote from John D'Emilio, *Sexual Politics, Sexual Communities: The Making of a Homosexual Minority in the United States, 1940–1970* (Chicago: University of Chicago Press, 1983), 24. See also Allan Berubé, *Coming Out Under Fire: The History of Gay Men and Lesbians During World War II* (New York: Free Press, 1990); Leisa Meyer, *Creating G.I. Jane: Sexuality and Power During World War II* (New York: Columbia University Press, 1996).

14. Margot Canaday, *The Straight State: Sexuality and Citizenship in the Twentieth Century United States* (Princeton, NJ: Princeton University Press, 2009); see also William Eskridge, "Challenging the Apartheid of the Closet: Establishing Conditions for Lesbian and Gay Intimacy, Nomos, and Citizenship, 1961–1981," *Hofstra Law Review* 25 (1997). Canaday's book focuses on the federal government, but the concerns about homo- and heterosexuality appeared at the state and local governments as well. Because the United States has a federated system of government, local and state officials have constrained, implemented, and expanded federal policies, including those related to sexuality. See Thomas Sugrue, "All Politics Is Local: The Persistence of Localism in Twentieth Century America," in Meg Jacobs, William Novak, and Julian Zelizer, eds., *The Democratic Experiment: New Directions in American Political History* (Princeton, NJ: Princeton University Press, 2003).

15. This does not mean that queer communities were invisible or in hiding in this period. Scholars of postwar LGBT history have painted elaborate portraits of the vibrancy of gay and lesbian communities after World War II. See D'Emilio, *Sexual Politics, Sexual Communities*; Brett Beemyn, ed., *Creating a Place for Ourselves: Lesbian, Gay, and Bisexual Community Histories* (New York: Routledge, 1997). All of these communities, however, grew in the context of increasing homophobia and government-sponsored repression.

16. Edward De Leon, *Left Coast City: Progressive Politics in San Francisco, 1975–1991* (Lawrence: University of Kansas Press, 1992).

17. For some of the best scholarship on these postwar communities, see John D'Emilio, "Gay Politics and Community in San Francisco Since World War II," in Martin Duberman, Martha Vicinus, and George Chauncey, eds., *Hidden from History: Reclaiming the Gay and Lesbian Past* (New York: NAL Books, 1989); Susan Stryker and Jim Van Buskirk, *Gay by the Bay: A History of Queer Cultures in the San Francisco Bay Area* (San Francisco: Chronicle Books, 1996); Nan Alamilla Boyd, *Wide Open Town: A Queer History of San Francisco to 1965* (Berkeley: University of California Press, 2004); Martin Meeker, *Contacts Desired: Gay and Lesbian Connections and Community, 1940s–1970s* (Chicago: University of Chicago Press, 2006); Josh Sides, *Erotic City: Sexual Revolutions and the Making of Modern San Francisco* (New York: Oxford University Press, 2008); Betty Luther-Hillman, "'The Most Profoundly Revolutionary Act a Homosexual Can Engage In': Drag and the Politics of Gender Presentation in the San Francisco Gay Liberation Movement," *Journal of the History of Sexuality* 20,

no. 1 (2011); Christina Hanhardt, *Safe Space: Gay Neighborhood History and the Politics of Violence* (Durham, NC: Duke University Press, 2013).

18. For studies of postwar LGBT communities in other places, see Elizabeth Lopovsky Kennedy and Madeline Davis, *Boots of Leather, Slippers of Gold: The History of a Lesbian Community* (New York: Routledge, 1993); Martin Duberman, *Stonewall* (New York: Plume, 1994); Brett Beemyn, *Creating a Place for Ourselves*; Marc Stein, *City of Brotherly and Sisterly Loves* (Chicago: University of Chicago Press, 2000); John Howard, *Men Like That: A Queer Southern History* (Chicago: University of Chicago Press, 1999); Lillian Faderman, *Gay L.A.: A History of Sexual Outlaws, Power Politics and Lipstick Lesbians* (New York: Basic Books, 2006); Kevin Murphy et al., *Queer Twin Cities* (Minneapolis: University of Minneapolis Press, 2010); Timothy Retzloff, "City, Suburb, and the Changing Bounds of Lesbian and Gay Politics in Metropolitan Detroit" (Ph.D. diss., Yale University, 2014); Timothy Stewart-Winter, *Queer Clout: Chicago and the Rise of Gay Politics* (Philadelphia: University of Pennsylvania Press, 2016); Ian Baldwin, "Family, Housing, and the Political Geography of Gay Liberation in Los Angeles, 1960–1985" (Ph.D. diss., University of Nevada, Las Vegas, 2016).

19. Paul Robinson, "Gays in the Streets," *New Republic*, 9 June 1979.

20. Kenneth Jackson, *Crabgrass Frontier: The Suburbanization of the United States* (New York: Oxford University Press, 1985).

21. James Clayton, "Defense Spending: Key to California's Growth," *Western Political Quarterly* 15, no. 2 (1962): 286.

22. For histories of the suburban Bay Area, see Robert Self, *American Babylon: Race and the Struggle for Postwar Oakland* (Princeton, NJ: Princeton University Press, 2003); Stephen Pitti, *The Devil in Silicon Valley: Northern California, Race, and Mexican Americans* (Princeton, NJ: Princeton University Press, 2003); Margaret Pugh O'Mara, *Cities of Knowledge: Cold War Science and the Search for the Next Silicon Valley* (Princeton, NJ: Princeton University Press, 2005); Charlotte Brooks, *Alien Neighbors, Foreign Friends: Asian Americans, Housing, and the Transformation of Urban California* (Chicago: University of Chicago Press, 2009); Aaron Cavin, "Fringe Politics: Suburban Expansion and the Mexican American Struggle for Alviso, California," in Christopher Niedt, ed., *Social Justice in Diverse Suburbs: History, Politics, and Prospects* (Philadelphia: Temple University Press, 2013). For histories of similar kinds of suburbs, see Rob Kling et al., *Postsuburban California: The Transformation of Orange County Since World War II* (Berkeley: University of California Press, 1991); Lisa McGirr, *Suburban Warriors* (Princeton, NJ: Princeton University Press, 2001); Lily Geismer, *Don't Blame Us: Suburban Liberals and the Transformation of the Democratic Party* (Princeton, NJ: Princeton University Press, 2015).

23. Melinda Beck et al., "The New Issue: Gay Teachers," *Newsweek*, 2 October 1978; Victor Zonana, "California Is Roiled by a New Initiative over Homosexuals," *Wall Street Journal*, 10 October 1978; "Briggs on a Crusade—This One to Save America," *Los Angeles Times*, 2 March 1979.

24. William Martin, *With God on Our Side: The History of the Religious Right in America* (New York: Broadway Books, 1996); Gallagher and Bull, *Perfect Enemies*; Sara Diamond, *Not by Politics Alone: The Enduring Influence of the Religious Right* (New York: Guilford, 1998); Janice Irvine, *Talk About Sex: Battles over Sex Education in the United States* (Berkeley: University of California Press, 2002); Beth Bailey and David Farber, *America in the Seventies* (Lawrence: University of Kansas Press, 2004); Thomas Frank, *What's the Matter with Kansas? How*

Conservatives Won the Heart of America (New York: Basic Books, 2004). This pattern reflects, in part, the tendency of American political historians to use the "New Right" as the most significant lens through which to understand electoral realignment since the 1960s. Not all of the books in this subfield necessarily focus on controversies over homosexuality, yet most of them attribute conflicts over "cultural issues" like gay rights or abortion primarily to organized social conservatives. See Alan Brinkley, "The Problem of American Conservatism," *American Historical Review* 99, no. 2 (1994); McGirr, *Suburban Warriors*; Donald Critchlow, *Phyllis Schlafly and Grassroots Conservatism: A Woman's Crusade* (Princeton, NJ: Princeton University Press, 2005); Daniel Williams, "Reagan's Religious Right: The Unlikely Alliance Between Southern Evangelicals and a California Conservative," in Cheryl Hudson and Gareth Davies, eds., *Ronald Reagan and the 1980s: Perceptions, Policies, Legacies* (New York: Palgrave Macmillan, 2008); Bruce Schulman and Julian Zelizer, eds., *Rightward Bound: Making American Conservative in the 1970s* (Cambridge, MA: Harvard University Press, 2008); Whitney Strub, *Perversion for Profit: The Politics of Pornography and the Rise of the New Right* (New York: Columbia University Press, 2011); Gillian Frank, "The Civil Rights of Parents: Race and Conservative Politics in Anita Bryant's Campaign Against Gay Rights in 1970s Florida," *Journal of the History of Sexuality* 22, no. 1 (January 2013); Andrew Hartman, *A War for the Soul of America: A History of the Culture Wars* (Chicago: University of Chicago Press, 2015).

25. Thomas Sugrue, *The Origins of the Urban Crisis: Race and Inequality in Postwar Detroit* (Princeton, NJ: Princeton University Press, 1996); Self, *American Babylon*. See also Jackson, *Crabgrass Frontier*; David Freund, *Colored Property: State Policy and White Racial Politics in Suburban America* (Chicago: University of Chicago Press, 2007); Eric Avila, *Popular Culture in the Age of White Flight: Fear and Fantasy in Suburban Los Angeles* (Berkeley: University of California Press, 2003); Lizabeth Cohen, *A Consumer's Republic: The Politics of Mass Consumption in Postwar America* (New York: Knopf, 2003); Kevin Kruse, *White Flight: Atlanta and the Making of Modern Conservatism* (Princeton, NJ: Princeton University Press, 2005); Matthew Lassiter, *The Silent Majority: Suburban Politics in the Sunbelt South* (Princeton, NJ: Princeton University Press, 2007); Scott Kurashige, *The Shifting Grounds of Race: Black and Japanese Americans in the Making of Multiethnic Los Angeles* (Princeton, NJ: Princeton University Press, 2008); Suleiman Osman, *The Invention of Brownstone Brooklyn: Gentrification and the Search for Authenticity in Postwar New York* (New York: Oxford University Press, 2010); Geismer, *Don't Blame Us*; N. D. B. Connelly, *A World More Concrete: Real Estate and the Remaking of Jim Crow South Florida* (Chicago: University of Chicago Press, 2015); Andrew Highsmith, *Demolition Means Progress: Flint, Michigan, and the Fate of the American Metropolis* (Chicago: University of Chicago Press, 2015). For a compelling critique of the limits of this subfield, see Andrew Needham, *Power Lines: Phoenix and the Making of the Modern Southwest* (Princeton, NJ: Princeton University Press, 2015).

26. For urban historians thinking about sexuality, see Bryant Simon, "New York Avenue: The Life and Death of Gay Spaces in Atlantic City, New Jersey, 1920–1990," *Journal of Urban History* 28, no. 3 (March 2002); Sides, *Erotic City*; Martin Meeker, "The Queerly Disadvantaged and the Making of San Francisco's War on Poverty, 1964–1967," *Pacific Historical Review* 81, no. 1 (2012); Timothy Retzloff, "The Association of (Gay) Suburban People," *Places*, April 2015; Baldwin, "Family, Housing, and the Political Geography of Gay Liberation in Los Angeles, 1960–1985."

27. John D'Emilio, "Capitalism and Gay Identity," in *Making Trouble: Essays on Gay History, Politics, and the University* (London: Routledge, 1992); D'Emilio, *Sexual Politics, Sexual Communities*; Lopovsky Kennedy and Davis, *Boots of Leather, Slippers of Gold*; Chauncey, *Gay New York*; Beemyn, *Creating a Place for Ourselves*; Stein, *City of Brotherly and Sisterly Loves*; Boyd, *Wide Open Town*; Sides, *Erotic City*; Stewart-Winter, *Queer Clout*. Most of this scholarship has focused on lesbians and gay men, but the growing field of transgender studies has followed a similar model. See Susan Stryker, *Transgender History* (Berkeley, CA: Seal, 2008).

28. Lisa Duggan, "Queering the State," *Social Text* 39 (Summer 1994); Canaday, *The Straight State*.

29. Lauren Gutterman, " 'The House on the Borderland': Lesbian Desire, Marriage, and the Household, 1950–1979," *Journal of the History of Sexuality* 46, no. 1 (2012).

30. Bar raids have been a recurring feature of LGBT history, but most historians have solely attributed them to the homophobia of the Cold War rather than also seeing them as products of metropolitan competition. D'Emilio, "Gay Politics and Community in San Francisco Since World War II"; Elaine Tyler May, *Homeward Bound: American Families in the Cold War Era* (New York: Basic Books, 2004); David Johnson, *The Lavender Scare: The Cold War Persecution of Gays and Lesbians in the Federal Government* (Chicago: University of Chicago Press, 2004); Boyd, *Wide Open Town*.

31. Carolyn Herbst Lewis, *Prescription for Heterosexuality: Sexual Citizenship in the Cold War Era* (Chapel Hill: University of North Carolina Press, 2010).

32. Many histories of the controversies over sex education begin their accounts in the late 1960s. See Irvine, *Talk About Sex*. Some begin in the Progressive Era but highlight the importance of the 1960s. See Luker, *When Sex Goes to School: Warring View on Sex Education Since the Sixties* (New York: W. W. Norton, 2006); Jeffrey Moran, *Teaching Sex: The Shaping of Adolescence in the Twentieth Century* (Cambridge, MA: Harvard University Press, 2000); Jonathan Zimmerman, *Whose America? Culture Wars in the Public Schools* (Cambridge, MA: Harvard University Press, 2002); Susan Freeman, *Sex Goes to School: Girls and Sex Education Before the 1960s* (Urbana: University of Illinois Press, 2008).

33. Matthew Lassiter, "Political History Beyond the Red Blue Divide," *Journal of American History* 98 no. 3 (December 2011); Lassiter, *The Silent Majority*, 7; Self, *American Babylon*, 1–2; Jennifer Brier, " 'Save Our Kids, Keep AIDS Out': Anti-AIDS Activism and the Legacy of Community Control in Queens New York," *Journal of Social History* 39, no. 4 (Summer 2006); Rachel Guberman, "The Real Silent Majority: Denver and the Realignment of American Politics After the 1960s" (Ph.D. diss., University of Pennsylvania, 2015).

34. D'Emilio, "Capitalism and Gay Identity"; Jonathan Ned Katz, *The Invention of Heterosexuality* (New York: Dutton, 1995); Jennifer Terry, *An American Obsession: Science, Medicine, and Homosexuality in Modern Society* (Chicago: University of Chicago Press, 1999). For research on queer subcultures that predated the gay-straight binary, see Nayan Shah, *Stranger Intimacy: Contesting, Race, Sexuality and the Law in the North American West* (Berkeley: University of California Press, 2011).

35. Chauncey, *Gay New York*. Historians have also demonstrated the ways that a more complicated array of sexual identities continued to exist in some places well past World War II. See Regina Kunzel, *Criminal Intimacy: Prison and the Uneven History of Modern American Sexuality* (Chicago: University of Chicago Press, 2008).

36. I borrow the term from George Lipsitz, *A Possessive Investment in Whiteness: How White People Profit from Identity Politics* (Philadelphia: Temple University Press, 1998).

37. My use of "political style" draws on Lassiter's analysis of "colorblindness" and Michael Kazin's study of the "language of populism." Michael Kazin, *The Populist Persuasion: An American History* (New York: Basic Books, 1995); Lassiter, *The Silent Majority*.

38. Wendy Wall, *Inventing the American Way: The Politics of Consensus from the New Deal to the Civil Rights Movement* (New York: Oxford University Press, 2008).

39. Lassiter, *The Silent Majority*.

40. Kathy Peiss, *Cheap Amusements: Working Women and Leisure in Twentieth Century* (Philadelphia: Temple University Press, 1986); John D'Emilio and Estelle Freedman, *Intimate Matters: A History of Sexuality in America* (New York: Harper & Row, 1988); Chauncey, *Gay New York*; Kevin Mumford, *Interzones: Black and White Sex Districts in Chicago and New York in the Early Twentieth Century* (New York: Columbia University Press, 1997); Chad Heap, *Slumming: Sexual and Racial Encounters in American Nightlife, 1885–1940* (Chicago: University of Chicago Press, 2009). For histories of early twentieth-century sex education, see Moran, *Teaching Sex*; Luker, *When Sex Goes to School*.

41. David Garrow, *Liberty and Sexuality: The Right to Privacy and the Making of* Roe v. Wade (New York: Macmillan, 1994); Marc Stein, *Sexual Injustice: Supreme Court Decisions from* Griswold *to* Roe (Chapel Hill: University of North Carolina Press, 2010); Robert Self, *All in the Family: The Realignment of American Democracy Since the 1960s* (New York: Hill & Wang, 2012); Leigh Ann Wheeler, *How Sex Became a Civil Liberty* (New York: Oxford University Press, 2013).

42. Several books critique middle-class gay politics. See Hanhardt, *Safe Space*; Stewart-Winter, *Queer Clout*.

43. There is a large literature on the state's support for marriage. See Michael Warner, *The Trouble with Normal: Sex, Politics, and the Ethics of Queer Life* (Cambridge, MA: Harvard University Press, 2000); Nancy Cott, *Public Vows: A History of Marriage and the Nation* (Cambridge, MA: Harvard University Press, 2000); Priscilla Yamin, *American Marriage: A Political Institution* (Philadelphia: University of Pennsylvania Press, 2012); Katherine Franke, *Wedlocked: The Perils of Marriage Equality* (New York: New York University Press, 2015).

44. For negative liberty, see Self, *All in the Family*. For accounts of privacy and sexual freedom, see David Garrow, *Liberty and Sexuality: The Right to Privacy and the Making of* Roe v. Wade (New York: Macmillan, 1994); Leigh Ann Wheeler, *How Sex Became a Civil Liberty* (New York: Oxford University Press, 2013). For a critical view of privacy and the courts, see Marc Stein, *Sexual Injustice*.

45. Gayle Rubin, "Thinking Sex: Notes for a Radical Theory of the Politics of Sexuality," in Peter Nardi and Beth Schneider, eds., *Social Perspectives in Lesbian and Gay Studies: A Reader* (London: Routledge, 1998); Warner, *The Trouble with Normal*.

46. Yamin, *American Marriage*. The exclusion of same-sex couples from these benefits was one of the strongest arguments of the marriage equality movement. See George Chauncey, *Why Marriage? The History Shaping Today's Debate over Gay Equality* (New York: Basic Books, 2004), 87–136.

Chapter 1

1. Lester Kirkendall, "Progress in Sex Education," *Clearinghouse*, October 1945; Howard Whitman, "The Biggest Taboo," *Collier's*, 15 February 1947; Harold Isaacs, "Shall Our Schools

Teach Sex?" *Newsweek*, 19 May 1947; Howard Whitman, "Sex and Early Marriage," *Better Homes and Gardens*, August 1947.

2. D'Emilio, *Sexual Politics, Sexual Communities*; Allan Bérubé, *Coming Out Under Fire: The History of Gay Men and Women During World War II* (New York: Free Press, 1990); Elizabeth Clement, *Love for Sale: Courting, Treating, and Prostitution in New York City, 1900–1945* (Chapel Hill: University of North Carolina Press, 2006), 242–58.

3. Chauncey, *Gay New York*, 33–46, 131–267; Paul Groth, *Living Downtown: The History of Residential Hotels in the United States* (Berkeley: University of California Press, 1997).

4. Chauncey, *Gay New York*, 35; Gwendolyn Wright, *Building the American Dream: A Social History of Housing in America* (New York: Pantheon, 1981), 112, 144. Josh Sides uses the term to describe San Francisco neighborhood groups after the war. See Sides, *Erotic City*, 7.

5. Historians have documented this surge in anxiety after World War II, but they have not distinguished between neighborhoods. See Estelle Freedman, "Uncontrolled Desires: The Response to the Sexual Psychopath, 1920–1960," *Journal of American History* 74 (June 1987); George Chauncey, "The Postwar Sex Crime Panic," in William Graebner, ed., *True Stories from the American Past* (New York: McGraw-Hill, 1993).

6. D'Emilio, "Gay Politics and Community in San Francisco Since World War II"; Boyd, *Wide Open Town*.

7. For more on California during the war decade, see Marilyn Johnson, *The Second Gold Rush: Oakland and the East Bay in World War II* (Berkeley: University of California Press, 1993); Kevin Starr, *Embattled Dreams: California in War and Peace, 1940–1950* (New York: Oxford University Press, 2002).

8. House Subcommittee on Naval Affairs, *Investigation of Congested Areas*, pt. 3 (San Francisco: House Subcommittee on Naval Affairs, 1943), 925.

9. California Committee for the Study of Transient Youth, *Transient Youth in California* (San Francisco: Rosenberg Foundation, 1948).

10. Joseph Jaines, "Profiles: San Francisco," *Journal of Educational Sociology* 19, no. 3 (November 1945): 168.

11. Many historians see the war as the most significant precursor of modern gay communities and politics in San Francisco. See Bérubé, *Coming Out Under Fire*; D'Emilio, "Gay Politics and Community in San Francisco Since World War II." Although they also see World War II as an important watershed, several historians have begun to draw out the histories of queer communities before the mobilization to stress the longstanding roots of queer life in America. See, for example, Boyd, *Wide Open Town*.

12. Alice Kessler-Harris, *Out to Work: A History of Wage-Earning Women in the United States* (New York: Oxford University Press, 1982), 276–77; Lochtin, "California Cities in the Hurricane of Change," 415; Charles Cox, *Investigation of Congested Areas*, 771.

13. Faderman, *Odd Girls and Twilight Lovers*, 120–22.

14. Workers of the Writers' Program of the Work Projects Administration of Northern California, *San Francisco: The Bay and Its Cities* (New York: Hastings House, 1940), 252–53; Anne Bloomfield and Arthur Bloomfield, *Gables and Fables: A Portrait of San Francisco's Pacific Heights* (Berkeley, CA: Heyday Books, 2007), xviii.

15. Albert Broussard, *Black San Francisco: The Struggle for Racial Equality in the West* (Lawrence: University of Kansas Press, 1993), 30–31; Paul Groth, *Living Downtown: The History of Residential Hotels in the United States* (Berkeley: University of California Press, 1994), 153–55; Shah, *Contagious Divides*, 84; Brooks, *Alien Neighbors, Foreign Friends*, 11–13.

16. James, "Profiles: San Francisco," 167. In San Francisco's Chinatown, white tourists frequently sought out racialized, sex-related entertainment in clubs in the neighborhood. Jim Kepner wrote a letter to a friend relating that when the military began cracking down on gay bars on the waterfront, queer soldiers and sailors began going to Li Po's nightclub in Chinatown. Bérubé, *Coming Out Under Fire*, 125. For more on the connections between vice districts and racial segregation, see Mumford, *Interzones*; Heap, *Slumming*.

17. Boyd, *Wide Open Town*, 49–62, 73–81.

18. J. C. Geiger, *Investigation of Congested Areas*, 661.

19. David Bohannon, Statement to Housing Clinic, San Francisco, 10–11 December 1945; Madeleine Butler O'Neill, letter to the editor, *San Francisco Chronicle*, 25 March 1947; Mr. L. Anderson, letter to the editor, *San Francisco Examiner*, 8 August 1949; "Disheartened," letter to the editor, *San Francisco Examiner*, 12 September 1949. For another grim assessment of the postwar housing crisis, see San Francisco Chamber of Commerce, *Observations on San Francisco Housing Situation* (San Francisco: Chamber of Commerce, 1948), Institute of Governmental Studies, University of California, Berkeley.

20. Don Cleary, "Worst Case of JapTown Housing Told," *San Francisco Chronicle*, 15 July 1943.

21. Lester Velie, "Housing: No Answer in San Francisco," *Collier's*, 11 January 1947, 42.

22. "Housing Problem," *San Francisco Chronicle*, 5 March 1947.

23. "The Great Housing Shortage," *Life*, 17 December 1945, 27; George Sessions Perry, "The Cities of America: San Francisco," *Collier's*, 16 February 1946, 58.

24. Julia Cooley Altrocchi, *The Spectacular San Franciscans* (New York: E. P. Dutton, 1949), 345.

25. Lester Velli and Frank Gervasi, "Housing: The Solution," *Collier's*, 8 February 1947, 12.

26. H. D. Davies, letter, *San Francisco Chronicle*, 29 October 1945; "New Homes Aren't Designed for Courtship," *San Francisco Chronicle*, 17 October 1948.

27. Ernest G. Long et al., *An Experiment in the Psychiatric Treatment of Promiscuous Girls* (San Francisco: City and County of San Francisco Department of Public Health, 1945), 20.

28. Edmund Brown, *Third and Final Report on Housing Conditions in San Francisco* (San Francisco: San Francisco District Attorney's Office, 1948), 11; Earl Warren Papers, Office of Planning and Research, California State Archives, Sacramento, CA.

29. Chauncey, *Gay New York*, 131–206.

30. Pat Bond, oral history with Allan Bérubé, May 1981, GLBT Historical Society of Northern California, San Francisco.

31. Jim Kepner, oral history with Allan Bérubé, 2 June 1981, GLBT Historical Society of Northern California.

32. Bérubé, *Coming Out Under Fire*, 40.

33. George Chauncey found a similar process at work in rooming houses in early twentieth-century New York City. See Chauncey, *Gay New York*, 153; Roland Bianchi, *Delivery Boy: Recollections of Life and Love in San Francisco* (McKinleyville, CA: Fithian, 2004), 73.

34. William Gaddis, letter to D——, n.d., Gaddis Papers, GLBT Historical Society of Northern California.

35. William Gaddis, letter to Dan, 2 June 1942, Gaddis Papers, GLBT Historical Society of Northern California.

36. This ideology gained adherents slowly over the course of the early to mid-twentieth century and did not include all middle-class Americans all at once. Many Catholics, for example, saw sex primarily as a procreative act, yet even a majority of Catholics had shifted their attitudes about sex's meaning by the 1940s and 1950s. See D'Emilio and Freedman, *Intimate Matters*, 241, 276–77.

37. For more on the gendered nature of the "home," see Sarah Deutsch, *Women and the City: Gender, Space, and Power in Boston, 1870–1940* (New York: Oxford University Press, 2000), 54–77.

38. Howard Whitman, *Let's Tell the Truth About Sex* (New York: Pellegrini and Cudahy, 1948), 82.

39. Edward Redford, cited in "Doctor to Give Advice to Parents in Sex Education," *San Francisco Chronicle*, 9 October 1946.

40. "Youth Crime," *San Francisco Chronicle*, 29 October 1943.

41. "Juvenile Troubles," *San Francisco Chronicle*, 6 February 1947.

42. Joseph Catton, *Behind the Scenes of Murder* (New York: W. W. Norton, 1940), 62.

43. Clarence Perry, *Housing for the Machine Age* (New York: Russell Sage Foundation, 1939), 18.

44. Clarence Perry, *The Neighborhood Unit: Neighborhood and Community Planning, Regional Survey*, vol. 7 (New York: Committee on Regional Plan of New York and Its Environs, 1929), 25; Perry, *Housing for the Machine Age*, 49–82. For more on Perry's neighborhood ideal, see Steven Conn, *Americans Against the City: Anti-Urbanism in the Twentieth Century* (New York: Oxford University Press, 2014), 77; Benjamin Looker, *A Nation of Neighborhoods: Imagining Cities, Communities, and Democracy in Postwar America* (Chicago: University of Chicago Press, 2015), 52, 55–56.

45. "Sunset May Be Rezoned as First Residential," *San Francisco Chronicle*, 17 April 1944.

46. H. Paul Douglas et al., *The San Francisco Bay Area Church Study* (San Francisco: San Francisco Council of Churches, 1945), 71; "Here Is List of School Sites Chosen by Education Board," *San Francisco Chronicle*, 24 November 1948; Herb Caen, *Baghdad by the Bay* (New York: Doubleday, 1949), 4; Lorri Ungaretti, *Stories in the Sand: San Francisco's Sunset District, 1847–1964* (Oakland, CA: Madison Street Press, 2012), 45–86; Ron Jones, *Growing Up in the Sunset* (Berkeley, CA: Regent, 2015). The privacy was only "modest" because many of the houses were very close to their neighbors and had thin walls. Herb Caen joked about the Sunset: "In the morning, when your wife asks you: 'How do you want your eggs, dear?' a husband seven houses down answers, 'Scrambled.'" Caen, *Baghdad by the Bay*, 244.

47. "West of Twin Peaks Group Fights Rezoning," *San Francisco Chronicle*, 4 July 1940.

48. "PTA Protests Liquor License," *San Francisco News*, 29 December 1949.

49. Parkside Improvement Club, History Notes, 1943, Parkside Improvement Club Records, San Francisco History Center, San Francisco Public Library, San Francisco.

50. Charles S. Johnson et al., *The Negro War Worker in San Francisco; A Local Survey* (San Francisco: American Missionary Association, 1944).

51. Herman Long and Charles Johnson, *People vs. Property: Race Restrictive Covenants in Housing* (Nashville, TN: Fisk University Press, 1947), 54.

52. Deirdre Sullivan, "Letting Down the Bars: Race, Space, and Democracy, 1936–1964" (Ph.D. diss., University of Pennsylvania, 2003), 146–200.

53. J. C. Geiger, *Investigation of Congested Areas*, 656; "Brown to Ask Cash for New Courts, Jail," *San Francisco Chronicle*, 16 October 1947.

54. San Francisco Board of Supervisors, *Journal of Proceedings*, 16 November 1942, 2553, accessed 1 July 2017, archive.org.

55. Ibid.

56. The new version eliminated the older draft's definition of "illegal sex" as any sex outside of marriage and instead substituted the vaguer terms "lewd acts," "assignations," and "fornication." San Francisco Board of Supervisors, *Journal of Proceedings*, 22 November 1942, 2585, accessed 1 July 2017, archive.org.

57. San Francisco Board of Supervisors, *Journal of Proceedings*, 6 March 1944, 397, accessed 1 July 2017, archive.org.

58. "San Francisco Women Leaders Urge Support for Mayoral Candidate," *San Francisco Chronicle*, 26 September 1947; "MacPhee Gets Women Voters," *San Francisco Chronicle*, 17 October 1947; "MacPhee Plan," *San Francisco Chronicle*, 19 October 1947; "Junior Museum: Corona Heights Recreation Project Blocked by Supervisors' Committee," *San Francisco Chronicle*, 18 April 1949.

59. Names taken from San Francisco Board of Supervisors, *Journal of Proceedings*, 6 March 1944, 403–4, accessed 1 July 2017, archive.org. Many of the people named in the report listed businesses as mailing addresses. Home addresses were gathered by consulting Polk's 1944 City Directory. Many of the people mentioned in the minutes occupied leadership positions related to youth, such as the Boy Scouts or YMCA, or downtown businesses, like the Market Street Association. Four of them had known addresses in Oakland, San Mateo, and Berkeley, and ten of them could not be found in the directory. The thirteen remaining San Franciscans from other parts of the city came from the Haight-Ashbury (3), Western Addition (2), Mission (2), Outer Mission (1), Telegraph Hill (1), Eureka Valley (1), Presidio Heights (1), Crocker Amazon (1), and Glen Park (1).

60. Second District PTA, Executive Board Meeting Minutes, 17 September 1947, San Francisco History Center.

61. Howard Whitman, "Terror in Our Cities," *Collier's*, 19 November 1949. See also "The Sex Rampage," *Newsweek*, 13 February 1950; Whitman, "Terror in Washington," *Collier's*, 24 June 1950; Chauncey, "The Postwar Sex Crime Panic," 175.

62. "Child Kidnap Try Blamed on Offender," *San Francisco Chronicle*, 10 November 1949; "Second District Urges Sex Offender Control," *San Francisco Chronicle*, 29 November 1949; "P.T.A. Urges Supervised Play in City's Park Area," *San Francisco News*, 20 November 1949; Mrs. Andy Crow, letter to Earl Warren, 8 December 1949, Earl Warren Papers.

63. "Grand Jury Calls for More Police," *San Francisco Chronicle*, 30 December 1949.

64. "New Restrictions Aimed at Parents," *San Francisco Chronicle*, 7 February 1950.

65. Moran, *Teaching Sex*, 43; "Experts Take on Child Hygiene," *San Francisco Chronicle*, 27 June 1915.

66. Jane Eads, "New Sex Education Goes Beyond the 'Birds and the Bees,'" *San Francisco Chronicle*, 2 October 1944.

67. Lester Kirkendall, *Sex as Human Relations: A Guidebook on Content and Methods for School Authorities and Teachers* (New York: Inor, 1950), 177.

68. Kirkendall, *Sex as Human Relations*, 125–26.

69. Ernst Wolff, "Trends in Child Psychiatry," *Journal of Pediatrics* 10, no. 1 (1937). See also Elizabeth Lunbeck, *The Psychiatric Persuasion: Knowledge, Gender, and Power in Modern America* (Princeton, NJ: Princeton University Press, 1994).

70. For examples of this thinking, see Anna Wolf, *The Parents' Manual: A Guide to the Emotional Development of Young Children* (New York: Simon & Schuster, 1941), 170–76.

71. Hale Shirley, *Psychiatry for the Pediatrician* (New York: Commonwealth Fund, 1948), 283–84. See also Philip Piker, "Sex Offenses as Seen by a Psychiatrist," *Journal of Health and Physical Education* 18, no. 9 (November 1947); Terry, *An American Obsession*, 307–8, 315.

72. Names and addresses pulled from Mental Hygiene Society of Northern California, "Introducing Our New Board of Directors and Officers," *Beacons* 3, no. 1 (January 1948), Institute of Governmental Studies, University of California, Berkeley.

73. Ellen Herman, *The Romance of American Psychology: Political Culture in the Age of Experts* (Berkeley: University of California Press, 1994); Moran, *Teaching Sex*; Rima Apple, *Perfect Motherhood: Science and Childrearing in America* (New Brunswick, NJ: Rutgers University Press, 2006).

74. See, for example, *Annual History and Reports, 1933–1934*, Second District PTA Records, San Francisco History Center; "Sex Education Series Arranged," *San Francisco News*, 21 February 1935; "News of Parent-Teachers," *San Francisco Chronicle*, 9 January 1938.

75. Hale Shirley, "Healthy Attitudes Towards Sex," *California Parent-Teacher*, November 1943, 8–9; "Second District P.T.-A President Reports on War Activities of Units," *San Francisco Chronicle*, 4 April 1943; "Doctors Give Parents Advice on Sex Education," *San Francisco Chronicle*, 9 October 1946.

76. " 'Human Growth' Movie to Be Shown Tomorrow," *San Francisco Chronicle*, 12 September 1948. For more on collaboration between the PTA and MHSNC, see "Two Oregon Films Brought to City," *San Francisco Chronicle*, 4 December 1949.

77. Frances Miller, "Sex Education for Parents," *California Journal of Secondary Education* 23 (February 1948).

78. The gender makeup of the PTA's leadership is taken from the annual reports filed in the Second District Records at the San Francisco History Center. For the total membership, see "P.T.A. Membership at All-Time High in S.F.," *San Francisco Examiner*, 19 January 1947.

79. Anne Meis Knupfer and Christine Woyshner, *The Educational Work of Women's Organizations, 1890–1960* (New York: Palgrave, 2008).

80. "News and Notes," *Marriage and Family Living* 11, no. 3 (August 1949): 108; "Institute Discusses Sex Education for Children," *San Francisco Chronicle*, 7 February 1950; Rebecca Davis, *More Perfect Unions: The American Search for Marital Bliss* (Cambridge, MA: Harvard University Press, 2010), 136–75; Heather White, *Reforming Sodom: Protestantism and the Rise of Gay Rights* (Chapel Hill: University of North Carolina Press, 2015), 15–42.

81. H. Paul Douglas et al., *The San Francisco Bay Area Church Study* (San Francisco: San Francisco Council of Churches, 1947), 18–19, 55.

82. Phebe Ward, "Adult Education Contributes to Family Life," *California Journal of Secondary Education* 24, no. 3 (March 1949): 152–53.

83. Noel Keys, "Youth and Marriage Today," *Marriage and Family Living* 8, no. 2 (May 1946): 41; Phebe Ward, "Adult Education Contributes to Family Life," 153.

84. William Issel, *Church and State in the City: Catholics and Politics in Twentieth Century San Francisco* (Philadelphia: Temple University Press, 2013), 4–5, 44–49, 99–100; Fred Sackett, "Gay, Young, and Good: San Francisco's Catholic Action," *Catholic Digest* 9 (February 1945): 33.

85. "Sex Education in SF Schools Debated," *San Francisco Chronicle*, 1 March 1944.

86. "Institute Discusses Sex Education for Children," *San Francisco Chronicle*, 7 February 1950.

87. "Sex Instruction," *Ave Maria*, 4 March 1944, 292–93. This logic was very common in Catholic writings on sex education in schools. See also Francis Connell, "Sex Instruction of the Young," *Journal of Religious Instruction* 15 (October 1944): 225–36.

88. "Catholic Women's Union Passes Resolutions," *San Francisco Chronicle*, 11 August 1949.

89. "Sex Education," *Journal of Religious Instruction* 14 (January 1944): 429; J. William Holt, "Sex Instruction of Youth," *Journal of Religious Instruction* 17 (September 1946): 36.

90. Mrs. Walter Ferguson, "Sex Education Dangerous? Mrs. Walter Ferguson: Kids May Test Knowledge," *San Francisco News*, 24 August 1949.

91. John Leffler, "Favoring Released Time," *Parent-Teacher Journal*, May–June 1944, ACLU Collection, California Historical Society, San Francisco.

92. George Gallup, "High School Courses in Sex Education Favored by Big Vote in National Survey," *Washington Post*, 4 June 1943.

93. "Sex Education in S.F. Schools Is Debated," *San Francisco Chronicle*, 1 March 1944.

94. "Senate Defeats Bill for Classes in Parenthood," *San Francisco Chronicle*, 10 June 1945; "School Board Opposes Bill on Bible Reading," *San Francisco Examiner*, 23 March 1949. Just two weeks prior to his statement on sex education, Alioto presided over a panel session at a conference on marriage sponsored by the San Francisco Archdiocese. See "Marriage Conference," *San Francisco Chronicle*, 6 March 1949.

95. "Proposed School Bills," *San Francisco Chronicle*, 23 March 1949.

96. "The Catholic Action Program" and "The Common Program—Practical Suggestions," in Catholic Men of the Archdiocese of San Francisco, ed., *Catholic Action: The Church in Action* (San Francisco: Archdiocese of San Francisco, 1939), 11.

97. "Teach Parents to Teach Sex," *America*, 27 August 1949.

Chapter 2

1. Alfred Kinsey, *Preliminary Report of the Subcommittee on Sex Crimes of the Assembly Interim Committee on Judicial System and Judicial Process* (Sacramento: Assembly of the State of California, 1950), 105.

2. Canaday, *The Straight State*; Margot Canaday, "Heterosexuality as a Legal Regime," in Michael Grossberg and Christopher Tomlins, eds., *Cambridge History of American Law*, vol. 3 (New York: Cambridge University Press, 2008). Canaday's work mostly focuses on federal policies. For material on state regulations, see Karen Graves, *They Were Wonderful Teachers: Florida's Purge of Gay and Lesbian Teachers* (Champaign: University of Illinois Press, 2009).

3. For earlier eras of regulation, see Shah, *Contagious Divides*; Horowitz, *Re-Reading Sex*. For the importance of the Cold War, see D'Emilio, *Sexual Politics, Sexual Communities*; May, *Homeward Bound*; Herman, *Romance of American Psychology*; Johnson, *The Lavender Scare*.

4. David Allyn, "Private Acts/Public Policy: Alfred Kinsey, the American Law Institute and the Privatization of American Morality," pt. 3, *Journal of American Studies* 30, no. 3 (December 1996): 405–28.

5. Canaday, *The Straight State*, 255–56.

6. Freedman, "Uncontrolled Desires"; Canaday, "Heterosexuality as a Legal Regime," 449–50.

7. Berubé, *Coming Out Under Fire*; Canaday, *The Straight State*, 141–42.

8. D'Emilio, *Sexual Politics, Sexual Communities*; Johnson, *The Lavender Scare.*

9. Canaday, *The Straight State*, 3.

10. Karl Bowman, *Sexual Deviation Research* (Sacramento: Assembly of the State of California, 1952), 12–14.

11. Risa Goluboff, *Vagrant Nation: Police Power, Constitutional Change, and the Making of the 1960s* (New York: Oxford University Press, 2016), 3, 148, 173–74.

12. Johnson, *The Lavender Scare*, 72–77.

13. In 1955, Karl Bowman, one of California's leading medical experts on homosexuality, complained that the "lavender scare" was getting out of hand: "The person even suspected of homosexuality is banned from any Government work. Almost no corporation or private business will hire a man with a stigma on his record." "S.F. Psychiatrist Assails Sex-Deviation 'Hysteria,'" *San Francisco Chronicle*, 10 May 1955.

14. Canaday, *The Straight State*, 256.

15. Letter to Chief Administrative Officers, 3 March 1948, Teachers Credentialing Commission, Investigative Files, California State Archives. Due to a confidentiality agreement required by the California State Archives, I am not allowed to reveal the names of anyone who is mentioned in these records.

16. When a private attorney from Southern California challenged the dismissal of a teacher who had been acquitted of a homosexual-related crime, state officials reacted by asserting in an internal memo, "The request of the attorney appears to be based solely on the fact that Mr. ——— had been acquitted of criminal charges. I do not think this information (which was previously known to the Commission) constitutes persuasive grounds for a reversal by the Commission or a reconsideration of its prior determination [to revoke the teacher's credentials]." Intradepartment Correspondence, 14 November 1961, Department of Education Records, Commission of Credentials, Investigative Files.

17. Intradepartment correspondence, 6 May 1960, Teachers Credentialing Commission, Investigative Files.

18. Ibid.

19. Everett Calvert, *A Report of the California Commission of Credentials of the State Department of Education* (Sacramento, CA: California Department of Education, 1963), 3, Department of Education Records, Commission of Credentials Reports, California State Archives.

20. Internal memo, no title, 20 January 1954, Teachers Credentialing Commission, Investigative Files.

21. Letter to San Francisco Board of Education, 19 October 1959, Teachers Credentialing Commission, Investigative Files.

22. Case report, no title, 17 December 1954, Teachers Credentialing Commission, Investigative Files.

23. Hearing on the Matter of the Applications for a General Secondary Credential in Correction of Speech Defects, and the Junior College Credential of —, hearing transcript, Minutes of California State Board of Education, November 1957. Final decision was rendered in 1958, Minutes of California State Board of Education, November 1958, 8210–17. The name of the teacher in this case is a matter of public record, but in order to protect his privacy, I have elected not to use his name here.

24. Intradepartment correspondence, Memo, 29 September 1954, Teachers Credentialing Commission, Investigative Files.

25. Letter, 9 June 1948, Teachers Credentialing Commission, Investigative Files.

26. Calvert, *A Report of the California Commission of Credentials of the State Department of Education*, 6.

27. Letter to Roy Simpson, 23 July 1952, Teachers Credentialing Commission, Investigative Files.

28. Letter, 1 September 1955, Teachers Credentialing Commission, Investigative Files.

29. Rafferty specifically alleged that the Board of Education cared too much about the "rehabilitation" of teachers than it did to "protecting children." "Rafferty Talks of Deviate Teachers," *San Francisco Examiner*, 18 June 1963; "Deviate Row on Board," *San Francisco Examiner*, 26 July 1963.

30. Intradepartment correspondence, 16 January 1950, "Mr. Hush" File, Teachers Credentialing Commission Investigative Files.

31. Letter, 8 December 1952, Teachers Credentialing Commission, Investigative Files.

32. Herb Caen, "Baghdad by the Bay," *San Francisco Examiner*, 19 January 1955.

33. It is important to note that the state relied primarily on tips from confidential sources to make its case and that it consciously played different political interests in San Francisco off one another. The state's stance on homosexuality subjected all educators to official surveillance and suspicion. In several instances, a confidential source within the San Francisco Department of Education provided investigators with hearsay and impressionistic evidence about their target. In one instance, the informant alleged that the administrator had hired a male secretary that she found "'queer' and 'odd' looking." Letter to Department Investigator, 12 August 1954, Teachers Credentialing Commission, Investigative Files. When state officials considered how to handle the Board of Education's refusal to fire the official, the informant alleged that the mayor was "queer" and was protecting the school administrator. The same informant counseled investigators to leak the incriminating letter to the Methodist minister because the clergyman believed the target of their inquiry had argued in favor of protecting Catholic parochial schools from taxation. Letter to Department Investigator, 24 January 1955, Teachers Credentialing Commission, Investigative Files.

34. Investigator with Santa Clara County District Attorney's Office, letter to Department of Education Investigator, 11 April 1952, Teachers Credentialing Commission, Investigative Files.

35. Calvert, *A Report of the California Commission of Credentials of the State Department of Education*, 67.

36. "Another S.F. Teacher Out as Morals Case Disclosed," *San Francisco Examiner*, 21 March 1957.

37. Canaday, *The Straight State*, 256.

38. Mental Hygiene Society of Northern California, "What's New," newsletter, April 1946, Institute of Governmental Studies, University of California, Berkeley.

39. "I Will Return, Tenney Warns as He Leaves Chico," *San Francisco Chronicle*, 28 February 1947.

40. This has been a common state-building practice. Brian Balogh, *The Associational State: American Governance in the Twentieth Century* (Philadelphia: University of Pennsylvania Press, 2015).

41. Federal Security Agency, Public Health Service, Mental Hygiene Division, *The National Mental Health Act and Your Community* (Washington, DC: Government Printing

Office, 1948); James Lowry, "How the National Mental Health Act Works," *Public Health Reports* 64, no. 10 (March 1949); National Institute of Mental Health, *The National Mental Health Act: Five Years of Progress, 1946–1951* (Washington, DC: Federal Security Agency, 1951).

42. University of California, *Announcement of the School of Medicine, 1950–1951* (Berkeley: University of California Press, 1950), 117; California Department of Mental Hygiene, *California Sexual Deviation Research* (Sacramento: Assembly of the State of California, 1953).

43. The U.S. Public Health Service, including its San Francisco office, encouraged all doctors, nurses, and hospital workers to learn about sex "aberrations", including homosexuality. See Henry Schumacher, "The Integration of Mental Hygiene Concepts and Practices in a Public Health Program," *Canadian Journal of Public Health* 39, no. 9 (September 1948): 354–55.

44. California Department of Mental Hygiene, *California Sexual Deviation Research*, 42.

45. Marion Faegre, *The Adolescent in Your Family* (Washington, DC: U.S. Children's Bureau, 1954), 22, 58.

46. Lester Beck et al., *Human Growth* (Eugene, OR: E. C. Brown Trust, 1947). See also Federal Security Agency, U.S. Children's Bureau, *Your Child from 6 to 12* (Washington, DC: Government Printing Office, 1947), 74, 101–2.

47. Marion Faegre, *Your Child from 6 to 12* (Washington, DC: U.S. Children's Bureau, 1949), 103; see also "Modesty Develops in Time," in Ralph Eckert, ed., *Sex Attitudes in the Home* (New York: Association Press, 1956), 40–51.

48. Eckert, *Sex Attitudes in the Home*, 46. Eckert worked for the State of California in the early 1950s, and this book came out after he left his government position. But his words reflect both his thinking on the subject and the larger field of child psychology promoted by the state.

49. Author unknown, Report on Parent Education, 1947, California Department of Education Records, California State Archives, Sacramento.

50. Ralph Eckert, "Growing Interest in Family-Life Education Is Statewide," *California Journal of Secondary Education* 25, no. 1 (January 1950): 43.

51. Ralph Eckert, "Changing Patterns in Summer Education," *Marriage and Family Living* 13, no. 1 (Winter 1951): 28.

52. Ralph Eckert, "Trends in Parent Education," *California Journal of Secondary Education* 22 (January 1947): 19–20.

53. "End of Free S.F. School Courses for Adults Seen," *San Francisco Chronicle*, 26 January 1958. City officials used state funding for a variety of different kinds of adult education, including parent education.

54. Phebe Ward, "A Community Conducts Its First Family Life Workshop," *Marriage and Family Living* 13, no. 1 (February 1951); Dorothy Westby-Gibson, "The San Francisco Family Life Education Service," *Marriage and Family Living* 13, no. 4 (November 1951). The family life education programs initiated at this conference included many different kinds of topics, but they included discussions of ways to promote normative sexuality.

55. Ralph Eckert, "The Role of the P.T.A. in Sex Education," *Marriage and Family Living* 13 (May 1951): 58.

56. See, for example, Harriet Randall, "He Loves Me . . . He Loves Me Not," *California Parent-Teacher*, December 1948; Ralph Eckert, "Ready for Marriage," *California Parent-Teacher*, March 1949.

57. For material on the two-tiered system, see Jackson, *Crabgrass Frontier*; Sugrue, *Origins of the Urban Crisis*; Freund, *Colored Property*. For more on San Francisco's public housing, see Amy Howard, *More Than Shelter: Activism and Community in San Francisco's Public Housing* (Minneapolis: University of Minnesota Press, 2014).

58. "Six Women Draw FHA Suspension," *Washington Post*, 31 October 1954; "List of Security Separations," *Washington Post*, 4 January 1955.

59. Housing and Home Finance Agency, *7th Annual Report* (Washington, DC: Government Printing Office, 1954), 381–82.

60. Howard, *More Than Shelter*, 6.

61. U.S. Federal Housing Administration, *Underwriting Manual*, section 1636 (Washington, DC: Federal Housing Administration, 1952).

62. Margot Canaday, "Building a Straight State: Sexuality and Social Citizenship Under the 1944 G.I. Bill," *Journal of American History* 90, no. 3 (December 2003): 956. See also Cohen, *A Consumer's Republic*, 143.

63. Federal Housing Administration, *Underwriting Manual*, 1952, section 1635.

64. Mary Wirth, "Point of Entry Work with Problem Families Proving Helpful," *Journal of Housing* 14 (April 1957): 128.

65. Else Reisner, *Homemaking and Family Adjustment Services in Public Housing* (San Francisco: Housing Authority of the City and County of San Francisco, n.d.), 11–12, 19, Bancroft Library, University of California, Berkeley.

66. Federal Housing Administration, *Your Home Buying Ability: FHA Credit Analysis for Home Buyers* (Washington DC: Government Printing Office,1960). For more on the ways that federal programs encouraged male breadwinning and disadvantaged women, see Cott, *Public Vows*; Cohen, *A Consumer's Republic.*

67. Howard, *More Than Shelter*, 13–15.

68. Jackson, *Crabgrass Frontier*; Cohen, *A Consumer's Republic*; Freund, *Colored Property*.

69. Federal Housing Administration, *Underwriting Manual*, 1952, section 1320.

70. Alice O'Conner, *Poverty Knowledge: Social Science, Social Policy, and the Poor in Twentieth Century U.S. History* (Princeton, NJ: Princeton University Press, 2001), 23–54.

71. J. S. Plant, "Some Psychiatric Aspects of Good Living Conditions," *American Journal of Psychiatry* 87 (March 1930): 849–60.

72. Edith Elmer Wood, *Slums and Blighted Areas in the United* States*: Housing Division Bulletin No. 1* (Washington, DC: Federal Emergency Administration of Public Works, 1935), 14. Wood also stated, "Overcrowding within the home, obtruding sights from uncurtained windows, obtruding sounds through thin partitions, thrust sex in its unloveliest aspects on the attention of young children." Edith Elmer Wood, *Introduction to Housing: Facts and Principles* (Washington, DC: U.S. Housing Authority, 1940), 59.

73. U.S. Housing Authority, *Dwelling Unit Planning* (Washington, DC: U.S. Housing Authority, 1938); "New Study on Health and Slum Conditions," *Public Housing* 1, no. 38 (April 1940).

74. Catherine Bauer, *A Citizen's Guide to Public Housing* (Poughkeepsie, NY: Vassar College, 1940), 44.

75. "Tenants Have Say on Low Rent Homes," *San Francisco Housing* 3, no. 3 (April 1946). These soundproofed walls also functioned as firebreaks and mirrored a promise made by the SFHA before World War II that it would "provision for privacy for each family within the home." Housing Authority of the City and County of San Francisco, *Annual Report*, 1940.

76. Lewis Mumford, *The Culture of Cities* (New York: Harcourt, Brace and Company, 1938), 432–33. See also American Public Health Association, Committee on the Hygiene of Housing, *Planning the Home for Occupancy* (Chicago: Public Administration Service, 1950).

77. Federal Housing Administration, *Underwriters' Manual*, section 428 (Washington, DC: Federal Housing Administration, 1947).

78. Ibid.

79. Freund, *Colored Property*, 192.

80. David Freund, "Marketing the Free Market: State Intervention and the Politics of Prosperity in Metropolitan America," in Kevin Kruse and Thomas Sugrue, eds., *The New Suburban History* (Chicago: University of Chicago Press, 2005).

81. For more on Kinsey, see Allyn, "Private Acts/Public Policy"; Miriam Reumann, *American Sexual Character: Sex, Gender, and National Identity in the Kinsey Reports* (Berkeley: University of California Press, 2005); Sarah Igo, *The Averaged American: Surveys, Citizens, and the Making of a Mass Public* (Cambridge, MA: Harvard University Press, 2007).

82. Alfred Kinsey, Wardell Pomeroy, and Clyde Martin, *Sexual Behavior in the Human Male* (Philadelphia: W. B. Saunders, 1948), 499, 552, 671.

83. Ibid., 623.

84. Ibid., 3.

85. Kinsey, *Preliminary Report of the Subcommittee on Sex Crimes*, 105.

86. "Kinsey Discusses Frustrations," *San Francisco Chronicle*, 21 August 1953.

87. Kinsey, *Preliminary Report of the Subcommittee on Sex Crimes*, 106.

88. "Kinsey's Report on U.S. Women Is Released," *San Francisco Chronicle*, 20 August 1953.

89. Ibid.

90. "S.F. Book Stores Stampeded—They All Want Kinsey's Book," *San Francisco Chronicle*, 21 August 1953; "Dr. Kinsey Topples Some Old Taboos," *San Francisco Chronicle*, 20 August 1953.

91. Arlene Meredith, letter, *San Francisco Chronicle*, 9 September 1953.

92. David Pressly, letter, *San Francisco Chronicle*, 15 September 1953.

93. Patricia Friedman, letter, *San Francisco Examiner*, 20 March 1958.

94. Olive Parker, letter, *San Francisco Examiner*, 2 April 1958.

95. "Post-Kinsey: Voluntary Sex Relations as Criminal Offenses," *University of Chicago Law Review* 17, no. 1 (Autumn 1949): 173.

96. Morris Ploscowe, *Sex and the Law* (New York: Prentice Hall, 1951), 213. Legal expert Isabel Drummond similarly argued that public opinion seemed increasingly open to decriminalizing private sex acts between consenting adults: "Doctors pronounce as ill virtually all perverts who indulge in 'unnatural' sex acts, and the collective conscience appears to be yielding more and more towards the extension of legal freedom to the adults who voluntarily indulge privately in sexual perversions with each other." Isabel Drummon, *The Sex Paradox* (New York: G. P. Putnam, 1953), 119.

97. Frank Kent Jr., "Sex Offenses Weighed for New Moral Code," *Washington Post*, 20 May 1955.

98. Ibid. and Allyn, "Private Acts/Public Policy."

99. Ibid.

100. Ploscowe, *Sex and the Law*, 279–83.

101. "Post-Kinsey," 182.

102. Ploscow, *Sex and the Law*, 282.

103. Louis Schwartz, "Moral Offenses and the Model Penal Code," *Columbia Law Review* 63, no. 4 (April 1963): 675. Schwartz's article looked back at some of the logic that helped create the first draft of thc ALI code in 1955.

Chapter 3

1. Federal Housing Administration, *The FHA Plan of Home Ownership* (Washington, DC: Government Printing Office, 1954); U.S. Savings and Loan League, *What You Should Know Before You Buy a Home* (U.S. Savings and Loan League, 1959); "Live in an Eichler—Discover the New Way of Life," advertisement, *San Francisco Chronicle*, 15 May 1959.

2. For other accounts of school crowding in other suburbs in the United States, see Jack Dougherty, "Shopping for Schools: How Public Education and Private Housing Shaped Suburban Connecticut," *Journal of Urban History* 38, no. 2 (2012); Highsmith, *Demolition Means Progress*, 116–17.

3. Linda Gordon, *Heroes of Their Own Lives: The Politics and History of Family Violence: Boston, 19860–1960* (New York: Viking, 1988); Reva Siegel, "The Rule of Love: Wife Beating as Prerogative and Privacy," *Yale Law Journal* 105, no. 8 (June 1996); Raphael Ginsberg, "Protecting the Prestige of the Family: The Politics of Domestic Violence Discourse," *Radical History Review* 126 (October 2016).

4. Paul Griffin and Ronald Chatham, "Urban Impact on Agriculture in Santa Clara County, California," *Annals of the American Association of Geographers* 48, no. 3 (September 1958): 198.

5. U.S. Bureau of the Census, *Sixteenth Census of the United States: 1940, Population*, vol. 4, *Characteristics by Age*, pt. 2 (Washington, DC: Government Printing Office, 1943), 186.

6. Yvonne Jacobson, *Passing Farms, Enduring Values: California's Santa Clara Valley* (Los Altos, CA: William Kaufmann, 1984). See also Robin Chapman, *The Lost Orchards of Silicon Valley* (Charleston, SC: American Palate, 2013).

7. Pitti, *The Devil in Silicon Valley*, 80–92; Cavin, "Fringe Politics"; Griffin and Chatham, "Urban Impact on Agriculture in Santa Clara County, California," 198.

8. Shah, *Contagious Divides*; Shah, *Stranger Intimacy*.

9. Richard McClure, interviewed by Allan Bérubé, 12 March 1979, Oral History Collection, GLBT Historical Society of Northern California.

10. *Nickola v. Monro*, 328 P 2d 271 (Cal. 1958). The case involved a raid on the bar, which included reports of white men dancing with black and Filipino men.

11. William Gaddis, letter to Harry, 22 September 1941, William Gaddis Papers, GLBT Historical Society of Northern California.

12. Pitti, *Devil in Silicon Valley*, 86–87.

13. V. B. Stanberry, *Economic Expansion in the San Francisco Bay Area, 1940–1947* (Washington, DC: U.S. Department of Commerce, 1948), 8.

14. Bay Area Council, *Facts About the Bay Area*, Economic Series P-10, 9 May 1950, Institute of Governmental Studies, University of California, Berkeley.

15. "Wanted . . . Housing," *California Real Estate Magazine*, April 1947.

16. Jackson, *Crabgrass Frontier*, 203–5; Freund, *Colored Property*.

17. Cohen, *A Consumers' Republic*, 141; Paul Wendt and Daniel Rathbun, *The Role of Government in the San Francisco Bay Area Mortgage Market* (Berkeley: University of California, Bureau of Business and Economic Research, 1952).

18. Jackson, *Crabgrass Frontier*, 206.

19. Ibid., 206; John Herzog, *Dynamics of Large-Scale House-Building*, report 22 (Berkeley: University of California Real Estate Research Program, 1963); Sherman Maisel, *Housebuilding in the San Francisco Bay Area* (Berkeley: Bureau of Business and Economic Research, University of California, Berkeley, 1951), 169.

20. Sunnyvale Chamber of Commerce, "Sunnyvale's Panorama of Progress," May 1956, Local History Collection, Sunnyvale Public Library, Sunnyvale, CA.

21. Branden Enterprises, *Tropicana Village: San Jose, CA*, 1958, Rare Books Collection Environmental Design Library, University of California, Berkeley.

22. Robert W. Travis, *A Development of Housing Research Techniques and Analysis of Housing Inventory and Estimate of Needs and Trends in San Jose, CA* (Sacramento: California State Library, 1960).

23. San Jose Planning Department, *Santa Clara Subdivision Activity, 1957–1967* (San Jose: San Jose Planning Department, 1967), Institute of Governmental Studies, University of California, Berkeley.

24. See, for example, Harold Wise Associates, *1955 Report: Palo Alto Interim General Plan*, (Palo Alto, CA: City of Palo Alto, 1955).

25. Federal Housing Administration, *Underwriting Manual*, 1952, sec. 1322.

26. National Association of Home Builders, *Home Builders Manual for Land Development* (Washington, DC: National Association of Homebuilders, 1958), 204.

27. Santa Clara County Planning Commission, *Planning Goals*, monograph 2 (San Jose: Santa Clara County Planning Commission, 1952).

28. San Jose Planning Commission, *Master Plan of the City of San Jose* (San Jose: San Jose Planning Commission, 1958).

29. "School Plant Trends," in American School and Publishing Corporation, *American School and University* (New York: American School Publishing, 1949), 116.

30. Ibid.

31. National Association of Home Builders, *Home Building Manual for Land Development*, 202.

32. William H. Claire, "The Church in the City Plan," *Journal of the American Institute of Planners* 20 (Fall 1954): 173.

33. Nazar Hajinian et al., *Interracial Prejudices in San Jose, California* (San Jose, CA: San Jose State College, 1950).

34. City of San Jose, County of Santa Clara, and City of Palo Alto Human Relations Commission, *Public Hearings on Housing Patterns, Zoning Laws, and Segregated Schools in Santa Clara County*, 4 August–22 September, 1975, 37. For a more detailed history of race and real estate in the South Bay, see Aaron Cavin, "The Borders of Citizenship: Race and the Politics of Metropolitan Space in Silicon Valley" (Ph.D. diss., University of Michigan, 2012).

35. National Association of Home Builders, *Home Builders Manual for Land Development*, 1953, 17.

36. San Jose Human Relations Commission et al. *Public Hearings on Housing Patterns, Zoning Laws, and Segregated Schools* (San Jose: San Jose Human Relations Commission, 1976), 33.

37. Hajinian, "Interracial Prejudices in San Jose, California"; "Negro Housing Problem Reported to City Council," *San Jose Mercury*, 1 July 1958, History San Jose.

38. Edwin Rios, *Improving Ethnic Balance and Intergroup Relations: A Report to the Santa Clara Board of Education* (San Jose: Santa Clara County Board of Education, 1968); Cavin, "Fringe Politics."

39. American Public Health Association, Committee on the Hygiene of Housing, *An Appraisal Method for Measuring the Quality of Housing: A Yardstick for Health Officers, Housing Officials and Planners, Part III, Appraisal of the Neighborhood Environment* (Chicago: American Public Health Association, 1950), 8.

40. "Hoboes Are Evicted from the Jungle," *San Francisco Chronicle*, 25 May 1947.

41. "Number of Hoboes Dwindles After Clean-up Drive," *Santa Clara Journal*, 21 July 1955.

42. *Nickola v. Monro*, 328 P 2d 271 (Cal. 1958). These raids on queer bars took place in other suburbanizing areas as well. For an example from Marin County, north of San Francisco, see "32 Held in Marin Tavern Raid," *San Francisco Examiner*, 1 July 1957.

43. " 'Dial a Doll' Cocktail Bar Promoter Gets Wrong Number," *Sunnyvale Daily Standard*, 12 April 1962; "So Much for Table Talk," *San Jose Mercury*, 13 April 1962.

44. Department of Alcoholic Beverage Control, *Report: Santa Clara County*, 1965–66, Department of Alcoholic Beverage Control, Subject Files, County Activity Reports, California State Archives. A note in the report singled out the South Bay by saying, "Santa Clara has more persons per license than any other county [in the state]."

45. Association of Bay Area Governments, "Bay Area Census," accessed 8 May 2017, http://www.bayareacensus.ca.gov/index.html.

46. Arthur Gimmy, *A Descriptive Survey of Urban Fringe Home Owners, Their House Buying Habits, and Their Mobility* (San Jose, CA: San Jose State Real Estate Research Bureau, 1958). For national trends, see U.S. Housing and Home Finance Agency, *What People Want When They Buy a House* (Washington, DC: U.S. Department of Commerce, 1955).

47. U.S. Bureau of the Census, *U.S. Census of Population and Housing: 1960, San Francisco–Oakland, California Standard Metropolitan Statistical Area* (Washington, DC: Government Printing Office, 1962); U.S. Bureau of the Census, *U.S. Census of Population and Housing: 1960, San Jose, California Standard Metropolitan Statistical Area* (Washington, DC: Government Printing Office, 1962).

48. U.S. Bureau of the Census, San Jose, California Standard Metropolitan Statistical Area, 1962.

49. Gimmy, *A Descriptive Survey of Urban Fringe Home Owners*, 19.

50. David Beers, *Blue Sky Dream: A Memoir of America's Fall from Grace* (San Diego, CA: Harvest Books, 1996), 43. For a similar story of parents imagining their home before they built it, see Chapman, *California Apricots*, 11–13.

51. Father 4, interview, 4 December 1957, 7–9, Lois Meek Stolz Psychology Case Interviews, Department of Special Collections, Stanford University, Stanford, CA.

52. Father 6, interview, 4 December 1957, 14, Lois Meek Stolz Psychology Case Interviews.

53. "Why Did You Choose the Peninsula for Home?" *San Francisco Examiner*, 4 June 1962.

54. "Why Did You Move Here?" *Santa Clara Journal*, 10 January 1962.

55. Father 11, interview, 21 February 1958, 22, Stolz Psychology Case Interviews. This father also says that he overcame the animosity of some of his neighbors in time.

56. Father 10, interview, 22 March 1958, 1, Stolz Psychology Case Interviews.

57. Bruce Schulman, *From Cotton Belt to Sunbelt: Federal Policy, Economic Development, and the Transformation of the South, 1938–1980* (New York: Oxford University Press, 1991); Elizabeth Tandy Shermer, *Sunbelt Capitalism: Phoenix and the Transformation of American Politics* (Philadelphia: University of Pennsylvania Press, 2013).

58. Self, *American Babylon*, 25–32, 100–11.

59. O'Mara, *Cities of Knowledge*, 140.

60. "Crisis in Schools: It Adds Up to Tax Dollars," *San Jose Mercury*, 15 April 1962.

61. "Squeezed Schools: They Battle Teacher, Space Shortages, with New, Old Tricks," *Wall Street Journal*, 3 September 1957; "Schools Get Bigger," *San Jose Mercury*, 24 January 1960.

62. "More Payrolls for a Bedroom Community," *Urban Land*, May 1953.

63. Mary Drury et al., *A Study of the School Building Program of the Laguna Salada Union Elementary School District* (Redwood City, CA, 1951), 9 Institute of Governmental Studies, University of California, Berkeley.

64. "High Income, High IQ Help Palo Alto, Calif. Grow Fast, Live Relaxed," *Wall Street Journal*, 10 August 1956.

65. "Predicted Crisis for San Mateo Schools at Hand," *San Francisco Examiner*, 27 February 1956.

66. "More Payrolls for a Bedroom Community," *Urban Land*, May 1953.

67. Palo Alto Planning Commission and Harold Wise Associates, *1955 Report*.

68. "Predicted Crisis for San Mateo Schools at Hand," *San Francisco Examiner*, 27 February 1956.

69. Drury et al., *A Study of the School Building Program of the Laguna Salada Union Elementary School District*.

70. Theodore Reller, *Problems of Public Education in the San Francisco Bay Area* (Berkeley: Institute of Governmental Studies, University of California, Berkeley, 1963), Institute of Governmental Studies.

71. San Mateo County Planning Commission, *Annual Report 1952–53* (Redwood City, CA: San Mateo County Planning Commission, September 1953).

72. Palo Alto Planning Commission and Harold Wise Associates, *Report on the Interim General Plan, City of Palo Alto* (Palo Alto, CA: Palo Alto Planning Commission, 1955).

73. James Clayton, "The Impact of the Cold War on the Economies of California and Utah, 1946–65," *Pacific Historical Review* 36, no. 4 (November 1967): 449.

74. Industrial Survey Associates, *Santa Clara County: Its Prospects of Prosperity* (Sacramento: California State Library, May 1948).

75. "IBM to Dedicate $16 Million San Jose Industrial Plant," *San Francisco Examiner*, 12 January 1956; "Lockheed Will Triple Sunnyvale Secret Missile Plant's Size," *San Francisco Examiner*, 2 May 1956; "Lockheed Moving Missile Division into San Francisco Bay Region," *Aviation and Space Technology*, 6 February 1956. For more on the importance of Stanford in this recruitment process, see O'Mara, *Cities of Knowledge*.

76. Clayton, "The Impact of the Cold War on the Economies of California and Utah," 460. Santa Clara County trailed Southern California as a whole, but it attracted more defense-related spending than Orange or San Diego counties.

77. Robert Wooley, "Industry Drive Is Getting Results," *San Francisco Chronicle*, 27 February 1955; "San Jose Discovers How It Feels to Be Rich," *Business Week*, 26 September 1964.

78. Glenn Matthew White, "The Challenge of the Century," *Ladies' Home Journal* 75 (May 1958).

79. Bill Boldenweck, "E. Palo Alto—The Other S.M. County Election," *San Francisco Chronicle*, 12 November 1967; "A Dramatic Difference in Tax Rates," *San Francisco Chronicle*, 21 September 1968. For more on the lack of services in some of the South Bay's suburbs, see Cavin, "Fringe Politics."

80. D'Emilio and Freedman, *Intimate Matters*, 241.

81. American Public Health Association, Committee on the Hygiene of Housing, *Planning the Home for Occupancy* (Chicago: Public Administration Service, 1950), 1.

82. Robert Woods Kennedy, *The House and the Art of Its Design* (New York: Reinhold, 1953), 113.

83. "Fresh Design = Fast Sales," *House and Home*, October 1952.

84. "H-Plan and V-Roof," *House and Home*, November 1952; "Built-in Merchandising Lifts California Joe Eichler into the Big Time," *House and Home*, July 1955.

85. "Four Bedrooms Solve Space Squeeze," *House and Home*, June 1954.

86. American Public Health Association, *Planning the Home for Occupancy*.

87. "Better Bathrooms and More of Them," *House and Home*, May 1954.

88. For an example of the living room as a "woman and children's space," see "Where Should You Put the Family Room?" *House and Home*, July 1955.

89. "Four Bedrooms Solve Space Squeeze," *House and Home*, June 1954. For more on the expectations of mothers in South Bay homes, see Annmarie Adams, "The Eichler Home: Intention and Experience in Postwar Suburbs," *Perspectives in Vernacular Architecture* 5 (1995).

90. "Two-Way Mirrors Allow Secret Surveillance of Students at Buchser and Wilson Schools," *Santa Clara Journal*, 13 November 1963.

91. "Stanford Drops 7 Students Seized as Sex Deviates," *San Francisco Examiner*, 14 February 1956; "Students Seized on Sex Charges Granted Leave," *Los Angeles Times*, 15 February 1956; "Cop Movies Net 24 in Sex Case," *San Francisco Examiner*, 27 January 1959.

92. "8 Nabbed on Morals Charges," *San Jose Mercury*, 6 February 1962.

93. Howard, *Men Like That*, 63–64.

94. Father 12, interview, 17 March 1958, Lois Meek Stolz Psychology Case Interviews, 22–24.

95. Father 1, interview, 26 November 1957, 17–18, Lois Meek Stolz Psychology Case Interviews.

96. Gutterman, "The House on the Borderland."

97. Richard Tooker, interview with Peter Toscani, 20 January 1998, GLBT Historical Society of Northern California.

98. "Area Doctor Faces 'Torture' Charges," *Sunnyvale Daily Standard*, 23 November 1964.

99. "Restaurant Partners Flee Sex Perversion Charges," *San Jose Mercury*, 5 January 1955.

100. *Statement by Judge and District Attorney Under 1203.01 (Penal Code)*, People v. Edward Goldstein, case 33009, 1955, Santa Clara County Superior Court Records, San Jose, CA.

101. *People v. Edward Goldstein*, 146 Cal. App. 2d (1956).

102. "Restaurant Partners Flee Sex Perversion Charges," *San Jose Mercury*, 5 January 1955.

103. Gordon, "Heroes of Their Own Lives"; Siegel, "The Rule of Love." For more on the legal near impossibility of marital rape, see Ruth Rosen, *The World Split Open: How the Women's Movement Changed America* (New York: Penguin, 2006), 182–86. For a longer history of rape within marriage, see Estelle Freedman, *Redefining Rape: Sexual Violence in the Era of Suffrage and Segregation* (Cambridge, MA: Harvard University Press, 2013).

104. *People v. Edward Goldstein*, 146 Cal. App. 2d (1956).

105. The First Appellate District of the California Court of Appeals later overturned Talle's conviction due to prosecutorial misconduct. *People v. Thomas Talle*, 111 Cal. App. 2d (1952).

Chapter 4

1. "Sex Syllabus Starts Furore in High School," *San Mateo Times*, 28 February 1951; "Sex Teaching Probe Widens," *San Francisco Call-Bulletin*, 2 March 1951; "Prosecutor Asks Full Report on Sex Class," *San Francisco Call-Bulletin*, 7 March 1951.

2. "San Mateo Head Says Sex Course Ended," *San Francisco Examiner*, 1 March 1951; "Sex Education Protests Are Answered," *San Francisco Chronicle*, 3 March 1951; "Sex in Schools," *San Francisco Call-Bulletin*, 7 March 1951.

3. Father 4, interview, 4 December 1957, 7–9, Lois Meek Stolz Psychology Case Interviews.

4. Ibid. See also Mother 1, interview, 14 November 1957; Mother 2, interview, 8 May 1958, Lois Meek Stolz Psychology Case Interviews.

5. This discrimination did not necessarily mean that middle-class women did not work outside the home. In fact, they worked in the paid labor force in higher rates than before the war, but they frequently occupied low-paying and part-time positions in the "pink-collar ghetto." See Joanne Meyerowitz, ed., *Not June Cleaver: Women and Gender in Postwar America, 1945–1960* (Philadelphia: Temple University Press, 1994).

6. Mother 5, interview, 8 April 1958, Lois Meek Stolz Psychology Case Interviews.

7. In 1947, the *San Francisco Examiner* reported that the city's PTAs had 13,000 members. That figure grew to approximately 26,000 members in the mid-1960s. But by the early 1970s, membership dropped considerably to 14,000 members. "P.T.A. Membership at All-Time High," *San Francisco Examiner*, 19 January 1947; "'Streamline' PTA Chores," *San Francisco Examiner*, 21 June 1967.

8. Membership records often included male administrators and teachers who were formally a part of the organization but who spent little time volunteering. Sixth District PTA Historian's Report 1947–48, Sixth District PTA Records, San Jose, CA; ibid., 1952–53; ibid., 1964–65.

9. Barbara Kalish, interview with Shelly Garside, n.d., "Women's Lives, Women's Work," Digital Oral History Collection, California State University, Long Beach, accessed 14 August 2015, http://symposia.library.csulb.edu/iii/cpro/; Daniel Winunwe Rivers, *Radical Relations: Lesbian Mothers, Gay Fathers, and Their Children in the United States Since World War II* (Chapel Hill: University of North Carolina Press, 2014), 19.

10. South Bay newspapers regularly carried stories about the groups' activities, and when they listed names of its leaders, they almost always introduced them all with the title "Mrs." See, for example, "City's First PTA Council in History Takes Office," *Santa Clara Journal*, 16 June 1955; "New High School PTA Organizational Meeting Announced for February 14,"

Santa Clara Journal, 2 February 1956; "Mrs. Roland Squires Heads High School PTA," *Santa Clara Journal*, 16 October 1958.

11. Elizabeth Goodrich, "What Is the PTA Anyway?" *California Parent-Teacher*, September 1952.

12. John Howard makes a similar point about queer communities: "Circulation is as important as congregation, avenues as important as venues." Howard, *Men Like That*, 14.

13. Ibid., 46.

14. Mother 1, interview, 14 November 1957, 7, Lois Meek Stolz Psychology Case Interviews.

15. Father 1, interview, 3 December 1957, Lois Meek Stolz Psychology Case Interviews.

16. S. C. Peabody, Service Program, First Congregational Church, San Jose, Herbert C. Jones Papers, Sourisseau Academy for State and Local History, San Jose State University, San Jose, CA.

17. Sunnyvale Planning Department, *Preliminary Studies of a General Plan for the City of Sunnyvale, California* (Sunnyvale, CA: Sunnyvale Planning Department, 1955); Robert Wilson, *An Example of Local Church Planning in the First Methodist Church of Palo Alto, CA* (Philadelphia: Methodist Church Board of Missions, 1962), 2.

18. "New Evangelistic Association Calls Full-Time Evangelist," *Christian Standard*, 27 November 1954.

19. "California Church Remodels Building," *Christian Standard*, 1 May 1954.

20. Josiah Chatham, "Your Assignment: Build a New Suburban Parish," *Homiletic and Pastoral Review*, December 1955, 219.

21. "Your Church," *Methodist Story*, March 1957, 19–20.

22. See, for example, "Attend the Church of Your Choice," *San Jose Mercury*, 30 April 1960; Church of Christ, "God Has Spoken: You Are Without Excuse," photograph of billboard, William Jessup University Archives, Rocklin, CA.

23. Mrs. Milton Randolph, "Make Your Church Family . . . and Lead Families into Worship," *Methodist Story*, April 1959, 13.

24. Ladera Community Church, "Invitation to Worship," n.d., Santa Clara Council of Churches Records, San Jose, CA.

25. National Council of Churches in the U.S.A., *Churches and Church Membership in the United States: An Enumeration and Analysis by Counties, States and Regions* (New York: Bureau of Research and Survey, 1956). The census calculated that Catholic churches in San Mateo and Santa Clara counties reported a membership of 149,981 and that mainline Protestant churches reported a membership of 46,233. They stated that the Church of Jesus Christ of Latter Day Saints had 3,850 members in Santa Clara County. They also reported that 1,750 Jews lived in Santa Clara County, but they did not provide a similar figure for San Mateo.

26. "There's a Boom, Too, in Church Building," *San Jose News*, 2 February 1957.

27. "Survey Proves SV Is Religious," *Sunnyvale Standard*, 14 February 1957.

28. Benjamin Spock, *Common Sense Book of Baby and Child Care* (New York: Duell, Sloane, and Pearce, 1946), 308.

29. Ibid., 311.

30. Arnold Gesell and Frances Ilg, *The Child from Five to Ten* (New York: Harper & Brothers, 1946), 316.

31. Ralph Eckert, *Sex Attitudes in the Home* (New York: Association Press, 1956), 93.

32. Robert Topp, "The Parents' Job," *California Parent-Teacher*, February 1953.

33. Eckert, "Sex Education and the PTA," 59.

34. Lester Kirkendall, "Family Life Education in the High School: Looking Ahead," *Marriage and Family Living* 13, no. 3 (August 1951): 110.

35. This statement may have been a pragmatic decision by Eckert to broaden the reach of sex education without involving the controversial subject of teaching sex in public schools, but it also reflected the psychological theories of the era that stressed the importance of parents. Eckert, *Sex Attitudes in the Home*, 4.

36. Benedict Anderson, *Imagined Communities: Reflections on the Origins and Spread of Nationalism* (New York: Verso, 1991); Michael Warner, *Publics and Counterpublics* (New York: Zone Books, 2002).

37. Eckert, *Sex Attitudes in the Home*, ix–x.

38. See, for example, Mother 4, interview, 26 November 1957, Lois Meek Stolz Psychology Case Interviews.

39. Father 9, interview, 17 February 1958, Lois Meek Stolz Psychology Case Interviews.

40. Father 9, interviewer's summary, 3 September 1958.

41. Mother 9, interview, 18 February 1958, Lois Meek Stolz Psychology Case Interviews.

42. Father 9, interview, 10 February 1958; Father 24, interview, 23 April 1958, Lois Meek Stolz Psychology Case Interviews.

43. Father 12, interview, 17 March 1958, 22–23, Lois Meek Stolz Psychology Case Interviews.

44. Father 12, interview, 17 March 1958, 23–24, Lois Meek Stolz Psychology Case Interviews.

45. William Plute, "Do You Answer Their Questions?" *California Parent-Teacher*, April 1949.

46. "Sunnyvale P-TA Anniversary," *Sunnyvale Standard*, 13 February 1948.

47. Ruth Feldstein, *Motherhood in Black and White: Race and Sex in Postwar Liberalism, 1930–1965* (Ithaca, NY: Cornell University, 2000), 2.

48. Susan Ware makes a similar point about the significance of the League of Women Voters; see Ware, "American Women in the 1950s: Nonpartisan Politics and Women's Politicization," in Louise Tilly and Patricia Gurin, eds., *Women, Politics, and Change* (New York: Russell Sage Foundation, 1990).

49. Ralph Eckert, "The Role of the PTA in Sex Education," *Marriage and Family Living*, May 1951, 58–59.

50. Sixth District Historian's Notebooks, 1946–47 and 1947–48. In both school years, Eckert spoke at a countywide meeting of PTAs on "Home Responsibilities" and "Preparing for Marriage." During the 1952–53 school year, the district PTA welcomed Eckert's associate at the Department of Education for a talk on "Family Living" as well as a representative from the State Department of Mental Hygiene who spoke on "Mental Health." See ibid., 1952–53, Sixth District PTA Records.

51. Sixth District, Summary of Minutes, Sixth District History, 1950–51, Sixth District PTA Records.

52. Sixth District History, 1947–48, Sixth District Records.

53. County Board of Education Meeting Minutes, 1947–53, History San Jose. It should be noted that the archive does not have minutes after 1953, and that the Board of Education

did not indicate that teachers receiving credentials for adult education before 1951 had any specialties. This may be a shift in the way that they maintained their records or it may indicate a change in the way that teachers became certified in adult education. Records for the period after 1953 are not available.

54. Sixth District History, 1955–56, Sixth District PTA Records.

55. "Positive Relations is Parents' Topic," *Sunnyvale Standard*, 23 January 1957.

56. Helen Andres Snyder, "A Program of Parent Education and Public Relations in the Campbell Union High School District" (master's thesis, San Jose State College, 1958), 25.

57. Ibid., 28.

58. Rebecca Davis, *More Perfect Unions: The American Search for Marital Bliss* (Cambridge, MA: Harvard University, 2010), 154.

59. E. Brooks Hollifield, *A History of Pastoral Counseling in America: From Salvation to Self-Realization* (Nashville, TN: Abingdon, 1983), 271–72.

60. Davis, *More Perfect Unions*, 136–75. At the 1959 annual meeting of the American Psychological Association, the American Catholic Psychological Association held a series of panels on marital counseling from a Christian point of view. See William Bier and Alexander Schneiders, eds., *Selected Papers from the ACPA Meetings of 1957, 1958, 1959* (New York: American Catholic Psychological Association, 1960).

61. Davis, *More Perfect Unions*, 143.

62. Robert Odenwald, "Counseling the Homosexual," *Priest*, December 1953.

63. Alfred Gross, "The Homosexual in Society," *Pastoral Psychology*, April 1950, 38. See also J. F. Harvey, "Homosexuality as a Pastoral Problem," *Theological Studies*, 1 January 1955.

64. "The Consultation Clinic: On Homosexuality," *Pastoral Psychology*, September 1955, 44.

65. "The Consultation Clinic: The Church and the Homosexual," *Pastoral Psychology*, November 1951, 49.

66. John Cavanagh, "Homosexuality as an Important Impediment to Marriage," *Bulletin of the Guild of Catholic Psychiatrists* 7, no. 2 (April 1960): 97.

67. Mark Paulson, "Churches Are Taking the Lead in Sex Education," *Parents*, March 1962, 120.

68. "The Consultation Clinic," 48.

69. Odewald, "Counseling the Homosexual," 943. Similar advice appeared among Protestant writers. See Anonymous Minister, letter, "The Consultation Clinic," 51.

70. "The Consultation Clinic," 47.

71. Paulson, "Churches Are Taking the Lead in Sex Education," 120.

72. General Board of Education of the Methodist Church, Department of the Christian Family, *Home and Church Working Together: The Program of Leadership Education of the Methodist Church Courses for Church Workers* (Nashville, TN: Department of Leadership Education, 1955), Boston University School of Theology Special Collections; The Methodist Church, General Board of Education, *In Holy Matrimony: The Marriage Manual of the Methodist Church* (Nashville, TN: Methodist Publishing House, 1958).

73. United Presbyterian Church in the United States of America, Office of the General Assembly, *Responsible Marriage and Parenthood* (Philadelphia: United Presbyterian Church in the United States of America, 1962).

74. See, for example, Melvin Breckenridge, "Courtship and Marriage," *Christian Standard*, 5 September 1953; Batsell Barrett Baxter, "The Home and the Church," *Christian Standard*, 16 September 1953; "Make It Permanent," *Christian Standard*, 14 November 1953.

75. *The Pastor's Manual for Premarital Counseling* (Nashville, TN: Methodist Publishing House, 1958), 18. The Presbyterian Church cited research that sexually satisfied partners tended to be faithful to their spouses and therefore endorsed sex education as a tool for curbing adultery. See United Presbyterian Church in the United States of America, *Responsible Marriage and Parenthood*, 42.

76. Davis, *More Perfect Unions*, 165–66.

77. Sue Leong, "An Introduction to Integrating Sex Education in the Church and Home" (master's thesis, San Francisco Theological Seminary, 1958), 52.

78. Bernard Pisani, in George Kelly, *The Catholic Marriage Manual* (New York: Random House, 1958), 32.

79. "Teens Not as Smart on Sex as They Think, Pastor Says," *Chicago Tribune*, 21 June 1960; Edward Staples, "Facing the Family's Problems," *Methodist Story*, May 1958, 23–24.

80. Anna Rock, "How Not to Give Sex Instruction to Children," *Family Digest*, October 1955.

81. Bishops of the United States, issued through the National Catholic Welfare Council, "Not in the School but in the Home," *Catholic Digest*, January 1951; "Catholics Decry School Sex Classes," *Los Angeles Times*, 19 November 1950.

82. "Children Should Get Early Sex Education, Group Agrees," *San Francisco News*, 7 February 1950.

83. L. Nelson Bell, "A Layman and His Faith," *Christian Standard*, 8 June 1959.

84. William Orr, "What the Bible Says About Sex," *Moody Monthly*, February 1958.

85. American Institute of Public Opinion, 12 August 1962, *The Gallup Poll: Public Opinion, 1935–1971* (New York: Random House, 1972), 1779.

86. "Religious Instruction Approved by Parents," *San Jose Mercury*, 17 October 1962.

87. What's Wrong at Home," *Los Angeles Times*, 4 December 1955; Paulson, "Churches Are Taking the Lead in Sex Education," 63.

88. Mother 9, interview, 28 February 1958, Lois Meek Stolz Psychology Case Interviews.

89. Father 3, interview, 9 December 1957, Lois Meek Stolz Psychology Case Interviews.

90. Eckert, "The Role of the P.T.A. in Sex Education.

91. "San Mateo School Head Says Sex Course Ended," *San Francisco Examiner*, 1 March 1951.

92. "Sex in San Mateo," *San Francisco Chronicle*, 1 March 1951; "Sex Education Protests Are Answered," *San Francisco Chronicle*, 3 March 1951.

93. "School Sex Course Issue Held Settled," *San Mateo Times*, 2 March 1951; "Sex Education Protests Are Answered," *San Francisco Chronicle*, 3 March 1951.

94. "Means Sought to Bar Sex Course Recurrence," *San Mateo Times*, 1 March 1951. Parentheses are in original source.

95. "DA 'Concerned' by Pornography," *Santa Clara Journal*, 14 January 1960; "DA Urges Boycott of Stores Selling Smut Literature," *Santa Clara Journal*, 16 January 1960; "D.A. Asks Women: Help Remove Pornography," *San Jose Mercury*, 19 October 1960.

96. Eileen Davis, letter, *Santa Clara Journal*, 25 January 1960.

97. "Inherently Unsound," *Santa Clara Journal*, 20 January 1960.

98. Inquiring Reporter, "Is Sex Being Overplayed?" *Santa Clara Journal*, 6 June 1960.

99. Joan Delfattore, *The Fourth R: Conflicts over Religion in America's Public Schools* (New Haven, CT: Yale University Press, 2004), 76.

100. Ibid., 101.

101. "Religious Issue Hits Jefferson Trustees Again," *Santa Clara Journal*, 20 November 1963.

102. "Inquiring Reporter: Bible Okay in Classroom?" *Santa Clara Journal*, 28 March 1962.

103. "Basic Sex Education Is Asked Here," *Santa Clara Journal*, 14 February 1962.

104. "Sex Education—Yes," *Santa Clara Journal*, 21 February 1962.

105. Ibid.

106. "PTAs Endorse Sex Education," *Santa Clara Journal*, 28 February 1962.

107. "Inquiring Reporter: Sex Education?" *Santa Clara Journal*, 28 February 1962; Letter, *Santa Clara Journal*, 7 March 1962.

108. Letter, *Santa Clara Journal*, 21 February 1962.

109. Letter, *Santa Clara Journal*, 7 March 1962.

110. "PTAs Endorse Sex Education," *Santa Clara Journal*, 28 February 1962.

111. "Sex Education Class Proposed," *Santa Clara Journal*, 21 March 1962; "Huxtable Gives Approval to Sex Education Panel," *Santa Clara Journal*, 28 March 1962.

112. "Sex Education Experts to Speak Here," *Santa Clara Journal*, 18 April 1962; "New Date Set for Panelists," *Santa Clara Journal*, 25 April 1962.

113. "Sex Education Vote Questioned," *Santa Clara Journal*, 16 May 1962.

114. Ibid.; "Wandering Around with Linn Brown," *Santa Clara Journal*, 6 June 1962.

115. "Sex Education Ignored; PTAS Shy from Controversy," *Santa Clara Journal*, 9 January 1963.

116. "Family Life Education Meeting Set Tomorrow," *San Jose Mercury*, 9 May 1962.

Chapter 5

1. Arthur D. Little, Inc., *San Francisco Community Renewal Program: Purpose, Scope, and Methodology*, August 1963, George Christopher Papers, San Francisco History Center, San Francisco.

2. Arthur D. Little, Inc., *Community Renewal Programming: A San Francisco Case Study* (New York: Praeger, 1965), 55.

3. The percentage of "Negroes" and "other races" rose from just over 10 percent in 1950 to over 18 percent in 1960. U.S. Bureau of the Census, *Selection Population and Housing Characteristics, San Francisco, California*, vol. 3, chap. 49 (Washington, DC: U.S. Bureau of the Census, 1952); U.S. Bureau of the Census, San Francisco–Oakland, California Standard Metropolitan Statistical Area, 1962.

4. Census tracts A-10, A-12, A-15, A-16, A-17, A-18, A-19, A-20, A-21, A-22, A-23, J-1, J-9, K-1, K-2, K-3, and K-4. U.S. Bureau of the Census, San Francisco–Oakland, California Standard Metropolitan Statistical Area, 1962.

5. Census tracts A-13, A-14, A-15, J-2, J-3, J-6, J-7, J-8, and L-5A; U.S. Bureau of the Census, San Francisco–Oakland, California Standard Metropolitan Statistical Area, 1962.

6. Daniel Crow, *Prophets of Rage: The Black Freedom Struggle in San Francisco* (New York: Garland, 2000); Deirdre Sullivan, "Letting Down the Bars: Race, Space, and Democracy in San Francisco, 1936–1964" (Ph.D. diss., University of Pennsylvania, 2003); Brooks, *Alien Neighbors, Foreign Friends.*

7. See, for example, tracts K-1 and K-2, South of Market. U.S. Bureau of the Census, San Francisco–Oakland, California Standard Metropolitan Statistical Area, 1962.

8. Tom Redmon, interview with Len Evans, 17 May 1984, Oral History Collection, GLBT Historical Society of Northern California.

9. Paul Groth, *Living Downtown: The History of Residential Hotels in the United States* (Berkeley: University of California Press, 1994), 305.

10. James Sobredo, "From Manila Bay to Daly City: Filipinos in San Francisco," in James Brook, Chris Carlsson, and Nancy Peters, eds., *Reclaiming San Francisco: History, Politics, Culture* (San Francisco: City Lights Books, 1998), 278.

11. Shah, *Contagious Divides.*

12. Groth, *Living Downtown*, 140.

13. Ibid., 140.

14. Gerald Fabian, interview with Jim Breeden, n.d. 1995, Oral History Collection, GLBT Historical Society of Northern California.

15. Allan Berubé, "'Dignity for All': The Role of Homosexuality in the Marine Cooks and Stewards Union (1930s–1950s)," paper presented at Reworking American Labor History Race, Gender, and Class Conference, Madison, WI, cited in Gayle Rubin, "The Miracle Mile," in *Reclaiming San Francisco*, 251.

16. "Police Order Renews Drive on Sex Deviates," *San Francisco Examiner*, 26 May 1955.

17. Fabian, interview with Breeden, 1995.

18. Steve Tonkovish, interview with Paul Gabriel, 20 April 1994, GLBT Historical Society of Northern California, Oral History Collection.

19. Fabian, 1995; Reba Hudson, interview with Jim Breeden, 23 August 1995, GLBT Historical Society, Oral History Collection.

20. D'Emilio, "Gay Politics, Gay Community"; Boyd, *Wide Open Town*; Sides, *Erotic City*.

21. Sherri Cavan, *Liquor License: An Ethnography of Bar Behavior* (Chicago: Aldine, 1966), 23.

22. Ibid., 23.

23. Department of Alcoholic Beverage Control, *Report: Santa Clara County*, 1965–66, Department of Alcoholic Beverage Control, Subject Files, County Activity Reports, California State Archives. Cavan noted that San Francisco had 224 bars in its downtown area in 1965, with 41 percent of those in the Tenderloin District. Although she did not give the number of bars in North Beach, she singled out the area as a site with a high concentration of bars.

24. San Francisco Department of City Planning, *Modernizing Downtown San Francisco* (San Francisco: San Francisco Department of City Planning, 1955), 9.

25. Cavan, *Liquor License*, 28–30.

26. Nancy Achilles, "The Homosexual Bar" (Ph.D. diss., University of Chicago, 1964), 19.

27. Ibid., 20.

28. For more on tourism and San Francisco's queer businesses, see Boyd, *Wide Open Town.*

29. Gerald Fabian, interview with Bill Walker, 20 November 1989, Oral History Collection, GLBT Historical Society of Northern California.

30. Reba Hudson, interview with unnamed researcher, n.d. 1981, Oral History Collection, GLBT Historical Society of Northern California; Dean Tomich, a self-identified gay man who lived in San Jose in the early 1960s, similarly drew a sharp distinction between the city and suburb: "I was not completely out of the closet [in the 1960s], nobody was completely

out then. . . . But if you really wanted to have a good time and feel a little freer, you had to go to San Francisco." Tomich, interview with Ted Sahl, n.d., Ted Sahl Papers, Special Collections, San Jose State University, San Jose, CA.

31. Boyd, *Wide Open Town*, 11. See also D'Emilio, *Sexual Politics, Sexual Communities*, 32; Sides, *Erotic City*, 39.

32. Charlotte Coleman, interview with Paul Gabriel, n.d. 1997, Oral History Collection, GLBT Historical Society of Northern California.

33. Donald Webster Cory, *The Homosexual and His Society: A View from Within* (New York: Citadel, 1963), 106–7.

34. For histories of the homophiles, see D'Emilio, *Sexual Politics, Sexual Communities*; Boyd, *Wide Open Town*; Johnson, *The Lavender Scare*; Meeker, *Contacts Desired*; Sides, *Erotic City*.

35. Nan Alamilla Boyd argues that the DOB was founded by a group of working-class women, but the group attracted more middle-class members after its early years; Boyd, *Wide Open Town*, 168–69.

36. Del Martin and Phyllis Lyon, *Lesbian/Woman* (San Francisco: Glide, 1972), 28.

37. Ibid., 89. Some of the leadership of the Mattachine Society made similar decisions. Don Lucas bought a house in San Francisco in 1966. See Don Lucas, interview with Paul Gabriel, 30 December 1996 to 28 February 1998, Oral History Collections GLBT Historical Society.

38. Daughters of Bilitis, San Francisco Chapter Membership List, Lyon Martin Papers, GLBT Historical Society of Northern California. The ratio of "suburban" members grows even larger if one includes cities near the urban core in the East Bay, such as Berkeley and El Cerrito, or North Bay communities like Napa and Mill Valley.

39. Mattachine Society, Address Lists 1959–1962, Don Lucas Papers, GLBT Historical Society of Northern California. This list's purpose is not exactly clear, but it's likely that it was for correspondence of some sort.

40. Marie Monier, letter, 6 October 1962, Lyon-Martin Papers, GLBT Historical Society of Northern California.

41. "Public Discussion Meeting," *Mattachine Newsletter*, October 1956; "Calendar of Events," *Ladder*, July 1957; "February Calendar of Events," *Mattachine Newsletter*, February 1957.

42. A.S. letter, *Ladder*, November 1956. Leaders of the group hoped to accomplish this very goal: "The therapy of group discussion of mutual problems, of talking it over with others in similar circumstances, cannot be denied." Del Martin, "Why a Chapter in Your Area?" *Ladder*, February 1957.

43. Meeker, *Contacts Desired*, 84.

44. Wes Knight, "Take Me Off This Mailing List!" *Mattachine Review*, September–October 1955; D. Griffin, "President's Message," *Ladder*, November 1956.

45. "Purpose of the Daughters of Bilitis," *Ladder*, January 1957; Untitled Description of Organization, *Mattachine Newsletter*, August 1957.

46. "Purpose of the Daughters of Bilitis."

47. "In Case You Didn't Know," *Mattachine Newsletter*, June 1956.

48. "Books in the San Francisco Area Council Reference Library," *Mattachine Newsletter*, September 1956; "Growing Pains Don't Hurt," *Ladder*, October 1957; "Publications Department Plans Banquet," *Mattachine Newsletter*, November 1958.

49. "Raising Children in a Deviant Relationship," *Ladder*, January 1957; "Relationship Not So Deviant if Child Has Love and Security," *Ladder*, April 1957.

50. Martin and Lyon, *Lesbian/Woman*, 135; for gay and lesbian parents, see Rivers, *Radical Relations*.

51. "Growing Pains Don't Hurt."

52. "Mental Health Society Announces 2 Lectures at San Francisco," *Mattachine Newsletter*, 15 January 1954; "Langley-Porter Staff Member to Speak at Banquet May 15th," *Mattachine Newsletter*, 14 May 1954.

53. "An Open Letter to Mr. and Mrs. America," *Mattachine Review*, September–October 1955.

54. Boyd, *Wide Open Town*, 160.

55. Wes Knight, "A Psychiatrist Asks: Why So Much Hysteria?" *Mattachine Review*, July–August 1955, 15.

56. "Sex Charges Against 23 Men," *Mattachine Newsletter*, February 1956. For more on this raid, see Chapter 3.

57. "Delinquents in S.F. Still Increasing," *San Francisco Chronicle*, 23 May 1954.

58. "Needed: A Cleanup," *San Francisco Examiner*, 28 June 1954.

59. Carolyn Anspacher, "Tommy's Bar Called Perverts' Haven," *San Francisco Chronicle*, 21 December 1954. For more on the raids at Tommy's Place, see Boyd, *Wide Open Town*, 83–92; Christopher Agee, *The Streets of San Francisco: Policing and the Creation of a Cosmopolitan Liberal Politics, 1950–1972* (Chicago University of Chicago Press, 2014), 82–84.

60. "Schoolgirl 17, Tells of Buying Drugs, Liquor at 'Thrill Spot,'" *San Francisco Examiner*, 16 December 1954.

61. "Clish in Surprise Appearance at P-T-A District Meeting: Asks Members to Back Move to Revoke Two Liquor Licenses," *San Francisco News*, 23 September 1954.

62. "PTA Letter Demands Revocation of Licenses," *San Francisco Chronicle*, 30 September 1954.

63. "PTA Fight on Bar," *San Francisco Examiner*, 4 December 1954; "Schoolgirl 17, Tells of Buying Drugs, Liquor at 'Thrill Spot.'"

64. "PTA Fight on Bar."

65. Letter, *San Francisco Examiner*, 6 September 1955.

66. Letter, *San Francisco Examiner*, 26 December 1955.

67. "Queer Characters Peril Kids in Park," *San Francisco Chronicle*, 28 March 1958.

68. Letter, *San Francisco Examiner*, 12 December 1957.

69. "Polk Street," *League for Civil Education News*, 12 November 1962.

70. Sullivan, "Letting Down the Bars," 146–255.

71. Commission on Race and Housing, *Where Shall We Live?* (Berkeley: University of California Press, 1958), 18–19.

72. Arthur Hoppe, "Daily Violence Protests Ghetto, White Injustice," *San Francisco Chronicle*, 14 January 1959; Arthur Hoppe, "Negroes and Crime—The Police Problem in S.F.," *San Francisco Chronicle*, 15 January 1959; George Draper, "The Other City: A Reporter's Journey into the Ghettos," *San Francisco Chronicle*, 15 July 1963; D. Manning Jackson, letter, *San Francisco Chronicle*, 26 July 1963.

73. Letter, *San Francisco Examiner*, 27 June 1957.

74. Letter, *San Francisco Examiner*, 9 July 1957.

75. Letter, *San Francisco Examiner*, 1 December 1958.

76. "Judge Urges Schools, Churches to Help Fight Juvenile Crime," *San Francisco Examiner*, 1 December 1958.

77. "S.F. Marriage Figures Drop," *San Francisco Examiner*, 4 October 1955.

78. "SF Housing Problem," *San Francisco Examiner*, 24 January 1960.

79. "Report Urges Shakeup in Vice Units," *San Francisco Examiner*, 17 December 1957.

80. "Too Many Bars," *San Francisco Examiner*, 14 January 1959.

81. "S.F. Master Plan or Suburbia," *San Francisco Examiner*, 21 February 1956.

82. San Francisco Planning and Housing Association, *A Report to the Community*, no. 1 (San Francisco: San Francisco Planning and Housing Association, February 1957).

83. San Francisco Department of City Planning and the San Francisco Redevelopment Agency, *A Preliminary Plan for a Project in the South of Market Redevelopment Area "D"* (San Francisco: The City, 1957).

84. Ibid.

85. George Dorsey, *Christopher of San Francisco* (New York: Macmillan, 1962).

86. "Christopher Reveals Plan to Improve Police," *San Francisco Examiner*, 23 December 1955.

87. "Wolden in 'Smear' Campaign," *San Francisco Examiner*, 8 October 1959.

88. "Sex Deviates Make S. F. Headquarters," *San Francisco Progress*, 7–8 October 1959.

89. "Wolden in 'Smear' Campaign," *San Francisco Examiner*, 8 October 1959.

90. " 'Plant' Revealed in Wolden's Smear Drive," *San Francisco Examiner*, 9 October 1959.

91. "Wolden Launches His Campaign for Mayor," *San Francisco Examiner*, 2 September 1959.

92. American Public Health Association, *An Appraisal Method for Measuring the Quality of Housing*, 8.

93. Edmund Brown, *Report of Attorney General on Liquor Law Enforcement in California* (Sacramento: California Department of Justice, 1954), 14, California State Library, Sacramento.

94. James Reinhardt, *Sex Perversions and Sex Crimes* (Springfield, IL: Charles C Thomas, 1957), 21.

95. "S.F. Judge Voids Vagrancy Law," *San Francisco Examiner*, 23 July 1961. Legal historian Risa Goluboff describes this kind of policing as a way of ordering the city. Vagrancy laws were a way of ensuring that everyone stayed in their "proper place." Goluboff, *Vagrant Nation*, 3.

96. Charles Abrams, " 'J.D.'—Symbol of a Larger Disorder," *Community Planning Review* (December 1959): 117. See also Anthony Wallace, "Planned Privacy: What's Its Importance to the Neighborhood," *Journal of Housing* 13 (January 1956): 13.

97. Jane Jacobs, *The Death and Life of Great American Cities* (New York: Vintage, 1961), 97–98; Stein, *City of Sisterly and Brotherly Love*, 84–85.

98. Jacobs, *The Death and Life of Great American Cities*, 58–60.

99. John Calene, "Districts to Discuss Downtown Problems," *San Francisco Chronicle*, 7 May 1954.

100. "Knight Signs Bill to Fight Vice in Bars," *San Francisco Examiner*, 24 June 1955.

101. "New Drive on Vice," *San Francisco Examiner*, 11 May 1955; "Police Order Renews Drive on Sex Deviates," *San Francisco Examiner*, 26 May 1955; "State Set to Accuse Four

Deviates' Bars," *San Francisco Examiner*, 8 June 1955; "9 Men Held as Vagrants," *San Francisco Examiner*, 19 June 1955.

102. Frank Fullenwider, "Statement to the Press," 9 June 1955, Department of Alcoholic Control Records, California State Archives, Sacramento, CA.

103. "Ahern Maps New Shakeup to Fight Vice," *San Francisco Examiner*, 2 February 1956; "Vice Squad Gets Broad Powers in New Shakeup," *San Francisco Examiner*, 15 February 1956; "Ahern to Form Own Elite Vice Intelligence Unit," *San Francisco Examiner*, 21 February 1956. For more on the significance of the Christopher election, see Boyd, *Wide Open Town*, 110–11; Sides, *Erotic City*, 30; Agee, *Streets of San Francisco*, 30–31.

104. "State, S.F. Police to Join in Crackdown on Bars," *San Francisco Examiner*, 2 March 1956; "Ahern Tightens Up Liquor Enforcement," *San Francisco Examiner*, 18 March 1956.

105. "Healy Moves to Curb Bar Licenses," *San Francisco Examiner*, 17 September 1955.

106. "State Maps Drive on Three S.F. Night Life Areas," *San Francisco Examiner*, 23 February 1956.

107. Malcolm Harris, letter to William Gilliss, 5 May 1958, Governor Goodwin Knight Records, Department of Alcoholic Beverage Control, California State Archives, Sacramento.

108. Frank Fullenwider, letter to Harold Spears, 19 April 1957, Department of Alcoholic Control Records, California State Archives, Sacramento.

109. "Ahern Opens War on Armed Teen Hoodlum Gangs," *San Francisco Examiner*, 23 June 1956.

110. "10 More Arrested in City Cleanup," *San Francisco Examiner*, 3 October 1957.

111. "Schoolteacher Arrested on Morals Charge," *San Francisco Chronicle*, 30 June 1957; "Police 'Operation S': Secret Crime Patrol Expands," *San Francisco Examiner*, 14 March 1959; "ACLU Clashes with Police on Vagrancy Arrests, 'Waterholes,'" *San Francisco Examiner*, 21 May 1957. The teacher subsequently lost his state credentials and his job.

112. Dean Jennings, "A Night with the S Squad," *Saturday Evening Review*, 21 April 1962, 36.

113. Elizabth Lenhart, letter to Ernest Besig and American Civil Liberties Union, 2 June 1959, ACLU Records of Northern California, California Historical Society, San Francisco.

114. Jennings, "A Night with the S Squad." California courts later sided with the ACLU and demanded that the police revise their treatment of "vagrants." For more on Operation S, see Agee, *The Streets of San Francisco*, 36–39.

115. Housing and Home Finance Agency, *Urban Renewal Provisions of the Housing Act of 1949, as Amended Through August 1955 and Excerpts from Other Federal Laws Authorizing Federal Assistance to Slum Clearance and Urban Redevelopment and Urban Renewal* (Washington, DC: Office of the Administrator, Housing and Home Finance Agency, 1955).

116. "Skid Row Gives Renewalists Rough, Tough Relocation Problems," *Journal of Housing* 18 (August–September 1961): 327. For a definition of "family," see Housing and Home Finance Agency, Urban Renewal Administration, *Local Plans for Residential Redevelopment and Family Relocation: Continental United States Through December 1954* (Washington, DC: Housing and Home Finance Agency, 1954).

117. Ibid.

118. Privacy was one of the key justifications for tearing down parts of the Fillmore District. Planners looked at the neighborhood in 1947 and declared, "There isn't much privacy in the Geary-Fillmore District." See San Francisco Planning and Housing Association, *Blight*

and Taxes (San Francisco: San Francisco Planning and Housing Association, 1947); San Francisco Department of City Planning and San Francisco Redevelopment Agency, *Replanning the Geary Area in the Western Addition* (San Francisco: San Francisco Department of City Planning, 1952). For plans to build "suburban-style" housing in Diamond Heights, see San Francisco Department of City Planning and Redevelopment Agency, *A Report to the Board of Supervisors: Redevelopment in Diamond Heights* (San Francisco: San Francisco Department of City Planning and Redevelopment Agency, March 1950); San Francisco Department of City Planning and Redevelopment Agency, *Diamond Heights: A Report on the Tentative Redevelopment Plan* (San Francisco: San Francisco Department of City Planning and Redevelopment Agency, November 1951).

119. Chester Hartman, *City for Sale: The Transformation of San Francisco* (Berkeley: University of California Press, 2002), 19.

120. For other histories of urban renewal in the Bay Area, see John Mollenkopf, *The Contested City* (Princeton, NJ: Princeton University Press, 1983); Hartman, *City for Sale*; Self, *American Babylon.*

121. San Francisco Redevelopment Agency, *The Effect of Redevelopment on Residents and Property Owners in Western Addition Project Area Number One* (San Francisco: San Francisco Redevelopment Agency, 1952), 4.

122. Arthur D. Little, Inc., *Community Renewal Programming*, 55.

123. San Francisco Redevelopment Agency, *Progress Report to Mayor George Christopher*, 5.

124. Ibid., 6; "What Are Needs of S.F. Housing?" *San Francisco Examiner*, 14 April 1963.

125. Bay Area Real Estate Research Committee, *Bay Area Real Estate Report* (San Francisco: Bay Area Real Estate Research Committee, 1960), 84, Institute of Governmental Studies, University of California, Berkeley.

126. The Project Service Company, prepared for the San Francisco Redevelopment Agency, *The Population of Western Addition 2, San Francisco, California: A Sample Survey of the Residents and Their Relocation Needs*, (San Francisco: San Francisco Redevelopment Agency, April 1962).

127. "Fabulous Barbary Coast Gives Way to Redevelopment," *San Francisco Examiner*, 18 January 1959.

128. "Spectacular Plan for New 'City' on Waterfront," *San Francisco Examiner*, 3 February 1960.

129. San Francisco Department of City Planning, *Issues in Housing, Housing Report II*, 1969, in Hartman, *City for Sale*, 63.

130. Hartman, *City for Sale*, 66.

131. Ibid., 54.

132. Ibid., 60.

133. Groth, *Living Downtown*, 277.

134. "Pockets of Blight," *San Francisco Examiner*, 13 November 1956.

135. Coleman, interview with Gabriel, 1997.

136. "Housing Promise," *San Francisco Examiner*, 22 March 1960.

137. "Eichler Big Diamond Hts. Buyer," *San Francisco Examiner*, 25 April 1961.

138. "S.F. Crime Drops from 1958 Peak," *San Francisco Examiner*, 18 February 1959; "Half of S. F. Deviate Bars Face License Loss," *San Francisco Examiner*, 29 May 1960.

139. "Guided Tours of S.F. Gay Bars," *Mattachine Review*, February 1963.

140. For more on the "Gayola" scandal, see Boyd, *Wide Open Town*, 207–10; Agee, *The Streets of San Francisco*, 73–108.

141. U.S. Comptroller General, *Review of Slum Clearance and Urban Renewal Activities of the San Francisco Regional Office, Housing and Home Finance Agency, October 1959* (Washington, DC: Comptroller General, 1960), 37–42.

142. Bay Area Real Estate Research Committee, *Bay Area Real Estate Report*, 82. The report also noted that the sharpest increase in rents actually came for white residents displaced from the Western Addition since black residents already paid disproportionately higher rents than whites in the city.

143. Roy Wenzlick and Company, *Market Analysis and Land Utilization Study, San Francisco, California* (St. Louis, MO: Roy Wenzlick and Company, 1963), 87–88.

144. Ibid., 87–88.

145. Citizens Emergency Task Force for a Workable Housing Policy, *The Shame of San Francisco* (San Francisco: Citizens Emergency Task Force for a Workable Housing Policy, 1969), 1–2.

146. Ibid., 9.

Chapter 6

1. William Beardemphl, "Dianne: The Goddess of Politics," *Bay Area Reporter*, 15 May 1971; "Windmills of My Mind," *Bay Area Reporter*, 1 June 1971; "Dianne," *Vector*, June 1971; "Windmills of My Mind," *Bay Area Reporter*, 15 June 1971.

2. Justin David Suran, "Coming Out Against the War: Antimilitarism and the Politicization of Homosexuality in the Era of Vietnam," *American Quarterly* 53, no. 3 (September 2001).

3. Colin Williams and Martin Weinberg, *Homosexuals and the Military: A Study of Less Than Honorable Discharge* (New York: Harper & Row, 1971), 53.

4. Paul Welch, "The 'Gay World' Takes to the City Streets," *Life*, 26 June 1964.

5. "The Homosexual in America," *Time*, 21 January 1966.

6. Meeker, *Contacts Desired*, 219.

7. Percentages derived from dividing the number of "husband-wife households" (1960) and "married couple households" (1970) by "total occupied households" in 1960 and 1970 housing censuses. U.S. Bureau of the Census, "Household Structure," 1960, prepared by Social Explorer, accessed 13 June 2014; U.S. Bureau of Census, Housing, 1960, prepared by Social Explorer, accessed 13 June 2014; U.S. Bureau of the Census, "Population in Households by Household Type and Relationship," 1970, prepared by Social Explorer, accessed 13 June 2014, https://www.socialexplorer.com.

8. Bay Area Census, "San Francisco City and County," accessed 8 August 2014, http://www.bayareacensus.ca.gov.

9. According to a group of housing activists in the 1970s, "We had already heard that real estate agencies were encouraging white gays to move to the Haight-Fillmore and Hayes Valley neighborhood. What became clear was that these new tenants were desired not because they are gay, but simply because they are white." Housing Rights Study Group, "A Look at the Neighborhoods," date unknown, Ray Broshears Papers, GLBT Historical Society of Northern California.

10. Mary Ragison O'Shea, interview transcript, *The Castro*, directed by Peter Stein (San Francisco: KQED-Television, 1996), GLBT Historical Society of Northern California. See also Castells, *City and the Grassroots*, 156; Sides, *Erotic City*, 107–8. San Francisco journalist Randy Shilts reported that during the 1950s and 1960s, while "some of the older people stayed" in the neighborhood, most of the younger generations "moved to subdivisions near San Jose, buying into the ranch houses of the new American Dream." Randy Shilts, *The Mayor of Castro Street: The Life and Times of Harvey Milk* (New York: St. Martin's, 1982), 82.

11. Sharon Johnson, interview transcript, *The Castro*, GLBT Society of Northern California.

12. "The Gay Rental," *Vector*, April 1968.

13. Timothy Stewart-Winter, "The Castro: Origins to the Age of Milk," *Gay and Lesbian Review Worldwide*, January–February 2009, 13.

14. For information about bank policies, see Castells, *City and the Grassroots*, 160. Realtor ads taken from advertisement, *Vector*, February 1965; "Bulletin Board," *Vector*, August 1965.

15. Stewart-Winter, "The Castro: Origins to the Age of Milk," 13.

16. Quoted in Sides, *Erotic City*, 109.

17. Unnamed teenagers cited in Donal Godfrey, *Gays and Grays: The Story of the Gay Community at the Most Holy Redeemer Church* (Lanham, MD: Lexington Books, 2007), 9–10.

18. These statistics refer to tracts J0018000, J0019000, N0003000, N0005A00, and N0006000 in the 1960 census and tracts 169, 170, 203, 205, and 206 in the 1970 census. The tract lines remained the same in both censuses. Household statistics include the number of "married couple households" listed in the 1960 census divided by the total number of "occupied housing units" and the number of "husband-wife households" divided by the total number of occupied households in 1970. In 1960, 55 percent of occupied housing units were "married couple households." In 1970, 37 percent of occupied households were "husband-wife households." These changes happened despite population growth. U.S. Bureau of the Census, U.S. Census of Population and Housing, San Francisco–Oakland Standard Metropolitan Statistical Area (Washington DC: Government Printing Office, 1972).

19. U.S. Bureau of the Census, *1960 Census* (Washington, DC: Government Printing Office, 1961). The census listed the area's population as 97.3 percent white, including 9.8 percent with "Spanish surnames." U.S. Bureau of the Census, *1970 Census* (Washington, DC: Government Printing Office, 1971).

20. For examples, see "Bulletin Board," *Vector*, April 1965; "Bulletin Board," *Vector*, June 1965); "Bulletin Board," *Vector*, August 1965; "Classified Ads," *Vector*, July 1969; "Classified Ads," *Vector*, April 1970; Castells, *The City at the Grassroots*, 148.

21. Gale Whittington, *Beyond Normal: The Birth of Gay Pride* (Gale Whittington: 2010), 94. For more on gay life in Nob Hill, see Sides, *Erotic City*, 103; Sesto Chiarello, "North Beach Revisited," *Vector*, March 1969.

22. This survey included chapters across the country and was not confined to San Francisco. Sidney Abbott and Barbara Love, *Sappho Was a Right On Woman* (New York: Stein and Day, 1972), 55.

23. Names taken from the 1966–70 newsletters of the San Francisco chapter of the DOB. The newsletter appeared irregularly, and not all of it was captured on microfilm. The sample included the names of all of the women listed as elected officers and the addresses of the group's monthly "Gab 'n Java" coffee klatch. Not all of the women named in the newsletter

are listed in the 1966 and 1968 phone books. The list included eighteen elected officers and eight "Gab 'n Java" addresses. Only seven women were listed in the phone books, and only seven of the addresses were found on present-day maps of San Francisco. *Polk's City Directory* (Monterey Park, CA: R. L. Polk, 1966); ibid., 1968.

24. Sides, *Erotic City*, 113.

25. Sue-Ellen Case, "Making Butch: An Historical Memoir of the 1970s," in Sally Munt, ed., *Butch/Femme: Inside Lesbian Gender* (London: Cassell, 1998), 37.

26. For examples, see "Bulletin Board," *Vector*, April 1965; "Bulletin Board," *Vector*, February 1967; "Classified Ads," *Vector*, October 1969.

27. Local preservationists described Pacific Heights as a neighborhood with "ample but not showy residences, freestanding . . . in a city where most housing is crowded onto narrow lots or apartments." Anne and Arthur Bloomfield, *Gables and Fables: A Portrait of San Francisco's Pacific Heights* (Berkeley, CA: Heyday Books, 2007), xvii.

28. "FHA Joins Tenants' War Against Noise," *Architectural Forum*, March 1964, 96–97; U.S. Department of Housing and Urban Development, Federal Housing Administration, *Minimum Property Standards for Multifamily Dwellings* (Washington, DC: Government Printing Office, 1970), 86. Section on acoustics revised March 1967.

29. "FHA Joins Tenants' War Against Noise," 96–97. See also "Noise Control in Architecture: More Engineering Than Art," *Architectural Record*, October 1967, 193–203.

30. George Stephen, *Remodeling Old Homes Without Destroying Their Character* (New York: Knopf, 1972), 142, 160–62.

31. Department of Housing and Urban Development, *Manual PG-50*, quoted in Stephen, *Remodeling Old Homes Without Destroying Their Character*, 223.

32. Stryker, *Transgender History*, 69.

33. Between 1960 and 1970, the percentage of people living in the neighborhood categorized by the census as "black" or "other race" increased from 3.3 percent in 1960 to 11.5 percent in 1970. Percentages based on 1960 census tracts A0020000, A0021000, A0023000, and A0022000 and 1970 census tracts 122, 123, 124, and 125. The total population in these tracts changed very little between 1960 and 1970.

34. Tenderloin Ethnographic Research Project, *Final Report* (San Francisco: Central City Hospitality House: 1978), 43–44.

35. Galye Rubin, "The Miracle Mile: South of Market and Gay Male Leather, 1962-1997," in Brook et al., *Reclaiming San Francisco*, 253.

36. The Tenderloin Committee, *Youth in the Tenderloin*, March 1967, Don Lucas Papers.

37. "100 Girls Seized in Tenderloin Raids," *San Francisco Chronicle*, 14 October 1966.

38. Harold Nawy, "The San Francisco Erotic Marketplace," *Technical Report of the Commission on Obscenity and Pornography*, vol. 4 (Washington DC: Government Printing Office, 1971), 211.

39. "Biggest S.F. Raid on Homosexuals," *San Francisco Chronicle*, 14 February 1965.

40. "100 Girls Seized in Tenderloin Raids," *San Francisco Chronicle*, 14 October 1966.

41. Susan Stryker, director, *Screaming Queens: The Riot at Compton's Cafeteria* (San Francisco: KQED-TV, 2006).

42. Census tracts 123, 124, and 125. Tract 125 had the highest number of units with a ratio of more than 1.51 people per room living in them in the city. Tracts 123 and 124 were also among the top five tracts for numbers of units with a ratio of 1.51 people per room. Tract 122, which straddled the Tenderloin and the more affluent Nob Hill neighborhood, also

exhibited a high number of units with a ratio of 1.51 people per room. U.S. Department of the Census, *1970 Census of Population and Housing: San Francisco–Oakland, CA Standard Metropolitan Statistical Area* (Washington, DC: Government Printing Office, 1972).

43. Stryker, *Screaming Queens.*

44. Ron Silliman, "A Statistical Portrait of the Tenderloin," in Clark Taylor et al., eds., *Final Report of the Tenderloin Ethnographic Research Project* (San Francisco: Hospitality House, 1978), 57.

45. Wheeler, *How Sex Became a Civil Liberty*, 104–14.

46. D'Emilio, *Sexual Politics, Sexual Communities*, 144.

47. Wheeler, *How Sex Became a Civil Liberty*, 104.

48. Harriet Pilpel, "Sex and the Law," *Harper's*, 1 January 1965, 35.

49. "The Homosexual in America," *Time*, 21 January 1966.

50. Rowena Gurner and Zad Leavy, "Court Challenge," in *Abortion Law Reform: A Report of the California Conference on Abortion* (Santa Barbara, CA: Association for the Repeal of Abortion Laws, 1968).

51. Self, *All in the Family*, 134–60; "Law, Police, and Patricia McGinnis," *Society for Humane Abortion Newsletter* 3, no. 1 (January–February 1967).

52. *Griswold v. Connecticut*, 381 U.S. 479 85 S. Ct. (1965).

53. "Reagan Will Sign Two Antismut Bills," *New York Times*, 22 June 1969; Philip Hager, "Court Bars Lifting of Teacher's Credential for Homosexual Act," *Los Angeles Times*, 21 November 1969.

54. The San Francisco Board of Education formally reprimanded a teacher for assigning a text that called the nation's sex laws "archaic and inhumane" because they encroached on the "privacy of our bedrooms." "Sex vs. Law Angry Parents," *San Francisco Examiner*, 17 March 1965.

55. Stein, *Sexual Injustice.*

56. *Loving et Ux. v. Virginia*, 388 U.S. 1 (1967). For a similar argument about the limits of the courts' attitudes on the sexual revolution, see Stein, *Sexual Injustice.*

57. Six justices ruled that Massachusetts could not arrest a doctor for giving a contraceptive foam to a woman he met at a lecture. The judges writing the majority opinion came to their decisions through different legal logics. Justice Brennan, who wrote the decision, justified it on a broad reading of the Fourteenth Amendment's equal protection clause, but Justices White and Blackmun argued that public officials, including the Supreme Court, could not ascertain whether or not the woman in the case was married. They, therefore, concluded, "There was no reason to reach the constitutional question whether the state could restrict or forbid the distribution of contraceptives to unmarried persons." *Eisenstadt v. Baird*, 405 U.S. 438 (1972).

58. *Morrison v. State Board of Education*, 1 Cal. 3d (1969).

59. Marc Stein, *Rethinking the Gay and Lesbian Movement* (New York: Routledge, 2012), 63.

60. "The Year Ahead: A Forecast," *Mattachine Review*, January 1965. This article came out while courts were facing cases testing the legality of sex laws but before the U.S. Supreme Court issued its ruling in *Griswold.*

61. "Kansas City Conference Finds: Specific, Immediate, Realizable Goals," *Vector*, March 1966.

62. Carol Muller, "Engaging the City—With Love," *Together*, May 1965; Lewis Durham, *Glide Foundation: From 1962 Through 1967*, n.d. Glide Memorial Church Archive; Donald Stuart, *I'm Listening as Fast as I Can: The Night Ministry in San Francisco* (Claremont, CA: Regina Books, 2003).

63. Ted McIlvenna, interview with author, 20 April 2009; Del Martin, "The Church and the Homosexual: A New Rapport," *Ladder*, September 1964.

64. Kuhn, *The Church and the Homosexual*, 32.

65. McIlvenna, quoted in Division of the Local Church, *Metropolitan Young Adult Ministry: San Francisco* (Nashville, TN: General Board of Education of the Methodist Church, 1966), 5; Muller, "Engaging the City with Love."

66. Bill Beardemphl and John DeLeon, interview with Paul Gabriel, July 1997, Oral History Collection, GLBT Historical Society of Northern California; Bill Plath, interview with Paul Gabriel, April 1997, Oral History Collection, GLBT Historical Society of Northern California; Herb Donaldson, interview with Paul Gabrial, 19 April 1997, Oral History Collection, GLBT Society of Northern California; "SIR's Statement of Policy," *Vector*, December 1964; Donald Lucas, "Social Policy on Homosexuality Developing," *Vector*, August 1965. For more on SIR's early years, see Boyd, *Wide Open Town*, 225.

67. D'Emilio, "Gay Politics and Community in San Francisco Since World War II," 464.

68. Herb Donaldson, interview with Martin Meeker, 31 January 2008, Regional Oral History Office, Bancroft Library.

69. Beardemphl and DeLeon, interview with Gabriel, 1997.

70. Larry Carlson, "Dorr Jones Is Our Man on the Go," *Vector*, March 1967.

71. "Angry Ministers Rip Police," *San Francisco Chronicle*, 3 January 1965; Boyd, *Wide Open Town*, 234–35.

72. Council on Religion and the Homosexual, *A Brief of Injustices: An Indictment of Our Society in Its Treatment of the Homosexual* (San Francisco: Council on Religion and the Homosexual, 1965).

73. "Legal Panel Cites Need to Litigate Homosexual Reforms," *Vector*, September 1966.

74. "SIR's Statement of Policy," *Vector*, December 1964.

75. "So. Cal. ACLU Policy on Sex," *Vector*, February 1966; Evander Smith, "The Judicial Branch of Government: The Watchdog of Liberty," *Vector*, March 1966. Although this article specifically focused on the Southern California ACLU, the national office of the organization adopted the same policy on homosexuality at approximately the same time. See Wheeler, *How Sex Became a Civil Liberty*.

76. Council on Religion and the Homosexual, *A Brief of Injustices*, 11.

77. "Entrapment and the Vice Squad," *Vector*, August 1966.

78. Herb Donaldson, interview with Paul Gabriel, 19 April 1997, Oral History Collection, GLBT Historical Society of Northern California.

79. Meeker, "The Queerly Disadvantaged and the Making of San Francisco's War on Poverty, 1964–1967."

80. "Glide Church—A Bold Path to the Fringes of Society," *San Francisco Sunday Examiner and Chronicle*, 10 September 1967; "Nearer My Church to Me," *Los Angeles Times*, 22 October 1967; Daryl Lembke, "Glide Church—Religion with a Beat: Church Winning Spirit of Young with Soul," *Los Angeles Times*, 16 May 1971. For more on the War on Poverty in the Tenderloin, see Meeker, "The Queerly Disadvantaged."

81. Boyd, *Wide Open Town*, 229–30.

82. Wheeler, *How Sex Became a Civil Liberty*, 154–55. ACLU, *Policy Handbook* (San Francisco: ACLU of Northern California Records, California Historical Society, 1967).

83. Council on Religion and the Homosexual et al., *The Challenge and Progress of Homosexual Law Reform* (San Francisco: Council on Religion and the Homosexual, 1968), 5.

84. Lewis Maddocks, "The Homosexual and the Law," *Social Action* 34, no. 4 (December 1967): 19–20.

85. "Reagan's No Bias Hiring," *San Francisco Chronicle*, 13 November 1967.

86. "Reagan Veto of VISTA in Tenderloin," *San Francisco Chronicle*, 4 January 1968; "Reagan Vetoes Poverty Fund for Program in S.F.," *Los Angeles Times*, 4 January 1968. Reagan's antipathy to the Central City program erupted a year after he faced a sex scandal in his administration. Syndicated columnist Drew Pearson alleged that the California governor had covered up a homosexual "orgy" among his staffers. See "Reagan Denies Report by Drew Pearson of Homosexual Ring Involving Staff," *New York Times*, 1 November 1967; Rowland Evans and Robert Novak, "Reagan's Denial of Staff Problems Seen as First Serious Political Error," *Washington Post*, 5 November 1967.

87. Ruthie Stein, "A Helping Hand in the Tenderloin," *San Francisco Chronicle*, 29 May 1972; Carolyn Anspacher, "Where the Scared and Sick Youth Can Turn," *San Francisco Chronicle*, 7 September 1972.

88. Judy Stone, "25 Million Americans Need Help," *San Francisco Chronicle*, 19 April 1970.

89. Council on Religion and the Homosexual, *A Brief of Injustices*, 4.

90. Council on Religion and the Homosexual, meeting minutes, 13 July 1965, Lyon-Martin Papers, GLBT Historical Society of Northern California.

91. Del Martin, letter, *Vector*, November 1968.

92. Don Lucas, interview with Paul Gabriel, 30 December 1996 through 28 February 1998, Oral History Collection, GLBT Historical Society of Northern California.

93. Ibid.

94. Ibid. It is possible that Lucas conducted these meetings as a part of his role in the Central City Community Action Program.

95. Council on Religion and the Homosexual, meeting minutes, 3 October 1968, Lyon-Martin Papers, GLBT Historical Society of Northern California.

96. Evan Golder, "A Glimpse of the Gay Life," *San Francisco Chronicle*, 2 January 1972; "Symposium for Parents of Homosexuals," *San Francisco Chronicle*, 5 August 1974.

97. Stein, *Rethinking the Gay and Lesbian Movement*, 81–111.

98. Dorr Jones, "President's Column," *Vector*, March 1967.

99. "SIR Candidates' Night," *Vector*, October 1966.

100. Jerry Roberts, *Dianne Feinstein: Never Let Them See You Cry* (New York: HarperCollins, 1994), 99.

101. "Consensual Sex and SIR," *Vector*, June 1969.

102. Roberts, *Dianne Feinstein*, 98–99, 134.

103. "Legal Panel Cites Need to Litigate Homosexual Reforms," *Vector*, September 1966.

104. Stokes, interview with author, 30 June 2014.

105. Don Collins, "Interview with Dorr Jones," *Vector*, September 1969.

106. Irene Fiske, "On the Rejection of the Status Quo," *Ladder*, February 1967.

107. Collins, "Interview with Dorr Jones."

108. Irving Reichert, letter to John Deluca, 12 October 1970, Alioto Papers, San Francisco History Center, San Francisco.

109. For a more in-depth explanation of these divisions, see Luther-Hillman, " 'The Most Profoundly Revolutionary Act a Homosexual Can Engage In.' "

110. "Open Forum: The Wearing of Drag," *Vector*, April 1967.

111. Abbott and Love, *Sappho Was a Right On Woman*, 64.

112. "In the Streets for the Revolution," *San Francisco Sentinel*, 1–15 November 1969.

113. "British Deviant Law Has Little Effect," *San Francisco Sentinel*, 7–21 December 1969.

114. Jerry Weiss, "Why Are We Rocking the Boat?" *Committee for Homosexual Freedom Newsletter*, 22 April 1969.

115. Gary Alinder, "My Gay Soul," *Gay Sunshine* 1, no. 1 (August–September 1970). See also Morgan Pinney, "Out of Your Closets," *Gay Sunshine* 1, no. 2 (October 1970).

116. "In the Streets for the Revolution," *San Francisco Sentinel*, 1–15 November 1969.

117. Hillman, "Most Profoundly Revolutionary Act a Homosexual Can Engage In."

118. Christopher Plummer, "Letter from the Sugar Plum Fairy," *Gay San Francisco Free Press* 1, no. 2 (December 1970).

119. "Report on the July Business Meeting of the DOB," *Daughters of Bilitis of San Francisco Newsletter*, 19 July 1970.

120. S. Willer, "The Lesbian, the Homosexual, and the Homophile Movement," *Vector*, October 1966.

121. Sally Gearhart, "Lesbianism Is a Political Statement," *Sisters*, December 1970.

122. Del Martin, *Battered Wives* (San Francisco: Glide Publications, 1972), 10, 17.

123. "Drag Queens Protest Tenderloin Housing Pinch," *San Francisco Chronicle*, 7 September 1973.

124. Plummer, "Letter from the Sugar Plum Fairy," December 1970.

125. Perry George, "The Gay Revolution (?) and SIR?" *Vector*, January 1970.

126. "S.F. Homosexuals' Political Machine," *San Francisco Chronicle*, 18 October 1971; "S.F.'s Gays—A New Political Force," *Berkeley Barb*, 1–7 October 1971.

127. "Gay Picket Set," *Berkeley Barb*, 14–20 January 1972.

128. "Gay Militants Zap S.I.R. Dinner," *Bay Area Reporter* 2, no. 3 (February 1972).

129. "Plea to Stop City Hiring on Sex Basis," *San Francisco Progress*, 2 May 1971; Northern California Council of Churches, press release, 15 November 1971; Archdiocese of San Francisco, Chancery Office, press release, 3 May 1971, SIR papers, GLBT Historical Society of Northern California.

130. Don Jackson, "Employment Rights Law," *Bay Area Reporter*, 17 May 1972.

131. "Boondocks Go After a Good Law," *San Francisco Chronicle*, 25 June 1975.

Chapter 7

1. Guy Wright, "The Sex Teachers," *San Francisco Examiner*, 28 May 1972; Guy Wright, "Homosexual Lessons," *San Francisco Examiner*, 5 June 1972; "Furor on Sex and Schooling," *San Francisco Chronicle*, 9 June 1972; "A Probe of Sex Education Classes," *San Francisco Chronicle*, 10 June 1972; Sasha Gregory, " 'Teaching Perversion,' " *Advocate*, 5 July 1972.

2. Tracts 166, 167, 171, and 301 border the south side of the Golden Gate Park panhandle, including the Haight-Ashbury intersection. Both percentages exceeded the average for San Francisco as a whole by 5 to 10 percentage points.

3. David Farber, "The Intoxicated State/Illegal Nation: Drugs in the Sixties Counterculture," in Peter Braunstein and Michael William Doyle, eds., *Imagine Nation: The American Counterculture of the 1960s and 1970s* (New York: Routledge, 2002).

4. "Inside Look at the Hippies," *San Jose Mercury*, 11 April 1967.

5. David Smith and John Luce, *Love Needs Care: A History of San Francisco's Haight-Ashbury Free Medical Clinic and Its Pioneer Role in Treating Drug Abuse Problems* (Boston: Little, Brown, 1971), 218–19.

6. Dave Felton, "Hippies Merely a Nuisance, SF Police Officer Insists," *Los Angeles Times*, 10 April 1967.

7. Eric Schneider, *Smack: Heroin and the American City* (Philadelphia: University of Pennsylvania, 2009), 155.

8. "A Letter from David the Hustler," *Vanguard* 1, no. 2 (n.d.).

9. G. Thomas Gitchoff, *Kids, Cops, and Kilos: A Study of Contemporary Suburban Youth* (San Diego: Malter-Westerfield, 1969), 95.

10. James Donait, "Normalcy and the Peeping Toms," *Santa Clara Journal*, 30 April 1969.

11. "Students, Parents Advocate 'Hip' Dress at High Schools," *San Jose Mercury*, 2 February 1968; "New Dress Code Battle Looms," *San Jose Mercury*, 10 February 1968; "Drop Dress Code, Students Argue," *San Jose Mercury*, 2 April 1969; "Suspended Buchser Coeds Threaten to Wear Slacks Again," *Santa Clara Journal*, 16 April 1969; "Girls Can Wear Slacks, Boys Allowed Mustaches," *Santa Clara Journal*, 11 June 1969.

12. "'Some School Segregation Here,'" *San Jose Mercury*, 11 January 1963; "Sequoia High Picketed by Civil Rights Group," *San Francisco Examiner*, 30 July 1963.

13. "School Integration, Busing Sought," *Santa Clara Journal*, 26 February 1969; "All Sides Agree, Busing's Not Answer to Racial Imbalance," *San Jose Mercury*, 27 March 1969; Eleanor Curry, "The Human Touch," *Peninsula Bulletin*, 23 January 1971.

14. "Wilcox Protesters Stage Walkout," *Santa Clara Journal*, 2 October 1968; "Protesters Picket at Wilcox," *Santa Clara Journal*, 25 December 1968; "Dress Code No Longer 'Law,'" *Santa Clara Journal*, 19 March 1969. Student protesters at the predominantly black Ravenswood High School in East Palo Alto pushed the district trustees to hire African American administrators. "A Negro Principal for Ravenswood," *San Francisco Chronicle*, 19 September 1968.

15. "Well-Read Jury Gets S.J. Obscenity Case," *San Jose Mercury*, 27 April 1967.

16. "S.C. Closes Curtain on 'Hard Core' Films," *San Jose Mercury*, 29 December 1971; "X-Rated Sunnyvale," *San Jose Mercury*, 9 December 1972.

17. Theodore Scott, letter, *Santa Clara Journal*, 29 March 1967.

18. "The Flower Children—Fad or Fantasy?" *Santa Clara Journal*, 6 September 1967.

19. "The Family: Pot and Parents," *Time*, 30 August 1968.

20. Millard Bienvenu Sr., "Why They Can't Talk to Us," *New York Times*, 14 November 1969.

21. "Teen 'Love-Ins' Spark Closure of Ballroom," *Santa Clara Journal*, 15 November 1967.

22. "Critics Attack Youth Library," *Santa Clara Journal*, 5 February 1969.

23. "'Tired Blood' the Winner in Banana Ranch Denial," *Santa Clara Journal*, 21 January 1968.

24. "Plan to Open M.V. Bar Protested by Residents," *San Jose Mercury*, 12 April 1969.

25. Ibid.

26. James Lincoln Collier and Sex Information and Education Council of the United States, *Sex Education U.S.A.: A Community Approach* (Pleasantville, NY: Guidance Associates/ Harcourt, Brace and World, 1968), title page.

27. Irvine, *Talk About Sex*, 29.

28. Moran, *Teaching Sex*, 160–63; "U.S. Policy on Sex Education," *San Francisco Chronicle*, 20 September 1966.

29. Lester Kirkendall, *Sex Education: Study Guide No. 1* (New York: SIECUS, 1965), 11. Emphasis added.

30. Collier et al., *Sex Education U.S.A.*, 3–5.

31. Calderone implicitly acknowledged this shift in a 1970 article: "The Christian churches today find themselves today in a dilemma about sex education. . . . Roman Catholics, in their schools, are free to teach sex within the context of their own religious dogma, but in the public schools this cannot be. For most Protestant denominations, this poses little or no difficulty. They recognize that education for sexuality in a sound public school curriculum must inevitably include . . . discussion of the basic moral values that underlie all human relationships. Beyond that, the moral values specific to each denomination have been found to be easily taught within the church itself." Mary Calderone, "Sex Education for the Society: The Real Stumbling Block," *Pastoral Psychology*, 22 November 1970, 50.

32. James McCary, *Human Sexuality: Physiological and Psychological Factors of Sexual Behavior* (New York: Van Nostrand Reinhold, 1967), 15.

33. Lester Kirkendall and Roger Libby, "Trends in Sex Education," in Carlfred Broderick and Jessie Bernard, eds., *The Individual, Sex, and Society* (Baltimore: Johns Hopkins University Press, 1969), 14. See also Lester Kirkendall and Elizabeth Ogg, *Sex and Our Society* (New York: Public Affairs Committee, 1964).

34. Steve Scarvele, "Before Sex Education—A Groundwork of Values," *Family Coordinator*, July 1968, 189.

35. McCary, *Human Sexuality*, 330.

36. "New Group Spurs Education in Sex," *New York Times*, 9 January 1965.

37. He also critiqued the "ostrich-like position that there should not be any sex education." McCary, *Human* Sexuality, 2–3.

38. Moran, *Teaching Sex*, 165.

39. H. S. Hoyman, "Should We Teach About Birth Control in High School Sex Education?" *Education Digest* 34 (February 1969): 20. Kirkendall and Libby frequently spoke about "responsible decision making." Kirkendall and Libby, "Trends in Sex Education," 16.

40. James Moore, "Problematic Sexual Behavior," in Carlfred Bartholomew and Jessie Bernard, eds., *The Individual Sex and Society* (Baltimore: Johns Hopkins University Press, 1969), 354.

41. Ibid., 354.

42. "New Group Spurs Education in Sex," *New York Times*, 9 January 1965.

43. Mary Calderone, "Sex Education and the Very Young Child," *PTA Magazine*, October 1966, 18.

44. John Kolber, "Sex Invades the Schoolhouse," *Saturday Evening Post*, 29 June 1968, 64.

45. For more on the Moynihan report, see Thomas Sugrue, *Sweet Land of Liberty: The Forgotten Struggle for Civil Rights in the North* (New York: Random House, 2008); Marisa

Chappell, *The War on Welfare: Family, Poverty, and Politics in Modern America* (Philadelphia: University of Pennsylvania Press, 2010); Self, *All in the Family.*

46. Boone Hammond and Joyce Ladner, "Sexual Behavior in a Negro Slum Ghetto," in *The Individual Sex and Society*, 51.

47. The authors refrained from making their suggestions explicit, but they attributed higher rates of teen pregnancy and sexually transmitted diseases to the allegedly promiscuous attitudes of their subjects. Their call for reforms only made general statements about the need for better housing, but given their diagnosis of the problem, it is likely that they understood improved housing to include private bedrooms.

48. Lester Kirkendall and Peter Anderson, "Authentic Selfhood: Basis for Tomorrow's Morality," *Pastoral Psychology* 21, no. 9 (October 1970).

49. John Phillips, *Sex Education in Major Protestant Denominations* (New York: National Council of Churches in the U.S.A., 1968).

50. Church leaders endorsed school-based sex education in the early 1960s in a larger discussion about sex and Christianity in Green Lake, Wisconsin. See Elizabeth Steel Genné and William Henry Genné, eds., *Foundations for Christian Family Policy* (New York: National Council of Churches of Christ in the U.S.A., 1961). By the late 1960s, newspapers merely mentioned the National Council's support for sex education in schools. See, for example, Howard Rusk, "Sex Education in U.S." *New York Times*, 5 October 1969.

51. Leslie Woodcock Tentler, *Catholics and Contraception: An American History* (Ithaca, NY: Cornell University Press, 2004), 204–63.

52. Ibid., 229–30.

53. Ibid., 223.

54. Ibid., 247.

55. Ann Lucas, "Why Teach Sex Education in the Schools?" *Catholic Educator*, April 1969, 32.

56. "Sex Education in Schools," *America*, 3 February 1968, 140–41; National Council of Churches et al., *Interfaith Statement on Sex Education* (n.p., 8 April 1968).

57. "Sex Education in Public Schools," *Catholic Mind*, December 1969, 3.

58. National Council of Churches, Commission on Marriage and Family, *Interfaith Statement on Sex Education.*

59. John Phillips, *Sex Education in Major Protestant Denominations* (New York: National Council of Churches of Christ in the U.S.A., 1968).

60. Richard Hettlinger, *Living with Sex: The Student's Dilemma* (New York: Seabury, 1966), 158–59.

61. Joseph Breig, "A Plea for Christianizing Sex," *Family Digest*, January 1966.

62. Conrad Baars, "Rhythm—An Expression of Marital Love," *Proceedings of the Second International Symposium on Rhythm* (Washington DC: National Catholic Welfare Conference, 1968), 25–26.

63. James Huffman, "Sex Education in Public Schools," *Christianity Today*, 26 September 1969.

64. "NAE Hits Hard at Pornography," *Christianity Today*, 9 May 1969.

65. "Foes Fail to End Sex Education Spread," *Washington Post*, 3 June 1969.

66. Jack Langguth, "Campaign Starts on School Prayer," *New York Times*, 13 April 1967.

67. "Dirksen Loses Fight for School Prayer," *New York Times*, 22 September 1966.

68. Walfred Peterson, "Can Anyone Be Against Dirksen's Amendment?" *Eternity*, April 1967.

69. John Baird, "Theology and Violence," *Christian Standard*, 8 October 1968.

70. "NAE Hits Hard at Pornography," *Christianity Today*, 9 May 1969.

71. B. L. Smith, "Homosexuality in the Bible and the Law," *Christianity Today*, 18 July 1969.

72. Huffman, "Sex Education in Public Schools."

73. George Steiner, "Pornography and Privacy," *U.S. Catholic*, February 1966, 59.

74. Glenn Cunningham, "A New Way to Discourage Pornographers," *Catholic Digest*, June 1968.

75. "PTA Groups Face Topical Issues," *Santa Clara Journal*, 23 December 1964.

76. "Family Life Title Preferred," *Sunnyvale Register Leader*, 23 September 1966. This article does not mention Dyer and Hansen by name, but it claims that FLEA grew out of conversations by volunteers working in Dyer's family life education program in Palo Alto in 1963.

77. "Family Life Education Not About Sex Alone," *San Jose News*, 29 May 1969.

78. " 'Family Life' Session Is Due," *Santa Clara Journal*, 19 May 1965.

79. "Family Life Education Not About Sex Alone," *San Jose News*, 29 May 1969.

80. Dorothy Dyer, Workshop on Family Life Education, Proceedings of the First County-wide Conference on Delinquency Prevention and Youth Welfare, Sunnyvale, CA, 31 May 1964.

81. California State PTA, "Family Life Education in Public Schools," formal resolution, 11 May 1967, California PTA Records, Sacramento, CA.

82. "Two Showings for School Sex Films," *Sunnyvale Daily Standard*, 12 February 1964.

83. "Sex Education Varies," *San Jose News*, 3 June 1969.

84. "School Sex Project OKd in San Jose," *San Francisco Examiner*, 22 September 1966; "Sex Teaching Approved for 4th Grade," *San Francisco Chronicle*, 27 September 1966.

85. " 'Family Life' Institute Slated Next Thursday," *San Jose Mercury*, 28 October 1966. Sister Alfread Marie presented a panel called "Action in Private Schools" and Reverend Herbert Summers presented "Action in Church."

86. Bonnie Fitzgerald, letter to Archbishop McGucken, 19 April 1968; Mrs. Robert Purcell, letter to Archbishop McGucken, 21 April 1968; Mr. and Mrs. Richard Bauer, letter to Archbishop McGucken, 29 April 1968, Archdiocese of San Francisco Records, St. Patrick's Seminary, Menlo Park, CA.

87. Advisory Committee on Family Life Education, "Recommendations on Family Life Education," 9 November 1967, Archdiocese of San Francisco Records. The recommendations named the members of the advisory committee, and it included FLEA leaders Helen Hanson and Bernadette Barton.

88. "Sex in School: Parents Urge Start from Kindergarten to Senior," *San Francisco Examiner*, 15 December 1967.

89. "Sex Education in Schools," *San Francisco Progress*, 9 November 1967; "S.F. Schools Ready Pilot Program on Sex Education," *San Francisco Sunday Examiner and Chronicle*, 12 November 1967; "Family Life Classes Considered for District School Curriculum," *Santa Clara Journal*, 31 January 1968; "Family Life Course Set," *San Jose Mercury*, 9 February 1968; Senate Bill One Committee, Dean Inglis, chair, *Final Report* (Sacramento: Santa Clara Unified

School District Records, California State Archive, 1970). Officials in later years insisted that "sex education" was not being offered in Santa Clara schools because they worried about controversy, but significant evidence suggests that they introduced classes on the subject in 1968 or, at latest, 1969.

90. FLEA, for example, held events in the First Methodist Church of Los Gatos and the Church of the Valley in Santa Clara. PTAs in Santa Clara made regular announcements about FLEA's work and asked its members to attend meetings organized by the group. Jefferson Union Council PTA, meeting minutes, 23 September 1965, Santa Clara Council PTA records, Santa Clara, CA. David Treat and his wife led a series called "Home and Church Responsibilities for Sex Education" at the Santa Clara Methodist Church in 1968. "Couple Plan Class in Sex Education," *Santa Clara Journal*, 28 February 1968.

91. Lester Kirkendall and Elizabeth Ogg, *Sex and Our Society* (New York: Public Affairs Committee, 1964), 25. Recommended in "Parents Keep Pace with Change," *PTA Magazine*, April 1968, 37.

92. "Illegitimate Births Soar in County," *San Jose News*, 30 May 1969.

93. Barbara Hawkins, "How One City Teaches Sex Education and Family Life," *PTA Magazine*, June 1969, 25.

94. "Sex Study Program Gets Tentative OK," *San Jose Mercury*, 22 September 1966; "School Sex Project OKd in San Jose," *San Francisco Examiner*, 22 September 1966. See also "Sex Teaching Approved for 4th Grade," *San Francisco Chronicle*, 27 September 1966.

95. Marjorie Holmes, "A Plea for Privacy," *PTA Magazine*, March 1971, 10–11.

96. "Obscenity Proposition Raises Stormy Dispute," *Los Angeles Times*, 6 October 1966.

97. "Reagan Backs Prop. 16, 'Anti-Obscenity' Measure," *San Francisco Chronicle*, 16 October 1966; "Evangelical Unit Backs Obscenity Amendment," *Los Angeles Times*, 5 November 1966.

98. U.S. Commission on Obscenity and Pornography, *Technical Report of the Commission on Obscenity and Pornography*, vol. 4 (Washington, DC: Government Printing Office, 1970), 186.

99. "Obscenity Proposition Raises Stormy Dispute," *Los Angeles Times*, 6 October 1966.

100. "Faults in Clean Initiative," *Los Angeles Times*, 22 June 1966. In a sign that moderates could oppose both Proposition 16 and sexually explicit material, the church leaders opposed the measure on pragmatic ground, noting that "sweeping censorship has been known to enhance rather than limit the appeal of pornography."

101. "We Urge 'No' Vote on CLEAN Amendment," *Sunnyvale Register Leader*, 29 September 1966.

102. "Pornography OK in the Home?" *San Jose Mercury*, 14 April 1969.

103. Ibid.

104. "S.C. Acts to Curb Topless Shows," *San Jose Mercury*, 1 February 1968.

105. "Topless Shimmy 'Busted,'" *San Jose Mercury*, 3 May 1969; "Council Approves Protest Against Topless Nightclub," *San Jose Mercury*, 26 March 1969. See also "Board Broadens Ban on Nudity," *San Jose Mercury*, 20 June 1973.

106. Eric Damian Kelly and Connie Cooper, *Everything You Always Wanted to Know About Regulating Sex Businesses* (Chicago: American Planning Association, 2000).

107. "SC Adopts Skid-Row Ordinance," *Santa Clara Sun*, 1 March 1977.

108. "Sex Education Plan Kept Alive; 4–3 Vote," *San Jose Mercury*, 4 October 1966.

109. "School Board Against Busing Amendment," *San Francisco Examiner*, 19 March 1968; "A Quarrel Over Sex Ed Films," *San Francisco Chronicle*, 7 August 1968.

110. Constance De Grey, letter, *Santa Clara Journal*, 26 March 1969.

111. Marilynn Hillyer, letter, *West Valley Times*, 30 April 1969.

112. "Family Life Group Outlines Position," *West Valley Times*, 1 September 1969.

113. "Anti-Family Life Education Group Tells Aims," *Santa Clara Journal*, 16 April 1969.

114. "A Bill on Sex Life and Schools," *San Francisco Chronicle*, 21 May 1970.

115. Santa Clara County Grand Jury, *Final Report 1969* (San Jose, CA: Santa Clara County, 1969), 28–29.

116. Stanley Elam, ed., *The Gallup Polls of Attitudes Towards Education, 1969–1972* (Bloomington, IN: Phi Delta Kappa, 1973), 76.

117. "Sex Education Gains Across Nation Cited," *Los Angeles Times*, 19 March 1970.

118. "More Family Planning, Sex Education Urged," *Los Angeles Times*, 20 September 1972.

119. Elizabeth Hendryson, "The President's Message: The Case for Sex Education," *PTA Magazine*, May 1969, 21.

120. *Citizens for Parental Rights v. San Mateo County Board of Education*, 51 Cal. App. 3d (1975).

121. "Sex Text Stirs State Board Rift," *San Francisco Examiner*, 11 January 1973; "Sex Text Will Be Kept but Revised," *San Francisco Chronicle*, 12 January 1973.

122. "Sex Text Will Be Kept but Revised," *San Francisco Chronicle*, 12 January 1973; "State Wants 'Spiritual' Put in Sex Handbook," *San Francisco Examiner*, 12 May 1973; "Sex Education Book Approved," *San Francisco Chronicle*, 15 June 1973.

Chapter 8

1. "Gays on the March," *Time*, 8 September 1975; "Battle over Gay Rights," *Newsweek*, 6 June 1977.

2. Victor Zonana, "Drive to Limit Office Construction Stirs Ballot Controversy in San Francisco," *Wall Street Journal*, 9 October 1979; Hartman, *City for Sale*, 3.

3. Herbert Gold, "Homosexuals Step Out of Closets, Into Politics," *Los Angeles Times*, 6 November 1977.

4. "San Francisco Home Prices Cited as Highest in Nation," *Orange County Register*, 21 October 1978. For more on the housing crisis brought on by San Francisco's downtown revival, see Hartman, *City for Sale*.

5. Katy Butler and Gwendolyn Edwards, "Gay Migration into Black Neighborhoods," *San Francisco Chronicle*, 1 September 1979. See also "Gay Restaurant Not Wanted in the Mission," *Bay Area Reporter*, 30 September 1976.

6. Noel Hernandez and Ferris Fisher, "The Haight: The New Castro?" *Bay Area Reporter*, 27 April 1978; Butler and Edwards, "Gay Migration into Black Neighborhoods."

7. "Roommates Wanted," *Bay Area Reporter*, 8 August 1974; "Roommates Wanted," *Bay Area Reporter*, 15 August 1974. For a longer history of gentrification, see Osman, *The Invention of Brownstone Brooklyn*.

8. Philip Hager, "S.F.'s Tenderloin District Fighting Redevelopment Plans," *Los Angeles Times*, 1 December 1980.

9. Bruce Pettit, "1/2 Million for City's Gay Mental Health," *Bay Area Reporter*, 13 April 1978.

10. Federal Housing Administration, Department of Housing and Urban Development, *An Analysis of the San Jose, California Housing Market* (Washington, DC: Federal Housing Administration, 1972), 8.

11. O'Mara, *Cities of Knowledge*, 97–141; M. Gottdiener and George Kephart, "The Multinucleated Region: A Comparative Analysis," in *Postsuburban California*, 40–42.

12. Department of Housing and Urban Development, Federal Housing Administration, *An Analysis of the San Jose, California Housing Market* (Washington, DC: Federal Housing Administration, 1972), 7; "Recruiting in Silicon Valley, *Time*, 7 August 1978.

13. Mountain View Planning Department, *General Plan Data Book* (Mountain View, CA: Mountain View Planning Department, 1974); Deborah Daro, "Where Will Dick and Jane Live? The Impact of Local Government Policy Making on Young Families with Children," Childhood and Government Project Working Paper, Earl Warren Legal Institute, University of California, Berkeley, 1976, 56–57.

14. Department of Housing and Urban Development, *An Analysis of the San Jose California Housing Market*, 7.

15. "Where Do You Live If You're Divorced," advertisement, *San Mateo Times*, 6 January 1973.

16. U.S. Bureau of the Census, *Age: Less Than 18* Years, 1970; U.S. Bureau of the Census, *Total Population: Less Than 18* Years, 1980. Prepared by Social Explorer, accessed 13 April 2018, https://www.socialexplorer.com.

17. Daro, "Where Will Dick and Jane Live?" 23.

18. Joint Cities-County Housing Element Program, *The Cost to Occupy Housing: Santa Clara County* (San Jose, CA: County of Santa Clara Planning Department, 1970).

19. For examples of tracts that fell from over 50 percent "husband-wife households" to approximately a third "married couple households," see tracts 5091.3, 5093.1, 5115, 5091.1 (split into 5091.5 and 5091.4 in 1980), and 5085.1 (split into 5085.3 and 5085.4 in 1980). Other tracts with significant drops below 50 percent include 5076, 5110, 5093.2, 5098.1, and 5078.3. U.S. Bureau of the Census, *Total Occupied Households: Husband-Wife Family*, 1970; U.S. Bureau of the Census, *Households: Married Couples Family*, 1980, prepared by Social Explorer, accessed 13 April 2018, https://www.socialexplorer.com.

20. Census tracts that retained over 80 percent of their husband-wife households in 1980 include 5072.02, 5074.1, 5075, 5076, 5119.06, and 5123.02. Although it was a new tract in 1980, 5119.8 also had over 80 percent married couple households. U.S. Bureau of the Census, *Total Occupied Households: Husband-Wife Family*, 1970; U.S. Bureau of the Census, *Households: Married-Couple Family*, 1980, prepared by Social Explorer, accessed 13 April 2018, https://www.socialexplorer.com.

21. "We Shall Not Be Housed in Pumpkin Shells," *San Jose NOW News*, January 1974. The landlord's comment came from a statewide taskforce on sex discrimination in housing, but the NOW chapter claimed that women in Santa Clara County heard similar comments on a regular basis.

22. "San Jose Pastor Understands Pressure on Gays," *San Jose Mercury*, 12 September 1977.

23. Ted Sahl, *From Closet to Community: The Story of Santa Clara County's Gay and Lesbian Communities* (Campbell, CA: Ted Sahl Gallery, 2002).

24. Barbara Walters, "Awakening to Our Day Dream," *Lesbian Voices* 1, no. 4 (September 1975).

25. Jon Snell, interview with Ted Sahl, 2 November 1994, Ted Sahl Collection, Martin Luther King Jr. Library Special Collections, San Jose, CA.

26. Wiggsy Sivertsen, in Sahl, *From Closet to Community*.

27. Lyon and Martin, *Lesbian/Woman*, 277.

28. Don Jackson, "Gay Parade Coming to San Francisco," *Bay Area Reporter*, 1 March 1972.

29. Self, *All in the Family*, 225.

30. Gary Alinder, "Gay Liberation Meets the Shrinks," in Karla Jay and Allen Young, eds., *Out of the Closets: Voices of Gay Liberation* (New York: Jove, 1977), 141–45.

31. Ronald Bayer, *Homosexuality and American Psychiatry: The Politics of Diagnosis* (New York: Basic Books, 1981), 91–115.

32. "Doctors Rule Homosexuals Not Abnormal," *Washington Post*, 16 December 1973.

33. "Gay, Gifted Yet Closeted in City's Classrooms," *San Francisco Examiner*, 12 June 1975.

34. "Board Accepts Gay Teachers," *San Francisco Examiner*, 18 June 1975.

35. Ibid.; Ken Bowers, "Milestone: Teachers Can Now Teach!" *Alice Report*, July 1975, Alice B. Toklas Democratic Club Papers, Charles Deering McCormick Library, Northwestern University, Evanston, IL.

36. Boyce Hinman, letter, *Sentinel*, 3 July 1974.

37. "Catholic 'Dignity' for Gays," *San Francisco Chronicle*, 21 January 1973; John Joseph, "Archbishop Acknowledges 'Dignity,'" *Bay Area Reporter*, 21 July 1977.

38. Jean Caffey Lyles, "What's Good for the NCC," *Christian Century*, 1 December 1982.

39. Gary Miller, "President's Report," *Alice Reports*, July 1975, Alice B. Toklas Democratic Club Collection.

40. "Gays Get Demo Backing," *Alice Reports*, April 1976, Alice B. Toklas Democratic Club Papers; George Mendenhall, "Gay Politics Within CDC," *Bay Area Reporter*, 14 April 1977.

41. Harvey Milk, "Waves from the Left," *San Francisco Sentinel*, 28 March 1974.

42. Harvey Milk, "A City of Neighborhoods," speech, in *The Mayor of Castro Street*, 357–58.

43. Harvey Milk, "Milk Forum: The Elections Are Over: Now What?" *Bay Area Reporter*, 13 November 1974.

44. Castells, *City and the Grassroots*, 145–53.

45. O'Mara, *Cities of Knowledge*, 8.

46. Donna Hughes-Oldenberg, interview with author, 26 May 2015.

47. "Stanford GPU Gets $90,000 Grant," *San Francisco Sentinel*, 23 May 1974; Gay Community of Concern, "End of the Year Report: 74/75," Gay People's Union and Gay and Lesbian Student Alliance Collection, Stanford University, Palo Alto, CA.

48. Gay Community of Concern, "Contact Sheet: San Mateo Family Services," 9 October 1975, Gay People's Union and Gay and Lesbian Student Alliance Collection.

49. Boyce Hinman, letter, *San Francisco Sentinel*, 3 July 1974.

50. "Victory! At Bd. of Ed.," *GPU News*, December 1975, Gay People's Union and Gay and Lesbian Student Alliance Collection; James McLeod, letter to Rebecca Morgan, 11 November 1975, Gay People's Union and Gay and Lesbian Student Alliance Collection; George Wilson, letter to Palo Alto School Board, 18 November 1975, Gay People's Union and Gay and Lesbian Student Alliance Collection.

51. "Sexual Preference in Hiring Outlawed in School Policy," *Palo Alto Times*, 19 November 1975.

52. L. Peter Deutsch et al., letter, *Palo Alto Times*, 26 November 1975.

53. The *Bay Area Reporter* estimated that only thirty-nine American cities or counties had rules protecting gay workers in 1977. "Cities, States Advance Gay Rights," *Bay Area Reporter*, 14 April 177. See also "S.J. Gays and the 'Sexual Preference' Ordinance," *Bay Area Reporter*, 4 August 1977. Details about the Mountain View and Cupertino ordinances are rare, but they are regularly included in lists of cities with nondiscrimination laws protecting gay men and lesbians. See Kenneth Wald et al., "The Politics of Gay Rights in American Communities: Explaining Antidiscrimination Ordinances and Policies," *American Journal of Political Science* 40, no. 4 (November 1996).

54. "Homosexuals, Many Types, Many Causes," *Los Angeles Times*, 1 November 1978.

55. Rosen, *The World Split Open*, 43–157.

56. Pauline Bart, "The New Sex Education and the Women's Movement," in *The New Sex Education*, 34.

57. Mary Calderone, "Eroticism as Norm," *Family Coordinator* 23, no. 4 (October 1974): 339.

58. "SIECUS Position Statements," *SIECUS Report*, May 1974.

59. Mollie Stevens Smart and Laura Smart, *Families: Developing Relationships* (New York: Macmillan, 1976), vii.

60. David Newton, "Representations of Homosexuality in Health Science Text Books," *Journal of Homosexuality* 4, no. 3 (1979): 249.

61. Alan Ball, "The New Sex Education and Homosexuality," in *The New Sex Education*, 328.

62. "School Board Votes Gay Lifestyle Studies," *SF Examiner*, 25 May 1977.

63. "School Board Walks Curriculum Tightrope," *SF Examiner*, 8 June 1977.

64. The organization's leadership tried to attract new volunteers inspired by the antiwar movement, feminism, and civil rights. When the association changed its constitution to allow for greater involvement in school-related politics, PTA President Grace Baisinger told the *Washington Post*, "We couldn't keep the old by-laws. The schools today have a generation of parents who were the children of the 1960s who questioned all authority." Lawrence Feinberg, "PTA Seeks to Reverse Decline with Activism," *Washington Post*, 5 December 1977.

65. "State PTA Votes for Anti-Busing Proposal," *San Francisco Chronicle*, 10 May 1974; "PTA Leader Raps Anti-Busing Stand," *San Francisco Progress*, 15 May 1974.

66. Garden Grove Council PTA, "Convention Resolution Form," 18 January 1979, California State Parent-Teacher Association Records, California PTA Office, Sacramento.

67. Feinberg, "PTA Seeks to Reverse Decline with Activism."

68. "Santa Clara Unified Council of PTA Council Membership Report 1971–1972," *Council Chimes*, March 1972, Sixth District PTA Records.

69. Grace Baisinger, "Parents' Page: Focus on the Family," *Parents*, September 1977, 12.

70. "Gay Help for Schools?" *Bay Area Reporter*, 30 October 1974.

71. "School Board Walks Curriculum Tightrope," *SF Examiner*, 8 June 1977.

72. William Muehl, "Some Words of Caution," in Ruth Tiffany Barnhouse and Urban Holmes III, eds., *Male and Female: Christian Approaches to Sexuality* (New York: Seabury, 1976), 168.

73. Herbert Anderson, "The Sex Education of Ministers," in Herbert Otto, ed., *The New Sex Education: The Sex Educator's Resource Book* (Chicago: Follett, 1978), 200. The National Council of Churches debated the line between supporting public "civil rights" for homosexuals while allowing some of its members to refuse to ordain openly gay ministers. Kenneth Briggs, "Rights Advocated for Homosexuals," *New York Times*, 7 March 1975.

74. "Vatican Affirms Teachings on Sex," *National Catholic Reporter*, 23 January 1976.

75. Eugene Kennedy, *The New Sexuality: Myths, Fables, and Hang-ups* (Garden City, NY: Doubleday, 1972), 173, 179.

76. Muehl, "Some Words of Caution," 168.

77. Russell Chandler, "In Christian Schools, It's Boom—and Bus," *Los Angeles Times*, 13 May 1978; Dochuk, *From Bible Belt to Sun Belt*, 300–5.

78. Stephen Bloom, "Education at Home Is an Answer for Parents Who Want to Instill Their Own Values," *San Jose Mercury*, 5 October 1986.

79. James Dobson, *Family Under Fire: A Conference Book* (Kansas City, MO: Beacon Press of Kansas City, 1976), 67–68.

80. John Howell, *Teaching Your Children About Sex* (Nashville, TN: Broadman, 1973), 36–39.

81. Dochuk, *From Bible Belt to Sun Belt*, 16.

82. Dobson, *Family Under Fire*, 8.

83. Henry Hollis Jr., *Thank God for Sex: A Christian Model for Sexual Understanding and Behavior* (Nashville, TN: Broadman, 1975), 57.

84. Howell, *Teaching Your Children About Sex*, 109.

85. James Dobson, *Preparing for Adolescence* (Ventura, CA: Vision House, 1978), 89.

86. Dobson, *Family Under Fire*, 66.

87. John Drakeford, *A Christian View of Homosexuality* (Nashville, TN: Broadman, 1977), 133–34.

88. "New Religious Awakening Dawns," *San Jose Mercury-News*, 28 January 1968.

89. "Evangelism in Bloom," *San Jose Mercury-News*, 27 January 1980.

90. Rickard, *Let It Grow*, 9.

91. See, for example, Marvin Rickard, "Church Planting—It Can Be Exciting," *Christian Life*, January 1982.

92. "Evangelism in Blossom," *San Jose Mercury-News*, 27 January 1980.

93. "Seminar Series to Explore Psychological Maturity," *San Jose Mercury-News*, 29 April 1978.

94. Donald McGavran, *Understanding Church Growth* (Grand Rapids, MI: Eerdman, 1970), 163.

95. Rickard, *Let It Grow*, 40.

96. On one hand, Rickard argued that class and racial homogeneity made more coherent congregations. But, on the other hand, his desire to evangelize to as large a population as possible no doubt brought him into contact with groups of people he initially sought to exclude. In *Let It Grow*, he briefly mentions that worshippers came "from various social and racial backgrounds," and at one point in 1975, the LGCC welcomed a group of Vietnamese refugees who came to the South Bay after the U.S. military evacuated them from Saigon before the Communist takeover.

97. Grant Harden, "Bay Area Catholic Bishop Discusses State of American Church," *San Jose Mercury*, 23 April 1978.

98. "New Religious Awakening Dawns," *San Jose Mercury-News*, 28 January 1968. Schuck also expressed faith that young people would return to the Methodist fold in greater numbers. See also Paul Boyer, "The Evangelical Resurgence in the 1970s," in *Rightward Bound: Making America Conservative in the 1970s* (Cambridge, MA: Harvard University, 2008).

99. Douglas Walrath, "Social Change and Local Churches, 1951–75," in Dean Hoge and David Roozen, eds., *Understanding Church Growth and Decline* (New York: Pilgrim, 1979), 255–57. See also Dean Hoge, "A Test of Theories of Denominational Growth and Decline," in *Understanding Church Growth and Decline*; Lyle Schaller, "The Coming Crisis in Church Development," Report 40, Regional Church Planning Office, Cleveland, OH, 1967.

100. Ezra Earl Jones, *Suburban Churches in Trouble* (New York: Methodist Church, National Division of the Board of Missions, 1972), 4.

101. Hoge, "National Contextual Factors Influencing Church Growth," *Understanding Church Growth and Decline, 1950–1978*, 105.

102. Ibid., 121.

103. "Evangelism in Bloom," *San Jose Mercury*, 27 January 1980. Catholic churches faced similar declines. San Francisco Archbishop John Quinn attributed declining attendance at mass due to the "disintegration of family life." Harden, "Bay Area Catholic Bishop Discusses State of American Church."

104. "New Evangelical Group Elects Leader," *San Jose News*, 23 November 1974. For the reaction of the Santa Clara Council of Churches, see Kenneth Bell and Fred Hillier, letter to David Rupert, 18 November 1974, Santa Clara County Council of Churches Records, Santa Clara County of Churches, San Jose, CA.

105. Sahl, *From Closet to Community*.

106. Santa Clara County Council of Churches Membership Committee, "Statement Regarding the Metropolitan Community Church Application for Membership in the S.C. County Council of Churches," 1 October 1975, Santa Clara County of Churches Records; "Council to Take New Vote on Gay Church," *San Jose News*, 15 January 1976.

107. Lloyd Spiker and John MacDonald, letter to Santa Clara County Council of Churches Board of Directors, 23 December 1975, Santa Clara County of Churches Records.

108. Joy Wilson, letter to Frederick Hillier, 6 January 1976, Santa Clara Council of Churches Records.

109. David Beamer et al., letter to Santa Clara County Council of Churches, 29 December 1975, Santa Clara County Council of Churches Records.

110. "Council Explains Gay Church Decision," *San Jose Mercury-News*, 14 February 1976.

111. "Religious Leaders Face Dilemma over Gay Church," *San Jose News*, 13 December 1975; Kenneth Bell, letter to Nathan Vanderwerf and Lynn Hodges, 22 February 1976, Santa Clara County Council of Churches Records. Fred Hillier, the Council's president, told the *San Francisco Chronicle* that he had doubts about the future of the group because "the decision to admit a predominantly homosexual church would give people a 'distorted picture.'" "A Gay Church Offends Brethren," *San Francisco Chronicle*, 18 December 1975.

112. Bell, letter to Vanderwerf and Hodges. See also Kenneth Bell, "Phone Conversation with Rev. Nathan Vanderwerf," 29 December 1975, Santa Clara Council of Churches Records.

113. "Christian Crazies Lose Round One," *Bay Area Reporter*, 27 May 1976.

114. "AB607 Would 'Straighten' Out Marriage Code," *Bay Area Reporter*, 14 April 1977.

115. Bruce Petit, "S.F. Grants Gays Full Rights," *Bay Area Reporter*, 30 March 1978.

116. Ibid.

117. "Jimmy Carter's S.F. Gay Rights Statement," *Bay Area Reporter*, 27 May 1976.

118. "Sharp Split on Gay Issues," *San Francisco Chronicle*, 12 August 1977.

119. Ibid.

120. "Anita Wins: Miami Kills Pro-Gay Law," *San Jose Mercury*, 8 June 1977.

121. Jeff Prugh, "Florida Gays Tabbed Tuesday Losers," *San Jose Mercury*, 6 June 1977.

122. Sonia Bailey, letter, *San Jose Mercury*, 25 June 1977.

123. "Miami's Vote Shocks Valley Homosexuals," *San Jose Mercury*, 8 June 1977.

124. "Little Gaiety in Gay Rights Fight," *San Jose Mercury*, 9 June 1977.

125. Armando Acuna, "Gay Week Draws Wrath of Churches," *San Jose Mercury*, 11 March 1978.

126. "Council Divides 4–3 in Approving 'Gay Rights Week' in S.J.," *San Jose Mercury*, 15 March 1978.

127. "Most City Candidates Would Have Said No," *San Jose Mercury*, 16 March 1978.

128. Armando Acuna, "Gay Rights Week Killed by Council," *San Jose Mercury*, 5 April 1978.

129. Ibid.

130. Marvin Rickard et al., letter, California Save Our Children, 29 August 1977, Ted Sahl Papers, San Jose State University, San Jose, CA; "Senator Briggs Speaks at Baptist Church," *Santa Clara Sun*, 3 October 1978.

131. "Briggs Files Anti-Gay Initiative," *San Francisco Chronicle*, 2 May 1978.

132. Shilts, *The Mayor of Castro Street*, 368.

133. "Teacher Role Crux of Debate," *Anaheim Bulletin*, 3 November 1978.

134. Jan Swanson, letter, *San Jose Mercury*, 2 November 1978.

135. "Briggs Drive on Homosexuals Takes on Religious Zeal," *San Jose Mercury*, 16 September 1977.

136. "Bishop Myers Blasts Prop 6 Fundamentalists in Farewell," *San Jose Mercury*, 4 November 1978.

137. "Peninsula Clergy Oppose Propositions 6, 7," *San Mateo Times*, 28 October 1978.

138. Frank Gells, letter, *San Jose Mercury*, 2 November 1978.

139. "The Dangers in Proposition 6," *San Francisco Examiner*, 12 October 1978.

140. "Prop. 6 Vote to Mark Milestone in Homosexual Controversy," *Register*, 27 October 1978.

141. "Reagan Sees It Right," *Los Angeles Times*, 27 September 1978.

142. "Briggs to Try Antigay Move Again in 1980," *Los Angeles Times*, 9 November 1978.

143. "Briggs Crushed," *Bay Area Reporter*, 9 November 1978.

Epilogue

1. *Obergefell v. Hodges*, 576, 135 S. Ct. (2015).

2. Hamid Aleaziz et al., "Highest Court's Historic Rights Decision Generates Cheers, Horns, City Hall Visits," *San Francisco Chronicle*, 27 June 2015; Karen de Sa, "Pride Amplified," *San Jose Mercury News*, 29 June 2016.

3. Thomas Peele and Mark Emmons, "Equal Dignity: Gay Marriage Is Now Legal in All Fifty States," *San Jose Mercury News*, 27 June 2015.

4. Ken Yeager, "We've Come a Long Way, Baby," *San Jose Mercury News*, 5 July 2015.

5. David Louie, "Conservative Church Refuses to Marry Same-Sex Couples," ABC Action News, 30 June 2015, accessed 21 August 2015, http://abc7news.com/religion/conservative-church-refuses-to-marry-same-sex-couples-/819770/.

6. Nan Zender, letter to *San Jose Mercury News*, 31 August 2015. Zender was specifically addressing the case of Kim Davis, a Kentucky county clerk who refused to issue licenses to same-sex couples.

7. Pew Research Center, "Support for Same-Sex Marriage Grows, Even Among Groups That Had Been Skeptical," 26 June 2017, accessed 18 October 2017, http://www.people-press.org/2017/06/26/support-for-same-sex-marriage-grows-even-among-groups-that-had-been-skeptical/; Molly Ball, "The Marriage Plot: Inside This Year's Campaign for Gay Equality," *Atlantic*, 13 December 2012, accessed 5 August 2015, https://www.theatlantic.com/politics/archive/2012/12/the-marriage-plot-inside-this-years-epic-campaign-for-gay-equality/265865/.

8. Jeanne Sager, "The Power of Inclusive Sex Education," *Atlantic*, 17 July 2017, accessed 18 October 2017, https://www.theatlantic.com/education/archive/2017/07/the-power-of-inclusive-sex-ed/533772/. California has one of the most progressive sex education laws in the nation, requiring all schools to speak to students about sexual consent, contraception, and LGBT relationships. Yet most of the LGBT-related material is focused on disease prevention and overcoming stereotypes. See Martha Kempner, "California Schools Required to Teach Comprehensive Sex Ed in 2016," *Rewire*, 9 October 2015, accessed 18 October 2017, https://rewire.news/article/2015/10/09/california-schools-required-teach-comprehensive-sex-ed-2016/. For controversy around teaching about anal, oral, and vaginal sex, see Khalida Sarwari, "Let's Talk About Sex: School Districts Attempt to Navigate New Sex Ed Law," *Mercury News Online*, 12 May 2017, accessed 18 October 2017, https://www.mercurynews.com/2017/05/12/lets-talk-about-sex-school-districts-attempt-to-navigate-new-state-law/.

9. For a similar critique, see Lassiter, "Political History Beyond the Red-Blue Divide."

10. Pew Research Center, "Support for Same-Sex Marriage Grows, Even Among Groups That Had Been Skeptical."

11. Gallup Poll, "Americans Split over New LGBT Protections, Restroom Politics," 18 May 2017, accessed 12 March 2018, https://news.gallup.com/poll/210887/americans-split-new-lgbt-protections-restroom-policies.aspx.

12. Ariel Levy, "The Perfect Wife," *New Yorker*, 20 September 2013.

13. It is unfair to say that Freedom to Marry completely ignored gender or racial diversity. Their website features a few examples of interracial families and gay couples of color. However, these testimonials largely focused on the sexual respectability of the couples, particularly their monogamous commitment to one another, and highlighted types of people whom straight-identified moderates might find sympathetic, including small business owners, veterans, homeowners, taxpayers, and parents. In any society that values whiteness as "normal," white same-sex couples will have stronger claims on rights than nonwhite ones. Quote from Jamie Cunningham and Courtney Seals, "Preparing for Our Family's Future in Tennessee," Freedom to Marry, June 2014, accessed 12 March 2018, http://www.freedomtomarry.org/stories/entry/preparing-for-our-familys-futures-in-tennessee.

14. For a similar critique see Warner, *The Trouble with Normal.*

15. This formulation has structured a great deal of urban LGBT history. See D'Emilio, *Sexual Politics, Sexual Communities*; Beeymn, *Creating a Place for Ourselves*; Boyd, *Wide Open Town.*

16. Patrick Sanders, "LGBT Activist Woolard: 'I'm Gonna Run Hard for Mayor,'" *Georgia Voice*, 12 March 2015; James McKinley, "Houston Is Largest City to Elect Openly Gay Mayor," *New York Times*, 13 December 2009; Jeremy Peters, "Openly Gay and Openly Welcomed in Congress," *New York Times*, 26 January 2013.

17. Richard Florida, *The Rise of the Creative Class . . . and How It's Transforming Work, Leisure, Community, and Everyday Life* (New York: Basic Books, 2002), 249–66.

18. Most books on church planting stress the need to bring the Gospel to a range of people, and they encourage pastors to consider the different demographics of the communities surrounding their new churches. But they also recognize new suburbs as good places for pastors to find new worshippers. See Ed Stelzer and Daniel Im, *Planting Missional Churches: Your Guide to Starting Churches That Multiply* (Nashville, TN: B and H Academic, 2016), 149.

19. Molly Worthen, "Southern Baptist Convergence," *New York Times*, 18 June 2012, accessed 16 August 2015, https://campaignstops.blogs.nytimes.com/2012/06/18/southern-baptist-convergence/; Michael Lipka, "Many U.S. Congregations Are Still Racially Segregated but Things Are Changing," Pew Research Center, 8 December 2014, accessed 3 April 2018, http://www.pewresearch.org/fact-tank/2014/12/08/many-u-s-congregations-are-still-racially-segregated-but-things-are-changing-2/. For more on church planting and the demographics of the suburbs, see Collin Hansen, "Love Where You Live," *Christianity Today*, July 2010. Part of this trend toward racial homogeneity comes from the church planting literature itself. Not all authors agree, but many writers on the subject encourage building "monoethnic churches." Aubrey Malpurs, *The Nuts and Bolts of Church Planting: A Guide for Starting Any Kind of Church* (Grand Rapids, MI: Baker Books, 2011), 129; Stelzer and Im, *Planting Missional Churches*, 107–9.

20. Jonathan Mahler, "The Soul of the New Exurb," *New York Times Magazine*, 27 March 2005.

21. The Los Gatos Christian Church in 2003, for example, had roughly one-sixth of the members it had in the late 1980s. Joan Connell, "From 88 Members to 6,000 Members in 3 Decades," *San Jose Mercury*, 21 June 1988; Shirley Wiesberg, "Los Gatos Christian Church," *San Jose Mercury*, 24 May 2003.

22. Suein Hwang, "The New White Flight," *Wall Street Journal*, 19 November 2005; U.S. Census Bureau, "State and County QuickFacts." On racial and class diversity in the suburbs, see Becky Nicolaides and Andrew Wiese, "Suburban Disequilibrium," *New York Times*, 6 April 2013.

23. Harris Interactive, "Americans Favor Safety over Privacy, Though Majority Recognize Need for Balance," 2014.

24. Bill Saporito et al., "Inside the New American Home," *Time*, 14 October 2002; Caroline Hertzel, "10 Favorite Master Bedrooms," *Sunset*, accessed 13 March 2018, https://www.sunset.com/home/architecture-design/master-bedroom.

25. Michelle Robertson, "A Shocking Number of Americans Have Roommates, but That Number Is Even Higher in SF," *SFGATE*, 14 December 2017, accessed 21 December 2017, https://www.sfgate.com/realestate/article/sf-bay-area-rent-roommates-parents-study-12432178.php.

26. John Wildermuth and Neal Riley, "S.F. Shelter for LGBT Homeless Nearing Approval," *SFGATE*, 14 August 2013, accessed 21 December 2017, https://www.sfgate.com/bayarea/article/S-F-shelter-for-LGBT-homeless-nearing-approval-4733425.php; Kevin Fagan,

"As Housing Costs Rise, So Does California Homelessness Report Shows," *SFGATE*, 7 December 2017, accessed 21 December 2017, https://www.sfgate.com/bayarea/article/As-rents-rise-so-does-California-homelessness-12410366.php; Devin Katyama, "The Suburbs: The New Face of Bay Area Homelessness," KQED Online, 26 June 2017, accessed 21 December 2017, https://www.kqed.org/news/11533683/the-suburbs-the-new-face-of-bay-area-homelessness.

27. Movement Advancement Project, "Equality Maps," accessed 13 March 2018, http://www.lgbtmap.org/equality-maps.

28. Kit Roane, "Gay Couples and the Law, at Odds over the Right to Marry," *New York Times*, 2 February 1997. For a forceful argument about the rights denied to same-sex couples, see Chauncey, *Why Marriage?*

29. Ball, "The Marriage Plot."

30. Ibid.

31. Self, *All in the Family*, 11–12.

32. This figure represents only the money allocated by Congress from 2006 to 2011. In 2011, the Obama administration made another $150 million available for marriage education and fathering programs. Yamin, *American Marriage*, 133–36.

33. Because of the diversity of households in the United States, there is no simple comparison to draw between married and unmarried Americans, and between 1969 and 2003, married couples generally paid higher taxes than single people. But beginning in 2003, Congress and the Bush administration changed the rules in a manner that largely benefited married Americans. James Alm and J. Sebastien Leguizamon, "Whither the Marriage Tax?" *National Tax Journal* 68, no. 2 (June 2015).

34. Kate Ashford, "11 Things You Never Thought of When You Decided Not to Get Married," *Forbes*, 26 September 2014, accessed 7 August 2015, https://www.forbes.com/sites/kateashford/2014/09/26/deciding-not-to-get-married/#26222eb7edf3.

35. Michael Cobb, "The Supreme Court's Lonely Hearts Club," *New York Times*, 30 June 2015. This disparity has caused a critique of same-sex marriage from the left because it is insufficiently inclusive. See Warner, *The Trouble with Normal*; Nancy Polikoff, *Beyond (Straight and Gay) Marriage: Valuing All Families Under the Law* (Boston: Beacon, 2008).

36. This does not mean that proponents of sex education have decisively won their battle. In fact, many sex educators vigorously oppose "abstinence-only" programs. However, a 2012 survey found that 93 percent of Americans believe it is important for teens to receive strong messages encouraging them to delay sex. A separate poll from 2004 found that only 7 percent of Americans believe schools should play no role in the sex education of young people. There is considerable debate about how to teach the subject, but there is a near consensus that schools should teach it. When they do so, only a relatively small fraction of people think of it as "big government." NARAL/Pro Choice America Foundation, "Americans Support Responsible Sex Education," 1 January 2017, accessed 14 April 2018, https://www.prochoiceamerica.org/report/americans-support-responsible-sex-education/; National Public Radio, "Sex Education in American," 24 February 2004, accessed 14 April 2018, https://www.npr.org/templates/story/story.php?storyId=1622610.

37. Eddie Arruza, "LGBT Senior Housing," WTTW Chicago Tonight, 19 December 2012, accessed 21 August 2015, https://chicagotonight.wttw.com/2012/12/19/lgbt-senior-housing; Rucks Russell, "Homeowners Protest Controversial Proposed Housing Facility," KHOU 11 News, 9 June 2015, accessed 21 August 2015. This fact should come as little surprise to

suburban historians. For over a generation, scholars in this subfield have stressed the ways in which the biggest recipients of housing assistance from the federal government have been among the largest critics of a robust safety net. Jackson, *Crabgrass Frontier*; Self, *American Babylon*; Lassiter, *Silent Majority*; Freund, *Colored Property*.

Index

Page numbers in italics indicate illustrations.

Acknowledgments

As I finish this project, I am extremely conscious of the ways in which I relied on the collective efforts of numerous friends, loved ones, archivists, and historians. The people whom I will thank below do not necessarily know each other, yet their physical, intellectual, and emotional support jointly helped me complete this book. I hope that this section can give them some kind of recognition for their work, even if it's just a matter of putting their name in print. I am so very, very appreciative of their help.

Matthew Lassiter played an enormous role in my intellectual development, and he has served as a role model for me as a scholar and a teacher. I owe a great debt to the intellectual community he helped build in Ann Arbor, and his generous critiques made this book stronger. Thank you, Matt. Jay Cook was an incredibly thoughtful reader as well, and I still think about the ideas that he introduced to me in his seminar on U.S. popular culture. My thanks also go to Scott Kurashige and Gayle Rubin for their thought-provoking questions. And no paragraph about my life in Michigan would be complete without an expression of gratitude to the following people from whom I learned so much: Allison Abra, Rabia Belt, Tamar Carroll, Nathan Connolly, Sam Erman, Laura Ferguson, Lauren Hirshberg, Monica Kim, Emily Klancher, Sara Lampert, Sharon Lee, Suzi Linsley, Daniel Livesay, Alex Lovit, Will Mackintosh, Diana Mankowski, Elspeth Martini, Tiffany McClain, Drew Meyers, Andrew Needham, Isa Quintana, Tim Retzloff, Dean Saranillio, Kisha Simmons, Alice Weinreb, and Matt Wittman.

Numerous archivists and librarians helped me find the sources that I used to write this book. I am indebted to the hard work of the reference librarians at the California State Archives, Stanford University's Special Collections, History San Jose, the California Historical Society, the Bancroft Library, and San Jose State University's Special Collections. I did not initially intend to write this book about San Francisco, but I was lucky to find so many fantastic archivists in the city. My thanks go to Tim Wilson, Tami Suzuki, Susan Goldstein, and the rest of the staff at the San Francisco History Center. The GLBT Historical Society of Northern California is an amazing place, and I have a special debt to Daniel Bao, Joanna Black, and all of the other staff and volunteers who work there. I am also grateful to the people who opened up their personal archives or shared their memories with me during interviews. I thank the Santa Clara Council of Churches, the Glide Memorial Church, and the San Francisco Archdiocese for allowing me to look at some of their records, as well as Barbara Emerich, Deloris Feak, Donna Hughes-Oldenberg, Marvin Rickard, Wiggsy Sivertsen, Rick Stokes, Mary Thompson, and Hank Wilson for talking about their lives with me.

Margot Canaday and Bob Lockhart have made working with the University of Pennsylvania Press a truly remarkable experience. Margot generously supported this project in its earliest form, and she offered brilliant comments on the first complete draft of the manuscript. Bob Lockhart's reputation as a first-class editor is well deserved. I am particularly grateful for his close reading of the manuscript during my final edits. Bryant Simon and Sarah Igo offered enormously helpful critiques, volunteered to answer my questions, and helped me see this history in new ways. Finally, Tom Sugrue expressed faith in my ideas at a preliminary stage, and I am very fortunate to have had his support.

Numerous friends and colleagues have shared beneficial comments on my work. I thank Stanford's Lane Center for the Study of the American West, the University of Minnesota's Quadrant Initiative, the Los Angeles History and Metro Studies Group, and Boston University's Political History Seminar for asking me to share pieces of this book. Tim Stewart-Winter and Gill Frank organized an incredibly useful mini-conference where we discussed histories of sexuality and politics. Aaron Cavin, Erika Gasser, Betsy More, Andrew Ross, and Dale Winling read portions of this manuscript and offered great suggestions on how to make them better. Jacqui Shine gave some much-needed last-minute advice on the introduction. Andrew Highsmith looked at the entire manuscript, and while he gave me numerous good ideas, he deserves an extra thank you for helping me to shorten it. Lily Geismer read just about every page in this book at one point or another. She helped me with her smart comments and great sense of humor. This book and I are better off for her friendship.

The Ohio State University provided me with many resources to help me complete this project. The College of Arts and Sciences and Department of History generously supported its publication with a subvention grant. I thank the faculty and staff of OSU's Department of History for their help finishing this project. Jerry Mount from the Center for Urban and Regional Analysis created the maps for this book and impressed me with his geographic knowledge. David Lincove, Josh Sadvari, and Mary Ries helped me locate crucial sources. Amna Akbar, Jim Bach, Ashley Bowerman, Steve Conn, Jason Courtney, Sarah Courtney, Lilia Fernandez, Dana Howard, Robin Judd, Liz Lee, Katherine Marino, Dodie McDow, Ben McKean, Joachim Moortgat, Tan Nguyen, Corinne Reczek, Amanda Robinson, Jenny Siegel, Birgitte Soland, Dave Steigerwald, Kristina Ward, and Ying Zhang have helped make Columbus feel like home.

When you move as much as I have, many friends feel a lot like family. I am so grateful for the friendship of the following people, whom I have met both in and out of the history world: Anna Armentrout, Marco Araujo, Nora Beck, Anne Blaschke, Ryan Blitstein, Katherine Brown, Katie Brownell, Camille Castillo, Michael Dube, Leanne Hartmann, Liz Jellema, Dena Kesselman, Alison Lefkovitz, Jess Lepler, Josh Long, David Leopold, Taylor Rielly, Abby Rubinson, Kaveh Ryndak, Sai Samant, and Maggie Shrout. I am glad that Sharon Larson did not give up on me after I refused to speak French with her in the ninth grade. Ken Eaton still makes me laugh even though we graduated from college a long time ago. Angelica Tsakaridis is like a sister to me. This project benefited from her love in many intangible ways. However, she also made one significant concrete contribution to it: she let me sleep on her couch for six weeks while I struggled to find an apartment in San Francisco. Maybe that is a favor only a lifelong friend can give.

Finally, I want to thank the rest of my family. Dan and Dianne Romanos and the entire Romanos-Shadroui clan have made me feel like I have known them my whole life, and I am still humbled by their willingness to include me in the mysteries of Joe's Pond. My mother, Suzanne Howard, has sustained me through countless moves and personal crises. Her love and support have made more than just this book possible. Scott Howard will never read this book, but I hope he knows that I love him. Catherine

Romanos is my beloved partner and best friend. I have struggled to find the right way to thank everyone in these acknowledgments, but I am truly at a loss here. No words can do justice to the happiness she has brought me in the decade or so that it has taken me to finish this project. This book is dedicated to Catherine, and I hope that it conveys at least a fraction of my gratitude to her.